The Beer Brewing Guide

EBC Quality Handbook for Small Breweries

Christopher and Nancy McGreger

The Brewers of Europe

Lannoo

"This Guide provides you with up to date insights and practical guidelines for your daily operations to guarantee the highest quality standards for your beers."

Gert De Rouck, Brew Master, KU Leuven, Belgium

"A lot has been said and written about the taste of beer and there is probably a lot more to come. Preferences and taste differences between drinkers are evident but, at the end of the day, good beer is just good beer. And it is very important, but quite difficult, for today's brewers to bring good beer to the market. Not only one time, but on a repeatable basis. Not only a few days after filling, but even after months of storage in warehouses all along the supply chain. Not only with limited offers and very special recipes, but also and above all with his/her flagship beers dedicated to the majority of beer lovers. This very practical and easy to read handbook gives technical guidance to brewers who want to achieve success in this fantastic job. Other aspects are also addressed by the author like, among others, efficient quality control, safety for workers and food safety culture, traceability and process recording. Readers will find a lot a qualitative advice which can steer a brewer to his goal: give to his/her beer the taste he wants it to have".

Paul Lefebvre, Brasserie Lefebvre, Belgium

"Every once in a while, a brewing handbook hits the shelves that manages to put scientific principles governing the production of beer into understandable clear language, enlightening and informing the reader on finer points of successfully brewing beer. Thorough explanations on what exactly happens during the various stages of beer production are interspersed with well-founded advice on how to ensure quality - quality in process, as well as quality for the final product. This book is a must for all brewers regardless of their portfolio of brands, or size, of their breweries."

John Brauer, Brew Master and EBC Executive Officer

"A useful and comprehensive guide, outlining the full breadth of topics involved in the production of good quality beer. Ideal for small scale breweries. A good read. Detailed enough to be of useful, but not overwhelming."

Sandra Stelma, Head of Science, Diageo, Ireland

"Dave and I embarked some 25 years ago into the unknown world of American craft beer. We were two home brewers with only a dream and simply put, quality is all you have in this competitive space. As a small brewer, you must master the art before you can sell beer. Books and periodicals like these are the manuals for success and a must read for anyone considering our industry."

Mike Stevens and Dave Engbers, Founders Brewing Company

Foreword By The EBC President

Humanity has been brewing beer for thousands of years. Different cultures held beer in high esteem, as a most valuable beverage and liquid food source, since the Neolithic era. The big challenge has been always how to repeat and control the natural process of fermentation, which leads to delicious beer in a consistent manner.

Egyptians, Sumerians, medieval monks, modern brewers of all sizes, have always been improving procedures and recipes to nourish and satisfy their consumers' palates and senses. History shows this as a magnificent achievement. Currently, more than two thousand million hectolitres of beer are being produced all over the world and many new brewers are launching themselves vigorously onto the scene. This amount partitions into the more than one hundred beer styles and leading to thousands of traditional and creative recipes.

New brewers start off small, full of passion and creativity, overcoming scarcity of resources. Sometimes great success often leads to fast growth; consequently, this implies an expansion to new geographical regions and an increase in production volumes which can compromise those quality standards – this becomes the challenge I was referring to.

Essentially, "quality" may be defined as fulfilling expectations in so many aspects: firstly, how the final beer matches the recipe that brewers have developed (brewer specifications). Secondly, how this beer matches consumers' expectations along its entire shelf-life (safety, taste and stability in the market). In all cases, science and technology are corner stones upon which this goal is founded: a brewer can have a great idea, translate it in a recipe, but to make it happen – consistently, brew after brew, with enough robustness and resilience to be appealing to the consumer in a shop or pub – that's neither easy nor always evident. It requires theoretical and also practical knowledge with the application of best management standards, from both an intrinsic as well as extrinsic point of view.

In today's world of fast-moving consumer goods, the development of process management protocols (for example, QA/QC, TQM, WCM, 6-Sigma, etc.) have become part and parcel of an overriding quality ethic. This is how we do business: food safety, product consistency, traceability and, ultimately, consumer satisfaction are almost unthinkable these days without best practices rooted in solid quality management.

It is in this context of more than two decades of having witnessed an explosion of new brewers in the sector. Coupled with heightened expectations in process and product quality in global beverage manufacturing, the EBC Executive Team and The Brewers of Europe opted in favour of developing this complete brewing quality handbook, including covering good brewing practices geared primarily, but not exclusively, at smaller breweries. In this aspect, I should also like to express my gratitude to the authors, Christopher and Nancy McGreger, for drawing up such an exemplary work of science, technology and practical applicability to the end-to-end beer value chain. Undoubtedly, it will prove to be an essential day-to-day guide on every brewer's desk or bookshelf.

Cheers!

Benet Fité Luis
EBC President

About the Authors

Christopher and Nancy began as enthusiastic homebrewers and went on to work in several breweries in the burgeoning US craft brewing industry. In 1997, they moved to Germany where they were also able to gain valuable experience in the Bavarian brewing industry. They attended the *Technische Universität München-Weihenstephan*, receiving degrees as *Diplom Braumeister* and subsequently in Brewing Science and Beverage Technology (MSc).

This book grew out of the knowledge they have accumulated in their studies and through their work as freelance consultants, authors, teachers and technical translators for the brewing and beverage industry. As avid book worms with an unquenchable wanderlust, they are often in pursuit of exceptional, traditional and unusual beers and brewing techniques. Their articles regularly appear in the English edition of *Brauwelt*. Christopher teaches *International Beer Styles and Brewing Methods* and *Technical English for Brewers and Maltsters* in Germany and *The Natural and Cultural History of Brewing* in the US.

Website: mcgreger-translations.com

Acknowledgements:

The authors would like to extend their sincere gratitude to the following colleagues and friends: John Brauer, Mathieu Schneider, Prof. Werner Back, Prof. Fritz Jacob, Prof. Martin Krottenthaler, Prof. Winfried Russ, Prof. Mirjam Haensel, Dr. Martin Zarnkow, Dr. Matthias Hutzler, Winfried Sahlmann, Yuseff Cherney, Dr. Chip McElroy, Dusan Kwiatkowski, John Hannafan, Kristian Huber, Alan Sheppard, Lance Snow, Dr. Christopher White, Dr. Karen Fortmann, Brian 'Swifty' Peters, Achim Nieroda, Mark Zunkel, Cassie Poirier, Wolfgang Lindell, Thomas Brandt and Petra Stich.

About the European Brewery Convention and The Brewers of Europe

The Brewers of Europe

The European Brewery Convention looks back on an illustrious history of almost 75 years' dedication to brewing excellence. Founded in 1947, EBC is the technical, European-based association for brewers. Initially, EBC helped to address the variable quality of raw materials and this became a main impetus for cooperation; later, the EBC Analysis Committee and Brewing Science Group have been facilitating research in industry and thus become the main technical committees for EU-wide collaboration. EBC is perhaps best known for the organising of brewing technical and scientific events (EBC congresses and symposia), as well as publishing a compendium of analytical and laboratory methods (Analytica-EBC).

With the membership base of EBC and The Brewers of Europe becoming more and more harmonised, the two brewing associations merged in 2008. The Brewers of Europe is "The Voice of the Beer Sector in Europe", representing and promoting the interests of Europe's brewers towards European legislators and working on initiatives ranging from societal and fiscal to product / regulatory issues in the world of beer. EBC defines itself as the technical and scientific arm of The Brewers of Europe. The important topic of sustainability is enjoying high priority for greener and cleaner brewing. Both associations are headquartered at the European Brewers House at Rue Caroly 23-25 in 1050 Brussels. For more information: https://brewersofeurope.eu and https://europeanbreweryconvention.eu

| Table of Contents

PREFACE

Brewing in the pre-industrial age

Beer is not rare, but exceptional beer is. This is largely due to pitfalls in the lengthy processes of malting and brewing and also to the fact that beer is a food that is relatively sensitive to environmental stresses. Like many traditional foods (cheese, yoghurt, wine, vinegar, bread, sauerkraut, salami, etc.), beer is a product of 'controlled spoilage'. This refers to the means by which humans developed methods for allowing food to undergo fermentation in a deliberate and systematic manner for the purpose of preserving it and thus keeping it edible prior to the invention of refrigeration. In doing so, the food remained uncontaminated with harmful microorganisms. Similar to cooking, fermentation makes many of the nutrients in foods more accessible and more digestible. This results not only in preservation of the food but also in increasing its nutrient value in its fermented state. Over the many millennia of its existence, beer has been difficult to keep palatable for an extended period and therefore has almost always been consumed relatively fresh. And yet, the longevity of our sustained relationship with 'the juice of the barley' attests to more than a mere craving for 'liquid bread'. It is deeply 'engrained' in our cultures and by harnessing its energy through domestication and farming, beer – along with its solid counterpart – have been a boon for humanity.

Why is this the case? The answer lies in beer itself. The fermented liquid is an aqueous solution of compounds derived from malted grain that has nourished us in one form or other since we began cultivating crops. This cereal-based beverage served as a staple upon which ancient civilisations were founded. Beer's nutritional properties are complemented by a number of barriers to the growth of pathogenic microorganisms.

Ultimately, the first quality control came about by trial and error in order to ensure that the beer – being a staple food – was flavourful, safe and nutritive.

In Mesopotamia and Egypt, beer nourished the first city dwellers and protected them against dangerous water-borne microorganisms. Pathogens do not survive for very long or at least cannot multiply in the final product, due to the anaerobic, slightly acidic (pH < 4.5), slightly alcoholic (> 2.5% ABV) conditions. Early beers were more or less spontaneously fermented, fairly sour and drunk fresh. This, of course, preceded the discovery of the effects of boiling hops in the mash or wort, though it is suspected that early Celtic brewers learned to influence the direction of their fermentations with additions of certain herbs. The oldest extant beer styles still maintain a level of acidity (pH 3.0–3.5) now considered outside the norm for most modern beer. This level of acidity would have been advantageous in the absence of boiled hops. Though they continue to exist in some areas of Europe, craft brewers are exploring how refreshing sour beers produced with a mix of microorganisms can be.

Though direct-fired kettles are still in use, boilers producing hot water and steam are common in modern brewing. Heating the combined ingredients in the brewhouse almost entirely eliminates any surviving microorganisms in the wort and paves the way for brewing yeast. Over about a thousand years, this practice steadily became widespread in medieval European beer production once it was discovered that beer remained drinkable for longer when hops were boiled in at least a portion of either the mash or the wort. The hops increased the microbiological stability and therefore the flavour stability of beer; of course, heating also pasteurised the wort. As a consequence, the wort was infused with bacteriostatic substances derived from the hops made soluble through the process of boiling. These practices favoured certain microorganisms, primarily those we now perceive as brewing yeast, *Saccharomyces cerevisiae*. Though conditions facilitated the dominance of this species of yeast, other undesirable microorganisms still lurked in the recesses of fermentation vessels and on brewing equipment, most of it made of wood. Fortunately, these problems were solved as well, as an industry arose around brewing.

Beer-making expanded beyond the dominion of most households in the Late Middle Ages, and facilities dedicated to its production became increasingly more industrialised through the Enlightenment and over the intervening centuries. Brewing has been a constant learning process for humanity and has borne fruit extending well beyond the realm of beer. As our understanding of the brewing process has improved, so has our knowledge of microbiology, biotechnology, food science, molecular biology, process engineering, thermodynamics and material science, among others. These innovations have found application in numerous scientific and technical fields but also in the brewing process directly. Thereby, brewing has undergone constant improvement.

After the Roman Empire spread north of the Alps, most of the population of Central Europe dedicated itself to viniculture, that is, until the chill of the Little Ice Age forced the inhabitants of the region to do otherwise. Unless they occupied lands along rivers or areas similarly conducive to growing grapes for wine, they began brewing and fermenting wort at lower temperatures, outside of the 'comfort zone' of many bacteria. A hybrid bottom-fermenting yeast, *Saccharomyces pastorianus*, could withstand the chill and facilitated the development of lager beer. Consequently, this hybrid beer yeast had much less competition under such conditions and could easily outcompete its rivals. Continental brewers were also some of the first to use boiled hops in wort production. These developments would have an enormous impact on the quality of beer as we know it. Therefore, well before Louis Pasteur and the advent of microbiology, procedures for manipulating the complicated goings-on in fermenting wort were devised, though the microorganisms themselves remained a mystery.

Techniques were also established which encouraged high cell counts of vigorous 'normal' (top-fermenting) brewing yeast, such as those in Burton-upon-Trent in the early 19th century. In order to mass produce English ales for the expanding British Empire, the brewers of Burton provided optimal conditions for yeast propagation and growth, allowing the strain of *Saccharomyces cerevisiae* fermenting their wort to rapidly outcompete other microorganisms. They could also effectively harvest the yeast in the Burton unions invented to separate the yeast from the green beer.

With the development of microbiological techniques, advances in steam production and refrigeration in breweries as well as innovations in metallurgy and measurement technology, it is not much of a stretch to reach the point we find ourselves today. In the broad strokes of history, brewing consisted of developing better raw materials and processes while also narrowing the window of opportunity for the microorganisms involved in beer spoilage. This remains the focus of our endeavours as brewers, maltsters, brewing scientists and the suppliers of raw materials.

| Modern brewing

The legacy of the brewers preceding us through the ages is manifested in the beverage itself and in the production techniques we inherited from them. Through their efforts, the 'controlled spoilage' of beer brewing has become much more fine-tuned and reproducible. This has allowed beer to be brewed in a consistent and systematic manner, virtually independent of the whims of nature.

Nevertheless, even given this progress, many strive for but never quite reach the three primary aspirations of every brewer in beer production: quality, drinkability and stability. Smaller breweries possess a few advantages over larger ones, one being that of the three important qualities of beer, stability is less of an issue for them. As in past centuries, smaller breweries usually serve their beer on or near their premises at local or regional retail outlets. This allows them to plan on their customers drinking their beer within one or two months of it being packaged.

The role of beer has shifted in the societies where it has traditionally been brewed. It is no longer the staple it once was; hence, we have a new category of beer known as 'craft beer' in which brewers find joy in experimentation for its own sake. These beers are brewed in small batches with less conventional ingredients, methods and microorganisms. For this reason, this book also contains some information on, for instance, barrels for fermenting and ageing beer as well as methods for evaluating sour and aged beers.

Although larger brewing companies make use of costly measuring devices in their laboratories, smaller breweries have neither the resources nor the need to do so. Quality management in smaller breweries is often not quite as comprehensive and is also less reliant on finely calibrated, expensive equipment. Perhaps, for this reason, small-scale brewing is somewhat more akin in its approach to a time in the past when brewers trusted their experience and the observations made with their five senses. And yet, given the latest technological advances and intimate understanding of the process, smaller breweries are not stuck in the Dark Ages. They can – with a few essential devices and quality control procedures – dependably brew flavourful, satisfying beers.

THE PURPOSE AND SCOPE OF THIS BOOK

This text was designed to be a handbook for those working in small to mid-sized breweries. It provides a basic understanding of quality management to facilitate the production of flavourful beer with a high level of drinkability and stability. This applies not only to the beer when it is fresh but also for a good while after it has been packaged. The book does not provide detailed descriptions of complex analyses and procedures but is rather a general manual for avoiding pitfalls commonly encountered in modern brewing that can negatively impact quality. References for a more in-depth understanding of brewing and quality assurance are included at the end of the book.

Brewers in smaller facilities often have to perform tasks in every part of production but may not have the requisite knowledge to maintain a high level of quality in each of those areas. Similarly, they may also be so busy with day-to-day operations that quality assurance falls by the wayside. Though compromising and setting priorities are part of managing a brewery, cutting corners should be avoided.

This book was not written as an exhaustive reference text. It is intended, however, to serve as guide for those wishing not only to improve the quality of their beer but also to maintain a consistent level of quality over time. Hopefully, it will awaken readers to the idea of quality assurance and raise their awareness concerning how merely sticking to a cleaning regimen or taking and recording measurements with inexpensive equipment can be used to recognise change over both the short and long term, providing them with the information they require to respond to sudden aberrations as well as gradual trends.

Who benefits from this book?

The target audience for this book are those working in smaller breweries with few resources. In larger facilities, a team of individuals dedicates their working hours to monitoring quality and responding to any fluctuations they notice in the measurement data they collect on a daily, weekly and monthly basis. In smaller facilities, quality assurance is performed by personnel who have other duties and squeeze it in when they have time. Always keeping an eye on things, establishing and following protocols, being careful at critical points in the process and applying common sense are half the battle. This book will hopefully help those brewers who have little time for quality assurance to approach their production process with this in mind.

GENERAL PRINCIPLES OF QUALITY AND QUALITY CONTROL

| What is quality?

In the pursuit of quality, one must first define the notion itself. The following terms are used in this book:

Quality, within the scope of this book, is defined as to what extent attributes meet expectations, e.g. whether drinkers find the flavour, appearance, foam and stability of a beer to be satisfactory or not. The absence of a high level of quality means disappointment on the part of the beer drinker.

Addressing quality in a brewery is rooted in the following concepts:

> **Quality management (QM)** is described as all of the coordinated activities for directing an organisation in its pursuit of quality.

> **Quality assurance (QA)** can be summed up as the actions necessary to guarantee an adequate level of confidence in the quality of the product. Quality assurance measures are relatively inexpensive when compared with the costly consequences of a lapse in quality.

> **Quality control (QC)** can be understood as the process of monitoring the myriad factors that affect the quality of beer. Only what brewers are able to observe and measure can be controlled.

Quality management is frequently divided into steps, known as the Deming Cycle after the engineer who developed the concept of continuous quality improvement:

- **Plan:** formulate objectives; evaluate conditions; develop a strategy for achieving the objectives.
- **Do:** implement the strategy; describe the operations; outline staff responsibilities.
- **Check:** are the operations going as planned? Have the objectives and improvements been achieved?
- **Act:** formulate responses to irregularities; modify the previous strategy if the objectives were not achieved.

An example of putting the Deming Cycle into practice is described below:

Our objective as brewhouse personnel is to increase and maintain mash and wort quality by taking samples and performing simple measurements, such as the extent of the mash conversion, the pH of the mash and wort as well as gravity readings at the appropriate points in the process. Monitoring these parameters and taking action, if necessary, ensure consistency in brewhouse operations, for example, when producing the brewery's flagship beer. Because this beer is brewed on a regular basis, the quality must not only reach a high standard but has to be maintained at that level. Moreover, the flavour profile, appearance and other characteristics should remain relatively constant to satisfy consumer expectations.

Plan: What are we attempting to do? In the planning phase, standard operating procedures (SOPs) are created for brewhouse operations, and the points at which the brewer takes and records measurements are defined in the process. The target parameters are also defined. In this case, the gravity, pH and time required for saccharification are to be measured and recorded. The brew log should be modified to include a section under mashing where this information can be documented.

Do: How will we achieve it? The brewer is made aware of his/her responsibilities to follow the SOPs and to take the specified measurements and record the data. The brewer responsible for implementing these tasks receives instructions on the proper procedures for taking the specified measurements and documenting the results in the brew log.

Check: Have the objectives been achieved? Do the data show that brewhouse operations and measurements are consistent? Who will monitor and determine if the objectives are being met and if the plan is being properly executed? Brewhouse procedures are performed and at the end of every production day, the brew log is reviewed. This task is overseen by the production director to ensure that no data are incomplete and that all brewhouse staff are following the instructions and fulfilling their duties. Any irregularities are to be addressed by the production director together with staff members.

Act: If the data reveal fluctuations in the quality of the raw materials or in the brewing process, measures are formulated or revised on how to best address and compensate for these deviations (modifying the milling procedures, mashing regime, the sparge liquor volume or temperature, the duration or intensity of the boil, etc.). Brewhouse personnel may also require additional training to ensure that they are carrying out operations consistently and to a high standard. Further improvements in quality can be achieved by repeating the process.

LAYING THE GROUNDWORK FOR QUALITY

Quality as a goal

When thinking about quality, a reasonable amount of time should be devoted to deciding how quality will be measured and what the brewery is trying to achieve. There are many reasons to strive for better quality beer. Is it to reduce customer complaints, to prevent beer from being dumped due to microbiological spoilage or perhaps to increase brewery sales by offering a consistent product?

From the outset, decisions should be made regarding which specifications are desirable for each beer. Product specifications provide the basis for evaluating whether a beer meets the quantifiable expectations the brewery has defined for a 'quality' product. Out-of-specification beers, even if drinkable, would not meet these expectations and would not be released for consumption until they do. An action plan should also be drafted on how to deal with out-of-specification products and how to implement corrective measures.

Further consideration should be given to establishing who will be responsible for quality, even though everyone at the brewery should keep quality foremost in their minds and should always be working towards this objective. However, key duties for ensuring quality need to be assigned to individual staff members who are best equipped and positioned to do so.

Literature and further reading

Heyse, K. (ed.), *Praxishandbuch der Brauerei*. Behr' s GmbH, 2000

Miedaner, H. *Technologische Betriebsüberwachung und Qualitätsoptimierung*. Vorlesungs-skriptum, Wissenschaftszentrum Weihenstephan, 1999

Pellettieri, M., *Quality Management: Essential Management for Breweries*. Brewers Association, 2015

THE GENERAL TYPES OF BREWERY QUALITY CONTROL

Comprehensive brewery quality control can be divided into the following general categories:

- microbiological
- physico-chemical (aka chemical-physical)
- sensory

Microbiological quality control

The main point of microbiological quality control is to know which microorganisms are doing the fermenting or are otherwise growing in the brewery. If they are the wrong ones, like beer-spoilers, then where are they lurking? Where might they be entering the process? What measures can be taken to eliminate them?

The harmful, the harmless and the indicators – sources of microorganisms in the brewery

Where do microorganisms come from?

- water
- malt, adjuncts, hops
- yeast contamination
- processing aids
- operating materials
- additives
- ambient air
- secondary contamination
- containers, e.g. kegs, returnable bottles
- personnel, e.g. workers in the fermentation, maturation or filter cellar or on the filling line, etc.

Most microorganisms are harmless in a brewery setting; however, some are not. For instance, bacteria can impart off-flavours to beer and even render it undrinkable. Some of the microorganisms in the brewery serve as indicators for the presence of beer spoilers, which the quality control team may not have found. Indicator microorganisms are often present when undiscovered beer spoilers are hiding out in the brewery and may also be able to harbour them in biofilms though the indicator flora themselves do not harm the beer. However, it is advisable to take steps in the form of targeted cleaning measures against undetected beer spoilers when indicator microorganisms are present.

Physico-chemical quality control

This kind of quality control involves characterising and measuring the physical and chemical attributes of sampled materials for the ultimate purpose of increasing or maintaining the quality of the raw materials, intermediate and finished products:

- analysis of raw materials, such as malt and water, for beer production (most often performed by suppliers or specialised laboratories)
- general testing of intermediate and finished products, that is, the wort, green beer and finished beer

Sensory quality control

Fortunately, brewers already possess excellent tools for assessing the raw materials and their products – their senses and awareness. Given that the human sensory apparatus is so sensitive and can be honed with practice, simply being familiar with the flavours and aromas of the product at each stage of the process and/or developing a tasting panel at a brewery to evaluate the finished beer is an inexpensive and effective means of quality control.

A brewer and/or tasting panel can evaluate the following:

- **raw materials**: malt, hops, water and to some extent yeast
- **intermediate and finished products**: wort, green beer and beer

HOW TO USE THIS BOOK

The following symbols appear at the top of the page at the beginning of each major section, so readers thumbing through the book can find out relatively easily which section they are in:

General safety and product quality

General safety

SOPs

Traceability

Hygienic design and cleaning practices

Cleanliness and hygienic design

Cleaning and sanitising

Brewery pumps

Raw materials

Water

Malt

Hops

Yeast and other microorganisms

Raw materials – sections

The following symbols appear at the top of each page next to one of the symbols for the raw materials. These symbols denote the subsection of raw materials under discussion:

General information   Analysis reports   Visual inspection   Storage

Beer production

After the section on raw materials is a section on beer production, indicated by this symbol:

The brewing process – hot side   The brewing process – cold side   The brewing process – clarification

The brewing process – barrels   The brewing process – packaging

Beer quality

The section on beer quality is divided into discussions on beer and basic food safety, sensory analysis of raw materials and the finished beer as well as the challenges to beer once it has left the brewery:

Beer and basic
food safety

Sensory analysis of
malt, hops and beer

Challenges to
good beer in trade

Monitoring quality

The procedures for checking quality are divided into two main sections, which are subdivided into two sections each, laboratories and analyses.

Laboratories

Equipping and setting
up a laboratory

Basic laboratory
techniques

Analyses

Microbiological
analysis

Physico-chemical
analysis

GENERAL SAFETY

Breweries are full of hazards to the uninitiated. The proper safety measures must be observed day in and day out in breweries, even for those only there for a visit. Breweries are, of course, required to comply with all regulations on the federal and local level regarding health and safety. These may vary by country or region.

Training and orientation

Newly hired workers are usually eager to learn and get started with their tasks at the brewery. However, thorough training prior to commencing work is essential, because new employees are usually the ones involved in accidents. General safety for the entire brewery should be part of everyone's training, and specific instruction for their respective work area is obligatory. Of course, when learning the layout of the brewery, the locations of eyewash stations and chemical showers and other safety equipment should be communicated to them. A test covering hazardous materials and processes in the brewery could be provided at the end of the training.

Even though beer is omnipresent at a brewery, personnel should only partake of beer or any other alcoholic beverages after their shifts are over.

Periodic meetings, generally every fortnight or perhaps monthly, should be held to ensure that the employees understand the safety precautions and preventative measures that need to be taken in the brewery. Any meetings, training or instruction in standard operating procedures (SOPs) should be documented, and upon completion, employees should sign off on having received the training (refer to the section below on SOPs). Should an accident happen, the appropriate measures to correct the situation must also be described in detail in the SOP.

The following are common aspects of brewery safety training.

Personal protective equipment

Shatterproof, non-vented goggles and face shields, gloves, work boots, aprons, hard hats, ear protection, reflective vests and respiratory masks may be required at various stages of production. Personnel are obliged without exception to wear the appropriate attire when working in specific production areas. In brewery inspection reports, an often-cited deficiency pertains to personnel failing to wear protective gear.

Material safety data sheets (MSDS)

MSDS, as they are known, must be readily accessible by all personnel in their work area, and they should be kept current, as cleaning and production processes, ingredients, processing aids, cleaning chemicals, etc. can change over time. Personnel should not have to ask for them and should be trained in how to read and interpret them. Material safety data sheets conform to globally harmonised systems that must provide the same information worldwide. They are divided into the following sections:

1. identification of the substance/mixture and of the manufacturer
2. hazards identification and classification of the substance
3. composition and information concerning the ingredients
4. first aid measures
5. firefighting measures and extinguishing media
6. accidental release measures, protective equipment, environmental precautions, cleaning up and containment
7. handling, storage conditions and uses
8. exposure controls and personal protection
9. physical and chemical properties
10. stability, reactivity, incompatibility, decomposition
11. toxicological information
12. ecological information, including toxicity, degradability
13. disposal considerations, wastewater treatment
14. transport information, special precautions
15. regulatory information: safety, health, environmental, legislative
16. other information

Chemical exposure

Information concerning toxic, reactive, flammable and explosive chemicals are available on the MSDS, including any first aid measures. Because cleaning, sanitising and other tasks in a brewery involve mixing solutions of chemicals and using them, sometimes in confined spaces, all of the necessary precautions should be taken. For example, ammonia is an effective refrigerant but is also toxic and flammable at certain concentrations. It must be handled with care. Luckily, it has a distinctive odour and is detectable by humans even at very low concentrations. Thus, minor leakages can usually be discovered by brewery personnel rapidly.

Carbon dioxide and other gases

Fermentation results in the evolution of large volumes of carbon dioxide gas. Generation of copious amounts of carbon dioxide in the latter part of the brewing process requires that certain safety measures be heeded when working around it, as there is danger of asphyxiation. Good ventilation or fans at the bottom of a space where fermentation takes place are essential. Alarms, which alert employees to dangerous levels of carbon dioxide, are highly recommended. If nitrogen or a mixed gas is used in an area, it would be wise to install low oxygen alarms in addition to the carbon dioxide alarms.

Pressure regulators and gauges should be regularly inspected for proper function to prevent carbon dioxide leaks, which can be easily detected using soapy water.

Fine particulates

In the milling area, in close proximity to the mash tun as well as in the filtration area where filter aids are employed, wearing a respirator or a suitable breathing mask is essential. For example, grain dust can induce asthma in some individuals but is hazardous to everyone. Diatomaceous earth, being microscopic pieces of silica, is very dangerous if it enters the lungs, though once it is wet, it does not pose a threat. Exposure to high levels of airborne crystalline and even amorphous silica in the form of diatoms or the quartz dust used to make countertops can result in silicosis, a serious lung disease for which there is no cure.

Confined spaces

Confined spaces with health or safety hazards exist in breweries. These include boilers, underground and other storage areas, tanks, silos, hoppers and rubbish containers.

Confined spaces in breweries possess these characteristics:

- of a sufficient size to allow a person to enter and perform work
- not designed for long-term occupancy, e.g. a tank, hopper, lauter tun
- restricted ingress or egress, e.g. manway
- a hazardous atmosphere, e.g. carbon dioxide, grain dust
- material that can engulf a person, e.g. water, wort, beer, grain

A hazard analysis and written procedures must be developed for confined spaces. If entering the confined space, such as a lauter tun or wort kettle, personnel must have the ability to lock out anyone from turning the equipment on. If entering a confined space such as a horizontal maturation tank, the manway door should be removed or otherwise blocked so that it cannot close, and the piping or hoses removed or otherwise blocked so that liquid or gas cannot enter the tank. A warning sign should be placed in an obvious position to indicate that personnel are working in the confined space.

Ergonomic injuries

Brewers deal with heavy sacks of grain and kegs and also perform repetitive tasks. Bending the knees, avoiding twisting while lifting and using lifting equipment will help prevent injury.

Electricity

At breweries, one finds large amounts of aqueous media and high voltage electricity. For this reason, certain precautions must be taken, most of which are common sense. Installing, repairing or otherwise working on exposed wiring or other electrical equipment should be avoided without the proper training. Any electrical equipment, like a pump, must be in good working condition (no worn or damaged cables, switches, etc.). All faulty or damaged equipment should be removed from operation. Electrical outlets, power strips or extension cables should not be overloaded. A brewery is a wet environment and all cords should be waterproof.

Brewhouse

Heated mash vessels and wort kettles, steam and hot water lines, tanks, boilers, etc. present hazards from the thermal energy stored in water or wort. Brewery personnel must be trained concerning the risks and appropriate behaviour when working around these aggregates and processes.

There are also moving parts in the brewhouse vessels, such as the mill, the raking arms equipped with sharp knives or tines and pumps. These also require the proper training in safety and operation.

Should the brewhouse contain copper in addition to stainless steel, personnel working with the copper vessels must be trained with regard to how they are different, since certain chemical cleaners can react with the copper.

Panels and pumps

A transfer panel with swing pipes can sometimes be connected incorrectly. Prior to turning on the pump, it is recommended that the operator or any other personnel not stand in front of the panel especially when transferring hot liquids. Pumps have moving parts and precautions should also be taken with this in mind.

Wet surfaces

Brewery floors should be installed so that they drain properly with minimal accumulation of liquid on the surface. They should possess a surface coating that is not slippery when wet (refer to the section on brewery floors). When liquids accumulate on a floor, especially beer, wort or other liquids containing nutrients, microorganisms tend to establish themselves rather quickly. Therefore, where liquids tend to accumulate, the floor should be cleared with a squeegee or other tool as soon as possible.

Kegs

Kegs are very often under pressure when they are full or empty. Prior to opening a keg to inspect it, replace a gasket or repair it, first ensure that the pressure has been released.

At many smaller breweries, kegs are cleaned and sanitised by hand. Purge kegs of cleaning and sanitising solutions with compressed air, not with carbon dioxide. Once the cleaning process is finished, the keg can be purged of air with carbon dioxide.

Bottles

Glass can shatter at any point in the filling process. The process of filling bottles can also be loud. Exposure to noise at that level for very long can be damaging to one's hearing. Therefore, safety goggles and ear protection are both required on the bottling line. Should a bottle shatter, the protocol for removing a set number of open bottles on either side of the shattered one must be followed.

Forklifts and pallet jacks

Although this is not always the case in smaller breweries, forklift drivers need to receive the proper training before getting behind the wheel. Many forklifts steer with the back wheel(s) and are thus a bit counterintuitive to drive and manoeuvre. The maximum speed, load and lift capability (weight and height) and distribution of the load when moving are essential to understanding forklift operations. Training should include the following:

- formal instruction: classes, written materials
- practical training: trainer demonstrations, exercises by personnel
- evaluation of the person's competence

Increasing the visibility of other personnel by wearing reflective vests to alert forklift drivers to their presence should be mandatory. Physical barriers with reflective surfaces to foster awareness where pedestrians and forklifts have to share the same space are advisable.

Pallet jacks do not require certification but nevertheless warrant a brief training session as their operation is not entirely intuitive.

STANDARD OPERATING PROCEDURES (SOPs)

What are SOPs?

A standard operating procedure (SOP) is a written set of instructions describing how to perform a routine activity. It is, in effect, the documentation of a process. At the hectic pace of everyday operations in the brewery, it is often difficult to find the time to commit to creating a set of SOPs that describe what is required for a specific procedure and how to go about it properly. Employees who are responsible for certain procedures as part of their job duties will obviously know what the task entails. However, a circumstance may arise in which these experienced employees are unavailable. At this point, an SOP becomes quite valuable in ensuring that operations continue smoothly. Furthermore, the chance of beer quality suffering as a result of unexpected circumstances is greatly reduced. As a brewery grows and increases output, SOPs also provide a welcome source of support for everyone involved.

The purpose of the SOP is to ensure that a procedure is performed in a consistent way and that it is carried out in a safe and efficient manner. The standard operating procedure should be clearly worded and brief. It should be easy to understand with action steps listed in the order they are to be performed. It should also contain warnings regarding any potential safety hazards. The SOP document should be readily available in close proximity to where the procedure is to be carried out.

Key areas where SOPs should be available include the following:

- brewhouse (mill and malt stores)
- fermentation, maturation and conditioning
- filtration
- filling and packaging
- laboratory
- cleaning and disinfection

Why are SOPs important?

- **Consistency:** they ensure that a standard procedure is in place regardless of which employee is performing the task, enhancing consistency in operations among all employees.
- **Communication:** SOPs take the guesswork out of the procedure to be performed. Employees can refer to the SOP to know which steps must be taken to perform the task at hand.
- **Saves time and money, increases efficiency:** everyone approaches a task differently. Having a written SOP in place ensures that all employees accomplish the task in the same way, saving time, increasing efficiency and allowing staff members to move on to the next task.
- **Accountability:** having a written set of instructions in place on how to perform tasks to meet expectations allows supervisors to fairly evaluate employee performance in an objective manner.
- **Safety:** performing a task in an unsafe manner not only jeopardises the safety of the employee and others, but it is also a liability for the company.
- **Training:** SOPs are valuable tools not only for existing employees but for new ones as well, helping them to learn new duties more quickly.

How to write an SOP

1. Draw up a list of the routine processes that occur at your company every day. Include the job duties associated with these processes.
2. Decide how the process can best be described, step-by-step instructions, flowchart, etc. Also consider how the information will be made available to the employee (online, printout at the workstation, etc.)
3. Gather input from the employees who regularly carry out the process. In some cases, suppliers may be the best source of information on how to best perform a procedure.
4. Write the process down and revise the standard operating procedure.
5. Update the SOP on an annual basis. Include the date the SOP was reviewed and updated, if applicable. Modify SOPs as conditions change.

Elements of an SOP

- **The title page** lists the name of the procedure and the department to which it applies.
- **A table of contents** can be helpful if the SOP is a longer document.
- **The procedure**, that is, the scope, terminology, procedure and any additional information that is relevant include the location of tools, equipment and warnings pertaining to occupational health and safety:
  - A description of the procedure can take the form of a checklist or a workflow diagramme.
  - The procedure should also indicate which tools are required and which methods to use.
- **Define the typical metrics** to review efficiency, such as the amount of time expected to complete the task, and consider possible options to streamline the process.

TRACEABILITY

The term traceability refers to the act of recording an identifying code or reference number for all of the materials used at every step within the production process. Should anything occur requiring some knowledge of what has gone into producing a particular batch of beer, these data records provide the information and, if necessary, some level of insurance for the brewer should there be a question about a particular beer. Traceability can provide essential information and perhaps even legal defence in response to complaints concerning beer in trade.

What is traceability?

Traceability is the capacity to identify and track the entire development of a product throughout the supply chain using documents or records – starting with all materials used to make it, through every step of the production process until the product is distributed and sold to the consumer. In essence, records should be maintained for everything along the supply chain that impacts the product. If traceability is practiced at every step in the supply chain, then for instance, the field the barley comes from, the lot of malt it belonged to, the batch of beer it went into and anything about its entire history and provenance is known because it has been recorded.

Why is traceability important and necessary?

Documenting the raw materials, the production process as well as the distribution and sale of the finished products enables quick and accurate traceability along the supply chain. Brewery products must be safe for consumers and must comply with all food safety legislation. Should any question arise regarding the safety of the product at any point, having accurate documentation in place makes the relevant information easily accessible. Documentation provides a reference to determine what point in the process should be reviewed and also helps pinpoint exactly what measures must be taken.

A comprehensive traceability programme involves the accurate collection and maintenance of records which document the following:

- Materials or goods received: all materials used in the production process obtained from suppliers such as water, malt, adjuncts, hops, yeast, process aids, additives, cleaning and disinfection agents and packaging materials.
- All products created, processed or packaged: wort, beer, spent yeast, spent grains, packaged products (kegs, bottles, cans), label information/codes.
- All products dispatched from the brewery: transportation, storage and delivery within the distribution network including wholesalers, retailers and customers.

| Record keeping

Record keeping is essential for recognising problems in the brewing process from the outset so that appropriate measures can be taken. Key measurements include starting gravity, final gravity, fermentation time, temperature, pH and yeast pitching rates.

For reasons of traceability but also of quality control, brewers should keep careful records of all operations, including water treatment, brewhouse, fermentation, maturation, filtration and filling. Keeping a meticulous history of brewery operations is of great importance. The more detailed and pertinent records are, the easier it will be to brew consistently and identify anomalies before they turn into problems. Furthermore, if a particular batch of beer is better or worse than others, one can find possible causes in the production records. Provided on the next two pages are examples of the kinds of sheets used to record brewhouse and fermentation/maturation cellar operations. For those needing a more detailed record of the mashing regime, refer to figure 1b. This mash report can be altered to fit the needs of the brewery and printed on the back of the log sheet in figure 1a:

Date				Brewer's name	
Beer		Batch no.		Brewing liquor	
Grain bill			kg		
				Mashing regime and notes	
				Mash pH reading:	
				Mash acidification	
				volume:	
				concentration:	
Total				adjusted to:	
Lautering programme and notes				time:	
				notes:	
				Equipment notes	

Wort run-off	extract [°P]	pH	Notes on pH
first wort, vol:			
sample 1, vol.:			
sample 2, vol.:			
sample 3, vol.:			
Final lauter wort			

Wort kettle — Kettle wort volume: — Cast-out wort volume:

boil time	hop variety	% alpha	utilisation	IBU	kg	Notes on wort boiling process

Wort acidification	Wort chilling
volume of acid/concentration:	time:
adjusted to:	
time:	temperature of pitching wort:
notes:	

Whirlpool	Brewhouse efficiency
whirlpool rest duration:	
whirlpool hop addition:	
notes:	

Figure 1a: Brewhouse log sheet

Mash Report   Mashing regime: _____

Grist to liquor ratio: _____ : _____

Grist [dt]: _____

Brewing liquor [hl]: _____

	Temperature [°C]	Time from	to	Duration	Volume [hl]
Total mash					**Volume [hl]**
Mash-in	at:				
Rest	at:				
Heated	from: to:				
Rest	at:				
Rest mash					**Volume [hl]**
Rest	at:				
Decoction mash 1					**Volume [hl]**
Decoction	at:				
Heated	from: to:				
Rest	at:				
Heated	from: to:				
Rest	at:				
Heated	from: to:				
Rest	at:				
Heated	from: to:				
Boiled	at:				
Return decoction mash to the main mash					
Mixed	from: to:				
Total mash					**Volume [hl]**
Rest	at:				
Rest mash					**Volume [hl]**
Rest	at:				
Decoction mash 2					**Volume [hl]**
Decoction	at:				
Heated	from: to:				
Rest	at:				
Heated	from: to:				
Rest	at:				
Heated	from: to:				
Boiled	at:				
Return decoction mash to the main mash					
Mixed	from: to:				
Total mash					**Volume [hl]**
Rest	at:				
Iodine test:	positive: ☐ negative: ☐				
Heated	from: to:				
Mash-out	at:				

Figure 1b: Mash report (on the reverse of the brewhouse log sheet)

| Fermentation tank no. | | | Brewer's name | | | | |

Beer

Tank CIP/sanitation and notes

Chilled wort date brewed:

batch number	wort volume	original gravity

total volume:
temperature:
original gravity:

Propagation (if applicable)

date/time	step	volume	aeration	°C	cell count

Yeast pitching

yeast strain:
yeast origin:
generation:
viability:
cell count:

Fermentation

date/time	sample [°C]	sensor [°C]	set [°C]	pH	gravity	cell count	Notes

Conditioning/maturation

date/time	sample [°C]	sensor [°C]	set [°C]	pH	gravity	cell count	Notes

Attenuation   final attenuation: limit of attenuation: Δ: (apparent)

Figure 2: Fermentation log sheet

The following form (fig. 3) can be printed with the values saved for the target values (min, normal, max), and the measurement data can be recorded by the member of the staff taking the readings. This form is useful for maintaining the consistency of products. If a particular batch is above or below the normal range, then blending may be in order.

Beer	Tank	Date

Target values	
Gravity reading	Attenuation

maximum		maximum	
normal		normal	
minimum		minimum	
measured values		measured values	

Target values	
pH	Carbon dioxide

maximum		maximum	
normal		normal	
minimum		minimum	
measured values		measured values	

Remarks

Figure 3: Target and measured values

| Additional points

- Accurate and easily accessible record keeping is key to a successful traceability programme. Records are usually a written description of an event that has occurred. Good record keeping makes it possible to trace and link all materials and processes used to create a product simply by looking up a batch number or similar label code on the package.
- Records also serve as proof of compliance with laws or governmental stipulations.

- Records may be printed on paper or stored digitally using software or programmes developed expressly for this purpose.
- Records should be created and stored in a well-organised manner which is clear to all persons involved. The cost of record keeping can be very low depending on the method chosen, limited to a few supplies and a short amount of time.
- Invoices and other delivery paperwork in paper form can be filed and stored in binders located in a designated location. They may also be scanned directly into some software programmes or the information can be entered manually, for example, in a spreadsheet programme.

Records should contain the following information:

Delivery invoices for goods received:

- date of the transaction
- name of business/supplier and contact information
- business identification information
- name of recipient
- name of persons responsible for traceability
- dispatch and receipt of product
- name of product, product identification number
- product description
- country or place of origin
- quantity
- best before date
- shelf life of the product
- any applicable specifications or analytical data
- storage information batch or lot numbers
- identifier or serial numbers
- sales receipt number
- price by unit or weight

Product sheets for all products created, processed or packaged in the brewery:

- brewhouse logs which document each batch of wort produced
- production sheets detailing the cold side of beer production including wort aeration, yeast pitching, fermentation, maturation, filtration, pasteurisation, carbonation, filling and packaging, label information/codes
- delivery invoices for all products dispatched from the brewery: storage and transportation in the distribution network and deliveries to wholesalers, retailers and customers

Delivery invoices for goods leaving the brewery:

- date of the transaction, name of brewery and contact information, business identification information, name of recipient, name of persons responsible for traceability, dispatch and receipt of product, name of product, product identification number, product description, country or place of origin, quantity, best before date, shelf life of the product, any applicable specifications or analytical data, storage information, batch or lot numbers, identifier or serial numbers, sales receipt number, price by unit or weight

Brewhouse log sheets are a record of brewhouse operations. These data can be compared to other batches later on to troubleshoot the cause of problems or optimise the process. A log sheet typically includes the following:

- date, person(s) on duty
- the name of the beer and the batch number for traceability
- grain bill with quantities and type of malt including information for traceability
- mashing and lautering information based on measurements made during mashing, temperature, pH, conversion, etc
- time entries for each step of the brewing process and notation of event
- transfer of wort to kettle, measurements of the gravity in the kettle, volume of wort, pH and temperature
- additions to the kettle during wort boiling, hops, variety, type, quantity and time added
- transfer of wort to the whirlpool and time entries

Yeast pitching and fermentation

- Yeast pitching sheets should be maintained (date, time, batch number, batch description, cell count, viability, pitching temperature, etc.) tank number, yeast strain.
- Gravity plotted vs. time provides quick visual confirmation of how a fermentation is progressing. Anomalies can be easily recognised simply by looking at the shape of the graph.
- Yeast brinks or yeast storage vessels have detailed information attached securely to the vessel. This may include variety, date transferred to container, viability, cell count, weight/volume, etc.
- Finished products should be labelled with clearly visible, systematic and understandable information regarding the batch number, date packaged and expiration date/best before date.
- Fermentation profiles chart the progress of fermentation. The time required for fermentation may vary according to season, especially if ambient temperature can influence fermentation. Therefore, the specific gravity should be measured daily during fermentation and the values plotted over time. This can be done manually, using software such as Microsoft Excel or a brewing application. In cases where a decision has to be made, information such as the gravity at packaging compared to the gravity measured on the market, could provide crucial evidence for recalling a batch (product recall, traceability).

Essential quality control in the brewery

- general measurements: time, pressure, temperature, fill level, dissolved oxygen, dissolved carbon dioxide
- grist composition, colour (digital meter, comparator, spectrophotometer), starch conversion, gravity (most will use hydrometer or digital meter), pH, yeast pitching rate, fermentation capacity
- beer: turbidity, IBU, alcohol concentration, foam stability, sensory evaluation, sulphur dioxide

Microbiology

- yeast cell counts
- culture media
- bacteria counts (aerobic, anaerobic)
- pure yeast cultures/propagation
- viability
- efficacy of cleaning procedures

Administrative records

- procedures and policies
- customer complaints and product returns
- personnel training and certification
- inspection reports
- documentation of corrective measures
- maintenance records

Developing a system

There are a variety of systems available; some of them are bundled with the brewery's automation system while others are simply computer spreadsheets. Either way, trends should be graphed and able to be tracked in a brewery. Being able to step back and view trend lines together, especially for different aspects of production, is very useful. This applies to every aspect of brewing and quality control: an increasingly positive result for the kinds of microbes that accompany beer spoilers can point to a weak spot in the cleaning regimen even before it becomes a problem affecting product quality. The more records are taken, the more carefully organised they are, the more accessible, trackable and visually displayed they are, the better.

OVERVIEW: CHALLENGES TO QUALITY

Quality is not just an assortment of measurements and numbers; it is a philosophy that brewers live by. All endeavours to constantly improve beer quality should be approached in a systematic manner. Every brewer should decide what constitutes the level of quality they are striving to attain and quantify and describe it to the best of their ability. Only through monitoring the most relevant parameters and by measuring the extent to which they vary can brewers expect to control the outcome.

The subsequent sections of this book will explore challenges to quality in breweries. First, cleaning and hygiene will be addressed, followed by raw materials, the brewing process and finally the finished beer. The points discussed here will provide the personnel at small breweries with a guide for improving quality and consistency in their beers while avoiding some of the pitfalls common in beer production.

Appendices outlining key laboratory techniques and recommendations for launching a brewery laboratory are included at the back of the book.

CLEANLINESS AND HYGIENIC DESIGN

Practical hygiene for breweries

Since brewers do more cleaning than almost anything else, hygienically designed equipment can not only help brewers maintain a high level of hygiene, it can keep the emergence of contamination at bay. Contrary to popular belief, hygienic design is not aseptic processing, which involves packaging vulnerable foods in sterilised containers in a sterile environment. Beer is not so vulnerable (unless it is non-alcoholic or low-strength beer) and therefore does not need to be packaged aseptically. Hygienic design refers to the fact that any internal or external surface coming into contact with the product at a given point in the production process must be so constructed that contamination and soil cannot easily persist on it. Furthermore, every single surface must be constructed so that it can be thoroughly cleaned.

Fundamental principles

The following criteria should be strictly observed regarding brewery equipment:

- All equipment must be installed with cleanliness in mind and must be able to be cleaned to a satisfactory microbiological level and maintained in such a state.
- Every part of the brewery must be accessible for inspection, maintenance, cleaning and disinfection and must also be hygienically compatible with other parts of the production process.
- Nothing in the brewery should be able to adulterate the products with fuel, foreign materials, lubricants, metal fragments, contaminated water, etc.
- All equipment and aggregates that come into contact with the product must be resistant to corrosion, must consist of non-toxic materials and be designed for the conditions under which they are intended to be used.

| Stainless steel

Stainless steel is an alloy of various metals, primarily steel, chromium and nickel, with additions of other elements. Stainless steel is practical in places where carbon steel cannot be utilised, such as when the steel comes into regular contact with liquids. The quality and the grade of the stainless steel employed in building tanks, lines and other equipment are central to hygienic design.

Specific designations

As mentioned, there are many grading systems; these include:

- European Standards (EN)
- British Standards (BS)
- International Organization for Standardization (ISO)
- German Standard (DIN)
- The Society of Automotive Engineers (SAE)
- The American Society for Testing and Materials (ASTM)
- Japanese Industrial Standards (JIS)
- Chinese Standard (GB)

The European numeric designations of common stainless steel grades are listed below. Their equivalents are provided in parentheses.

Alloying elements

Simply stating that a material is composed of 'stainless steel' is not enough to understand its properties and whether it is suitable for certain applications. There are over 100 grades of stainless steel and different ways to classify them. Various grades of stainless steel alloys are available for applications in the food and beverage industry. All around the world, one hears in conversations or reads terms referring to stainless steel like 'chrome-nickel', 'V2A', 'V4A', '304', '316', etc. Some of the terms are historical or specific to certain regions. A standardised classification system now exists to avoid any confusion regarding the grades of stainless steel. The older terms still persist, however, and it is beneficial to know the most common ones, in order to understand what one hears or reads on the subject, especially when sourcing equipment for a brewery.

Table 1 (not an exhaustive list) provides a summary of the common alloying elements found in stainless steel:

Table 1: Alloying elements in stainless steel

Element	Purpose
aluminium (Al)	hardener, deoxidiser
carbon (C)	strengthener, forms carbides
chromium (Cr)	improves resistance to oxidation, ferrite stabiliser
copper (Cu)	improves resistance to sulphuric acid, hardener with titanium and aluminium, austenite stabiliser
manganese (Mn)	increases nitrogen solubility, combined with sulphur to prevent hot cracking, austenite stabiliser
molybdenum (Mo)	improves resistance to chlorides, prevents pitting and crevice corrosion, ferrite stabiliser
nickel (Ni)	improves resistance to mineral acids, austenite stabiliser
nitrogen (N)	improves resistance to chlorides, austenite stabiliser
sulphur (S)	increases weldability, machinability, but reduces resistance to pitting corrosion
titanium (Ti)	hardens stainless steel, ferrite stabiliser

One critical element in stainless steel is chromium, an element – not chrome, which is a coating. Chromium is classified as a transition metal on the periodic table and is resistant to corrosion. Chrome refers to the layer of electroplating, a chromium oxide coating, one sees over the surfaces of metal on motorcycles, tools, etc. For stainless steel to be resistant to rust, the alloy must contain at least 13% chromium.

Less expensive stainless steel grades contain less chromium and/or nickel and are often employed in automotive applications and in the manufacture of, for example, countertops, sinks, washing machine drums or housewares but should not be utilised in the manufacture of tanks or other equipment.

Passivation

The resistance to corrosion and rust of stainless steel is improved by passivation, which refers to treatment of stainless steel surfaces with acid in order to remove free iron particles. Mechanical stress caused, for instance, by cutting or grinding or chemical stress, such as pitting or corrosion can damage stainless steel in such a way that it necessitates passivation. After passivation, an inert, uniform, chromium oxide layer exists on the surface. A mild oxidant is used for passivation. Impellers, agitators and similar devices are generally passivated and electropolished, a further means to improve the surface quality of stainless steel and to make it more resistant to corrosion. Unlike paint or other coatings, there is no chipping or peeling. Passivation is, however, not possible with all grades of stainless steel (those lacking adequate levels of chromium and nickel) or with just any kind of acid. Damage from welding or brazing cannot be alleviated by passivation. A nitric acid solution (1–1.5%) can be used, but many brewers are wary of nitric acid because it is dangerous, environmentally hazardous, requires higher temperatures and can emit toxic gases.

Thus, a method for citric acid passivation has been developed for almost every grade of stainless steel, which is much safer, environmentally friendly, can be carried out at room temperature and does not emit noxious gases. Citric acid can impart resistance to corrosion similar or even superior to nitric acid passivation. There are commercial products containing citric acid available for stainless steel passivation and instructions on how to carry out the process correctly.

Literature and further reading

DeBold, T.; *Passivating Stainless Steel Parts*. Machine and Tool Blue Book, November 1986

Narziss, L. *Abriss der Bierbrauerei*. Wiley-VCH Verlag GmbH & Co., 2017

Yasensky, D., Larson, C. Reali, J., *Citric Acid Passivation of Stainless Steel*. United Space Alliance M&P Engineering, Chad Carl, NASA M&P Engineering, 2009

Other considerations

Surface roughness and welds

The surfaces of tanks and piping and all of their welds must be cleanable, meaning that the roughness of the surface in contact with the product must correspond to the basic requirements for food production. Welds can be especially problematic if a manufacturing company is not familiar with the construction of food-grade equipment.

Surface roughness

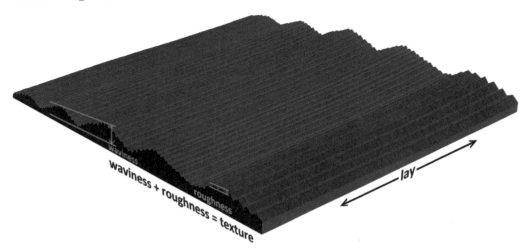

Figure 4: Surface roughness

Surface roughness (fig. 4) is defined as deviations in the direction of the so-called 'normal vector' of an actual surface compared to an ideal surface. If the actual surface deviates significantly from its ideal form, then the surface would be considered rough. On the other hand, if they are small, the surface is deemed to be smooth. Roughness is measured in micrometres (μm). To provide a point of reference, a single brewing yeast cell is around 8 to 10 μm. The finish on tank walls and the like can be expressed by the abrasive belts used in their manufacture ('polished to grit 180'). This is, however, not an objective measurement of the surface roughness.

Measurements of roughness describe the following:

Average roughness (R_a): Average distance above and below the centre line for the sample length; also known as **Centre Line Average (CLA)**. These measurements should be taken in areas where the greatest roughness is presumed to exist on the surface.

An upper limit can be specified for this value. In EN ISO 4288 (see below), there is a rule on maximum roughness. It states that all roughness values labelled with the subscript 'max' represent the maximum value for the mean measured in five lengths of the surface in question. This maximum value should not be exceeded – no exceptions.

Why should this be of interest to a brewer?

Suffice it to say that larger deviations in surface roughness diminish the efficacy of the cleaning cycle and promote the growth of microorganisms. These minute irregularities on the inner wall of a tank, for example, are interesting from the viewpoint of hygienic design. If the surface is smooth from a hygienic perspective, it diminishes the surface's adhesive properties and facilitates cleaning. The inner surface of the cone of a cylindroconical tank must be especially smooth, in order to allow the yeast to slide down the cone towards the opening at the bottom.

Manufacturers, who build equipment for smaller breweries, must of course also adhere to hygienic design requirements. Upper limits for the finish on the inner surface of tanks and their welds should be stipulated in equipment contracts.

The EHEDG (European Hygienic Engineering & Design Group) recommends the following:

Surfaces that come into contact with the product should meet the following criteria:

- The surface finish must exhibit an acceptable R_a value, preferably $R_a \leq 0.8$ μm, unless test results can prove that it is cleanable with a higher value for roughness.
- The surface must be free of imperfections, such as scratches, cervices, pitting and folds.

The surface of stainless steel can be finished by brushing, polishing or bead blasting. Resistance to corrosion is one important factor determining the finish on stainless steel. The grit on the fine abrasive belt used to produce a certain finish provides no guarantee that the whole surface will exhibit a roughness corresponding to that grit number. The higher the grit number, the finer the lines on the surface and thus the more reflective the stainless steel will be. The most common finish when stainless steel exits the mill is referred to as a 'matte finish'. The number 4 or 'brushed finish' is often classified as 'food-grade', while the number 8 finish is called a 'mirror finish'.

Welds

Joining pieces of metal together using heat requires skill and knowledge. The quality of hygienic welds on equipment can vary widely depending upon the manufacturer. This is why inspecting equipment is of the utmost importance, prior to agreeing to purchase it or pay for work done on it. The surface of the weld should at least correspond to the level of roughness expected for the non-welded stainless steel.

The two pictures in figure 5 show the same weld on the inside and outside of a stainless steel pipe. A mistake has been made: the pipe was not purged with inert gas and 'sugar' or burnt metal has created an unhygienic surface, one that is completely unfit for wort or beer. Pinhole-sized leaks are also often present with such welds. Unfortunately, these kinds of welds can be encountered from time to time; however, this example is quite extreme:

Figure 5: Unacceptable welds, 'sugar'   Photos: *Yuseff Cherney*

Although the following weld (fig. 6) looks good from the outside, there was not sufficient penetration by the orbital welder, and the two pieces were not joined completely on the inside. There is an unhygienic gap present between the two pieces (the arrow in the next photo points at the gap):

Figure 6: Unacceptable welds, insufficient penetration   Photos: *Yuseff Cherney*

Figure 7 shows a hygienically welded – as yet unpolished and unpassivated – stainless steel pipe fitting (the arrow points to the weld):

Figure 7: An acceptable weld with sufficient penetration – prior to passivation and polishing
Photo: *Yuseff Cherney*

Literature and further reading

Details concerning definitions of these and other terms as well as how to perform and evaluate surface measurements can be found in the EN ISO 3274 (1997), EN ISO 4288 (1997) and EN ISO 4287 (1998) standards.

| Piping and valves

Concerning water/wort/beer lines, it is imperative that any piping or tubing be installed in the brewery so that it is as straight and direct as possible and in such a way that liquids flow downwards with gravity and can be drained (fig. 8). An incline in the opposite direction, results in upward flow having to occur. There is a chance that some 'backwashing' and thus contamination might happen.

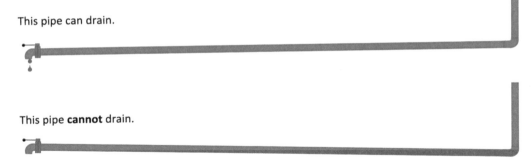

This pipe can drain.

This pipe **cannot** drain.

Figure 8: Pipes must be able to drain

Dead ends and similar pipe layouts should ideally be entirely avoided or at least fitted with a threaded cap (figs. 9 and 10) which can be removed to allow cleaning. After making alterations to equipment, for instance, any redundant piping has to be removed to prevent contamination with microorganisms. Any branching, intersections or piping diverted away from the main line must be equipped with some means for sealing them off, such as with a valve. Valves must also be installed where the side branch begins and not several metres

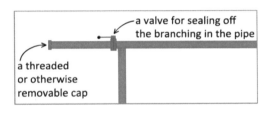

Figure 9: A dead end

in. Though one does occasionally see them, capped dead ends extending outward from tank domes should likewise be avoided, as spray shadows are inevitable inside of them, meaning that the cleaning solution cannot reach them. At the bottom of a tank – in the example below (fig. 11), a cylindroconical tank – it is not uncommon to see an elbow welded directly to the bottom of the cone. This is problematic, as disassembly and thus thorough cleaning are impossible. The valve above the elbow also prevents yeast cells from sedimenting out into the uncooled pipe. In the uncooled elbow, they rapidly undergo autolysis, a process which occurs when the enzymes in dead yeast cells degrade the cellular constituents. These compounds become soluble and can produce unpleasant off-flavours in the finished beer.

Figure 10: Two examples of pipe layouts one should avoid. Liquids become trapped in the pipe on the left, while gases become trapped in the pipe on the right.

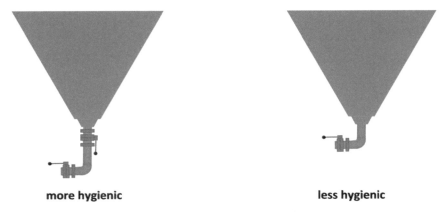

more hygienic   **less hygienic**

Figure 11: More and less hygienic valves and piping on a tank cone

Thermometers, manometers and other sensors should not be connected via a simple T-fitting with a threaded dairy coupling as these cannot be adequately cleaned. Other hygienic connectors for this purpose are available.

Ball valves should be completely avoided in beer production as they are considered unhygienic and cannot be properly cleaned. Butterfly valves are recommended for use in breweries, since they have fewer 'dead spots' than ball valves. In a butterfly valve, the disc in the centre of the pipe is turned by an actuator on the outside. If the disc is completely parallel to the flow of the medium in the pipe, the valve is open. If the disc is turned so that it is completely perpendicular to the flow, the valve is closed (fig. 12).

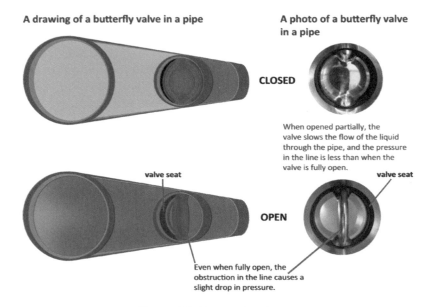

Figure 12: Butterfly valves
Photos: *Yuseff Cherney*

Valve seats and gaskets

Valves are only as good as their seats and gaskets, so they must be inspected frequently and regularly without fail. In critical areas, two butterfly valves can be connected in series with a short length of pipe between them (perhaps even with a sight glass) to prevent leakage. For extra safety and security on a more permanent basis, double-seated valves with a controlled leakage space are recommended for keeping products safe and uncontaminated, especially during switching operations. If one of the valve seats is leaking, it is immediately apparent, and the seal can be replaced. They can, however, be expensive and thus may be impractical for smaller breweries.

Given the rigours of pH and temperature, to ensure safety and a long service life, the material used for the valve seats must be carefully chosen. The material must meet the following criteria:

- capable of withstanding a range of temperatures from below the freezing point (< 0 °C) to well above the boiling point (> 150 °C) of water, resistance to steam
- resistance to detergents, sodium hydroxide (NaOH)
- tolerant of a wide pH range

Though other materials exist, ethylene-propylene (EPDM) has proven to be the best for seats and gaskets in a brewery setting, given its resistance to a range of temperatures, pH values and cleaning chemicals (acid, caustic, hot water).

Other fittings and hoses

As mentioned above, disassembly is necessary for cleaning and inspection of valves, temperature probes, sight glasses and other fittings. Dairy fittings, which are common in breweries, are not sufficiently hygienic and should either be avoided from the outset or replaced at the earliest convenience. Brewers using dairy fittings can produce quality beer; however, they must be vigilant and ensure that they clean behind the gaskets with every CIP cycle.

Hygienic couplings designed for aseptic and pharmaceutical applications exist (e.g. EN 14420-2/3/4/5/6/7/8), but dairy fittings can also be made more hygienic by replacing the standard gaskets with, for example, hygienic k-Flex gasket inserts. These gasket inserts are certified by the EHEDG, since they eliminate gaps between fittings.

Any process lines, including compressed air, nitrogen or CO_2 lines, can become contaminated should flow occur in the wrong direction. Backflow preventers and hygienically designed piping are therefore highly recommended. However, the lines must be planned and installed with this in mind. Even with backflow preventers, piping should nevertheless be regularly inspected and cleaned.

Refer to the section on the brewing process below for information on aeration and carbonation equipment.

Air compressors

Breweries require compressed air in the production area, most notably the brewhouse where the wort is aerated. Compressors concentrate airborne contaminants (micro-organisms, dust, rust, oil and water vapour, pollen and other pollutants). Airborne contaminants have to be reduced to acceptable levels in order to protect a brewery's products and by extension, its customers. The air compressor should be one manufactured expressly for use in food production, not one simply fitted with an attached oil separator.

The air supplied by the compressor should be clean, oil-free and dry. The oil used for lubrication of the compressor must nevertheless be food-grade should any bleed through. Since some traces of food-grade compressor oil will likely migrate downstream, thereby feeding any microorganisms present along the way, some food production facilities install additional sterile air filters downstream at the point of use, rather than only far upstream near the compressor.

Steam for cleaning

If a brewery requires steam for cleaning (e.g. kegs or tanks), the steam should not come directly from the boiler. Boiler feed water should never be in contact with the product or any vessel used in production. The steam from the boiler should only be employed to heat water of at least drinking water quality by means of a heat exchanger to create hot water or steam for cleaning.

Brewery hoses

Hoses not currently in use should always be hung up with the ends down so they can drain. The ends should not touch the floor or hang over a gutter, drain or other sources of contamination.

When working with hoses, they should <u>never</u> be crimped to stop the flow of liquid through them. This will destroy the lining, creating an unhygienic surface where microorganisms can hide.

Hoses have what is known as a 'bend radius', which refers to the

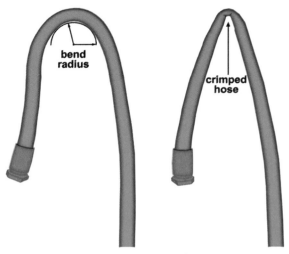

Figure 13: Brewery hoses

minimum extent to which a hose should curve. At a smaller radius, the hose lining can be damaged. Hoses with a small bend radius are manufactured for use in breweries where space is limited. Should hoses extend across spaces where forklifts or other heavy equipment may be in operation, crushproof hoses or protective ramps are available to avoid damage to hoses.

Hoses rated for the pressure, temperature and chemicals present in a brewery should be the only hoses that come into consideration for beer production; for instance, non-food-grade hoses should never come into contact with water, wort, beer or any products intended for human consumption, and vinyl hoses should never be used for CIP cleaning with hot cleaning chemicals.

Wastewater piping

Any wastewater pipes should not be directly connected to a drain but should end in front of it, since a connection with the sewage system allows microorganisms to migrate more readily upwards into the brewery.

Filling equipment

Aside from normal CIP procedures, fillers should be sprayed down with cold water (drinking water quality) after every filling run, in order to remove any residual beer or soft drinks still on them. They should be sprayed off carefully and thoroughly, as beer and soft drinks provide a source of nutrients for microorganisms, which will not hesitate to become established there.

Heat exchangers

Breweries are full of equipment where heat conductivity is key to the proper function of the equipment and to the overall success of the brewing process.

If the wort kettle or fermentation tanks are not cleaned properly, not only does the quality of the beer suffer but energy is wasted and costs increase. Learning to inspect and remove scale, soil and beer stone from heat transfer surfaces is important. This may at times require mechanical cleaning. Depending upon the quality of the brewing liquor, the shell and tube heat exchanger in the hot liquor tank may also need to be inspected for hard water deposits.

Fouling, the accumulation of a layer of scalded wort, must be removed in internal and external calandrias (refer to the section on thermal stress below). This layer acts as insulation, greatly reducing the efficiency of the calandria. This is particularly a problem if a calandria is not equipped with a pump below the heating tubes to push the wort through and out of the heat exchanger. If a calandria is not equipped with a pump, brewers generally heat the wort in the wort kettle (usually equipped with additional steam heating at the base or on the sides) and then begin heating it in the calandria when it is near boiling to reduce fouling.

A common problem in brewhouses performing several shifts per day, especially with heavily hopped beers, is that the heat exchanger rapidly becomes inefficient at heat transfer due to soil accumulation on the stainless steel surfaces – and perhaps also contaminated with wort bacteria. Therefore, it is recommended that the product side of the heat exchanger be backflushed with water after every brew cycle to remove any soil accumulation. If possible, this should be done at a slightly higher velocity than the wort is pumped in the opposite direction during normal production. Depending upon how frequently the brewhouse is in operation, the heat exchanger should be cleaned with a caustic cleaning solution (backward and forward) during the cleaning cycle, either at the end of every day or every week, at the latest. It should also be taken apart and inspected every three to six months. Not only can soil become baked on and require mechanical cleaning, but gaskets can wear out and become cracked.

Refrigerants and coolants

A refrigerant is a substance in liquid form, such as R-717 (ammonia), R-134a (tetra-fluoroethane) or R-404A (a blend of chemicals), that is capable of becoming a gas at low temperatures and thus can be employed in mechanical refrigeration to chill foods or air. The refrigerant does not normally come into direct contact with the equipment containing the wort or beer to be chilled.

A coolant, on the other hand, is a liquid chilled in a heat exchanger by the refrigerant. The coolant circulates through, for instance, the jackets of a tank to reduce or maintain a suitable temperature for fermentation and maturation. Food-grade coolants, such as propylene glycol, should be employed so that any accidental contact with the beer will not result in adulteration of the wort or beer with hazardous chemicals, for example in a heat exchanger with a leaky gasket, through a damaged tank wall or beer dispensing line. If the cooling jacket on a tank is leaking, before it can reach the inner wall of the tank, the glycol should flow down through the cladding to the so-called 'weep hole' at the bottom of the tank where it can drip out. If this occurs, the tank would need to be repaired immediately.

The coolant pumped to a fermentation or maturation tank has to be turned off prior to commencing the cleaning cycle. If the heat exchanger in the brewhouse is connected to the same circuit as the fermentation and maturation tanks, they should be shut off briefly while the coolant in the reservoir returns to a suitable temperature. This is one reason breweries are equipped with either two separate circuits or a refrigeration system with enough capacity to rapidly chill the coolant, whether it be ice water, cooling brine or a mixture of food-grade glycol and water. Figure 14 shows a schematic of a refrigeration

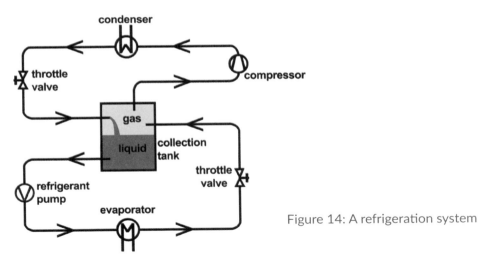

Figure 14: A refrigeration system

system. In the case of a walk-in cool room for packaged beer, air is blown across the evaporator coils to cool the room. Fans propelling air across these coils spread the microorganisms harboured there which are sometimes present as biofilms. As they are difficult to clean, it is highly recommended, especially in cool rooms housing maturation or serving tanks, that food or other sources of contamination <u>not</u> be stored there to avoid promoting adulteration by microorganisms. Not only can these microorganisms harbour beer spoilers, but especially if given nutrients, they can grow quickly enough to greatly reduce the efficiency of the heat exchange surfaces, thus creating more expense through greater energy usage or failed compressors. Cooling coils need to be inspected regularly for the presence of bacterial and mould growth. There are products designed to keep the coils in cool rooms free of contamination. These should be taken into consideration, in order to keep cool rooms running efficiently and relatively free of unwanted microorganisms.

Brewery floors

Brewers generally expend most of their initial capital outlay on a building and brewing equipment and have little left over for much else. The importance and practical benefits of a good brewery floor are quite often underestimated. The flooring has to be suitable for industrial applications and capable of bearing heavy loads, and along with the drains, needs to promote overall brewery hygiene.

Drains and gradients

Floor drainage is an important aspect of hygienic production:

- The slope should be sufficient to allow drainage, so that puddles do not form on the surface. A 1% grade is probably sufficient in most cases, but a 2% grade from each corner to the drain can compensate for any unevenness of the floor to prevent 'shelving', still allowing complete drainage over longer distances.

- Linear channels are the most practical floor drains for breweries, as the volume of liquid can be too great during day-to-day production to flow to a single point.
- The metal drainage components are best manufactured from the appropriate grades of stainless steel. They should be passivated or electroplated after the components have been manufactured to reduce the incidence of corrosion.

Flooring

There are a variety of options for breweries, such as various types of tiles as well as cement-based, polyurethane and epoxy surface coatings; however, regardless of the material, the following is advisable for floors in a brewery production area:

- The material should be of a consistency or texture that does not promote microbial growth.
- Both the surface and arrangement of equipment on the floor should be easy to clean and to maintain.
- The surface should be robust enough to allow frequent high-pressure steam or hot water cleaning.
- Resistance to mechanical force is necessary, both for the surface and the underlying structure (heavy tanks and other equipment).
- With the range of chemicals employed in production, the floors must be as non-reactive as possible, resistant to a range of chemicals and stain-proof.
- The surface should tolerate a wide range of temperatures.
- The floor should exhibit a high resistance to abrasive forces, chipping or flaking.
- A non-slip surface is required (floors are rated for this).

Selecting a floor that is HACCP-certified and recommended by the EHEDG for hygienic food production would be prudent.

Figure 15: Brewery floor tiles, before and after installation

Literature and further reading

The European Hygienic Engineering & Design Group (EHEDG); refer to ehedg.org

Website: haccp-international.com/business-directory/wpbdp_category/flooring

Fairley, M., Smith, D., Timmerman, H. *Hygienic Design and Operation of Floor Drainage Components*. Journal of Hygienic Engineering and Design, Review paper UDC 631.62

Spare parts

Keeping spare parts on hand is also important, as broken components are, at the very least, unhygienic. Those that are critical for brewery operations should be kept on site in sufficient numbers, while those less critical might not need to be in stock at a supplier but available for pickup or delivery on relatively short notice.

Finding sources of contamination

A brewer must always be circumspect about whether the production facility is harbouring microorganisms capable of directly or indirectly contaminating the raw materials, processing aids, intermediate or final products, which include the brewing liquor (water), malt, hops, yeast, compressed air, CO_2, diatomaceous earth, process water, wort and beer. The raw materials, processing aids and intermediate products can be infected and then become a source of microbial contamination as well. Microorganisms able to adulterate beer are not the only ones at issue, since non-product-spoiling bacteria and wild yeast can form cooperative communities that can provide safe haven for a whole host of microorganisms (refer to the section on beer-spoiling microorganisms).

One must keep in mind, that if soil and other contaminants are present on the outside of, for example, a tank or piping, the higher the probability is that microorganisms capable of damaging the product will find their way inside. With hygienically designed equipment, keeping microbial contaminants under control is much more straightforward.

CLEANING AND SANITISING

Clean-in-place (CIP)

Cleaning the inner surfaces of brewing equipment (vessels, piping, hoses, etc.) can be performed by establishing a closed circuit, which includes a vessel containing cleaning solution. The cleaning solution is pumped around at the proper concentration, pH, temperature and velocity. In this way, the piping, vessels, etc. are cleaned in the process. If only a single tank has to be cleaned, the cleaning solution can be created in the bottom of the tank and pumped in a circuit through the CIP arm and the spray ball. Valves, temperature probes and other fittings in the cleaning circuit should be removed for inspection and cleaning. Gaskets and any other removable parts should likewise be examined and cleaned thoroughly to ensure no soil is present in crevices or other spaces. Alas, gaskets, washers, rings and other parts wear out and may need replacing at some point. Gas lines (compressed air, carbon dioxide, nitrogen) must be cleaned and sanitised as well, as they may also be a source of microbial contamination (see below).

Cleaning and sanitation practices

It goes without saying that a large part of brewing process involves cleaning and maintaining hygienic production conditions at every step. Luckily, if the brewer takes the appropriate measures during production, once the beer is finished and packaged, there is not much that can happen to the beer aside from ageing. However, a key aspect is to prevent potential beer spoilers from contaminating beer or wort, especially at the most critical stage before the yeast becomes the dominant organism in the medium, i.e. immediately after chilling the wort. Therefore, it is essential to effectively clean all surfaces and objects which come into direct contact with the chilled wort and later, the beer.

Cleaning involves physically or chemically removing any residues from the brewing process and is followed by disinfection to render any microorganisms inactive which could cause damage to the beer through spoilage. Without proper cleaning to remove soil and residues, the subsequent sanitising step cannot be effectively carried out.

Sanitising is meant to reduce – not entirely eliminate – the occurrence and growth of bacteria. As mentioned, cleaning must occur first, since sanitising soils or biofilms is a waste of time and resources.

Sterilising a surface will eradicate (kill, denature, deactivate and/or destroy) all viable microorganisms and their spores on a surface, including viruses and fungi. Refer to the section on autoclaving under laboratory procedures.

Brewers only sanitise surfaces that come into contact with the product because they want to ensure that the microorganisms capable of spoilage are inactivated. Additionally, the fact that brewers do not sterilise tanks and piping indicates a certain level of dependence upon beer's inherent properties to hinder the growth of many of the microorganisms which naturally occur in the environment (refer to section on the inherent properties of beer). Compare the level of cleanliness at a brewery to the much more stringent level common in the dairy industry. Surfaces that do not come directly into contact with the product can nevertheless harbour microorganisms. Even if they are not direct beer spoilers, they can support microbial communities that can facilitate the growth of beer spoilers.

One must also think of the environment when washing these cleaning and sanitising agents down the drain. Reusing them as often as possible and neutralising them before disposal are common practices in breweries and may even be required by the local water authority. One must, however, ensure that in neutralising cleaners and sanitisers that no harmful gases are produced, like chlorine gas. Refer to the warnings on the packaging of the respective cleaning and sanitising agents for more information.

The basic principles of cleaning

Cleaning is accomplished through a combination of the following elements: chemical strength, temperature, contact time and mechanical action.

- Select the most suitable chemical agents in the appropriate concentrations.
- Determine the optimal temperature of the chemical solution.
- Determine the necessary contact time for wetting, cleaning and rinsing.
- Apply mechanical force in the form of flow rate, turbulence or scrubbing with a brush, where necessary.

These four elements can be adjusted as needed to achieve the targeted cleaning result. Some breweries rely exclusively on manual cleaning while others have equipment to carry out CIP procedures (clean-in-place – see below) which may be partially or fully automated. Regardless of the method employed, safety is of the essence when working with chemicals and other potential hazards. Rubber gloves, the appropriate boots, safety glasses and protective clothing should be readily available and worn by all employees who are entrusted with the task of cleaning.

Sinner's Circle

This has nothing to do with brewers sitting in a circle confessing their transgressions with regard to cleaning their equipment. Rather, it is a concept summarising the four fundamentals of cleaning developed in the 1950s by Dr Hubert Sinner, which are as follows:

1. temperature
2. chemistry
3. time
4. mechanical cleaning

Each one of these is fundamental to properly cleaning brewing equipment and, within reason, if one of these factors is diminished to some degree, another must take up the slack.

For instance, pre-rinsing with hot water or pre-cleaning with previously used cleaning solution can increase the temperature, time, chemistry and/or mechanical cleaning. Or, if the temperature, time and exposure to chemical cleaners is lessened for some reason, for example, in a difficult-to-reach area, disassembly and manual cleaning with a brush or other tool may be required (fig. 16).

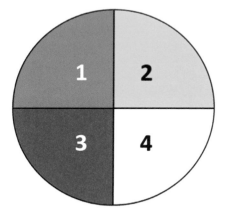

When the cleaning solution is prepared and heated in accordance with the instructions provided by the chemical supplier and applied with sufficient mechanical force and time, each factor equally affects the efficacy of the cleaning process.

Figure 16: Sinner's circle

Temperature

As Louis Pasteur discovered, heat damages microorganisms. Heated cleaning solutions are also more effective at removing organic soil. The higher the temperature is within certain limits, the greater the efficacy of the cleaning process. There are some soils that can become more difficult to dislodge if heated to high temperatures during cleaning and allowed to dry. However, heating the cleaning solution usually makes the process more effective. The key is not to damage gaskets, seals, etc. in doing so. Therefore, cleaning is normally performed between 60 °C and 80 °C. The MSDS and usage instructions for the cleaning solution should be consulted concerning the recommended temperature. If the recommendation is that the cleaning solution be at least 60 °C to achieve maximum efficacy, then the solution may need to be heated to above that temperature to ensure that this temperature is maintained in the equipment subjected to cleaning.

Vessels containing heated liquids, especially if steam is involved, must be vented shortly after the cleaning cycle is finished, because tanks can implode when the liquids or vapours contract.

Chemistry

The chemicals used to clean and sanitise brewing equipment are formulated to target the type of soils and the microorganisms commonly found in beer production.

Cleaning and sanitising agents

Cleaning agents are generally alkaline and may contain chlorine. They are formulated to remove soil and create a clean surface, which can subsequently be sanitised. Because they are alkaline, a neutralising step is recommended after rinsing. With stainless steel, it is generally best to avoid chlorinated cleaners.

Surfaces can be sanitised or disinfected physically through the application of heat, such as hot water or steam. This can become expensive due to the generation of steam or hot water, but no chemicals are used which can contaminate the product. Chemical sanitisers include alkaline agents (e.g. quaternary ammonium) and acidic agents (e.g. phosphoric acid) as well as oxidisers (e.g. hydrogen peroxide). Phosphoric acid may include iodine, known as iodophor, to increase the microbiocidal spectrum.

Some sanitisers are designed not to be rinsed off. If these are used, then one must be very careful that the solution is mixed correctly. As mentioned, acids also neutralise the caustic agents used in cleaning.

Chemicals and mixtures one should avoid

Cleaning and sanitising agents should never produce harmful liquids or gases when mixed. These agents should be purchased from reputable companies who produce chemicals for cleaning and sanitising brewing equipment.

Chlorine bleach (sodium hypochlorite) is not often employed in breweries for good reason.

Bleach + acetic acid (vinegar) → chlorine gas

Chlorine gas makes breathing difficult, induces coughing and results in burning and watery eyes.

Bleach + ammonia → chloramine

Chloramine is also a toxic gas, inducing shortness of breath and chest pain.

Bleach + isopropyl alcohol → chloroform

Chloroform is a highly toxic chemical.

Essentially, mixing bleach with any chemical except water is dangerous. There are other ways to sanitise surfaces.

Another chemical mixture to avoid would be the following:

Hydrogen peroxide + acetic acid → peracetic acid/peroxyacetic acid

The product is highly corrosive.

Concentration and water composition

The composition and correct concentration of these chemicals are important as corrosion can result from excessively high concentrations or use of the wrong chemicals. Following the MSDS and the instructions on the packaging and preparing the cleaning solution according to the manufacturer's directions are important. 'More is better' does not hold true for cleaning chemicals, plus it increases cleaning expenses. This, of course, requires carefully measuring the amount used to create the solution and not 'guesstimating'. The chemistry of the water used to prepare the cleaning and sanitising solutions also plays an important role. For example, high concentrations of chloride in drinking water can combine with hydrogen from certain cleaning chemicals to create hydrochloric acid, which is strongly corrosive. Hygienically smooth stainless steel surfaces can become pitted and unhygienic with exposure to excessively high concentrations of chemical solutions.

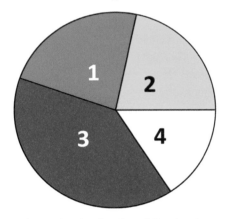

Increasing the duration of the cleaning process can to some extent compensate for the other three factors or simply add to the overall efficacy of the process.

Figure 17: Increasing the duration of cleaning

Time

Follow instructions for the minimum duration for cleaning. If none is given, this is one case where increasing the duration will do little harm and, in fact, will often improve the efficacy of the cleaning cycle, especially when the recommended temperature, concentration or pH are close to the lower limit. The more soil in a vessel (e.g. tank) or other equipment, generally the greater the duration of the cleaning cycle, as increasing the time of the exposure to cleaning chemicals increases their efficacy, and it costs very little. If the temperature, concentration and/or mechanical cleaning are somehow lacking, increasing the time can make up for these shortcomings – within reason (refer to fig. 17). Spraying soil with cleaning solution and allowing it to soak may also be an option in certain cases. That being said, prolonged exposure of stainless steel to certain chemicals, like chlorinated cleaners, can cause pitting. Consult the instructions and the MSDS carefully in such cases.

Mechanical cleaning

This type of cleaning involves the application of mechanical force in the cleaning process, for instance, by the cleaning solution exiting a spray ball at a high velocity or by brewery personnel through the use of brushes, spray wands, sponges, etc. Some surfaces cannot be satisfactorily cleaned by a CIP system (refer to the section on cleaning-in-place below) or cannot be connected to it and necessitate cleaning by hand, such as open fermentation vessels, sensor housings in pipes, recesses in the walls of tanks or some lauter tun screens. Metal brushes are not recommended but rather those made of materials like stiff plastic, because metal can damage the surface of stainless steel.

In cleaning a tank as part of a CIP regimen, the mechanical cleaning is, as mentioned, provided by the spray ball and the velocity of the cleaning solution hitting the tank wall. This is the reason that larger tanks may require a different type of spray ball or nozzle or even multiple spray balls. In a pipe, the level of mechanical cleaning increases as the flow becomes more turbulent (refer to the section on flow rate and the Reynolds number below). For difficult-to-reach areas, some disassembly and cleaning with brushes are required. Spray shadows prevent mechanical cleaning in CIP systems (refer to the section on spray shadows below).

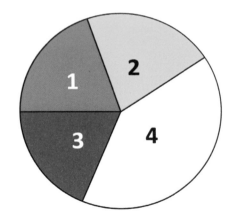

Increasing mechanical cleaning, such as with a brush, can compensate for less exposure to cleaning solution in a difficult-to-reach area.

Figure 18: Increasing mechanical cleaning

Flow rate and the Reynolds number

In the study of how fluids behave, a key metric to describe what happens when liquids move was established. This metric is known as the Reynolds number. It elegantly captures the opposition between the forces holding a fluid together, i.e. the fluid's resistance to flow or viscosity, and those moving the fluid and creating shearing forces. With a cleaning solution, for instance, as the flow rate increases, the liquid reaches a point where the inertial forces surpass the power of the viscous forces to keep the liquid flowing smoothly, and chaotic turbulent flow ensues. The Reynolds number is a means to predict when this transition from smooth flow, known as laminar flow, to turbulence will occur.

If the numerous variables governing the flow of the cleaning solution remain below a certain value for the Reynolds number, the liquid will not transition to turbulence. Think of a glassy mountain lake; though the water is moving, it is nevertheless moving slowly enough that the surface is very tranquil and almost mirror-like.

In the cross-section of the pipe that follows (fig. 19), the liquid has not yet reached the point that turbulent flow will commence. This idealised image shows the discrete layers of the liquid moving in parallel in the direction of laminar flow in a cutaway view of a section of pipe. Those along the surface travel more slowly due to the friction created by the walls of the pipe.

Laminar flow in a section of pipe full of cleaning solution

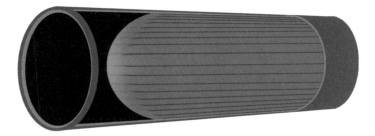

Figure 19: Laminar flow in a pipe

With cleaning in place, one definitely wants to induce turbulent flow, as the overall cleaning effect is much higher when the inertial force of the liquid is increased, as this generally aids in the removal of soil from the walls of tanks or piping. The cleaning solution is also much more likely to reach every corner and curve if the flow is turbulent. Think of a stormy sea tossing ships around as if they were toys. This kind of flow is more likely to dislodge any biofilms or soil that may be present in the piping. The idealised image below illustrates the currents, eddies and vortices that develop with the transition to turbulent flow in a cutaway view of pipe.

Turbulent flow in a section of pipe full of cleaning solution

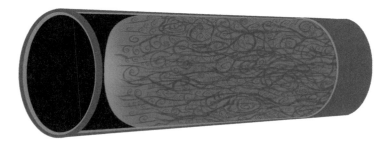

Figure 20: Turbulent flow in a pipe

How does one ensure that the Reynolds number reaches the point where the transition to turbulence is achieved? Looking at the parameters used to define the Reynolds number, it becomes apparent that the easiest variables to control are the velocity and temperature of the cleaning solution as it moves around the piping and other equipment. Heating the cleaning solution lowers the viscosity and consequently increases the Reynolds number. Besides, heat is advantageous for microbiological reasons and should be high enough to contribute to the elimination of the microorganisms regardless of its effect on fluid dynamics. One is only faced with ensuring that the pump provides sufficient force to raise the velocity of the cleaning solution to the extent that turbulence occurs. Generally, pumps are capable of doing this if they are sized correctly.

However, turbulence is useless if there is not enough cleaning solution, for instance, in the piping. If pipes are half-full of cleaning solution, then biofilms can take hold, which later may require mechanical removal after they become established. After a certain point, no amount of turbulent caustic solution will break their hold on the surface of the equipment. Since the length and diameter of pipes are generally known or can easily be estimated, and the calculation is simple one, the reservoir for the cleaning solution should be of an adequate volume to ensure that the pipes are completely filled during the CIP cycle. Hoses must also be positioned so that the solution fills them completely in the CIP circuit and no air bubbles are formed.

Turbulent flow in a section of pipe half full with cleaning solution

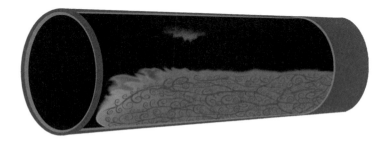

Figure 21: Turbulent flow yet half full

In the figure above, a patch of biofilm is lurking on the inner surface of the pipe where the cleaning solution does not normally reach, even though the piping in its entire length is subjected to routine cleaning. Once a biofilm is established, mechanical cleaning is often required to remove it.

In considering the efficacy of the clean-in-place (CIP) system, one must choose pipe diameters and runs or routing that allow the cleaning and sanitising solutions to fully fill the space, completely purging the pipes of air, so that these solutions reach all of the internal surfaces during standard cleaning procedures. The flow rate should also be rapid enough that it is turbulent, as opposed to laminar (refer to the section on pumps below). Should branching or junctions be necessary, a downstream pipe diameter should be chosen that nevertheless allows turbulent flow of the cleaning solution through the entire volume of the pipe.

In a CIP circuit (refer to the section on cleaning-in-place), if the piping or hoses are not all the same size, the cleaning circuit should be so constructed that a change in diameter occurs from larger to smaller in the direction of flow.

Spray shadows

In order to be able to clean-in-place, spray balls, jets, nozzles and various other devices apply cleaning solution (or sanitiser) evenly and forcefully across soiled production surfaces, like the walls of tanks. Though they are very effective, if obstructions prevent the cleaning solution or sanitiser from reaching certain areas, a spray shadow forms. Within a spray shadow, soil can collect, allowing microorganisms to take hold and establish themselves. Therefore, prior to CIPing vessels or other equipment with fittings, sensors, manways or anything else with a profile that will create a spray shadow, they must be removed. Spray shadows are usually inevitable under or around most types of manway doors. For this reason, this area should be inspected without fail after every CIP cycle. Manual cleaning will more often than not be required.

Figure 22: Spray shadows

Figure 23: A tiny soil deposit inside a stationary spray ball

Figure 24: Rotary spray head

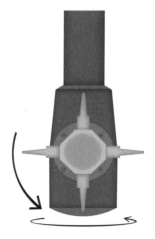

Figure 25: Rotary spray jet

Once caustic has recirculated through the tank and/or the lines, soil can accumulate inside the spray ball. Therefore, after a cleaning cycle, it is recommended that the spray ball be removed, inspected and, if necessary, cleaned out (fig. 23)

A stationary spray ball requires longer cleaning times, more cleaning chemicals and more water. Thus, the expenses related to cleaning and rinsing tanks are higher. There are alternatives. Rotary spray heads with holes or slits or rotary spray jets allow cleaning solution to be distributed more evenly across the walls of a vessel (figs. 24 and 25). They are able to wet and remove soils more quickly than a stationary spray ball in smaller tanks. They clean tanks more effectively, while also using less cleaning solution. Savings are substantial, and downtime is minimised. Their rotation is brought about by the liquid pressure flowing through them. Rotary spray jets are especially efficacious against stubborn soils and save even more time, cleaning chemicals and water. Tanks with stationary spray balls can be retrofitted with rotary spray heads or jets.

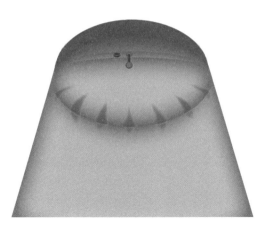

Figure 26: The image above depicts the inside of a tank, looking up through the manway. On its walls towards the top, there remains soil which has evaded cleaning due to installation of a static spray ball too small or otherwise unsuitable for the tank.

As tanks grow in size, so does the need for greater pressure and reach. If a spray ball that works well in a smaller tank is installed in a larger tank, cleaning may be insufficient.

It may be advantageous for a brewery to use a burst nozzle or a cleaning procedure in which pulses of chemical cleaners are utilised. Soil accumulated during fermentation or other brewing processes may come clean more effectively with chemical soaking. During the intermittent periods between the bursts, the soil on the tank walls is wetted, allowing the chemicals to react with the soil. Using bursts in this manner utilises the chemicals more effectively and saves both cleaning chemicals and water.

Proper cleaning of the inside of a larger tank can be achieved by a rotary spray jet, which sprays the entire surface of a larger tank with a narrow, focused stream of cleaning solution. They require a minimum pressure and are especially applicable in primary fermentation tanks or similar vessels with a considerable amount of otherwise unyielding soil. Modern rotary jets are motorised and controlled by a processor. They can be programmed to linger over areas where heavier soil is likely to adhere to the walls of the tank.

To ensure that housings for temperature sensors and the like are cleaned well, it is imperative that the flow rate is sufficient and that the flow is in the right direction. The direction of flow should always be towards any kind of housing as seen in figure 27:

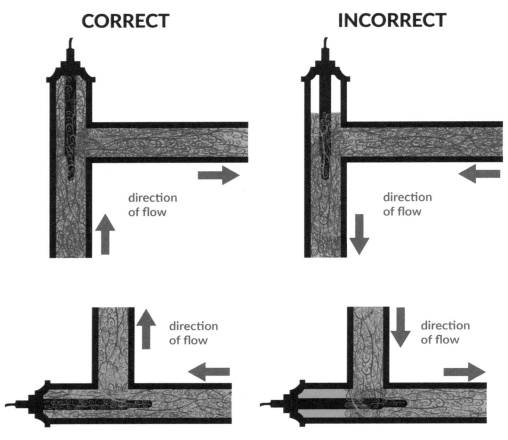

Figure 27: Cleaning temperature sensor housings

Literature and further reading

Fairley, M., Smith, D., Timmerman, H. *Hygienic Design and Operation of Floor Drainage Components*. Journal of Hygienic Engineering and Design, Review paper UDC 631.62

The European Hygienic Engineering & Design Group (EHEDG); refer to ehedg.org: The European Hygienic Engineering and Design Group (EHEDG) is an independent organisation dedicated to all aspects of hygienic design in the food industry.

Website:

haccp-international.com/business-directory/wpbdp_category/flooring

H. L. M. Lelieveld. *Hygienic design of food processing equipment*. DOI: 10.1533/9780857098634.2.91

Winfried Sahlmann. *Hygienic Design – Practical Applications*. Brauwelt International 2018/II, p. 132

| Stages of cleaning a tank

Purge

If the equipment to be cleaned is a fermentation vessel or a maturation tank or another kind of vessel containing CO_2, it must be purged. CO_2 neutralises caustic, plus when the two react, they can implode a tank (see below).

Refer to the section on safety concerning general precautions, CO_2 sensors, fans at floor level, etc.

Pre-rinse

Prior to cleaning, spraying with water removes some organic soil due to its solubility and also by mere brute mechanical force. This will reduce the soil in the caustic cleaning solution, so that it can be reused.

Pre-clean

An initial cleaning to soften up tanks with a heavy layer of organic soil prior to the primary cleaning cycle can be carried out with previously used caustic solution. Larger breweries routinely reuse caustic solution. Its efficacy and value as a means for pre-cleaning tanks is determined not only by the soil freight but the pH of the solution. The pH should be similar to that of a fresh solution. If it is not, it may require topping up with a small volume of fresh solution.

It is very important to vent a tank when cleaning it with a caustic solution. Vacuum collapse can occur when the carbon dioxide gas reacts with sodium hydroxide liquid to produce sodium bicarbonate (solid). The pressure relief valve (vacuum break) may not be able to react quickly enough or may only work in the opposite direction. Removing the valve on the racking arm and the sample port and removing the manway door will protect against implosion.

Clean

All of the soil should be removed during this process. Fresh caustic is employed at this step. The temperature and pH of the caustic should be monitored to ensure that cleaning will be effective. Refer to the information above concerning the concentration, time, temperature, cleaning-in-place, etc.

NOTE: Caustic and other kinds of powdered chemicals <u>must</u> be dissolved in water and not added directly to the tank prior to adding water, though it can save time. Caustic granules sprinkled over stainless steel will corrode the surface, which then generally entails mechanical treatment using abrasive means (grinding/polishing) and repassivation.

Rinse

It is imperative that all of the equipment subjected to caustic cleaning be thoroughly rinsed. Prior to the next stage, the caustic solution must be removed from the tank. Once rinsing has taken place for the allotted time, brewers have been known to allow the last bit of water draining from the tank to drip on their thumb and forefinger. When they rub them together, if any caustic is left in the rinse water, it will feel 'slick', whereas pure water does not. This is, nevertheless, no longer recommended for reasons of safety. Much more preferable are pH strips with a range around 7. The rinse water coming from the tank should be as close to neutral (pH 7) as possible. Rinse water is often collected and used for the pre-rinse or for mixing more caustic solution.

Most tanks can be rinsed using two or three bursts of water, about 30 seconds each, followed by about a minute of draining. Piping, on the other hand, should be rinsed in a continuous flow of approximately one to two times the volume of the piping. If there is a junction then each section requires this volume of rinse water.

Acid rinse

Phosphoric acid neutralises any residual caustic solution, since alkaline cleaners do not rinse off as readily as acids do. An acid rinse can also dissolve any beer stone that may have accumulated. The acid rinse solution can be captured and reused. One must simply monitor the pH and top up the solution when necessary.

Rinse

See the rinse step above. This rinse water can also be captured and used for mixing the solution for the next acid rinse.

Sanitise and rinse

As discussed, there are a number of different types of sanitisers; some are rinsed off and some are not. Follow the instructions very precisely concerning how to mix the solution, especially if it will not be rinsed off.

| Surface hygiene

Clean, sanitised and sterile

The differences between clean, sanitised and sterile are often confused. These were mentioned above but bear repeating.

The act of **cleaning** reduces soil on a surface.

By **sanitising** a surface, the number of microorganisms capable of growth is significantly diminished.

A surface is **sterilised** when all of the microorganisms on it are killed.

Refer to the section on microbiology for swab tests and ATP testing.

BREWERY PUMPS

Without pumps, modern breweries could not function. Older breweries and malthouses were built to take advantage of gravity fed processes, but now pumps are the workhorses of a modern brewery. Some understanding of what they do and how they do it is essential. The wide variety of pumps available for use in breweries and the details of their operation are well beyond the scope of this text. The basic information presented below is intended to provide some orientation on this topic from the standpoint of hygiene and quality control for brewers.

Selecting a pump

Pumps are primarily utilised to accomplish the following in small breweries:

1. moving beer, wort, water and sometimes yeast
2. recirculating the mash
3. cleaning-in-place

Centrifugal pumps

The majority of pumping operations in small breweries are carried out by centrifugal pumps. If another type of pump is required to perform some operation in the brewing process, then it is almost always a positive displacement pump (refer to "Other types of pumps" below). The impeller of a centrifugal pump is secured to the shaft of the pump. The liquid enters through the so-called eye at the end and centre of the pump and flows into the rotating impeller, causing the liquid to move outward along the vanes of the impeller by means of centrifugal force. Aside from their design, the diameter and rotational speed are important parameters

Figure 28: Centrifugal pump

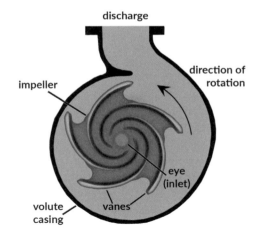

Figure 29: The impeller inside of a pump

in the function of the pump. The impeller can be open or closed. (A pump with an open impeller is depicted in figure 29.) A closed impeller has a cover over both sides. Each finds applications in breweries: the open ones tend to be used for liquids containing some suspended solids or sludge and exert higher shearing forces, while closed ones are better for moving materials solely in liquid form (solids become stuck between the vanes) and can withstand more pressure due to their robust design. For instance, closed impellers are preferable for pumps in CIP applications.

Generally speaking, however, a brewery pump must meet hygienic standards for food safety (easy to clean internally) and be gentle on the wort and beer as well as exhibit considerable chemical resistance. For example, the stainless steel surface should have an electropolished finish or similarly hygienic surface.

The sum of the pressure on the pump from the column of liquid, that is, the pressure on the discharge side minus the pressure on the suction side is known as the total dynamic head. The total energy output of a pump is dependent upon the total dynamic head and flow rate. These are expressed in the pump curve.

If the discharge of a centrifugal pump were going straight up a vertical pipe, as depicted in the figure below, and at evenly spaced points up the line, holes were bored in the pipe, then the pressure required to move the water higher would increase incrementally, and the flow rate of the water exiting each bored hole would decrease. The rotational speed of the pump's impeller does not change. There would be a point further up the pipe where no water would come out of one of the holes bored highest on the pipe because the flow rate had reached zero. This is known as the maximum head.

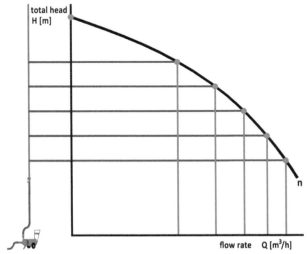

Figure 30: Total dynamic head and flow rate at a constant rotational speed n

It is obvious that certain pressures and flow rates are optimal for a given pump. Without taking the conditions under which the pump is operating into account, the optimal pressures and flow rates are determined by the diameter of the impeller and its rotational speed as well as energy needed to run the pump, usually expressed in horsepower.

The efficiency of a pump is the energy input to the pump and its output to the system. On each side of the point of highest efficiency (70 to 80% and 110 to 120% of the flow rate), the pump can operate reasonably well. Running a pump outside of this range, that is, above or below this flow rate, can be detrimental to the gaskets and seals as well as the impeller, volute casing and shaft, causing the pump to fail or causing it to become unhygienic. At flow rates well above this range, cavitation can occur (refer to the section on cavitation below).

Net positive suction head

There are two terms engineers use under the term net positive suction head (NPSH):

NPSH available (NPSH$_A$): the absolute pressure at the inlet (suction) side of a pump

NPSH required (NPSH$_R$): the minimum pressure required at the inlet (suction) side of a pump to prevent the pump from cavitating

This ultimately boils down to the fact that the brewer operating the pump must make more pressure available to the pump at the inlet than is inherently required by the pump.

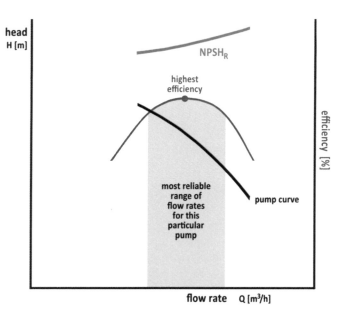

Figure 31: Net positive suction head

These aspects of pump performance are illustrated in the diagramme above, which is the type of composite pump performance curve that one receives from pump suppliers.

Cavitation

When gas bubbles, or cavities, form in a liquid passing through a pump due to a drop in pressure around the impeller, this is referred to as cavitation. When this gas returns to the liquid state on the discharge side of the pump, the shockwaves of the implosion can damage the impellers, resulting in undue wear on pumps and piping. This will shorten their service life and cause their internal surfaces to become unhygienic. As mentioned, the net positive suction head thus refers to the pressure (the sum of the positives and negatives) on the suction side of the pump necessary to prevent cavitation. However, if the temperature of the liquid is high, it is closer to the boiling point, and this increases the likelihood that cavitation will occur.

Positioning the pump so that it is below and as close as possible to the source (the tank or other vessel) of the liquid being pumped with few obstructions between the two is very important. This means that one should not try to 'pull' liquid through piping, hoses and equipment but rather 'push' it through by placing any valves, etc. on the outlet (discharge) side, avoiding long pipe runs or small pipe diameters on the inlet (suction) side.

System curve and operating point

The system in which the pump is operating, meaning the size, length and orientation of the piping and equipment, among other factors, determines the pressure and friction

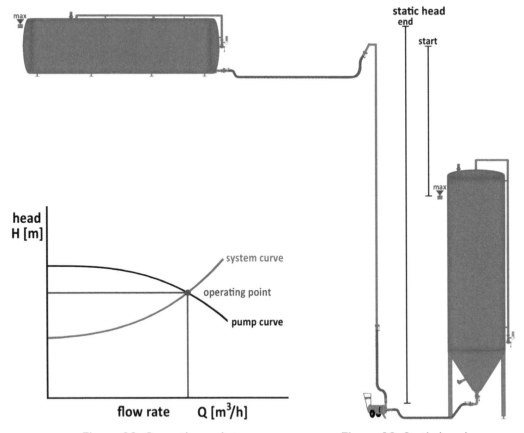

Figure 32: Operating point   Figure 33: Static head

the pump must overcome. This is known as the system head and is the curve upon which a pump must operate within a given piping system. The static head refers to the net force of gravity acting upon the pump. Figure 33 illustrates the static head and how it can change over the course of pumping green beer from a cylindroconical fermentation tank to a horizontal maturation tank situated on a floor above it. (For the sake of simplicity, the image does not show the blending device, which allows deaerated water to push the remaining green beer out of the line.) Along with the static head, friction losses through the piping, hoses, valves, elbows, etc. must also be taken into account. The velocity of the liquid being pumped also plays a role so that the total system head can be calculated as the static head, the friction losses and the velocity head added together. Because the sum of these variables increases with the flow rate, they form a curve. This is known as the system curve. Where the system curve meets the pump curve is known as the operating point, because this point is where the pump must operate under those conditions. In figure 33 showing the green beer being transferred from one tank to another, the static head changes and the pressure on the discharge side increases.

Moving a mobile pump from one location to another will change the system curve because the piping, equipment and other factors change.

Engineers and pump manufacturers take all of the above information and calculate, using a pump curve, the size of pump a brewery needs. This is based upon the flow rate required, the diameter and type of impeller and the horsepower of the motor. Most brewery pumps are equipped with a variable frequency drive, so that the speed at which the impeller rotates can vary within a certain range. This is depicted in

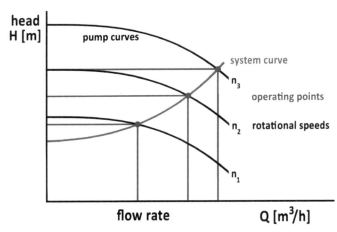

Figure 34: Centrifugal pump

figure 34. The three curves represent only three of the rotational speeds of a centrifugal pump equipped with a variable speed drive. Any of the rotational speeds between n_1 and n_3 are possible. The pump curves also vary in the same way if the rotational speed remains the same and the diameter of the impeller is increased or decreased.

Other types of pumps

Viscous liquids can be detrimental to the performance of a centrifugal pump. A positive displacement pump provides an alternative for pumping thick liquids containing solids, especially those sensitive to shearing forces (refer to shearing forces in the brewhouse and with yeast below). Positive displacement pumps can be operated at almost any point on the pump curve.

Maintenance

The function and integrity of seals on the pump must be checked regularly as part of routine maintenance according to the manufacturer's instructions. Sets of seals (internal and/or external) can be purchased from the pump supplier if replacements are needed. Mechanical seals for pumps should be checked periodically according to the manufacturers' instructions. For brewery application, these seals usually consist of graphite and stainless steel. For steam applications the materials will be different, e.g. silicon carbide.

Literature and further reading

MacKay, R., *The Practical Pumping Handbook*. Elsevier Advanced Technology, 2004

Wagner, W., *Kreiselpumpen und Kreiselpumpenanlagen*. 3. Auflage, Vogel Buchverlag, 2009

RAW MATERIALS: WATER

General information

On a molecular level, water only consists of two hydrogens and an oxygen atom bound together at an angle to form H_2O; however, its remarkable properties epitomise the expression 'the whole is greater than the sum of its parts'. Brewers need to understand the properties of water in order to utilise them, not only because water is the primary ingredient in beer but because these properties also play a central role in production and cleaning.

Liquor versus process water

Water serves as an ingredient in beer and is also vital to the brewing process. Any water entering the brewery should be of drinking water quality at the very least. Beyond that, the water separated for use as an ingredient in beer is generally treated much more stringently prior to entering the brewing process. Once treated, this water is known as *liquor*, while the water utilised, among other things, for dissolving cleaning chemicals and heating the brewhouse is known as *process water*. Process water should meet the requirements for drinking water, but since it may contain contaminants or chemicals undesirable in beer, it must be kept entirely separate. Obviously, the rinse water used in the cleaning cycle should be free of microbiological contaminants.

Water – properties, phases and dissolved solids

Water is found in the liquid phase over much of the Earth's surface and possesses polarity due to the oxygen (−) and two hydrogens (+) which are bound together at an angle slightly greater than 90°. Thus, it can serve as a solvent for a vast range of polar substances. Strongly non-polar substances, like fats, oils, etc. can be suspended in water but never dissolve in it, though if water can sufficiently surround and penetrate such substances, it can 'wet' them to the point that they disperse evenly in water. Carbon chains, like those comprising fats, oils, etc. are non-polar, meaning they won't dissolve in water; this includes the carbon chains in alcohols, which are defined as compounds containing a hydroxyl group (OH⁻) bound to a carbon. However, it turns out that in alcohols with extremely short carbon chains, like methanol (C_1) and ethanol (C_2), the charge of the OH group is strong enough to attract water, since the short carbon chain is simply too small to override the molecule's polarity. Alcohols with longer carbon chains, that is, four carbons and above, are increasingly less miscible in water for this reason. Higher alcohols, i.e. those consisting of seven or more carbons, cannot dissolve in water at all.

What we generally think of as water is more than H_2O. The polarity of water causes some solids to dissociate and dissolve. These are usually the carbonates, sulphates and chlorides of calcium, sodium and magnesium, depending upon their occurrence and solubility, such as calcium carbonate (chalk or limestone), calcium sulphate (gypsum), sodium chloride (table salt) and calcium chloride, among others (refer to the section below on mineral ion content).

Water is cohesive, which means hydrogen bonds form between the molecules causing them to be attracted to one another, one reason that water exhibits surface tension. For this reason, water is also adhesive, referring to the fact that it clings to surfaces. These properties become apparent when racking against gravity or reading a hydrometer.

Due to its high specific heat, water is difficult to heat and cool, especially beyond the bounds of the liquid phase. This is both an advantage and disadvantage to brewers. Though it takes a substantial amount of energy to heat water, once hot, the water will retain its heat for a long time. These properties make water an excellent medium for storing heat energy.

H_2O in its solid form (ice) floats on top of its liquid form because H_2O is densest at 4 °C. Since beer largely consists of water and many operations are conducted using water, the density of water is extremely relevant to the process, for example, in a storage tank for hot process water, in a wort kettle heated by saturated steam or in a cylindroconical maturation tank for lager beer.

Being the main ingredient in beer, water is obviously important for beer quality. Two main aspects are of concern with regard to water quality:

- **Impurities:** suspended solids, organic compounds, microorganisms, pesticides, chlorine, chloramines, other unwanted or harmful substances, like heavy metals, nitrates, etc.
- **The mineral ion content:** central to quality for its effect on the flavour, aroma, body, clarity and other attributes of beer.

A detailed review of water treatment methods, especially for breweries drawing their water from non-municipal sources, is beyond the scope of this book. However, below is a brief overview of the requirements for drinking water and brewing liquor which is followed by a selection of treatment methods and practices.

Impurities

The level of impurities in the water largely depends on the source of the water and whether it has been treated prior to arriving at the brewery. Municipal water sources should be relatively free of impurities, but this is not always the case. In order for water to become brewing liquor, it must be freed of not only suspended solids, heavy metals, fertiliser residues (nitrates), organic compounds, odorants, e.g. earthy or musty aromas, and microorganisms but also of the chlorine and/or chloramines dissolved in the water, which are found in some municipal water supplies around the world.

If a brewery has its own well, then independent testing of the water is necessary at regular intervals. The results of this analysis will inform the brewery concerning what kind and level of treatment will be required for the water to reach the standard of quality for brewing liquor.

Suspended solids must be removed as a part of the pre-treatment of surface water and recycled water. Sand filters and self-cleaning screen filters fulfil this purpose well. Heavy metals like lead are extremely dangerous in drinking water and are often leached from old fittings, joints, caulk and piping. Pesticide residues may be an issue, especially in rural areas. Maximum allowable values for these substances vary from country to country, and independent testing of the water at the tap may be advisable, in order to determine whether the maximum values are exceeded or not.

Removing chlorine from water

Municipal water undergoes extensive treatment and often at the end of this process, chlorine or chloramine is added in order to keep the microbiological flora in the water at a minimum. Since chlorine has been added to drinking water as a disinfectant, beginning in the early 1900s, waterborne diseases have declined dramatically. However, removal of these chemicals is necessary. If chlorine is not removed from brewing liquor, chlorophenols form during the brewing process which are perceptible in the flavour profile of the finished beer. Chlorine dioxide (ClO_2) disinfection does not lead to the formation of chlorophenols, unlike the use of sodium hypochlorite (bleach) which is cheaper. Chlorine can have a corrosive effect on stainless steel as well.

Trihalomethanes (THMs) are a group of volatile substances which form in the process of treating drinking water. They, as well as other substances, are among the disinfection by-products (DBPs) one wishes to avoid in brewing liquor.

There are a number of methods available for removing THMs:

- **Aeration:** Volatile THMs undergo a phase change from liquid to gas and are stripped away using air. Flavour and odour-producing compounds are greatly reduced.
- **Activated carbon:** In a powdered or granulated form, THMs are absorbed by the carbon. This method also eliminates organic contaminants, pesticides, etc.

from water. This is the most common method used in breweries to remove these undesirable compounds.

- **Ozonation + hydrogen peroxide + UV:** The THMs are destroyed by ozone (O_3) but the process is too slow if it is not accelerated with the addition of hydrogen peroxide (H_2O_2) and UV light, which result in hydroxyl radical (OH^-) formation.
- **Titanium dioxide (TiO_2) + UV:** Photocatalytic water treatment using nanocrystalline TiO_2 can mineralise organic compounds into harmless substances, e.g. water, carbon dioxide and inorganic ions. TiO_2 is inexpensive and is a strong oxidiser under UV light (< 385 nm). Coupling TiO_2 photocatalysis with other water treatment methods is advantageous, especially on a larger scale.
- **High-energy electron beam:** It effectively destroys all of the THMs but is quite costly.

Chlorine and/or chloramines dissolved in the water will also unnecessarily encumber the yeast or any other microorganisms used in the brewing process and can impart a medicinal flavour to beer in the form of chlorophenols.

However, once the chlorine and/or chloramines are removed, the brewer must be careful that the water remains free of contamination. Particular care must be taken to ensure that the carbon filter does not become contaminated with microorganisms (see treatment options below). This should be part of regular quality control and cleaning regimens. Although the water will ultimately be boiled in the brewhouse, the liquor used in other parts of the brewery may not be.

The water should be tested daily for chlorine/chloramines either with a test kit or, if unavailable, sensorially by personnel sensitive to it.

The mineral content

The dissolved minerals in the liquor play a central role in brewing. They react with the dissolved substances and the enzymes from malt, the hops in the wort and other ingredients and have a substantial influence on fermentation and the sensory attributes of the finished beer. The mineral content of the water has historically determined what kind of beer was brewed in some of Europe's most famous brewing cities. All of these brewing centres, even the extremely soft water of Pilsen, possess water containing some minerals. Therefore, good beer cannot be produced using water with no mineral content.

The mineral content of water is determined by the geological formations through which the water runs prior to it being used as brewing liquor. The mineral content affects the properties of the water, including its pH. Pilsner malt mixed with distilled water at a ratio of 1:4 results in a wort pH (prior to boiling) of around 5.8. Depending upon the mix of minerals, the mash and wort therefore may require some acidification, which is discussed below.

Brewing cities where famous beers originated have widely varying mineral compositions. Some of the beers and the cities that spawned them include:

Burton-on-Trent (pale ale): water that is hard and high in carbonate (temporary) hardness along with high concentrations of calcium sulphate (permanent) imparts the sulphurous 'Burton snatch' to water and makes for crisp pale ales.

London (porter): hard and high in carbonate (temporary) hardness; historically, earlier porters contained only brown malt, while later ones were brewed with additions of dark malt, like crystal and chocolate malt, to pale base malt.

Dublin (dry stout): similar to London; the high percentage of roasted barley in dry stout countered the carbonate hardness in Dublin's water.

Munich (*Dunkles*): also similar to London, hard and somewhat higher in carbonate (temporary) hardness. Munich malt, a darker malt capable of bringing about mash conversion, was developed for use in the region. Munich *Helles* is a beer style that was invented after water treatment was developed, so *Helles* is not brewed with Munich water as is. However, traditional Bavarian style *Weißbier* is brewed with liquor containing some temporary hardness.

Pilsen (pilsner): though the water is very soft, it still contains some minerals; reverse osmosis or distilled water cannot be used without the addition of brewing liquor containing minerals; soft water allows for the grist to consist entirely of very pale malt; another advantage of Pilsen's water is that it allowed substantial amounts of noble hops to be added during the boil without them imparting an unpleasant bitterness as they would in harder water.

The activity of enzymes such as those contained in the malt is also dependent on the pH, which is governed by composition of minerals present in the water. The pH is a measure of the concentration of hydrogen ions in a solution, or more simply, the acidity. The pH scale ranges from 0 to 14, with 14 being the most basic, 0 being the most acidic and 7 as neutral. Like other measurements such as temperature, the pH is simply an additional tool and reference point in the beer production process.

Sources, treatment and testing

The water source and the treatment method are both decisive in determining what testing should be implemented. If a brewery receives its water from a municipal source, then, as mentioned, it may make sense to have some independent testing done concerning certain minerals and other dissolved substances.

However, if a brewery does not tap into a municipal supply but rather has its own well or other source of water, whether from surface or well water, a considerable amount of effort must be put into treatment and/or testing on a regular basis.

Since testing water requires special laboratory equipment, most breweries submit their water to be tested externally at an accredited facility. Although water quality is always monitored at the brewery, brewers will rely on municipal water reports for detailed information regarding water composition and quality. For those wanting to independently test their water, water test kits are available. Using the materials provided in the kit, breweries can submit water samples for testing to accredited laboratories which specialise in water analysis. Some offer tests tailored to the needs of breweries. Refer to EBC method 2.1 for instructions on how to collect water samples.

Though some hardness is desired in the brewing liquor for dark beers, pale beers require water with less carbonate hardness and styles like pilsner can only successfully be brewed with low levels of total hardness. The advantages of carbonate removal or salt removal are manifold in the production of pale beers. Mashing is more efficient, lautering occurs more rapidly, the wort boiling process is more effective, brewhouse efficiency increases and final attenuation is higher. During wort boiling, however, more hops may need to be added to reach the same hop yield.

An addition of calcium ions (Ca^{2+}) in the form of calcium sulphate (gypsum or $CaSO_4$) or calcium chloride (CaCl) can counteract some of the adverse effects of bicarbonate in water. Calcium sulphate additions should not exceed 30 mg/hl because it can negatively influence the flavour of the beer. Calcium sulphate is the primary mineral salt in the waters of Burton-on-Trent, the city made famous for its dry, bitter pale ale. The gypsum in the water contributed to the pleasant dryness of that beer. Calcium chloride imparts a softer, milder flavour to beer.

HCO_3^- ions in brewing liquor neutralise acidic compounds in the mash and wort, so liquor with a significant carbonate hardness, if left untreated, will require some acidification to reach a suitable mash/wort pH. Prior to the advent of water treatment, brewers of the past, who only had carbonate waters available to them, knew that darker malts in the grain bill or the addition of wort fermented with a sourdough culture would achieve better conversion and produce more attenuated beer. German brewers still utilise something similar, called *Sauergut*, for this purpose. Modern brewers not subject to the *Reinheitsgebot* add phosphoric acid, an inorganic acid, or lactic acid, an organic acid, to their mash tuns and wort kettles. (By the way, lactic acid does not impart the flavour of sour milk to beer.) Brewers should never use sulphuric or hydrochloric acid for acidifying mash or wort. Chloride (Cl^-) and sulphate (SO_4^{2-}) ions may cause pitting in metal piping, chloride being the worst offender. The formation of protective oxide films on piping does not occur when they are present in the relevant concentrations.

How to interpret a water analysis

Common ions in brewing liquor

The most important minerals in the brewing process are as follows:

Calcium: This mineral is frequently present in large quantities, originating both from the brewing liquor and the malt. Calcium combined with minerals and other substances in the mash can increase acidity, that is, lower the pH. These substances reduce the buffering capacity of the wort. The drop in the pH during fermentation can be encouraged to a certain extent through the addition of calcium salts, such as calcium sulphate (gypsum) or calcium chloride. During mashing, calcium salts protect α-amylase against thermal degradation. They also promote the activity of the endopeptidases. Protein coagulation in the wort boiling process is stimulated as well. The formation of calcium oxalate and its negative effects on beer quality (gushing, oxalate turbidity) seems to be restricted through the addition of calcium ions. Calcium also slows yeast degeneration and compensates for excessive magnesium content.

Magnesium: If no adjuncts are added to the grist and milling and mashing are carried out properly, the malt supplies the wort with an ample amount of magnesium. The brewing liquor, of course, can also contribute magnesium to the wort. While reasonable levels of magnesium chloride have little to no effect on the beer, a high magnesium sulphate content in the brewing liquor produces beers with a less than satisfactory bitterness. Magnesium sulphate conveys a 'cold', hard quality to the beer. Lesser amounts, however, can be beneficial for the overall flavour. The capacity for magnesium to acidify the wort is less than that of calcium. Magnesium facilitates the activity of the enzymes from the malt, e.g. peptidases, and is a cofactor for various enzymes during fermentation.

Sodium: Sodium chloride at concentrations between 75 and 150 mg/l can make positive contributions to mouthfeel. However, above approximately 150 mg/l, sodium produces a salty harshness. This is the reason, for instance, in brewing *Gose* (a type of German wheat beer) that the sodium chloride content should be adjusted so that it is right at the flavour threshold and not far above. Sodium also plays an important role in yeast metabolism, that is, in maintaining potassium transport in yeast cells. Together with bicarbonate and carbonate (soda), sodium ions raise the pH of the mash and the wort. These produce unpleasant, harsh flavours in the finished beer. Sodium sulphate is likewise unpleasant but not as severe as other sodium salts.

Potassium: This mineral also produces a salty flavour in beer. The brewing liquor should not contain more than 10 mg/l of potassium, even though the malt contributes a lot to the mash, since potassium inhibits many of the enzymes in mashing. Potassium is, however, of great physiological importance to the yeast and therefore for fermentation.

Iron: If iron enters the process through the brewing liquor, it causes problems even at low concentrations, e.g. 0.2 mg/l. Iron can impede saccharification, diminishes the body of the beer and imparts a harsh bitterness. Concentrations above 1 mg/l cause degradation of the yeast. Iron also facilitates the oxidation of beer, can produce turbidity and initiate gushing. Nevertheless, during fermentation, a lack of iron (under 0.1 mg/l) can inhibit the synthesis of the yeast's enzymes involved in respiration. Fortunately, iron in the brewing liquor is usually retained in the spent grain and the hot break material, but changes to the wort are difficult to compensate for once they have occurred.

Ammonia: Though not damaging on its own, ammonia serves as an indicator for the putrefaction and decay of organic substances. Whether NH_3 or NH_4^+ is present depends upon the pH and temperature of the water. The dissociated form (NH_4^+) is referred to as ammonium and, unlike ammonia, it is not toxic to aquatic life.

Bicarbonate: Most significant are the negative effects of this ion on the acidity of the brewing liquor. In the presence of hydrogen (H^+) ions from chemical reactions or simply by heating the brewing liquor, the bicarbonate ion is altered to create water and carbon dioxide, which escapes as a gas, according to the following reaction:

$$HCO_3^- + H^+ \rightarrow H_2O + CO_2 \uparrow$$

Of course, bicarbonates have a negative effect on enzymatic activity because they increase the pH. The bicarbonates in the brewing liquor can influence the flavour of the hops and the colour of the wort.

Sulphate: The sulphates of calcium and magnesium bring about an increase in the H^+ ions, meaning, a drop in the pH of the mash. They directly stimulate the activity of the carboxypeptidases and the aminopeptidases and also indirectly affect enzymatic activity during mashing by lowering the pH. The sulphate content of the water determines the quantities found in the wort and beer. Sulphates can enhance the aromas described collectively as 'a hoppy bouquet' in the beer. Sulphates also impart a dry, bitter flavour to the finished beer.

Chloride: This mineral stimulates α-amylase activity. When calcium chloride is present in the beer, it imparts a full, soft flavour to the beer. Sodium chloride increases the mouthfeel; however, too much produces a salty, coarse flavour. In higher concentrations, chloride ions corrode equipment made of almost any kind of steel, even certain types of stainless steel. As calcium and magnesium chloride, it influences the pH of the mash, wort and beer.

Nitrate: These salts are indicative of contamination with organic compounds or of the presence of mineral fertiliser. At higher concentrations, yeast metabolism is negatively affected, and a musty, unpleasant flavour is evident in the beer.

Phosphate: These ions are also a sign of organic contamination. Phosphates are, however, also used by water treatment plants but can negatively impact the decarbonisation of water using lime.

Fluoride: This mineral is added to some municipal water supplies to aid in the prevention of tooth decay. Concentrations below 10 mg/l have no effect on fermentation; however, beers can exhibit a harsh flavour, especially with soft brewing liquor.

Other aspects of a water analysis

Not only is the mineral content of consequence but the general quality and the pollution levels of the water in question. Water supplied by a municipality must fulfil certain microbiological and chemical specifications up to the point that the water crosses the boundary from the public to a private distribution system. Upon entering the private distribution network, the responsibility of the municipality generally ceases. Brewers should consult the regulations governing the upper limits for chemical and microbiological contaminants in drinking water for their respective region. In some countries, however, these are untrustworthy; thus, the brewery may want to take over all water treatment if this is the case.

At smaller breweries, the personnel responsible for monitoring the quality of the raw materials need not concern themselves with extensive analysis of the municipal water supply – this is the responsibility of the public health authority. However, the status of the piping within the brewery and how it may affect the water used to brew the beer falls under the responsibility of the brewery. The chlorine level in municipal water supplies does require treatment on the part of the brewery, since chlorine can negatively influence not only the flavour of the beer but also the health of the microorganisms used to produce the beer.

Biochemical Oxygen Demand (BOD) and ammonia are indicators for contamination with organic waste. This will be monitored closely and kept in check if the water is supplied by a municipal source.

Heavy metals, especially lead, are of consequence, since it acts as a blood and nerve poison in low concentrations. In the USA, no more than 15 ppb and in Europe less than 10 ppb (0.010 mg/l) lead is permitted in drinking water. Brewers using municipal water supplies should follow the laws governing drinking water in their respective regions. Those using well water or other on-site water sources must adhere to the laws governing the extraction of water from underground sources. As many small breweries are built in existing buildings, antiquated pipes and other equipment are particularly dangerous with regard to heavy metals. Most often, municipal water delivery systems are only respon-sible for the water quality to the boundary of the brewery's property. Contamination with heavy metals often occurs from the edge of the property to the point of dispense in corroding pipes; therefore, the water piping must be tested and either treated with an internal coating or replaced. If pipes are relatively old and soft enough to be scraped with a screwdriver to reveal shiny metal underneath, the pipes are probably made of lead. The corrosivity of the water in large part determines whether heavy metals can leach into the water. Most municipal water supplies are treated to prevent corrosion, but this may not always be the case.

For private water wells, an accredited authority should be engaged to take samples of the water and test them for the relevant substances and microorganisms on a regular basis.

For those attempting to brew a beer true to an established style, a water analysis is a good place to start. Water analysis reports may be limited to a few analyses or may be quite extensive in their scope. A water analysis carried out by a laboratory usually includes tests to determine the concentrations of the following ions: calcium, magnesium, carbonate, bicarbonate, chloride, iron, sodium, potassium, sulphate and nitrate. In addition, the estimated total dissolved solids, pH, total hardness, total alkalinity, the electrical conductivity, and total phosphorus are measured.

Electrical conductivity

The total dissolved solids (TDS) in water cannot be measured very easily. For this reason, it is usually carried out by a laboratory. However, a common alternative method for measuring the TDS in water is the electrical conductivity (EC). The electrical conductivity of the water is influenced by the dissolved salts in the water. For this reason, seawater is a much better electrical conductor than distilled water or water similarly treated. Furthermore, at a pH near 7, there are hardly any ions present in distilled water. The more salts are dissolved in the water, the better it conducts electricity, because more ions are present. The conductivity of water is measured at 25 °C in microsiemens per centimetre (µS/cm). Common values for various kinds of water are as follows:

pure water	0.05 µS/cm
R/O water	0.05 – 200 µS/cm
drinking water	200 – 800 µS/cm
fresh water	< 1500 µS/cm

Table 2: Electrical conductivity

The relationship between mg/l of TDS and EC is dependent upon the water source. Thus, for the factor K, figures ranging from 0.5 to 0.9 are often given, with the mean being about 0.7, where TDS = $K \times$ EC. Employing one factor K for all types of water leads to a substantial measurement error. However, a separate factor K for each type of water (e.g. distilled/RO water as well as various natural or brackish waters) has been proven to be linear and quite accurate. The laboratory performing the test or the documentation with the specific equipment employed to do so should be consulted for this information.

Hardness

Hardness simply refers to the concentration of mineral ions or salts dissolved in the water. When water comes into contact with stones or other kinds of mineral deposits, cations, primarily calcium (Ca^{2+}) and magnesium (Mg^{2+}) become dissolved in it and form salts with other minerals.

Total hardness: This refers to all of the calcium and magnesium salts in the water. The total hardness can be divided into carbonate hardness and non-carbonate hardness.

Carbonate hardness: Carbonate (CO_3^{2-}) and bicarbonate (HCO_3^-) ions combined with calcium and magnesium ions increase the alkalinity of the brewing liquor. Alkalinity represents the water's capacity to neutralise acids and is defined by the carbonate hardness, which is also referred to as temporary or non-permanent hardness. It is 'temporary' because it can largely be eliminated through the application of heat or lime softening (adding a calcium hydroxide solution to the water). In both cases, calcium carbonate ($CaCO_3$) precipitates out, and the brewing liquor can be decanted off of it. Deposits formed by heating water with a high temporary hardness have to be removed as they can damage or greatly reduce the efficiency of heating elements.

Non-carbonate hardness: This kind of hardness is essentially defined as the amount of calcium and magnesium salts other than carbonate and bicarbonate salts, such as calcium chloride (CaCl), calcium sulphate or gypsum (CaSO$_4$), etc. This hardness cannot be removed by boiling and is therefore known as permanent hardness.

Measuring hardness

Measurements are commonly expressed as follows. Millimole per litre is the currently preferred unit. There are a number of ways to express the hardness of water. In the past, French and German hardness were commonly used in Europe:

$$1.0 \text{ mmol/l} = 10.0 \text{ °fH (French)} = 5.6 \text{ °dH (German)}$$

Some of the standard units of measure are included below. The total hardness of water is divided into four groups: soft, medium, hard and very hard:

Soft water

    < 0.6 mmol/l of CaCO$_3$
    < 6.0 °fH
    < 3.4 °dH
    < 60 mg/l of CaCO$_3$
    < 34 mg/l of CaO
    < 60 ppm
    < 1.2 mval/l
    < 3.5 gr/gal (US)

Hard water

    1.2 to 1.8 mmol/l of CaCO$_3$
    12.1 to 18.0 °fH
    6.8 to 10.1 °dH
    121 to 180 mg/l of CaCO$_3$
    68 to 101 mg/l of CaO
    121 to 180 ppm
    2.4 to 3.5 mval/l
    7.0 to 10.5 gr/gal (US)

Moderately hard water

    0.6 to 1.2 mmol/l of CaCO$_3$
    6.1 to 12.0 °fH
    3.4 to 6.7 °dH
    61 to 120 mg/l of CaCO$_3$
    34 to 67 mg/l of CaO
    60 to 120 ppm
    1.2 to 2.4 mval/l
    3.5 to 7.0 gr/gal (US)

Very hard water

    > 1.8 mmol/l of CaCO$_3$
    > 18.1 °fH
    > 10.1 °dH
    > 181 mg/l of CaCO$_3$
    > 101 mg/l of CaO
    > 181 ppm
    > 3.6 mval/l
    > 10.6 gr/gal (US)

The pH of the mash and the wort can also be adjusted (refer to the section on mashing).

Water treatment

Filtration

Where breweries do not tap into a municipal water system and instead bore their own well, treatment options would need to be tailored to the characteristics of the water source. Generally, this would entail a sand or gravel filter to aerate the water to precipitate iron and manganese and to protect the carbon filter further downstream from any suspended solid material.

As mentioned, an activated carbon filter eliminates impurities and chlorine but must be subject to regular cleaning and maintenance. Municipal authorities may add more chlorine in summer than in winter; therefore, the carbon may need to be cleaned or replaced more frequently in warmer months. A carbon filter may work fine for months in winter and only for a couple of weeks in summer. Due to the introduction of chloramines in some water sources, a specific type of carbon filter ('catalytic carbon') may be required to fully remove the chloramines from the water. Though they are more effective, these types of carbon filters are also more expensive.

A simple depth filter, such as a polypropylene spun filter, can be installed downstream to capture any carbon fines that may be present in the water after carbon filtration. This must also be checked and maintained and, if necessary, replaced.

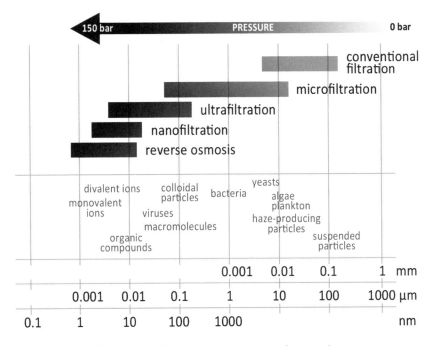

Figure 35: Filtration, pressure and pore size

A note on reverse osmosis

In the figure below, one sees a semi-permeable membrane through which only water molecules can pass. By means of osmosis, water (the solvent) will flow across a semi-permeable membrane towards the side with the highest solute concentration, i.e. the salts and other compounds. Reverse osmosis inverts the movement across the membrane through the application of pressure to the side with the greater solute concentration. A reverse osmosis membrane possesses a pore size of < 0.001 µm. Thus, an RO system is a very practical means for taking minerals and impurities out of water. The water exiting an RO system is almost as pure as distilled water.

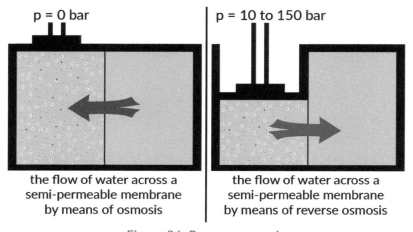

Figure 36: Reverse osmosis

However, RO water cannot be used solely as brewing liquor. Beer, like tea and coffee, has to be made using water with some minerals in it – even pilsner is brewed with liquor containing minerals, though the water is indeed very soft.

For this reason, some water with dissolved minerals must be available to mix with the RO water or in-line injection of mineral salts, e.g. CaCl, $CaSO_4$, etc. Therefore, the requisite equipment for taking out impurities (e.g. pesticide residues, suspended solids), microorganisms or treatment chemicals (e.g. chlorine or other substances) must be available. This allows the RO water to be mixed with the treated water to form the brewing liquor. A system for blending RO water with treated water containing minerals also allows brewers to tailor their liquor to every beer style they produce. For instance, when brewing a pilsner, the proportion of RO water would be higher than when brewing a porter.

Lime softening

This method is popular because it is effective, inexpensive and relatively simple for softening water and can be carried out at room temperature. Lime softening involves creating lime water (or "milk of lime"), a saturated aqueous solution of calcium hydroxide

(Ca(OH)$_2$) and adding it to the raw water. The so-called 'slaked lime' or calcium hydroxide combines with CO$_2$, raising the pH to create calcium carbonate (CaCO$_3$) and water. Due to its low solubility, the calcium carbonate precipitates out of the water. In more alkaline waters, magnesium can be removed as well, precipitating as magnesium hydroxide (Mg(OH)$_2$). This treatment usually takes place in a continuous reactor but can be carried out in large vessels. If the latter is the case, the precipitate must be removed periodically.

If there are no other issues with the water, then the slaked lime treatment will suffice. Otherwise, chlorine or heavy metals may need to be removed or microorganisms eliminated.

Ion exchangers

Using this method, ions one wishes to remove from the water are, as the name suggests, exchanged for others, namely H$^+$ and OH$^-$, which can then form water. Ion exchangers can be employed to soften hard water as the sole treatment or downstream as an additional treatment method for further improving water quality. Ion exchangers are composed of synthetic resins that are positively or negatively charged and that attract cations (positive ions) and anions (negative ions).

There are weakly acidic, strongly acidic, weakly alkaline and strongly alkaline ion exchangers. The combination best for a particular type of water must be determined on an individual basis.

A weakly acidic ion exchanger removes calcium (Ca^{2+}) and magnesium (Mg^{2+}) ions bound to bicarbonate (HCO$_3^-$), resulting in the creation of carbon dioxide (which must be removed) and water. The non-carbonate or permanent hardness remains in the water.

A strongly acidic cation exchanger can be used to soften the water used in boilers because it exchanges calcium (Ca^{2+}) and magnesium (Mg^{2+}) for sodium (Na$^+$), causing the alkalinity in the water to rise. All of the anions remain in the water, which is not suitable for use as brewing liquor.

A weakly alkaline anion exchanger can be used to remove sulphate (SO$_4^{2-}$), chloride (Cl$^-$) or even nitrate (NO$_3^-$). Through the ion exchange, alkaline substances are created which must be removed with, for example, a strongly acidic cation exchanger.

A strongly alkaline anion exchanger is employed to exchange all of the cations of mineral salts with hydroxide, even carbonic acid (thus removing CO$_2$), and for this reason a strongly acidic cation exchanger is recommended in tandem with this ion exchanger.

Ion exchangers are usually regenerated with either hydrochloric acid (HCl) or sodium hydroxide (NaOH). The resulting wastewater must also be disposed of responsibly.

UV sterilisation

Once the water has been treated to become brewing liquor, it is susceptible to microbial growth. Sterilisation of the liquor with UV light is an effective option for ensuring that brewing liquor stored in buffer tanks does not become a refuge for beer spoilers or microorganisms in whose company they find sanctuary. UV sterilisation unit(s) can be installed as follows:

- immediately upstream from the buffer tank
- at both the inlet and the outlet of the buffer tank
- in conjunction with a pump that is constantly recirculating the liquor through the sterilisation unit

Hot and cold liquor tanks would both need to be subject to some kind of treatment; though, depending upon the temperature of the hot liquor, the tank may not be as susceptible to microbial growth. Without some form of treatment, biofilms are apt to form, which could then possibly serve as a source for microbial contamination in the brewery.

De-aeration

De-aerating water or working as air-free as possible is an often-underestimated means for improving beer quality. Oxygen is the number one enemy of the brewer for a variety of reasons. Water can be de-aerated using vacuum or membrane technology. Nevertheless, a brewery must be of a sufficient size to make de-aeration worthwhile from an economic standpoint. The flavour stability of beer can be greatly improved by degassing the brewing liquor for use both on the hot side (mashing, lautering) and cold side of production, but particularly for pushing beer through long pipe runs. Regardless, every effort should be made to minimise the uptake of oxygen throughout the process. For diluting high gravity beer, the liquor must be practically free of oxygen (≤ 0.01 ppm). There are several different kinds of de-aeration and degassing equipment on the market. Which type best fits the specific needs of a particular brewery must be determined on an individual basis.

Practical water treatment

Treatment might include the following:

- sand filter (with well water, not municipal water)
- activated carbon filter
- a bypass
  - a portion is sent directly to a separate buffer tank
  - a portion is subject to further treatment
- reverse osmosis
- UV treatment at the inlet and outlet of each buffer tank

By splitting the water, depending upon the mineral content, a portion can be combined with the RO water at a ratio required to brew a certain beer style. Activated carbon filters should be replaced at regular intervals according to the manufacturer's guidelines.

Boiler feed water

Regular maintenance of the brewery's boiler will greatly extend its life. The total dissolved solids in the boiler should not exceed 1000 ppm. Boiler feed water should not be taken directly from the municipal supply without first being treated, because it may contain oxygen and chlorine, two substances that contribute to corrosion. Degassed, RO water is often employed for boiler feed water for a number of reasons. Water exhibiting a low hardness, particularly with regard to the carbonate and silica content, is best as boiler feed water due to scale and the evolution of carbon dioxide gas, which can give rise to corrosion, especially in the presence of oxygen. Additives can be used to ensure an optimal pH of 11 and to aid in the prevention of corrosion. Consult the manufacturer for further recommendations. Should any water or steam leaks be discovered in the system, it is best to repair them as quickly as possible. Common offenders found to be leaking steam or condensate are pump seals, vacuum relief valves and solenoid valves. If the boiler requires more water than usual, it could be that the float serving as a level indicator is faulty and need replacing.

Visual inspection and evaluation of raw water

The raw water must be evaluated at the brewery on a routine basis (daily). It is simple and requires no special instruments or measuring devices. The water, which will eventually become the brewing liquor and the primary ingredient in a brewer's beer, must be completely clear, free of any suspended solids, colour or other visual signs of impurities, and the odour and taste must be completely neutral.

Collect a water sample in a clean, clear glass and inspect it for the following:

- **Colour**: hold the glass up to a white piece of paper and look for any evidence of colouration. The water should be colourless.
- **Particulates and sediment**: no suspended solids, i.e. neither visible particles nor haze; no sediment after allowing the glass to stand for several minutes.
- **Appearance:** no oily film on the surface
- **Odour:** brewing liquor and all water used in beer production should be free of chlorine and other odours and be neutral in flavour.

Refer to the section on sensory analysis for evaluating the flavour of water.

Literature and further reading

Barceló, D. (ed.), Kostianoy, A. (ed.), *The Handbook of Environmental Chemistry*. Springer Nature Switzerland AG, 1980–2020

Glas, K. (ed.), Verhülsdonk, M. (ed.), *Wasser in der Getränkeindustrie*. Fachverlag Hans Carl, 2015

Mitteleuropäische Brautechnische Analysenkommission (MEBAK), *Water*. MEBAK (publisher), 2008

Narziss, L. *Abriss der Bierbrauerei*. Wiley-VCH Verlag GmbH & Co., 2017

Palmer, J., Kaminski, C., *Water: A Comprehensive Guide for Brewers*. Brewers Association, 2013

Walton, N.R.G., *Electrical Conductivity and Total Dissolved Solids-What is Their Precise Relationship? Desalination*, 12 (1989) 275–292

RAW MATERIALS: BARLEY MALT, OTHER GRAINS, SUGARS

General information

Malt is known as the 'soul of beer' for good reason. Besides water and sugar-metabolising microorganisms, malt has been central to beer production since its inception and is the foundation upon which it is built.

Why do we make malt instead of brewing with raw grain? Grain, unlike grapes for wine, cannot simply be crushed and fermented into beer. A certain amount of degradation must take place inside the kernel so that the starchy portion of the kernel (the endosperm) can be exposed and sufficiently broken down for the yeast to be able to access it. Beers today and the beers of the past have never been brewed from purely unmalted grains. Sprouted grains with some degree of endosperm degradation have always had to be in the grist to supply enzymes to the process. If unmalted grain is soaked in water and then subjected to the brewing process, the 'wrong' microorganisms will take hold. Nowadays, one must use exogenous enzymes, meaning those extracted from other organisms, to brew beer from unmalted grain.

An important concept for brewers and every food technologist working with fermented foods to remember is that the substrate determines which microorganisms thrive and survive in a medium. If malt is sprouted from the grain first and then mashed (i.e. starch degradation in an aqueous medium), the substrate will contain simple sugars that allow yeast to dominate, creating CO_2, alcohol and weak acids to deter the growth of foodborne pathogens (refer to the section on beer and basic food safety).

As there are many craft maltsters nowadays, brewers have more opportunities to order malt produced to the specifications they need for the beer they want to brew. The endosperm of a barley kernel has to undergo a certain amount of change before it can yield sugary wort in the brewhouse. For this reason, malt quality impacts brewhouse yield and performance as well as the consistency and quality of the finished beer. When selecting a type of malt, the primary focus tends to be on the colour, the degree of degradation, the protein content and the potential extract yield. These factors plus the enzymes in the malt have to be sufficient to convert the carbohydrates into soluble, fermentable sugars in the brewhouse, and for this to occur, the grain must contain an ample quantity of not only starch, but accessible starch.

Modification refers to the process of allowing the barley to sprout so that the little plant living inside the kernel (known as the shoot, plantlet, or embryo) releases enzymes, which induce other enzymes to begin breaking down the endosperm. The highly complex compounds (carbohydrates, proteins, etc.) in the endosperm are essentially broken down to provide fuel for the embryo's initial growth spurt. This allows the kernel to sprout and become a barley plant. However, before that first leaf (the acrospire) can reach for the sunlight, the maltster kilns the green malt. This process is gentle and does not involve roasting the grains, which is a much more intensive process. In doing so, the embryo is inactivated but the enzymes remain intact. The malt kernels have lost enough moisture that they can be stored for a considerably long period. This allows the enzymes in the kernels to be used by the brewer during mashing to bring about further degradation of the compounds in the endosperm.

These compounds, mainly sugars, become dissolved in hot water, i.e. the brewing liquor, (this solution is called 'wort'). Because the most common microorganisms in brewing are top and bottom-fermenting yeast (*Saccharomyces cerevisiae* and *Saccharomyces pastorianus*, respectively), the wort has to provide enough fermentable sugar that these types of yeast can change the wort into beer. If brewing is carried out with mixed microorganisms, like alternative yeast or bacteria, then some of the larger carbohydrates can be broken down by them as well, resulting in more highly attenuated beer with a wider range of flavour and aroma compounds as well as some acidity.

Modification of the endosperm starts from the area of the kernel just in front of the embryo (on the right side in figures 37 and 38) and works its way to the point (on the left side). Modification primarily involves breaking down several sets of compounds with enzymes. These are roughly grouped into three categories: proteolytic (proteins), cytolytic (structural components, e.g. cell walls) and amylolytic (starch) enzymes. The cell walls (mainly β-glucans) have to be degraded during malting; otherwise, the starch remains encased in them and cannot be extracted. Protein modification has to occur to the point that the yeast can be provided with nutrients, but not too far – otherwise the beer will have neither foam nor body. Maltsters attempt to free the starch from the structural elements surrounding it, making it accessible while also keeping it largely intact. This allows the enzymes to break down the starch into mostly fermentable sugars during mashing.

If modification is not complete, the kernel can be hard on the end. These unmodified parts have an appearance that has been termed 'glassy'. This portion of the kernel is made of large, insoluble molecules and will therefore not serve as food for the yeast. If there are too many glassy kernels, they can substantially slow the processes of lautering and beer filtration.

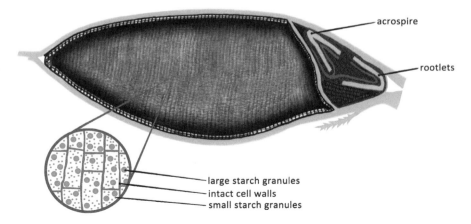

Figure 37: A simplified representation of a barley kernel prior to malting

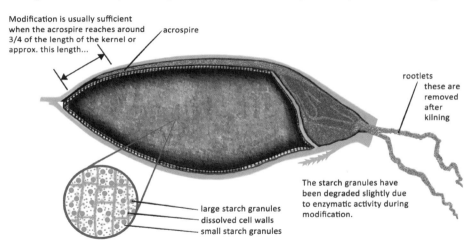

Figure 38: A simplified representation of a kernel of malted barley

Malting and the subsequent brewhouse work also results in the liberation of other molecules and minerals which serve as essential yeast nutrients. These include amino acids and zinc. If malting is not carried out properly, problems may arise in downstream processes (mashing, lautering, fermentation, filtration, etc.). Malt quality also directly affects the colour, flavour, consistency, foam formation and retention as well as the overall stability (colloidal, flavour, microbiological) of the finished beer. Given its central role in determining the quality of the finished beer, some scrutiny of the condition of the base malt is therefore warranted.

| Barley malt

Barley is the most common grain employed in brewing beer for several reasons:

- Its husks serve as a filter during lautering.
- The protein content is low.
- The extract content is high.
- Its enzymes break down starch during mashing (called 'starch conversion').
- The gelatinisation temperature is usually low – no gelatinisation means no starch conversion.

Barley is practically indispensable in beer production, even for brewers using admixtures like unmalted grains, rice or starch from other sources (adjuncts).

Perhaps one area where those in smaller breweries feel they have little or no control over the process would be the quality of the malt. Many brewers accept malt deliveries from reputable suppliers without question and also do not routinely review the quality of their malt, but it is a good idea to do so. Like all agricultural products, barley is subject to climate conditions and will exhibit, despite the best efforts of farmers and maltsters, regional variation and seasonal fluctuation. Maltsters are able to compensate to some extent for this natural variation, and though they do their utmost to produce malt of a consistent quality, this is not always physically possible. Brewers do, however, have some recourse in the brewhouse, if they know what to look for, how to react to it and have the equipment to do so. Even in smaller breweries, mashing regimes can be altered or adjusted to accommodate changes in malt quality.

The type of malt brewers choose is a significant factor in what kind of beer they want to brew. Even though this is the case, independent of the quality of the malt, brewhouse processes can at least to some extent be adapted to create wort with qualities more akin to those a brewer might have in mind – that is, if the brewhouse equipment allows it. Brewers have much more latitude in reacting to fluctuating malt quality if they can, for instance, control the temperature of their mash vessel or heat a portion of the mash separately from the main mash. This greater flexibility also contributes significantly to a brewer's creativity.

Among craft brewers, creativity is often expressed through recipe formulation, but choosing different types of malt, hops, fruit, herbs, etc. represents only the tip of the iceberg. Production processes, both on the hot and cold side, offer many opportunities for the creation of flavourful beers.

A note on starch

Starch is found behind the cell walls of the endosperm. In properly modified malt, the maltster has laid bare the starch by bringing about cytolytic and proteolytic degradation inside the kernel. Cytolytic degradation occurs during the stage of malting called germination. The cell walls in the barley endosperm are approximately 80% glucans and 20% pentosans. The cell walls of wheat endosperm contain more pentosans. The cell walls are not entirely dissolved; merely made much more permeable. Once this has occurred, the starch present in the cells in the form of large and small granules is accessible to enzymatic degradation. The brewer's job during mashing is to degrade the starch in the kernels with the barley's own enzymes so that they are broken down to smaller molecules for the yeast. Because yeast cells have evolved the ability to 'eat' simple sugars, these molecules must be quite small.

Both the large and small granules of starch have an appearance similar to that of an onion. They are layered and are formed around a central point called a hilum. Outwards from the hilum, concentric layers of amylose and amylopectin are present. The well-ordered layers contain starch helices and are crystalline, while those of the amylose layers are not well-ordered and are amorphous. If maltsters have done their job well, the starch behind the structural compounds of the endosperm have already been carefully exposed without, however, breaking it down in the process. Brewers now have to make sure this granule and all of its layers become exposed in the mash, so that the enzymes can gain access to them and the molecules composed of glucose they contain.

In *The Other Double Helix—The Fascinating Chemistry of Starch*, Robert Hancock and Bryon Tarbet describe the form and function of the starch molecule. Starch is not merely a chain of glucose molecules but rather is composed of branching helical chains

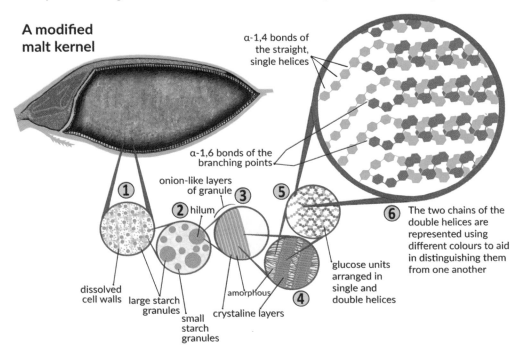

Figure 39: A modified malt kernel at various levels of magnification

tightly wound in semi-crystalline granules. It turns out that starch and DNA share a few similarities. Both have the capacity to densely pack together what they store very effectively; in the case of starch this would be energy and, in the case of DNA, of course, information.

The starch in the endosperm shown at different levels of magnification (fig. 39):

1. The starch granules become visible within the cell walls, which were dissolved during the malting process.

2. A closer view of the large and small starch granules is provided.

3. Zooming in, the onion-like crystalline and amorphous layers of the starch granules become visible.

4. The crystalline layers are interspersed with amorphous layers.

5. The individual glucose molecules come into focus. The crystalline portion consists of double helices of glucose molecules (depicted as two different colours in order to distinguish them).

6. The α-1,4 bonds of the straight chains, the α-1,6 bonds of the branching points and the well-ordered starch helices can be seen here.

During the work in the brewhouse, the helices have to unwind before the enzymatic scissors can get at the starch to cut it up in order to convert it to fermentable sugars. To unwind the starch, the mash has to be heated to above the

starch granule

Not swollen - alternating amorphous and crystaline layers are visible.

Swelling begins with fissures centred on the hilum.

The layers start to disappear. The cavity in the centre grows larger.

The fissures grow further; the outer layer still holds the granule together.

Above the gelatinisation temperature, the starch granule ruptures and the amylose and amylopectin inside the granule are exposed.

Figure 40: Gelatinisation of a starch granule

gelatinisation temperature. When the gelatinisation point is reached, starch granules grow in volume by a factor of 100 or more. In barley malt, this normally occurs at or just above 60 °C. Weather conditions during barley cultivation largely determine the gelatinisation point. By raising the mash above 60 °C, starch gelatinisation occurs. This 'opens' the starch to the amylases, i.e. the enzymes β-amylase and α-amylase which are critical in the generation of fermentable extract. Though they will work at temperatures above and below, that of the optimum of β-amylase is approximately 62 °C, while that of α-amylase is around 70 °C. If the gelatinisation temperature of the starch is above that of the maltose rest (62 °C), then it would be wise to separate part of the mash and heat it (almost) to boiling independent of the main mash. This exposes the starch to the enzymes that are still active in the main mash.

Amylose and amylopectin from a ruptured starch granule are depicted below. On the left, the strands of glucose in the amylopectin are still wound around one another in helices. On the right, the starch is fully gelatinised, i.e. the helices are completely unwound. Thereby, the starch loses its crystalline structure.

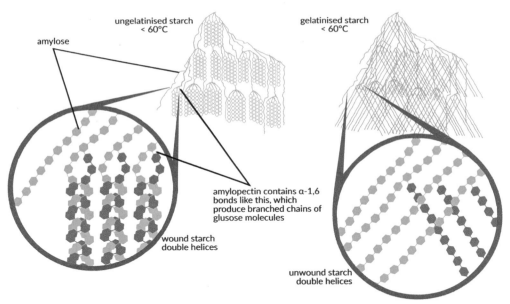

ungelatinised starch
< 60°C

gelatinised starch
< 60°C

amylose

amylopectin contains α-1,6 bonds like this, which produce branched chains of glusose molecules

wound starch double helices

unwound starch double helices

The two chains in the helix are represented using different colours to aid in distinguishing them.

Figure 41: Ungelatinised and gelatinised starch

The 'straight' chains of amylose molecules are actually single helices as shown in figure 42. They are depicted as completely uncoiled in most of the illustrations in this book, so that the reader can better visualise the structure of the starch molecule and its degradation products. The double helices are those that unwind to form the straight glucose chains when the starch is gelatinised. This is the reason gelatinised starch reacts with iodine, because the single chains are helical (refer to the iodine test).

The amylases in the mash have access to the glucose molecules in gelatinised starch. If the amylopectin is not enzymatically degraded into smaller glucose units, the process is reversible (the staling of bread is a consequence of the reversal of gelatinisation). The straight chains, meaning those without branches, are made of the same units (glucose). They are bound the same way over and over again,

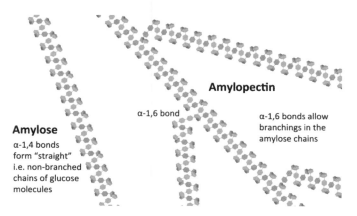

Figure 42: The single helices of amylose and amylopectin

whether they are only twisted into single strands of amylose or are further wound into the double helices in amylopectin. The repeating element of these straight chains is depicted below:

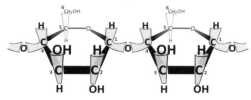

Figure 43: A two-glucose section of the repeating units that form an amylose chain. The molecules are linked together by an α-1,4 glycosidic bond.

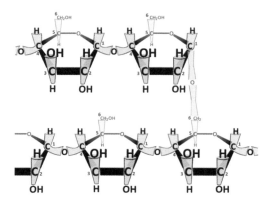

Figure 44: A close-up of two amylose chains linked together by an α-1,6 bond.

It is the branched chains in amylopectin that allow double helices to form from two strands. In every case, these repeating units are glucose molecules bound together by what are known as glycosidic bonds, which is a covalent bond linking one carbohydrate molecule to a molecule of another carbohydrate or a different group (e.g. protein). There are two types of glycosidic bonds that concern us: α and β.

The carbons are numbered and the bond between the glucose molecules joins them at carbon 1 on one glucose and at carbon 4 on the other with an α-glycosidic bond.

The carbons in the glucose molecules involved in the bond and the type of bond are important. If the glucose molecules are joined at carbons 1 and 6 with α-glycosidic bonds, another kind of enzyme is required to break the bond. The α-1,6 bonds create the branching points in the amylopectin (fig. 44).

Suffice it to say that the glucose molecules linked together at carbons 1 and 4 by α-glycosidic bonds (amylose, a type of α-glucan) are very different molecules than the β-glucans joined at the same carbons by β-glycosidic bonds (fig. 45) or, for that matter, even those joined at other carbons, such as 1 and 3 by β-glycosidic bonds.

Different enzymes are required to break each of these bonds (refer to the sections on malt analysis and on mashing). The β-glycosidic bonds joining glucose molecules are mostly found in the cell walls and other structural elements of the endosperm and must primarily be degraded during malting. As mentioned, these compounds are generally referred to as β-glucans.

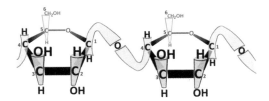

Figure 45: Two glucose molecules linked by a β-glycosidic bond; this kind of bond is not found in starch but rather forms chains of other compounds important in the structural elements in the endosperm, like cell walls. These compounds must be broken down during malting.

The α-glycosidic bonds joining glucose molecules are predominantly found in starch and are broken during mashing. The most prominent enzymes involved in starch modification, i.e. the degradation of large α-glucans to their smaller constituents, are α- and β-amylase. These enzymes both attack amylose molecules, i.e. chains of glucose molecules linked by α-glycosidic bonds at carbons 1 and 4, meaning they both incise the same types of bonds, simply at different places on the chain.

| Other malted grains

Malting barley varieties are bred and cultivated with brewers in mind, unlike wheat and other grains, which are mainly developed for bakers or for other applications in the food industry. Along with maize (corn), oats and soybeans, feed barley varieties are cultivated for livestock and differ significantly in their protein and carbohydrate composition. Wheat and other cereals are used primarily for other foods, like bread, and are not as suitable for brewing as malting barley, with its array of characteristics that make it almost ideal for beer production (starch content, ratio of proteins to carbohydrates, enzymes, husks, etc.). Therefore, difficulties with mashing, lautering, fermentation, filtration and other problems are common if the ratio of other malted grains in the grist is too high.

| Unmalted grains

Unmalted cereal grains have been used as an adjunct to barley malt throughout history, dating all the way back to the ancient Sumerians and Egyptians. Normally, they are added in relatively low quantities, at a maximum of 5–10%, though exceptions exist (e.g.

lambic) which require their own special brewing processes. If more than this percentage were added to the grist, brewhouse procedures would need to be altered in order to accommodate the unmalted grains.

Roasted barley is primarily used to brew dry stout (≤ 10% of the grain bill). Hulled barley and naked wheat are often utilised to make roasted grains for brewing, since the husks, when subjected to the extreme heat of the roasting process, can impart an unpleasant bitter flavour to beer. The kernels are not malted prior to being heavily roasted and thus contain very little fermentable extract. Their colour is very dark (1000–1300 EBC) and their aroma is reminiscent of heavily roasted coffee beans. If a beer turns out too roasty or bitter, it may be preferable to use less roasted barley, substituting part of it with chocolate malt or another dark, malted grain.

| Sugars and other additives

Kettle adjuncts can be dissolved in the wort during the boiling process. These include malt syrups (malt extract or grain-based syrups), honey, maple syrup (used by early American colonists), and brewing sugars (low molecular weight carbohydrates that provide additional fuel for fermentation). Brewing sugars are extracted from either sugarcane or sugar beets, or they can be derived from starch (glucose syrups). If desired, fermentable sugars can lighten the body of beer. They can be employed to increase the alcohol content of beer as well but should be used sparingly as beer can taste thin and empty with larger additions. Sometimes small amounts of 'primings' or simple sugars like glucose are added immediately prior to packaging (in the presence of living yeast) in order to bring about secondary fermentation and thus CO_2 production in the casks or bottles.

Sweetness and fermentability

Sugar is basically some combination of carbon, two hydrogens and an oxygen, i.e. $C/H_2/O$, such as glucose and fructose which are both $C_6H_{12}O_6$. It is well known that soft drinks made with sucrose do not taste like those prepared with high fructose corn syrup. The human sensory apparatus reacts to various sugars differently. Some, like sucrose or fructose impart a very sweet flavour to foods and beverages while others, like lactose, do not. Fructose has approximately 30% more sweetening power than sucrose.

Glucose, fructose, sucrose, maltose and maltotriose are the fermentable sugars normally encountered by brewing yeast. Because they are fermented, these sugars do not sweeten the finished beer unless they are added after flash or tunnel pasteurisation. If this is the case, the infection pressure on the packaged beer would increase, making it much more susceptible to microbial contamination.

Glucose, fructose, maltose and sucrose

Monosaccharides consist of a single sugar molecule and are the basic building blocks of carbohydrates. Glucose and fructose are monosaccharides and contain the same atoms, each with a different structure (isomers). Glucose is extracted from starch (corn, wheat, rice) and is generally available as syrup. Glucose and fructose form (with an α-1,4 glycosidic bond) the disaccharide sucrose, or table sugar, which is extracted from cane or beets. Two glucose molecules similarly bound together make maltose.

The prevalent isomer or type of glucose in nature is called dextrose or D-glucose. Like most monosaccharides, this sugar is 100% fermentable unless it has been treated enzymatically to adjust its fermentability. There are dozens of different types of applications for it in the food industry.

Fructose should not be confused with isoglucose or high fructose corn syrup. Fruit beers are frequently sweetened with fructose syrups owing to the synergistic effect of fructose and the flavour/aroma of the fruit. Fructose is an expensive adjunct.

The most common sugars used in the European brewing industry are hydrolysed starch syrup (nearly 100% fermentable) and high-maltose syrups. These are usually added in brewhouse.

Crystalline sucrose and free-flowing sucrose syrup are stable at room temperature. Sucrose syrup is approximately 67% dry matter to avoid crystallisation. They are almost 100% fermentable; however, yeast must secrete the enzyme invertase to break sucrose down to its readily fermentable constituents, glucose and fructose. Sucrose is added in the brewhouse at or near the end of the boil. Sucrose is also commonly referred to as 'candy sugar' or 'candy syrup'. In a brewing context, the term 'candy sugar' does not refer to rock sugar crystals, though this rumour persists.

Inverted sucrose syrup is processed to contain equal parts sucrose, glucose and fructose. It can flow freely and is very stable at room temperature. This is often used for bottle and cask conditioning. It is a common sweetener in European soft drinks.

Lactose

This disaccharide, consisting of the monosaccharides glucose and galactose, cannot be fermented by yeast. Many types of bacteria, however, are able to consume it. Though glucose and galactose by themselves can be fermented by yeast, it is the β-1,4 bond joining them that prevents brewing yeast from utilising it as an energy source. Lactose is the sugar found in milk and thus also in dairy products that has not been completely fermented by bacteria, such as yoghurt and ricotta. The Italian cheese, parmigiano reggiano, which is matured for a minimum of 12 months, contains no lactose. Though all infant mammals can digest lactose, many humans cannot, once they have reached adulthood. Therefore, if this sugar is used in beer, consumers must be made aware of the fact through an allergen declaration on the label in compliance with federal and local regulations. Likewise, where draught beer is served, customers must also be sufficiently informed of any additions of lactose to beer. Since it is unfermentable, lactose imparts body, smoothness and a complex sweetness to beers. Though it possesses a fraction of the sweetening power of glucose, it can nevertheless overwhelm the drinker if too much is added (> 8–10%). Craft brewers have sometimes been known to employ excessive amounts of lactose in beer, which achieves little except to create a beverage with an unpleasant mouthfeel and an odd sweetness. One must simply be aware that though brewing yeast cannot ferment lactose, other microbes can. Therefore, lactose increases the infection pressure on the beer to which it is added.

Ingredients containing sugar

Fresh fruit, maple syrup, molasses, malt extract, honey or other such additives ordinarily enter the process in the brewhouse, usually in the wort kettle. It is wise to pasteurise fresh fruit and honey, in particular, unless the fermentation is to be spontaneous. Heating the fruit or honey briefly by adding them, for instance, towards the end of the boil in the wort kettle and allowing it to mix well would be sufficient in most cases to retain a portion of their flavour and aroma compounds in the finished beer.

Honey consists of a mixture of fermentable sugars, mainly fructose and glucose with a few disaccharides, as well as a variety of other compounds. It also contains many volatile constituents which impart flavour and aroma to the honey. These are difficult to preserve in the finished beer. The honey can be treated separately by heating it slowly to 80 °C and holding it there for 30 min. Afterwards, it can even be added once primary fermentation is finished to induce a secondary fermentation. Less of the volatile compounds are driven out in this way, thus increasing the flavour and aroma of the honey in the beer. Additions are normally in the range of 2 to 10%.

Measuring sugar content

The amount of sugar in a solution can be expressed as follows:

Dry substance: this is a measure of the total dissolved solids in a given sugar solution. Dry substance is expressed as a percentage, which is analogous to the extract content of wort. This is not the same as degrees Brix.

Degrees Brix: this conveys the concentration of pure dissolved sucrose in solution, such that 1 g of sucrose in 100 g of water is equal to 1°Brix.

DE (dextrose equivalent): the content of reducing sugar or reducing power in a sugar product expressed as a percentage of dextrose on a dry matter basis.

Sugar spectrum: this provides the relative amounts of the various sugars present in a given sugar syrup and is expressed as a percentage. The individual sugars in the syrup can be adjusted to reach the desired composition.

Adding sugar in the brewing process

Sugars can be added at several points in the brewing process.

Wort boiling: Sugars are frequently added on the hot side because any microbiological risk is eliminated. They are added towards the end of the boil if any increase in colour is to be avoided. Some of the extract will be lost in the hot break material.

Upstream from the chiller: In-line injection avoids extract losses in the whirlpool; however, pasteurisation may be required because the sugar solution may not be heated long enough in the line to eliminate the microbiological risk.

Fermentation tank: This reduces the stress on the yeast. Of course, the sugar solution must first be pasteurised prior to injecting it into the tank.

Priming: Inverted sugar syrup, sucrose or dextrose can be mixed with the attenuated beer (with yeast if necessary) to provide sugar for cask or bottle conditioning.

Beers containing sugar

Adding sugar to beer is not unusual outside of Germany; for instance, anywhere from 10 to 25% of the fermentable extract in the beer styles Belgian tripel and blonde comes from the sugars, sucrose and isoglucose, respectively.

The beer style known as milk stout does not contain milk but rather lactose. This unfermentable sugar has traditionally been added to impart a complex sweetness. Lactose can also soften the edge of an overly sour beer in low doses. As mentioned above, the percentage of the lactose addition should not exceed 8–10%.

| Colouring agents

Colouring agents can increase or correct the colour of beer. Generally, dark malts are employed to add colour to beer. Although it would be preferable to add dark malt to the mash, dark malt extract can also be added to the wort kettle.

Brewers may at times prefer to bring about a more dramatic change in the colour of their beer without the accompanying change in flavour imparted by dark malts or roasted grains. Caramel colour may be used in brewing. If using it or other colouring agents, refer to the manufacturer's specifications regarding where the substance should be added and in what quantity per hectolitre per unit of colour.

Röstmalzbier / Farbebier

A product known in German as *Röstmalzbier* is a *Reinheitsgebot*-sanctioned liquid malt colouring agent made from fermented barley malt wort. Very little is required as it is extremely dark (8100–8600 EBC), very stable and can be added at almost any point in the process, from casting out of the wort kettle to packaging. It is best to add it where there is some mixing, such as in the wort kettle, when transferring to the maturation tank, immediately prior to filtration, in the bright tank, etc. The dosage rate of *Röstmalzbier* is ordinarily 14 grams per EBC unit of colour per hectolitre of product.

Caramel E150c

This colouring agent is dark brown and black and is produced through the controlled heating of sugar with ammonia. The most common sources for the sugar are beets and cane but also maize (corn) starch. Colours as high as 49,000+ EBC are possible. The colour is so high that scant amounts are needed, and thus little flavour is imparted through additions. This product is very viscous and therefore necessitates a brewhouse addition or proper mixing. Declarations on the label must conform to all applicable regulations. Natural, declaration-free colourants may be preferred if a brewery wishes to have a 'clean label'.

Literature and further reading

Belitz, H.-D., Grosch, W., and Schieberle, P., *Lehrbuch der Lebensmittelchemie*. 6. Auflage, Springer Verlag, 2008

Dziedzic, S., Kearsley, M. (ed.), *Handbook of Starch Hydrolysis Products and Their Derivatives*. Springer, 1995

Huber, K., Presentation at Doemens Academy (Aspera Brauerei Riese GmbH)

How to interpret a malt analysis

In this section, explanations are given for the values found in the analysis reports brewers receive from their malt suppliers. The analyses discussed below are available in the EBC collection of analyses for malt.

Low quality malt means not only poor beer quality but disruptions throughout the brewing process as well. Taking a careful look at the malt analysis accompanying a delivery is one way to find out the condition of this vital raw material. A malt analysis is essentially a document comprising a certificate of analysis (COA) and a malt specification sheet, which lists analysis results and other measurable characteristics of malt. The values are expressed in a standardised form to enable comparison among lots and suppliers. The term 'dry basis' or 'dry matter' refers to the values without any moisture, so that no adjustments are necessary. Some report average analysis results, while others report the values for each lot.

The analyses reviewed here are those important in providing information about 'base' malt, i.e. the primary malt a brewer uses in the grist to bring about starch conversion and yield fermentable extract in the brewhouse. Specialty malts are not included in this section.

Moisture content

For proper storage and prevention of mould growth, this value should be low. Standard values: < 4–6%. Refer to the section on malt storage for more details.

EBC Congress mash method

The EBC Congress mashing protocol is used to produce Congress wort. The procedure specifies how and with what equipment the malt must be milled, the amount of malt and liquor added, the level of agitation, the exact temperatures and rests, and filtration method, in order to obtain standard wort which can subsequently serve as the basis for a number of analyses. The Congress mashing protocol has been employed as a method since 1907 to produce standard wort for analysis, in order to assess the quality of malt for beer production. The Congress mash method is widely referenced; however, it is often replaced by the 65 °C isothermal mash method. The latter is deemed to be more useful, by many brewers, in terms of reflecting the brewing behaviour of modern malts.

Isothermal mash methods

The four isothermal mash methods used to evaluate barley are carried out at 20 °C (cold water extract), 45 °C, 65 °C and 80 °C. These mashes were devised during the mid-20th century by Hartong and Kretschmer, each created using a standard grist (amount, grind) and held for a set period of time (60 min) at a single temperature. They were intended to provide insight into the degree of modification, the amount of soluble extract in the malt and how effective the enzymes are in the malt.

Isothermal 45 °C mash method

The 45 °C mash, often expressed as VZ 45 °C ('VZ' for Verhältniszahl, German for 'ratio') and also known as the 'Hartong index' or the 'modification index'. This ratio compares the extract from the isothermal 45 °C mash with that of the Congress wort. For decades, a worthwhile tool for assessing the modification of malt samples and their inherent enzymatic activity, the VZ 45 °C has become less relevant with contemporary barley varieties. The 45 °C isothermal mash cannot deliver the same useful, practicable data it once did with modern malt, given its higher level of modification and powerful complement of enzymes.

Overly modified malt may, for instance, exhibit a favourable value, and likewise, malt well-suited for producing wort and beer without processing issues (e.g. wort clarification, fermentation, filtration) can be deemed to yield an unsatisfactorily low value. The analysis is presented below, however, because as a gauge for malt quality, it is still utilised in the industry.

Isothermal 65 °C mash method

The isothermal 65 °C mash method is becoming widely used, either alongside, or even replacing the EBC Congress method. It is an isothermal laboratory method utilised to evaluate various parameters of malt quality. The isothermal 65 °C method is considered to reflect current mashing practices more accurately than the EBC Congress mash method, which was developed when malting barley possessed a different quality altogether than it does now. The Congress method begins with a mash-in temperature of 45 °C. At this temperature, β-glucan degradation occurs. For this reason, the values for β-glucans in the Congress mash are too low compared to conventional brewing practice.

Rather than employing the Congress method, various standard malt analyses, such as extract, colour, soluble nitrogen and free amino nitrogen, are now carried out after mashing at a constant temperature of 65 °C for 60 minutes. On some malt specification sheets, this analysis method appears in addition to the EBC Congress method while others have already adopted the 65 °C mash method to produce wort for the various malt analyses. The β-glucan content determined according to Carlsberg in both the Congress wort and the 65 °C wort provides a clear indication of the cell wall modification and the homogeneity of cytolysis.

It should also be noted that the values for extract, soluble nitrogen, colour, free amino nitrogen and boiled wort colour are somewhat lower than those obtained with the Congress mash wort. The following values are also lower:

- Extract is lower by 0.3–0.5%.
- Soluble N is lower by 40–80 mg/100g (d.m).
- FAN is lower by 20–30 mg/100g (d.m.).

Therefore, values which involve calculations, such as the Kolbach index, will be impacted. The values for viscosity and β-glucans will also be a bit higher. Wort colour and boiled wort colour increase by about 0.4–0.7 EBC.

Colour

Colour is an indicator, one, for contamination and, two, for the degree to which the Maillard reactions (they make the crust of baked bread brown) and caramelisation took place during malting. Green, black or red blemishes on the surface of the malt likely indicate a fungal infection. Pale base malts, such as pilsner malt, should not be heated to the point that they undergo excessive browning due to exposure to heat. For this reason, they are very light in colour.

| Colour of pale malt: | ≤ 4 EBC |
| Colour of boiled wort: | ≤ 5 EBC |

The colour of the boiled Congress wort provides a more accurate indicator of the colour of the finished beer.

Degree of modification

This refers to the extent to which the compounds in the kernel have been broken down. There are a number of ways to characterise this in malt. The most relevant for understanding a malt analysis are discussed here.

Carlsberg method

This method is based upon the fact that cell walls containing β-glucans above a certain molecular weight (around 10,000 daltons) in an insufficiently modified endosperm of a sectioned barley kernel can be stained with calcofluor, and it will fluoresce under UV light. A 'Malt Modification Analyser' was developed by Carlsberg using this principle to measure the degree of modification.

Standard values:
Modification "M" > 85%
Homogeneity "H" > 75%

Friability

Friability is practical, simple to perform and widespread. Malt is dried to a specific moisture content, and then in a device similar to a mill called a friabilimeter, the malt kernels are forced against a stainless steel wire sieve drum by a roller. The amount of material retained by the sieve is the unmodified or non-friable portion of the malt. These are the so-called 'glassy' or 'vitreous' kernels. The amount falling through the sieve is the friable portion.

Results may vary according to whether the malt has been produced using spring or winter barley, due to the quantity of husk material. Suspicions that highly friable malt may be over-modified would need to be verified using other methods.

If kernels are glassy, i.e. they weren't modified during malting, the extract will not dissolve in the wort during mashing, plus there are various other problems that can arise in the brewing process, such as slow lautering and filtration. Specialty malts, e.g. crystal malts, may be glassy by design, so they are not subject to this analysis.

Results are usually expressed as follows. Sometimes half-glassy kernels are included (expressed as percentage by weight):

> Friable flour: > 80%
> Completely glassy   < 2%

Extract

Before we can ferment wort into beer, the extract must first be obtained from the malt. Wort obtained from the EBC Congress mash method or the 65 °C isothermal method is used to determine the extract content of the malt. First, the malt is finely ground and the laboratory wort is obtained by mashing according to a defined regimen. The extract, in this case, refers to all the compounds, brought into solution during this standardised process.

> Standard values:
> Extract, air-dried: 72–79%
> Extract, dry basis: > 80%

The extract content on malt analysis sheets is expressed in other ways as well:

Fine grind or FG: The fine grind extract is the maximum soluble extract yield possible or maximum extract potential. It is an indicator of modification of the carbohydrates (amylolysis) in malt.

> Standard values: > 78%.

Coarse grind or CG: The extract as determined by a specific setting for coarsely grinding malt – a truer representation of expected extract yield. It is an indicator for brewhouse yield, if the moisture content is taken into consideration.

> Standard values: > 78%.

Fine grind/coarse grind or FG/CG difference: This is an indicator of the uniformity of modification.

> Standard values: < 2.0%.
> For British-style single temperature infusion: 0.5–1.0%.

Hot water extract or HWE: An analytical measure of the quantity of dissolved solids extracted from the malt using hot water (65 °C).

> Standard values: 75–82%.

Cold water extract or CWE: An analytical measure of the quantity of dissolved solids extracted from the malt (20 °C) without the benefit of the malt's enzymes.

Standard values: 18–22%
Under-modified malt: < 18% (requires a protein rest)
Over-modified malt: > 22%

Hartong VZ 45 °C: Malt is milled, mashed at 45 °C and compared to the Congress wort. This value serves as an indicator for enzymatic activity (except for α-amylase) and protein modification. (Refer to the information above.)

Standard values: 36–41%

Dextrinising units (DU)

This value quantifies the activity of α-amylase. The unit represents the quantity of α-amylase needed to dextrinise 1 g of starch in 1 h at 20 °C. When using adjuncts, the value for DU should be at least 30.

Standard values: 40–48

Diastatic power (DP)

This is a measure of the complete enzymatic power of malt, i.e. the α-amylase and above all the β-amylase. The values are expressed in Windisch-Kolbach units (°WK).

Standard values: > 250
ca. 100–150 for British malts (well-modified)
ca. 300–400 for European lager malt
ca. 400 for American malt (two-rowed, high protein)
up to ca. 500 for American six-rowed brewer's malt

Another unit used to express this is degrees Lintner (°L). The following formulae can be used to convert between these units:

$$°L = (°WK + 16) ÷ 3.5$$
$$°WK = °L × 3.5 − 16$$

Saccharification rate

The amount of time required for the iodine test to be negative for the Congress mash.

Standard values: ≤ 15 min

The Congress mash is more dilute (1:6) than most are in practice. Thus, compared to the time required for saccharification in an actual brewery, it is much shorter.

Clarity of the run-off from the mash

The run-off should be relatively clear but not as clear as the finished beer. Clarity is an indication that mashing and lautering were successful. If the wort is too clear, however, it may lack some nutrients, such as low molecular weight proteins (e.g. FAN) or trace elements.

Limit of attenuation

This indicates the maximum amount of fermentable extract in the Congress wort.

> Standard values: > 80%

Since there is no β-amylase rest at 62 °C in the Congress mash method, the limit of attenuation is lower than most brewers can achieve in practice.

Viscosity

A high viscosity is caused by β-glucans in cell walls, which can lead to problems in the brewhouse and further downstream (lautering, fermentation, filtration, etc.).

> Standard values for viscosity: < 1.60 mPa·s.

The viscosity will be slightly higher (0.06–0.16 mPa·s) in the 65 °C wort. The acceptable upper limits for the β-glucan content in the Congress wort and the 65 °C wort will also be different:

> Congress wort: ≤ 200 mg/l
> 65 °C wort: ≤ 350 mg/l

Gelatinisation temperature

When the bonds within starch molecules are broken, the starch will dissolve in the mash and then be attacked by the enzymes. If the gelatinisation temperature is too high, e.g. 65 or 66 °C, i.e. above the 62 °C optimum for β-amylase, then the starch does not dissolve well in the mash and the β-amylase cannot attack the starch. This can create problems in the brewing process downstream and produce unsatisfactory beers. The mashing process would in this case need to be altered to compensate for this, e.g. double decoction (refer to mashing below).

Protein

Protein concentration is dependent on the variety of barley or other grain, provenance, growing conditions and the soil. Protein is inversely proportional to extract.

Total protein

This value expresses the percent of the kernel that consists of protein.

> Standard values (total nitrogen × 6.25): 9–11% for all-malt brewing
> Standard values (total nitrogen × 6.25): ≤ 12.8% for adjunct brewing

Soluble protein

This value expresses the quantity of the proteins found in malt, which go into solution under the conditions present during the Congress mash method.

> Standard values (total nitrogen × 6.25): 3.4–4.7% for all-malt brewing
> Standard values (total nitrogen × 6.25): 4.8–5.6% for adjunct brewing

Kolbach index

This value expresses the quantity of the soluble protein compared to the total protein in malt and is an indicator for the degree of proteolytic modification. The Kolbach index represents the percentage of soluble nitrogen present. The total protein content must always be taken into account when considering the Kolbach index.

> Standard values: 38–42% for barley malt with a protein content around 10.5%

Mashing processes may need to be modified to accommodate the degree of protein modification.

> Infusion mashing: 36–42%

For decoction mashing with lager malt:

> 30–33% is under-modified.
> 37–40% is over-modified.

For darker malts, like Munich malt, due to the depletion of low molecular weight proteins, the Kolbach index will be lower, approximately 37–40%.

Free amino nitrogen

The value for FAN provides the quantity of amino acids available for yeast nutrition.

> Standard values: > 140 mg/100 g dry basis (ppm) for all-malt brewing
> Standard values: > 210 mg/100 g dry basis (ppm) for adjunct brewing
> For more on yeast nutrition, refer to the section on yeast below.

Dimethyl sulphide precursor (DMS-P)

DMS-P is a compound called S-methylmethionine (SMM) and can be measured in cold extract or in the Congress mash. When SMM is boiled, DMS cleaves off of it, hence the name DMS-P. At very low concentrations, this volatile compound can impart a creamed corn or cooked vegetable aroma to beer, which is generally considered to be unpleasant.

> Standard values: < 5–7 mg/kg

In summary, the most important aspect of the raw material malt for brewers to understand is the fact that two-rowed barley malt can vary dramatically depending upon how it was malted, its provenance, whether it is spring or winter barley, etc. Other grains, like malted wheat or oats, do not possess the same properties as barley malt, since their composition is different, in part, because these grains are not bred with brewing in mind but rather for other purposes like baking. The three primary degradation processes during malting do not occur all at once but are somewhat staggered. Cytolysis should largely be taken care of by the maltster, proteolysis to a lesser extent and amylolysis as little as possible.

| Visual inspection and evaluation of malt

Maltsters and brewers have examined malt in this manner for as long as these professions have existed. The visual inspection consists of a physical examination of malt upon delivery. Even today, every shipment of malt should be evaluated in terms of odour, colour, appearance, flavour, aroma, homogeneity and for the presence of foreign material, pests, and contaminants. Though the senses are employed in inspecting the malt, a separate section in this book discusses a method for the sensory analysis of malt, which includes evaluation of the kernels by steeping them in hot water.

A representative sample of malt should be taken, if possible. In a well-lit area, the kernels should be spread over a clean, light-coloured surface to visually examine them. Smelling and tasting the kernels is also employed in the inspection, in order to evaluate the following attributes:

- **Homogeneity:** the kernels in the sample should be uniform in size, shape and colour. Kernels should be plump (contain more extract) and healthy. Greater uniformity in malt helps ensure a more consistent brewing process. More precisely concerning the size of the kernels, barley prior to entering a malting facility was sorted into 'malting barley' (fractions I/II sorted by 2.8 mm/2.5 mm sieves).
- **Foreign material or contaminants:** inspect the malt sample for the presence of seeds from weeds and foreign grains, husk remnants, culms (the rootlets from the germinating kernels during malting), holes bored by insects, dust or stones. The malt kernels should not be damaged, crushed or mouldy.

- **Colour:** the colour should be uniform and typical for the kind of malt. Base malts should be pale to golden while specialty malts can be much darker.
- **Appearance:** malt should appear polished, bright and glossy; it should not be grey or dull. The kernels should not have any green, red or black discolouration as this is a sign of fungal infection.
- **Odour:** high quality malt should exhibit a fresh, straw-like and pure aroma. Any musty or stale odours are an indication of inadequate storage conditions (damp), plant disease or fungal infection. A smoky odour is only acceptable in smoked malts.
- **Flavour:** taste the malt. Paler malt should be sweet but aromatic. Burnt or roasted flavours are typical for darker malts.

Refer to the section on sensory analysis for the sensory evaluation of malt.

| Delivery and storage of malt

Delivery

Suppliers can provide malt to breweries in bags of various sizes or in bulk. When a delivery arrives, the person receiving the malt should examine the malt for the proper colour, aroma and appearance. The number of sacks and pallets should be counted and compared to the invoice to ensure that the correct quantity is being delivered. If the malt is in sacks, check for any damage to the sacks and for any evidence of pests. Document any damage in writing on the delivery papers and take photos. When transferring bulk malt to silos, a filter should be positioned over the exhaust vent to reduce the amount of malt dust that escapes. If the malt is transferred pneumatically, care should be taken to move the malt at the appropriate speed so that the kernels do not sustain damage.

Storage

The storage area should be cleaned before the malt is delivered. If malt is stored in a silo, then the silo should be cleaned regularly (at least a couple of times per year); cleaning should be scheduled, of course, when the silo is empty. If malt is stored on pallets, once a pallet is empty, it should be moved, and the floor swept below it to avoid accumulation of malt dust in the storage area.

General quality guidelines:

- Store malt in a cool, dark, dry place.
  Malt and other grains should have a low moisture content when they are delivered, and they should remain dry until they are needed.
- Exposure to heat and oxygen diminish the quality of malt. Heat damages

important compounds in the malt, creating undesirable substances, which become oxidised, creating off-flavours in the beer.

- Moist conditions promote the growth of mould and bacteria on the malt. Pre-crushed malt is very susceptible to oxidation, so keep it in a sealed container in a cool area and use it quickly. Thus, outdoor silos or indoor storage rooms must protect malt from extreme temperatures (0 °C > 35°C) and moisture. Note that the malt temperature will affect the mash-in temperature.
- Malt sacks must be stored off of the floor on pallets (plastic) or on metal racks to facilitate air flow.
- The storage area must be monitored regularly for evidence of mice, rats, insects and other pests and the appropriate action should be taken at the slightest evidence of their presence (see below).
- The storage area should be free of any external odours. Malt sacks, big bags, etc. should be kept away from any exhaust, smoke, kitchen odours or gas emissions.
- Any containers used to store malt should be food-grade quality.
- Any dust or malt kernels should routinely be swept up and disposed of properly, i.e. away from the malt sacks. The storage area should be cleaned regularly and maintained appropriately. Hang a dedicated (and labelled) broom and dustpan on the wall.
- If removing a portion of malt from a sack, close the sack securely after use.
- Maintain an inventory system. Have a system in place for clearly separating the different types of malt and adhere to the first in, first out (FIFO) principle, e.g. stock should be rotated and used pallets or individual malt sacks should be labelled for quick identification.
- If the concentration of malt dust is high enough in the air, it can ignite. Therefore, adequate ventilation is essential to ensure safe working conditions. Not only should routine cleaning be carried out, but the area should be inspected regularly for dust.
- Malt stock on pallets should be rotated.

Malt suppliers usually provide an expiration date on their products. Malt should be purchased and delivered within a reasonable time of its use in the brewery. Although a malt supplier should check for the presence of mould on grains, especially those that form mycotoxins, it is always best to personally examine samples of malt as an additional check. Mould on malt can cause the beer brewed with it to taste musty. A general rule of thumb is one year for bagged malt and three weeks for pre-milled malt if stored under proper conditions. It is best to avoid pre-milled malt if at all possible.

Pest control:

- It is best to store malt away from the walls of the room so that the space can be cleaned and monitored for pests.
- Malt should be manually examined for an infestation or damage by pests (past or current).

- There should be a regularly scrutinised programme in place for controlling pests and rodents on premises, especially around the malt storage area. Documentation of a pest control programme and records of pest control measures should be on file.
- The pest control programme should define who is responsible for carrying out pest control measures, the schedule of activities, the names of chemicals or pesticides employed and indicate where the pest control devices are located. If pest control services are provided by another company, records and verification of preventive and corrective action should be filed.
- Ensure that the room or warehouse where malt is stored is secured against pests. Holes and cracks or even through an open door allow pests to gain access to the malt. Check the integrity of the roof, floors, walls and around windows.
- If the pests are present, eliminate them and dispose of any contaminated or damaged raw materials and document the actions taken.

Literature and further reading

Back, W., Gastl, M., Krottenthaler, M., Narziss, L., and Zarnkow, M., *Brewing Techniques in Practice*. Fachverlag Hans Carl, 2019

Bertoft, E., *Understanding Starch Structure*: Recent Progress. Agronomy 2017, 7, 56

Briggs, D., Malts and Malting, Blackie Academic & Professional, 1998

Craft Maltsters Guild Quality & Safety Manual, Craft Maltsters Guild, 2017

Gastl, M., Geißinger, C. Kupetz, M., Becker, T., *Isothermes 65 °C-Maischverfahren löst Kongressmaischverfahren bei der Analytik von hellem Gerstenmalz ab*, Brauindustrie, Vol. 11, 2019

Hancock, R., Tarbet, B., *The Other Double Helix – The Fascinating Chemistry of Starch*. Journal of Chemical Education, Vol. 77, No. 8, August 2000

Keßler, M., Kreisz, S., Zarnkow, M., Back, W., *Do brewers need a starch modification index?* Brauwelt International I 2008, 52–55

Malzanalytik: Branchenweite Umstellung der Analysenbasis für helles Gerstenmalz, Brauwelt 2019 (online)

Narziss, L. *Abriss der Bierbrauerei*. Wiley-VCH Verlag GmbH & Co., 2017

Narziss, L., Back, W., *Die Bierbrauerei, Band 1: Die Technologie der Malzbereitung*. 8. Auflage, Wiley-VCH Verlag GmbH & Co., 2012

Narziss, L., Back, W., *Die Bierbrauerei, Band 2: Die Technologie der Würzebereitung*. 8. Auflage, Wiley-VCH Verlag GmbH & Co., 2009

RAW MATERIALS: HOPS

General information

Given all the herbs that grow in Europe, why did brewers settle on hops? *Humulus lupulus* is the Linnaean taxonomic name for hops, a forest-dwelling, climbing bine indigenous to northern Eurasia. They belong to the same family as hemp (Cannabaceae) and are dioecious, meaning the male and female plants are separate. The cones or flowers from the female plants are harvested for use in beer brewing. The male plants are excluded from the hop cultivation areas to avoid pollination (except in Britain) and are only employed for breeding purposes as the seeds of fertilised hops contain fats and other substances undesirable in most beers. Hops require long hours of daylight to produce the cones that brewers greatly value and thus only grow satisfactorily in northern or southern latitudes between 34 and 55 degrees.

Figure 46: Hops on the bine

The primary incentive for European brewers to adopt hops was not their aroma, though very pleasant when hops are fresh, but their bacteriostatic characteristics. However, hops only first saw widespread adoption by brewers after large vessels and enough fuel became available for boiling their wort.

The female hop flowers, known as cones, have glands which produce lupulin, the substance in hops most valued by brewers. Lupulin is sticky to the touch and is greenish yellow in colour. The lupulin contains bitter compounds, including the α-acids, as well as the hop oils, which are extracted in the brewing process.

The figure below shows a whole hop cone (l.) and a cone that has been split open to expose the lupulin glands.

The α-acids present in hops have to be altered slightly at a molecular level through the application of heat so that they become soluble in water. This process is known as isomerisation. These soluble iso α-acids provide bittering power and can hinder the growth of Gram-positive bacteria like those of the lactic acid bacteria genera *Lactobacillus* and *Pediococcus*.

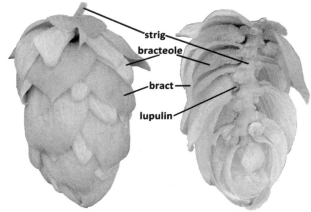

Figure 47: A hop cone

The iso α-acids are not the only substances in hops that can act as preservatives, provide bitterness or otherwise influence the finished beer. These include other types of acids, resins, polyphenols, nitrogenous substances, pectin and some minerals. The polyphenols in hops benefit not only the bitterness but also the body and flavour of beer. Humulinones and non-isomerised α-acids are examples of two substances which can contribute to bitterness from late/dry hopping. Research has shown that the intensity of the bitterness imparted to beer by high alpha hop varieties is perceived as greater and yet lacking in harmony compared to noble hop varieties. Thus, the high alpha varieties used to bitter a dry stout may not be suitable for brewing pilsner or pale ale, which benefit from the gentle bitterness imparted by noble varieties or traditional low alpha British varieties.

The noble European varieties represent old landraces and their derivatives from, for instance, the traditional hop-growing regions of Hersbruck, Spalt, Strisselspalt, Tettnang, Hallertau and Saaz (Žatec). Traditional British hops are derived from hops brought over by the hop farmers of the Low Countries approximately 500 years ago who subsequently began cultivating them in Kent. Varieties, such as Fuggles and Goldings, though fertilised by male plants in Britain, also produce a finer bitterness in ales than do high alpha varieties. The use of whole hops or type 90 pellets of noble or otherwise lower alpha hops containing a high proportion of polyphenols also imparts substantially more of these compounds and other beneficial substances found in hop plants to the wort and the finished beer. By way of example, in one study, in which various hop-derived compounds were measured in wort, the variety Hersbrucker brought 11 times the polyphenols into solution compared to Magnum at the same dosage of α-acids (8 g/hl). These polyphenols were shown to be instrumental in prolonging a beer's flavour stability.

In addition to imparting bitterness and protecting beer from microbial spoilage, hops contribute aroma, mouthfeel and flavour while also facilitating foam formation, head retention and lacing.

Among craft brewers, hops have become a means for creating distinctive flavours and aromas through various hopping techniques on both the hot and cold sides of the process. Late hopping in the whirlpool, additions in a special vessel known as a hopback (refer to the section on the brewing process), wet and dry hopping during fermentation and/or maturation as well as extract additions after filtration provide brewers with a wide palette for creating unique and individual beers.

Hops and hop products

Hops are available as whole leaf hops, hop pellets and hop extracts. Whole hops are generally dried and pressed into bales or ballots. Use of whole hops was routine into the 1960s. This is no longer the case for several reasons:

- their susceptibility to oxidation

- their large volume

- equipment required for separation (e.g. hop jack, filter)

- significant wort/beer losses

Hop pellets are ground hops which are extruded to form pellets. Pellets are packaged under an inert gas atmosphere in composite foil bags. Hop extracts are the viscous liquid products resulting from hop extraction with carbon dioxide or ethanol. They are packed in cans or drums for manual or automatic dosing.

Figure 48: Whole hops
(dried and compressed)

Whole hops

Whole hops cones are generally dried before they are sold, but they are also available fresh shortly after the harvest.

Whole leaf hops: whole leaf hops in this form are 100% whole hops which have been dried and compressed into bales or ballots (fig. 48). They are not as perishable during storage due to their low moisture and lower exposure to oxygen. Pressing increases the density of the product and thus lowers the amount of space required for storage.

Whole, wet hops: wet hops are harvested in the autumn and not dried. The whole cones are loosely packed with a moisture content of around 80%, hence the name 'wet hops'. These hops must be used immediately after harvesting due to their high perishability.

Brewers generally place the wet hops in a hopback or use wet hops on the cold side of the brewing process to transfer a distinctive 'green hop' character to beer.

Hop plugs: the whole hop cones are pressed into plugs in the required size and shape to fit through the bunghole of a cask. Hop plugs were widely used in the past in the British Isles for dry hopping cask-conditioned beers.

Aged, whole hops: in past centuries prior to refrigerated storage, properly ageing dried hops was considered essential. The aroma compounds in hops only became a significant part of brewing in the late 19th /early 20th centuries. Lambic brewers as well as modern craft brewers using a mix of microbes sometimes deliberately age their hops. With fewer α-acids, the hop-sensitive bacteria in mixed cultures are not as affected by the hop addition in the wort kettle. Aged hops do indeed need to be boiled. Over time, as hops age, the resins and oils become oxidised if they are not stored under an inert atmosphere. Many of these oxidation products are polar and thus water-soluble. They dissolve in the wort and their odour is reminiscent of cheese; however, this should be muted in properly aged hops. One lambic brewer stated, "Aged hops should smell like the feet of the gods." For this reason, aged hops must be boiled for quite some time in order to drive out any of the less appealing volatile compounds.

The polyphenols in aged hops usually come into contact with air, and once they are oxidised, they produce a harsh, unpleasant bitterness. However, even the polyphenols in aged hops contribute to the flavour stability of the beer. Lambic brewers employ aged hops but, due to the harshness of the polyphenols, in much smaller quantities.

Hops set aside for ageing should be noble hops (e.g. from the Hallertau or Saaz (Žatec) but not 'American noble hops'), pressed into ballots to reduce rapid oxidation and be stored in a cool, dark place (not freezing). If they are noble, they will be unfertilised, and their α-acid content should be ≤ 10%. They should be low in myrcene and possess no extreme aromas, such as an onion-like odour. They should be aged a maximum of 3 to 4 years. Over time they will turn light green or yellow but should not turn brown. They should still, even after this time, possess a bacteriostatic effect.

Hop pellets

Hop pellets: most brewers in smaller production facilities use pellets to brew beer. The hop cones are milled into powder and pelletised. Pellets are stored cold and packaged under nitrogen or other inert gas, thus prolonging their shelf life and protecting the constituents, e.g. polyphenols, oils, etc. from oxidation. If pellets are softer, they were pelletised as lower temperatures (≤ 50 °C) and pressures than harder pellets (≥ 55 °C). Therefore, softer, less dense pellets are qualitatively preferable to the higher density, harder ones.

- **Type 90:** similar to the content of whole hops; they are produced by milling whole hops along with any leaves and stems accompanying them. 100 kg of hops produces 90 kg of these pellets.

- **Type 75:** enriched hop pellets; 100 kg of hops makes 75 kg pellets.
- **Type 45:** enriched hop pellets; 100 kg of hops produces 45 kg of these pellets; undesirable plant material is removed, doubling the bitter acid content. Less undesirable plant material also results in a less grassy or vegetal flavour in highly hopped beers. Brewers must keep in mind that pellets added to the wort or beer and then subsequently removed from the brewing process absorb up to 10 litres of liquid (wort/beer) for every kg of pellets. Type 45 pellets would reduce these losses.
- **Type 25 to 35:** enriched hop pellets, similar to type 45, i.e. 100 kg of hops produces 25 to 35 kg pellets. Developed one year after a poor harvest, these enriched products are not always available. Excessive enrichment of pellets results in products that are unstable and rather soft due to the high concentrations of α-acids and hop oil. Losses during production are higher as well.

Hop powder

Hop powder is the result of a process in which the lupulin glands are separated from the hop cones and concentrated. Hop powder contains the resins and aromatic oils found in hops without the vegetal material.

Hop extracts

Hop extracts are the products of the extraction of bitter compounds from hops. The compounds are extracted and concentrated, leaving the plant material behind. Extracts are commonly used for bittering purposes and are standardised to a defined concentration of α-acids. Hop extracts can be used in the brewing process in place of whole hops and pellets. Care should be taken when making a transition to extract for beers that are highly hopped (> 40 IBU) because hop extract can contribute additional flavours and mouthfeel impressions to the beer at higher hopping rates due to the greater extraction of plant material in the production process.

Hop extract according to method and type:

- **CO_2 and ethanol extracts:** Both solvents for extracting hop compounds are found in beer and thus any slight residues are not harmful. The ethanol extracts are closer to the chemical composition of whole hops.
- **Hop essential oils:** Extracted with CO_2, these can provide hop aroma (floral, fruity, etc.) to beer.
- **Isomerised extracts:** The isomerised α-acids in the extract increase the bitterness of beer. Isomerisation of these acids normally occurs in the wort kettle during the boiling process. Some of these products are chemically altered so that they do not develop the skunky aroma of lightstruck beer.
- **Pre-isomerised hop pellets:** normally, isomerisation of the α-acids occurs

in the wort kettle. These pellets are chemically isomerised and impart more hop bitterness to the beer but do not conform to the stipulations of the *Reinheitsgebot*.

A note on nitrate and pesticides

Brewers of heavily hopped beers should be aware of the fact that the quantities of nitrate (NO_3^-) in hops is considerable (ca. 1% by weight). As mentioned under the section on water, nitrate can negatively affect yeast metabolism and should also be generally avoided in foods (European drinking water requirement: < 50 mg/l). Because it is highly soluble in water, it will end up in the finished beer, and the concentration can be higher than 50 mg/l. Transfer of nitrate from the hops into the finished beer through the brewing process increases linearly with the addition. Thus, brewers wanting significant amounts of the bitterness and aroma derived from hops in their beer and who will be hopping on both the hot and cold sides of production may want to avoid large additions of whole hops or type 90 pellets. For every 100 g of a bittering addition, up to 8 mg/l of nitrate is transferred to the beer. Most pilsners are hopped at a rate not generally in excess of 500 g/hl but American-style IPAs are. Nitrate concentrations from hop additions of this magnitude will exceed most legal limits for nitrate in drinking water. Type 45 pellets or extract can be used as an alternative for the first (bittering) addition, in order to avoid higher concentrations of nitrate. A bittering addition of 100 g of type 45 pellets per hl beer transfers much less nitrate, approx. 3.5 mg/l, to the finished beer. This, of course, partially depends upon the conditions in the brewhouse.

Farmers receive up-to-date information about pesticides (herbicides, insecticides, fungicides) along with their approval status. Of course, the extraction of pesticides in the brewing process largely depends upon their solubility in water, at what point the hops are added and the temperature of the wort or beer. Less soluble pesticides are generally removed with the spent hops or sediments. A significant percentage of the pesticides allowed for use on hops in most cultivation regions are generally detectable only at lower concentrations or are completely undetectable in beer because they are insoluble or possess a low solubility. However, there are others that are quite soluble in wort/beer. Thus, the concentration of these pesticides is substantial in highly hopped beers (> 200 g/hl). As the quantity of hops added to the beer increases (either on the hot or cold side), so do the traces of their pesticide residues in the beer. Even if they cannot be detected in beer, often their degradation products can be. The hop supplier should be able to provide information regarding the pesticides employed during a particular season at a specific location.

Even organically grown hops are treated with some form of pesticide, such as with fungicides containing copper. They have simply been approved for organic farming. Few hops produce enough yield to justify organic cultivation; high alpha varieties particularly do not fare well. What is true for nitrate is true for pesticides: usage of extracts or type 45 pellets for the bittering addition reduces the concentrations of their residues in the finished beer.

Other herbs

Craft brewers have experimented with hops in a number of applications (bittering, flavouring, aroma) and are now eagerly doing the same with various herbs, some of which were used in the past to flavour beer. Beers previously found in Europe known as gruit beer and *Gose*, which contained a variety of herbs in the past, are now being revived and reinterpreted by modern brewers. *Witbier*, a Belgian wheat beer, incorporates coriander and dried Curaçao orange peels as well. The herbs employed in brewing these beers do not possess the same bacteriostatic properties imparted by hops, nor in some cases are their effects on beer and beer drinkers fully known.

| Essential information from suppliers on hops

Individual hop varieties are described in great detail on the websites of hop suppliers, while the information on hop analysis sheets is limited to the results of the hop analysis. Hops purchased within Europe must be accompanied by the following, which should provide sufficiently specific information to allow traceability back to lot, production facility and grower:

- provenance, i.e. country of origin
- cultivation region
- harvest year
- variety
- lot number
- the code of the facility which issued the certificate (usually the production facility – see below)

The following analysis data should also be made available:

- certificate of analysis for every lot
- moisture content
- lead conductance value: conductometric titration of a solution of hop bitter substances in hops and hop powder/pellets but not specific for α-acids; the value is very close to the α-acid content of fresh hops (refer to EBC method 7.4)
- bitter substances (HPLC): an analysis for determining the α-acids and β-acids in hops and hop products (refer to EBC method 7.7)
- hop storage index (HSI): hops acids are not very stable; this serves as an indicator for the degree of ageing in whole hops and pellets (refer to EBC method 7.13)
- upon request: hop oil content

| Varietal information sheets

Varietal information sheets include the following:

- **provenance/growing area:** where the hop variety originated and/or where it was cultivated
- **variety:** the name of the variety
- **images and descriptions** of the hop cones and plants
- **usage:** intended purpose, aroma hop, bitter hop or combination
- **description:** aroma and flavour characteristics
- **maturity:** when the crop reaches maturity: early, mid-season, late
- **yield:** crop yield, important for hop farmers
- **agronomic characteristics:** resistance to disease and pests, ease of cultivation and harvest
- **suitability for storage**

Hops are evaluated and the data collected about them at each year's harvest. This information is provided in hop harvest guides or the like. The general information about individual varieties is demonstrated in the example provided in figure 49 (used with the kind permission of Joh. Barth & Sohn GmbH & Co. KG).

Lilac
Lemon
Red Currant
Apricot
Juniper

Analytical values	
Growing Area	Germany
Lineage	Land Variety
Alpha acids*	3.0 – 5.5 %
Beta acids	3.0 – 5.0 %
Total Polyphenols	4.0 – 5.0 %
Total oils	0.7 – 1.3 mL/100 g
Myrcene	20.0 – 28.0 % of total
Linalool	0.7 – 1.1 % of total
Alpha ø 2018	3.9 %
Oil ø 2018	1.1 mL/100g

Figure 49: Varietal Information

Aroma descriptors for hops

The tables below provide primary descriptors for categories of hop aromas, and below each descriptor is a set of attributes belonging to the respective category:

Table 3: Hop aromas grouped according to their character

Red Berries	Citrus	Menthol	Grassy, Hay-like
cranberries	tangerine	wine yeast	nettle
wild strawberries	ginger	menthol	green peppers
strawberries	lemongrass	camphor	tomato leaves
blackberries	bergamot	lemon balm	hay
raspberries	lemon	mint	freshly cut grass
blueberries	lime		green-grassy
red currant	orange		
cassis (blackcurrant)	grapefruit	**Herbal**	
		sage	**Woody Aromatic**
		maté tea	pine
Sweet Fruits	**Floral**	black tea	cedar
guava	lavender	green tea	earthy
mango	lilac	marjoram	resin
kiwi	carnation	rosemary	myrrh
cherry	geranium	thyme	incense
pineapple	rose	fennel	woodruff
dried fruit plum	apple blossom	dill	leather
lychee	jasmine	tarragon	barrique
passionfruit	lily of the valley	parsley	cognac
apricot	camomile blossom	basil	tobacco
peach	elderflower	thuja	
honeydew melon		lovage	
watermelon			**Spicy**
banana	**Cream Caramel**		fennel seeds
	tonka	**Vegetal**	gingerbread
	vanilla	wild garlic	cloves
Green Fruits	coffee	garlic	liquorice
white wine grapes	toffee	artichoke	nutmeg
gooseberry	caramel	onion	aniseed
apple	cream	leek	juniper
quince	honey	celeriac (root)	curry
pear	yoghurt	celery stock	chili
	chocolate		pepper
	butter		

Source: Drexler, G., et. al., *The Language of Hops: How to Assess Hop Flavor in Hops and Beer*. MBAA Technical Quarterly, vol. 54, 2017

Spider diagramme

A diagramme that resembles a spider web is used to characterise hop aroma. These are very practical for comparing the aroma profiles of hop varieties at a glance because they form a distinctive shape over the web-shaped scale. Two examples of spider diagrammes are provided below along with a blank one on the following page. The aroma impressions in the two examples were created not only as part of the visual inspection (rubbing the cones between one's hands) but also through a cold infusion of hops. For more information on the sensory analysis of hops, refer to hop tea sensory method in the sensory analysis section below (used with the kind permission of Joh. Barth & Sohn GmbH & Co. KG).

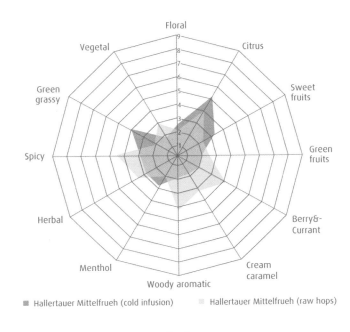

■ Hallertauer Mittelfrueh (cold infusion)   ▢ Hallertauer Mittelfrueh (raw hops)

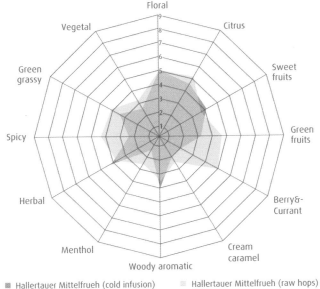

■ Hallertauer Mittelfrueh (cold infusion)   ▢ Hallertauer Mittelfrueh (raw hops)

Figure 50: Spider diagrammes for the aromas in the hop cones of Hallertau Mittelfrüh, raw hops and cold infusion

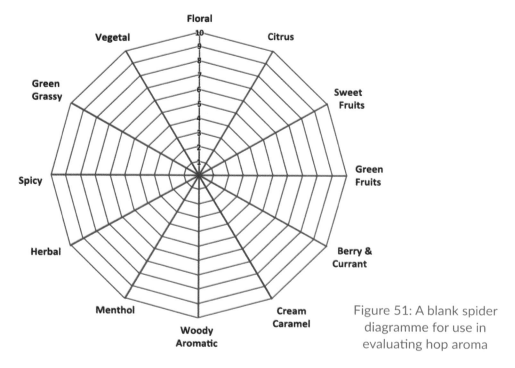

Figure 51: A blank spider diagramme for use in evaluating hop aroma

How to interpret a hop analysis

A hop lot analysis provides much more information about specific compounds in a particular lot of hops. Many suppliers now offer analysis results for a single lot of hops on their websites. Brewers must simply enter a code or otherwise indicate the lot they purchased in order to view the lot analysis. The α-acid content of each lot often also designates which analysis is utilised, so that comparisons between hops can be made with the analysis method in mind.

The three groups of compounds in hops

Most of the world's brewers are only interested in the amount of α-acids in hops. The other two groups of compounds, hop polyphenols and oils, normally never enter their minds. This is unfortunate because hops have a great deal to contribute to beer besides bitterness. Whole (pressed) hops or type 90 pellets would be most suitable for adding these other groups of compounds to beer.

Bitter compounds

Bitter compounds are present in the form of resin which can be further subdivided into soft and hard resins. The total resins comprise all of the bitter compounds in hops. The total resins are divided into the subgroups hard and soft resins. The soft resins contain the bitter acids present in hops, namely the α-acids and β-acids. Neither the α-acids nor β-acids exhibit a high level of solubility at pH values common in wort. However, during the wort boiling process, the α-acids are isomerised which makes them soluble in the aqueous solution of the wort. The isomerised α-acids are also much more bitter than in their unisomerised form and thus provide the primary source of bitterness in beer.

The α-acids and β-acids are divided into the humulones and lupulones, respectively. The three most relevant types of α-acids are the humulones, adhumulones and cohumulones. Hops possessing low cohumulone levels tend to impart a less harsh bitterness. The soft resins that do not comprise the α-acids and β-acids are classified as auxiliary bitter substances. The ratio of β-acids to α-acids provides some idea of the quantity of the auxiliary bitter substances present in the hops. These auxiliary compounds (resins) have been shown to make a positive contribution to bitterness, providing a more harmonious and rounded character to the finished beer. Aroma hops contain more auxiliary bitter substances. Non-isomerised α-acids entering the process through late hop additions, though scarcely soluble, enhance foam formation and head retention in the finished beer.

- α-acids in bitter and high alpha hop varieties: 10–20%
- α-acids in aroma hop varieties: 2–10%
- β-acids in bitter and high alpha hop varieties: 4–8%
- β-acids in aroma hop varieties: 4–7%

EBC method 9.8 is used to determine bittering units (IBU). It is unspecific and detects both alpha acids and iso-alpha acids in addition to auxiliary bitter substances. If this analysis does not yield the same results as an analysis for iso-alpha acids (e.g. using HPLC), this is attributable to the auxiliary bitter compounds. The use of aroma hops and older hops increases this proportion, as they both contain more of these substances.

Polyphenols

Hop polyphenols make a substantial contribution to the total polyphenol content of the wort. Low molecular weight polyphenols are antioxidants, positively impacting the flavour stability of the finished beer. They can also influence the bitterness of the beer as well as the mouthfeel and the body. High molecular weight polyphenols can darken the colour of the finished beer, especially if the wort is boiled for an extended period of time. These higher molecular weight compounds can also lend an astringency to the bitterness of the beer and can increase the beer's susceptibility to haze formation. Low alpha hops tend to contain not only higher amounts of polyphenols, but when adding them to the wort kettle, more are required to reach the same level of bitterness. Therefore, the polyphenol content of the wort derived from hops increases significantly when aroma hops are employed. This positively affects the quality of the bitterness, the body and flavour stability (anti-oxidative potential) of the finished beer.

- polyphenol content of bitter and high alpha hop varieties: 3–4%
- polyphenol content of aroma, low alpha hop varieties: 4–6%

Oils

The composition of hop oils is heavily dependent on the individual hop variety, the provenance, climate and processing conditions. Hop oils are the compounds that contribute most to the hop aroma in beer. The total hop oil is generally quantified in millilitres per 100 g. The composition of the oils in hops is so specific to the variety that identification keys have been developed based on the individual oils found in the hops and their respective proportions. The most prevalent oils present in hops are myrcene, farnesene, caryophyllene and humulene. Geraniol can also play a role in the aroma of some hop varieties. Humulene and caryophyllene are frequently expressed together as a ratio (H:C). If the ratio is weighted more heavily towards humulene, a brewer can expect herbal and spicy aromas in the finished beer. Less volatile hop oils are more likely to be carried through to the finished beer, while the more volatile oils are lost through evaporation in the brewhouse.

- oil content of bitter and high alpha hop varieties: 1.5–3%
- oil content of aroma hop varieties: 0.6–1.5%

The aroma characteristics of the prevailing hop oils are as follows:

- **myrcene:** green, resinous, herbaceous; fresh hop aroma; high volatility; generally viewed as a less desirable aroma; however, some craft brewers prefer the pronounced and distinctive aroma of myrcene in fresh hops; higher quantities in American hops (e.g. Cascade, Chinook, Centennial)
- **linalool:** floral and orange; lower volatility
- **caryophyllene:** woody, peppery; lower volatility
- **farnesene:** floral, noble hop aroma; higher volatility
- **geraniol:** rose-like, floral, sweet-smelling; desirable in beer, lower volatility

Hop storage index (HSI)

The hop storage index included on the documentation from the supplier provides a measure of the oxidised compounds present in hops. The HSI value is an indication of how much hops have aged or become oxidised. Brewers can use the HSI value provided to adjust their recipes accordingly, as the hops age.

- fresh hops: < 0.31
- processed hops (properly stored): 0.31–0.40
- aged hops: 0.50–0.60
- oxidised hops: > 0.60

Trials have shown that using hops with a lower HSI value, especially for those used in dry hopping, has a positive influence on the quality and intensity of hop aroma. When older hops are used, hop additions must be carefully calculated to ensure that appropriate levels of bitterness are imparted to the beer.

Testing for bitterness

The bitterness of hops or hop products is usually measured by the producer. If the hop yield differs from the expected value in wort or in the finished beer, samples should be collected and sent to an independent laboratory for confirmation (the bittering units in the cast-out wort – refer to EBC method 8.8 for more information). Some breweries regularly submit samples of packaged beer for analysis of bittering units according to EBC methods 7.4 through 7.7.

| Visual inspection and evaluation of hops

Whole hops

Whole hops are hop flowers and are also referred to as hop cones. Whole hops to be used for imparting aroma to beer, either in a late brewhouse addition or through cold-side hopping, can be chosen not long after the harvest in a process known as 'hop selection' at the supplier.

This involves standing over small piles of different hop varieties and first visually evaluating the cones, their homogeneity, their colour as well as the presence of any extraneous plant material. The procedure below describes how hops are selected from individual lots. Regardless of where the hops are evaluated, always take a representative sample of the hops if possible. Hops should be inspected in surroundings devoid of any unusual odours, be protected from wind, under bright, uniform halogen lights. As shown in the photo, the best background for the visual inspection of hops is blue with no reflective properties to eliminate glare. Like with most learned activities, continued practice makes perfect. Perfume and other toiletries should not be applied prior to the visual inspection. Scheduling the inspection before lunch is best (prior to dulling of the olfactory organ by food, coffee, etc.), and it should last no more than 90 minutes, given the sensory fatigue that occurs over time.

Figure 52: The visual inspection of hops involves more than merely looking at the cones

Although it is called a visual inspection, the aroma and texture are also assessed. There are many factors that influence hop quality, including the variety, provenance, the year's climatic conditions, pests, diseases, conditions and the timing of harvest, subsequent kilning and storage.

Since the human sensory apparatus is very well suited to this task, brewers visually examine the hops and then rub them vigorously between their hands in order to break the lupulin glands and release the aromatic oils contained in them. The following criteria can be used to assess their quality:

- **Varietal purity:** examine the hop cones for uniform size, shape and colour. Although the size of the cones may vary due to differing levels of maturity at harvest, most of the cones should be similar.
- **Appearance:** the colour, size and shape of the hop cones should be typical for the individual variety. They should largely be intact with few loose petals, which are known as bracts. Tighter, more compact cones, compared to those with loose bracts, can prevent some oxidation of the lupulin glands. Infestation by hop aphids or downy mildew should be immediately obvious to an observant brewer by the physical appearance of the whole hops. The hop cones should be bright and homogenous in colour and should not have any brown patches or discolouration and should be relatively uniform in colour. There should be a minimal amount of leaf and stem material from hop plants as well as from other vegetation. Examine the hop cones for damage caused by pests and disease. Shattered or excessively brittle cones and crushed lupulin glands are an indication of incorrect handling.
- **Aroma (uncrushed):** First, assess the hop aroma by simply smelling the hops without crushing them. The aroma emanating from the surface of the hops allows observations to be made as to whether the hops were incorrectly stored or handled. Hops with a scorched or smoky odour indicate that the hops were dried too rapidly at a high temperature. Poor storage conditions or inadequate drying result in spoilage of the hop cones. Musty notes point to mould growth due to a high moisture content. The presence of other atypical or foreign odours arises from poor storage conditions. There should be no oxidised or cheesy aromas in fresh hops. The aroma impressions should be recorded on an evaluation sheet for each sample for use in later comparison of each lot.
- **Aroma (crushed):** Next, rub the hop cones between both hands to crush the hops. This releases the hop oil contained in the lupulin glands, allowing the true aroma to be assessed. Naturally, it is to be expected that hops of the same variety grown in different geographical areas will exhibit subtle differences in aroma. One judges the harmony, complexity and intensity of the aroma. Hops of the same variety harvested from the same garden can nevertheless evince different aromas if one lot is harvested late and the other early, as this can alter the composition of the oils. This will be evident in the finished beer, if the beer is late/dry hopped to preserve the oils.

For more information on sensory analysis using a cold water extraction and the flavour and aroma properties of hops, refer to the section on sensory analysis.

Hop selection

Whole hops are evaluated for their sensory properties either for later use as cones or prior to pelletisation. Hops are often assessed by brewers at the supplier shortly after the harvest to determine which hops they would like to purchase for the following year.

Hop pellets

How to determine pellet quality:

- Upon delivery, inspect the bags of pellets. They are generally packed in foil bags under inert gas to eliminate oxygen. Open the cartons carefully and remove the foil bags, checking for any evidence of punctures or cuts that have occurred in transit.
- When opening each bag of pellets, always smell the contents and decide whether the aroma is typical for that specific hop variety. Refer to the descriptions on the supplier's website or the hop analysis sheet for more information on how pellets of a certain variety should smell and look. Cheesy notes indicate that the pellets have somehow been exposed to oxygen. If the bag appears to be intact, empty it and hold it against a light to check for the presence of tiny holes.
- Depending on the hop variety, pellets may vary in colour. They are generally green to brownish-green and should crumble under moderate pressure. The pellet surface should not appear hard or glassy as if it was exposed to excessive heat during processing.

| Delivery and storage of hops

Delivery

When accepting a hop delivery, the following should be taken into consideration:

- Place the relevant documentation of hop delivery in a binder or save it in digital form as part of a software programme so that traceability is assured at all times.
- Inspect all packaging to ensure that they are still sealed (check foil bags for punctures or loss of vacuum for products supplied as vacuum packs) or cardboard boxes for damage.
- Upon opening the package: check for proper colour and aroma, physical appearance, etc. Ensure that there is no evidence of infestation by pests (current or past). Also check that boxes or bags are not harbouring any pests which could then infest the brewery.

Storage

Some brewers prefer to purchase hops on an annual basis and have a dedicated area set aside (climate-controlled) for their storage. For others, it is more convenient to have the hop merchant take care of storage and shipment of smaller amounts to the brewery as needed. The supplier's recommendations should be consulted for each hop product because they can differ depending upon the production process. The hop storage index or HSI provides information on how rapidly the loss of bitter compounds is predicted to occur.

The following measures should be taken to preserve hop quality for as long as possible:

- The area where hops are stored should be monitored for pests and contaminants as part of a routine, preventative plan.
- If removing only a portion of the hops or hop products in a container, close it securely after use. Once a package is opened, the remaining pellets/whole hops should be stored in a closed container under cold conditions to protect against oxidation.
- Maintain an inventory system for on-site stock. Have a system in place for clearly identifying and separating the different hop varieties and adhere to the first in, first out (FIFO) principle. Stock should be rotated to utilise older stock before moving on to newer stock.
- The storage area should be free of any external odours that could be transferred to the hops.
- Any containers used to store hops should be food-grade quality.

A note on the storage of pellets:

- Pellets should also be stored under refrigeration after arrival at the brewery.
- Pellets may be kept for several years when stored properly and packaged under inert gas, but there will be a loss in bitter compounds over that time period.

A note on the storage of extracts:

- CO_2 pure resin extracts can be stored at 15 °C; however, at 0 °C to 5 °C, the shelf life is 10 years.
- Ethanol extracts can be stored at temperatures of 0 °C to 5 °C for up to five years.

Literature and further reading

Back, W., Gastl, M., Krottenthaler, M., Narziss, L., and Zarnkow, M., *Brewing Techniques in Practice*. Fachverlag Hans Carl GmbH, 2019

Basarova, G., Savel, J., Basar, P., Lejsek, T., *The Comprehensive Guide to Brewing from Raw Material to Packaging*. Fachverlag Hans Carl GmbH, 2017

Biendl, M., Engelhard, B., Forster, A., Gahr, A., Lutz, A., Mitter, W., Schmidt, R., Schönberger, C., *Hops: Their Cultivation, Composition and Usage*. Fachverlag Hans Carl GmbH, 2014

Forster, A., Schüll, F., Gahr, A. *Hintergründe und Update zur Lupulinanreicherung von Hopfen*. HVG Hopfenverwertungsgenossenschaft e.G., 2020

Hengel, M., Shibamoto, T. Method *Development and Fate Determination of Pesticide-Treated Hops and Their Subsequent Usage in the Production of Beer*. Journal of Agricultural and Food Chemistry 50(12):3412-8, July 2002

Kippenberger, M., Hanke, S., Biendl, M. *Transfer of nitrate and various pesticides into beer during dry hopping*. BrewingScience 67(1):1-9, January 2014

Narziss, L. *Abriss der Bierbrauerei*. Wiley-VCH Verlag GmbH & Co., 2017

Narziss, L., *Im Hopfen ist mehr als nur α-Säure*. Brauwelt no. 6, 122–126, 2009

RAW MATERIALS: YEAST AND OTHER MICROORGANISMS

General information

Brewing yeast is usually divided into two major categories: top-fermenting and bottom-fermenting. Classifying yeast cells by the fermentation temperature would actually be more practical, since some strains that ferment at higher temperatures may not be truly top-fermenting strains. Whether yeast rises to the surface or settles out on the bottom of the tank is determined by a number of factors:

- The degree to which yeast cells are hydrophobic: the more hydrophobic they are on the surface of the cells, the more they may tend to adhere to bubbles of carbon dioxide. They rise to the surface with the bubbles, forming a layer of yeasty foam on the surface.
- The pH of the wort/green beer interacting with the proteins and minerals in the yeast cell walls may play a role.
- The electrostatic repulsion between yeast cells drops as fermentation progresses, causing them to flocculate and settle.
- The amount of hot/cold break material left in the wort may, due to its opposite charge, cause it to stick to the yeast, enhancing flocculation.
- The formation of communities of cells, i.e. top-fermenting, causes them to rise to the surface on carbon dioxide bubbles as opposed to the separation of mother-daughter cells as seen in bottom-fermenting yeast (see below).

Top fermentation

Top-fermenting strains of yeast (*Saccharomyces cerevisiae*) became domesticated centuries ago in late medieval breweries. This means that similar to malting barley, brewing yeast is completely dependent upon humans and can no longer live in the wild. Over the process of domestication, these yeast strains lost undesirable characteristics, like the generation of unpleasant flavour and aroma compounds. Harvesting wild yeast has become popular among craft brewers; however, those existing in the surrounding environment may, for this reason, produce beer with unpleasant off-aromas and off-flavours (disagreeably acidic or medicinal substances or those reminiscent of solvent, tallow, nail polish remover, an electrical fire, etc.).

Ultimately, top-fermenting yeast strains can be categorised as fermenting at temperatures above 15 °C all the way up to about 30 °C (saison yeast) or even 40 °C (kveik), and thus fermentation occurs more rapidly than with the bottom-fermenting yeast. Typically, many of the cells do not completely separate and form connected communities. These are carried on the rising bubbles from the yeast in suspension to the top of the fermenting wort or green beer in a foamy, yeasty froth known as 'barm' in English. However, there are some differences between Central European and British top-fermenting yeast. For instance, a percentage of *Weissbier* yeast cells tend to cause beer to have a milky

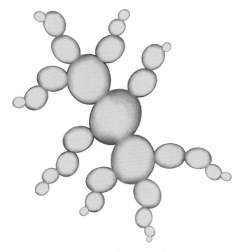

Figure 53: Top-fermenting yeast

appearance, since the yeast cells in suspension do not clump together and sediment out very readily, making them similar to the 'powdery' or 'dusty' bottom-fermenting yeast that continue to float around in the green beer when the majority of the yeast cells have already clumped together and sedimented out. British top-fermenting strains, on the other hand, are more similar in this regard to their bottom-fermenting cousins in their tendency to be flocculent and non-flocculent. British strains are referred to as 'ale yeasts' after the top-fermented beer brewed there.

Generally speaking, top-fermenting yeasts produce more fruity and floral volatile aroma compounds (esters, higher alcohols). These impart a degree of drinkability, even at lower concentrations. Top-fermented beers are also normally devoid of sulphurous characteristics.

Top-fermenting yeast strains, when they are not actively fermenting, will tend to undergo autolysis at a pH of approximately 4.7.

Bottom-fermenting yeasts can ferment the wort sugar, raffinose, a trisaccharide, consisting of galactose, glucose and fructose bound together. Top-fermenting yeast strains cannot, because they lack the enzyme melibiase, the enzyme that cuts the bond between the molecules in melibiose, the glucose/galactose portion of the molecule. Thus, top-fermenting yeast only ferment 1/3 of the raffinose molecule by cutting off the fructose. This trait is, of course, genetically determined. For this reason, a simple method, the raffinose test, has been devised for distinguishing top and bottom-fermenting yeast. A pure culture is aseptically injected into a sterile tube of a raffinose broth containing an indicator substance. If the yeast fully ferments it, the pH drops, bringing about a colour change which indicates that the strain is bottom-fermenting.

Bottom fermentation

Bottom-fermenting or lager yeast strains (*Saccharomyces pastorianus*, formerly known as *S. carlsbergensis*) are descendants of a hybrid species of yeast (*S. cerevisiae* and a wild strain *S. eubayanus*) able to ferment at cooler temperatures which results in less microbial competition and fewer fermentation by-products in the finished beer. These strains are employed to produce lager beers, such as pilsner, *Dunkles*, *Helles* and international-style lagers.

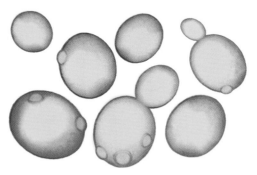

Figure 54: Bottom-fermenting yeast

These yeasts do not form clustered branched communities. When budding, upon reaching close to full size, the daughter cell cleaves off its mother cell. Therefore, they are not pushed upwards by the CO_2 bubbles to the surface of the wort during fermentation. Once they flocculate and sediment out, they form a layer on the bottom of the tank and are apt to undergo autolysis at a pH around 5.0 when in this state.

They prefer cooler temperatures during fermentation, usually between 9 °C and 12 °C. Fermentation and maturation take quite a bit longer with these strains of yeast. They can ferment the trisaccharide raffinose (refer to the discussion above about top fermentation). The white foam that crowns the wort and green beer during fermentation contains far fewer yeast cells and is known as *Kräusen* (a German noun for the rocky, white meringue-like head relatively free of yeast on bottom-fermenting wort/green beer). The term has been adopted by brewers around the world.

| How to interpret a yeast data sheet

Yeast strain selection

Selecting the proper yeast strain is one of the most important aspects in determining the type of beer that come out of the production process. Refer to the respective data sheets for information about what to expect from an individual strain. Suppliers will usually provide a chart or a table listing the various yeast strains and their characteristics for easy comparison.

Yeast data sheet

Yeast suppliers provide technical data sheets with a variety of information, including a description of the fermentation behaviour of each strain. Every strain exhibits a different combination of characteristics, including by-products such as esters, attenuation rate, flocculation behaviour, alcohol tolerance, storage suitability, resistance to mutation, tolerance of stress factors and overall brewing performance. All factors and their impact on the desired flavour profile of the finished beer should be considered when choosing a yeast strain.

| Visual inspection and evaluation of yeast

Most brewers today work with cylindroconical fermentation tanks, which allow timely removal of sedimented yeast from the cone of the tank and facilitate the cropping of yeast for repitching that settle out into the cone of the tank. True top-fermenting yeast are best cropped from open fermentation vessels. Regardless of the source of the yeast, it is always good practice to sensorially inspect the yeast before pitching it (examine the colour and texture, smell and taste the yeast).

Table 4 provides a selection of yeasts employed in making beer. Of course, *S. cerevisiae* and *S. pastorianus* are the two species most frequently utilised in beer production.

Table 4: Yeasts used in brewing

Yeasts used in brewing	Summary of information
Saccharomyces cerevisiae	Strains ferment at warmer temperatures (15–40 °C); wine/top-fermenting/distilling/bread yeast present throughout history among the microorganisms in sourdough cultures which were maintained to regularly leaven dough and brew beer; many strains of this species exist with a wide variety of characteristics; some are domesticated, others wild; incapable of digesting melibiose (raffinose test).
English ale yeast	These strains produce the fruity esters common in English ales; rapid attenuation; highly flocculent; like all highly flocculent yeast, green beer compounds (e.g. diacetyl) may not be effectively eliminated (e.g. diacetyl, acetaldehyde).
S.c. var. diastaticus	A super-attenuating (> 90%), warm-fermenting (mid-30s °C), wild variant exhibiting the enzyme amyloglucosidase (AMG, aka glucoamylase, coded by the STA genes). Found in saison yeast; if undesired, this yeast can be detected at low cost with fermentation on starch plates or in fully attenuated beer.

Table 4 (cont'd)

Yeasts used in brewing	Summary of information
Weissbier yeast	Both of these sets of yeast strains exhibit the wild attribute of producing phenolic aromas but in such a way that it is normally appealing in the beer styles produced with them if treated properly (clove-like, spicy, slightly smoky). Some of these strains do not flocculate well, hence the cloudy nature of many of the beers fermented with them. Refer to the POF test.
Belgian ale yeast	
Kveik (Norwegian term for farmhouse yeast)	Numerous strains of Norwegian origin exist; generally a mixed culture unless cells are isolated; ferment at temperatures near or even above 40 °C with few to no unpleasant fermentation by-products; lower pitching rates than other strains; slightly lower final beer pH; can be carefully dried.
Saccharomyces pastorianus	Bottom-fermenting strains ferment at cooler temperatures (9–12 °C) and in conjunction with cold maturation used to brew lager beer; are divided into two subgroups: Frohberg (majority of the modern, industrial yeast strains) and Saaz; many strains exist with a wide range of fermentation characteristics; can digest melibiose (raffinose test); generally produce fewer fermentation by-products than yeast that ferment at higher temperatures.
Brettanomyces (anamorph; teleomorph *Dekkera*)	Generally considered a wine-spoiler; a super-attenuating (> 90%) yeast that can ferment oligosaccharides up to 12 glucose molecules long at temperatures ranging from 10 to 35 °C; many strains are POF positive but also produce appealing fruity flavours
Brettanomyces bruxellensis	Originally the predominant species in Brussels and used for Orval bottle conditioning; imparts a slight 'horse blanket' earthiness to beer
Brettanomyces lambicus	Present in Flemish red and *Oud Bruin* and, of course, lambic; native to Brussels and the surrounding area; exhibits fruity aromas; most likely a strain of *B. bruxellensis*.
Brettanomyces anomalus	The strains are found in the stouts of the British Isles; produces delicate fruit notes.
Brettanomyces claussenii	Known for subtle fruitiness and is very closely related to or is perhaps a strain of *B. anomalus*.
Torulaspora delbrueckii	Some strains are maltose-negative, while some are maltose-positive; fermentation at approx. 20 °C; POF-negative (see below); popular among craft brewers in mixed cultures due to intense fruity notes (blackcurrant).
Kloeckera apiculata (anamorph; teleomorph *Hanseniaspora uvarum*)	Ferments glucose; found on fruit, particularly grapes; active early in spontaneous fermentation (esp. fruit beers); produces ethyl acetate, inactive above approx. 4% ethanol.
Schizosaccharomyces pombe	Rod-shaped yeast in African opaque millet beers and most likely in ancient Near Eastern beers, along with *S. cerevisiae*; ferments best at 24–26 °C; found in tropical and sub-tropical settings; asexual reproduction by fission rather than budding.

Sources, propagation and storage of yeast

Deciding what type of yeast to use

Beyond choosing a bottom-fermenting or top-fermenting yeast strain based on the style of beer being brewed, there are multiple factors to consider when selecting the form of yeast to use. Key aspects include production volume, equipment, type of brewery and the degree of expertise in handling yeast. Due to inherent constraints, most breweries opt for ready-to-pitch yeast from suppliers, which is available both in dry and liquid form. Others may choose to step up their yeast to pitchable volumes from a yeast culture or operate dedicated propagation equipment on-site to meet their needs; however, this option requires specific equipment and proficiency in sterile microbiology techniques.

- **Dry yeast**
- **Liquid yeast**
- **Propagating yeast on-site**: Larger breweries are more likely to have the equipment and personnel in place to propagate and maintain their own yeast cultures. Propagating yeast requires a high level of hygiene since mistakes can lead to contamination of the culture and spoilage of beer.

Dry yeast

With a shelf life of one to two years, this form of yeast offers the greatest flexibility, but the number of strains is limited. For dry yeast packed under a vacuum, the vacuum should still be intact, otherwise do not use it. Once opened, the package should be closed tightly, refrigerated and used within several days. The yeast should be used by the expiration date on the package. Upon examination of the contents of the package, the yeast should be dry and uniform in colour and flow freely when poured. No undesirable odours should be present. The information provided with the yeast contains instructions concerning how a particular package of dried yeast should be rehydrated and pitched.

Liquid yeast

This form of yeast must be used within a short time after delivery, so some advance planning is required. However, the selection of available strains to choose from is far greater. Sometimes yeast will require stepping up in order to reach the correct pitching rate. Some yeast is shipped in ready-to-pitch packages for a given tank size. Either way, the instructions should be included regarding how to best handle the yeast prior to pitching it.

Healthy yeast should have a thick consistency, be light in colour, almost white, and creamy but not slimy. The yeast should smell fresh and, for lack of a better word, 'yeasty'

– similar to rising bread dough. It may even smell of fruit like apricots or bananas, especially if it is top-fermenting. It should never exhibit mouldy odours or off-aromas. The flavour of yeast is also fresh and somewhat bitter but never sour or off in any way. CO_2 will give it a prickly feeling on the palate.

Treating yeast well keeps its viability and vitality high. Thus, less time is required for fermentation and maturation, meaning the decline in extract concentration, pH and diacetyl are all more rapid. Many off-flavours in beer can be avoided simply by pitching healthy yeast. The amount of fatty acids created during maturation is also lower and therefore foam formation and head retention are better. The perception of a beer's bitterness is also finer, cleaner and more pleasant. Beers fermented and matured with healthy yeast also age more gracefully, that is, their flavour stability is greater over time due to their increased reduction potential.

Propagating and harvesting yeast

For brewers with smaller operations, it is ordinarily considered impractical to maintain yeast cultures and to propagate them up from a single cell to a reasonable pitching volume, though the authors have been to a number of small breweries that do, in fact, grow their yeast from slants. Generally, these breweries employ personnel with experience in applied microbiology and use a wide variety of strains to produce their beers. Commercial yeast banks and even generous colleagues are the usual source for fresh yeast at a small brewery. If a small volume of yeast is purchased from a supplier, it can be grown up to a pitchable volume with a limited amount of equipment, using aseptic transfer techniques. The primary objective in the preparation of brewing yeast for pitching is to create conditions as ideal as possible for the yeast so that they are healthy and active when they are moved to production. The number of living cells should be as close to 100% as possible. Yeast is too often neglected in breweries and is held under poor conditions (high concentrations of CO_2, alcohol, high pressure and nutrient deficits).

During propagation, the conditions should be optimal, so that the yeast cells remain in the logarithmic growth phase. When yeast is subjected to anaerobic conditions, this is less than ideal for propagation; only during beer production should yeast ferment wort. The stresses on the yeast should be kept to a minimum until pitched for beer production. Figure 55 shows asexual budding as it occurs with *Saccharomyces pastorianus*.

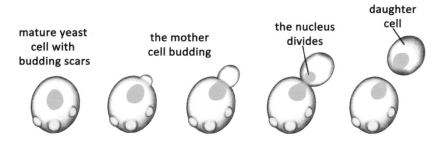

Figure 55: Budding bottom-fermenting yeast

Stepped propagation

For those who possess the basic skills required for aseptic technique, relatively little equipment is necessary to grow up yeast. Yeast can be cultivated from a pure culture, meaning that it can be 'stepped up' to create a large volume of pitchable yeast. Brewers can begin with an agar slant or a packaged liquid yeast culture (fig. 57).

In order to step up yeast from a pure culture, sterile cast-out wort is required. This can be collected from the brewhouse and then autoclaved in the laboratory (fig. 56). The wort should be well-aerated. Yeast should not be cultivated in sugar solutions (glucose, sucrose, etc.) because important metabolic pathways become inhibited in the process, and they 'forget' what to do in wort.

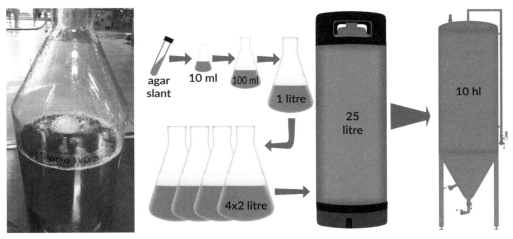

Figure 56: Sterile wort collected in the brewhouse

Figure 57: Yeast propagation from an agar slant

Should they be necessary, the steps beyond 10 hl would be 40 hl, then 80 hl and finally 800 hl.

Source: Back, W., Gastl, M., Krottenthaler, M., Narziss, L., and Zarnkow, M., *Brewing Techniques in Practice*. Fachverlag Hans Carl GmbH, 2019

There are different terms for the yeast cultivation techniques brewers employ to increase the cell mass prior to pitching. Traditional cultivation and propagation involve yeast in every phase of growth, while assimilation keeps them in the logarithmic phase (refer to these phases in the section on fermentation below). In modern assimilation systems, the temperature is maintained at 12 °C to 18 °C for bottom-fermenting yeast and 20 °C to 25 °C for top-fermenting yeast or no more than around 5 °C above the yeast's pitching temperature. At an initial cell count of approximately 10 million cells/ml, the yeast suspended in wort is gently circulated through the system equipped with a Venturi tube where sterile air enters the substrate. Head space of approximately 40% is necessary in this vessel. If continuous aeration is not possible, frequent aeration will suffice. When the yeast cell count reaches approximately 80 to 120 million cells/ml, which takes about 24 h, more wort can be added to the vessel or the yeast can be pitched – in either case, the yeast remains in the logarithmic phase. Approximately 10% or more is left in the vessel in order to repeat the process. If left in the assimilation vessel to reach higher cell counts, the yeast tends to enter the stationary phase, which is not desirable. Pitching only 20% yeast cultivated in this manner with 80% vital harvested yeast is enough to improve fermentation and the quality of the finished beer.

Refer to the instructions on aseptic technique in the appendix for how to transfer the yeast to the sterile wort.

Harvesting yeast

As mentioned above, when yeast sediments out, even if the tank is equipped with cone cooling, it can encounter a great deal of stress there, given the higher pressures and temperatures. For this reason, it is wise to purge the yeast in the cone at the proper time and at frequent intervals. If the yeast is under hydrostatic pressure in a cylindroconical tank, cropping yeast early is worthwhile, since the stresses on the yeast in the cone increase over time.

Losses in yeast vitality over several harvests and generations can be forestalled by early cropping and proper care. In order for yeast to be vital and ready for repitching, it needs to be freed of pressure and CO_2. It should, however, not be aerated if it is to be stored for several days prior to repitching. It is advisable to use yeast as soon as possible after harvesting in order to maintain its good health.

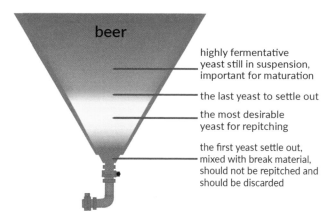

highly fermentative yeast still in suspension, important for maturation

the last yeast to settle out

the most desirable yeast for repitching

the first yeast settle out, mixed with break material, should not be repitched and should be discarded

Figure 58: Layers of yeast sediment in a tank cone

Not all of the yeast in the cone is the same. The most suitable yeast for repitching is found in the middle of the sedimented yeast in the cone (fig. 58).

When pulling yeast off of the bottom of the cone, one should do so slowly, because if performed too rapidly, mixing of the yeast layers will occur. The yeast laden with hot break material at the bottom of the cone comes out at the same time as the desirable pitching yeast and perhaps even some of the beer (fig. 59).

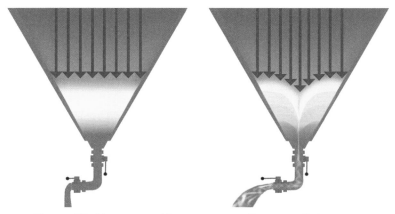

Figure 59: How to and how not to pull yeast off the cone

True top-fermenting yeast does not form layers at the bottom, but rather floats at the top (hence the name) and can be harvested there, if fermentation occurs in open tanks. However, as mentioned, some British ale strains are more flocculent. In fact, nowadays not all yeast strains that ferment at higher temperatures are top-fermenting, probably given the fact that there has been strong selective pressure in recent decades on all yeast to settle out, since those that do are harvested at the bottom of fermentation vessels and reused, while those in suspension end up in the filter or the finished beer.

Figure 60 represents an example of harvested yeast one would want to repitch. Note how light in colour and thick it is – incidentally, it also smells very fresh, somewhat like rising bread dough.

The slurry pictured in the glass (fig. 61) was taken from a lager tank and provides a good example of undesirable yeast, i.e. yeast one does not want to repitch. It is full of old, depleted yeast cells and harsh-tasting sediment that has to be removed from the production process as waste. It can, however, find application as a supplement in animal feed, if properly treated.

Refer to the section on beer production for yeast pitching information and to the section on microbiology for instructions on how to determine yeast cell count and yeast viability.

Figure 60: Healthy and vital harvested yeast in a tank with two agitators
Photo: *Wolfgang Lindell*

Figure 61: Yeast slurry from the bottom of a lager tank
Photo: *Lance Snow*

Yeast storage

There are a variety of methods to store yeast for longer periods of time. These include storage on agar slants or at low to extremely low temperatures (approx. -6 °C to -20 °C, depending on the method) in cryo tubes with special beads, under glycerine or in an isotonic salt solution.

If yeast slurry must be stored for several days, pre-sterilised 20 litre stainless steel soda kegs are a good option; however, a yeast brink is designed for this purpose. Yeast remains most vital when stored at 1 °C to 2 °C. The yeast must be stored in a vessel or container which is capable of releasing pressure. Kegs should be shaken and vented on a daily basis to prevent pressure from building up which can damage the yeast. The harvested yeast can be mixed with sterile, cold water for storage over a short period. All surfaces and containers used in yeast storage should be thoroughly cleaned and sanitised. The small components of the soda kegs, such as valves and gaskets, also need to be properly disinfected. One day before reusing the yeast, pour the beer off of the yeast sediment and reactivate it by resuspending it in some fresh, aerated wort (9–12 °Plato) and storing it at room temperature. If possible, determining the living/dead ratio and/or testing yeast for microbiological purity prior to pitching is always a good idea.

How to harvest and store yeast

Equipment: 70% ethanol, gas torch, sanitiser, cold water/sterile wort, tank or storage container

Yeast should be harvested when the beer is close to its final gravity, prior to the diacetyl rest.

1. Spray valve with ethanol and flame to sterilise. Sanitise all equipment which will come in contact with the yeast, including hoses.
2. Bottom-fermenting yeast will flocculate and settle out on the bottom of the tank. The layer at the bottom of the tank contains a lot of dead cells and particulate matter which sedimented out early in fermentation. The middle layer is cleaner, consisting primarily of yeast cells. The top layer of sediment usually contains impurities such as coagulated proteins and tannins that have sedimented out when the foam collapses at the end of fermentation.
3. If bottom-fermenting yeast is to be harvested from a cylindroconical tank, open the valve and purge the dark layer of yeast from the tank.
4. Once the colour of the yeast flowing from the tank becomes lighter and the consistency is creamy, collect the yeast to be reused in a sterile container and seal it.
5. Avoid collecting too much yeast and pulling off some of the darker yeast layer on the top of the sediment.
6. If top-fermenting yeast is to be harvested from a round tank, remove the yeast from the surface during the high kräusen stage with a sanitised stainless steel scoop or a paddle. Take care to harvest yeast that is light in colour and contains the least amount of particulate material.

Washing and sieving yeast

Yeast excretes cellular poisons (ethanol, CO_2) during fermentation and must be freed of them as soon as possible, if the yeast is to be repitched. With regard to the yeast vitality, the process of fermentation should be completed as quickly as possible and upon harvesting the yeast, they should be washed with treated, cold water, which rids them of the alcohol, and sieved, which aids in removing the carbon dioxide.

The yeast cells in the sediment located in the cone of a cylindroconical fermentation tank are under pressure as they are harvested. Carbon dioxide has a negative impact on yeast vitality and its ability to reproduce. This, in turn, ultimately affects the quality of the beer. Once the pressure has been released on the yeast, passing the yeast through a sieve will remove the majority of the carbon dioxide. The yeast slurry should be sieved first and then chilled to 3 °C. The yeast can be stored at this temperature for up to a week.

The majority of particulate matter can be removed from the cropped yeast with the help of vibrating sieves. After the yeast has passed through the sieve, it can be repitched in a new batch of wort. If the yeast will be used within two days, it can be stored under beer at or below 3 °C. If the yeast is kept for more than two days, it should be washed prior to using.

Yeast can be washed or rinsed to remove particulate material, dead yeast cells and alcohol trapped in the slurry. Cold water at a temperature of 4–5 °C with a hardness of 8–10 °dH is optimal. The water should be sterile, meaning that it is free of any microorganisms. A low level of chlorination (0.5 g/m³) is acceptable. When done correctly, this procedure simply removes physical impurities without affecting yeast viability. This procedure should not be confused with acid washing which is done to remove bacterial contamination. The following methods can be implemented to rinse yeast:

- The yeast is placed in a yeast brink or appropriate vessel. Cold water is added (at least double the amount of yeast) and the mixture is briefly stirred to suspend the cells. After the cells have settled to the bottom, the water is decanted. Fresh water is added, and the procedure is repeated.
- The yeast is placed in a vessel or funnel with a water supply fitted from below. The water flows upward through the yeast layer, carrying the impurities up the surface. The water containing the impurities is released through ports arranged at different heights in the vessel. With the funnel method, the yeast sediment is removed from the bottom of the funnel while the water remains in the funnel. The washed yeast is transferred to a yeast brink after the procedure.
- Yeast brinks can also be fitted with perforated rings which can be used to clean the yeast directly in the brink.

Instructions for rinsing yeast

1. Select one of the methods above and sanitise the equipment.
2. Transfer the yeast to the appropriate vessel and perform the rinsing procedure until the overflow water appears clear and free of visible particulates.
3. Remove the yeast and store in an appropriate vessel or immediately repitch.

Note: As breweries become more modernised and increasingly automated, yeast sieves become more difficult to integrate into the process. They are, however, quite helpful in freeing the carbon dioxide from the harvested yeast.

Bacterial contaminants, particularly Gram-negative bacteria, can be eliminated from yeast through acid washing. These microorganisms will negatively impact beer quality over time if they are not removed from the process. Bacteria are generally more sensitive to acid than yeast, and therefore, brewers may choose to wash their yeast with a food-grade phosphoric acid to inactivate any bacterial contaminants, although certain microorganisms, such as lactic acid bacteria, may be more difficult to eliminate. Acid washing is also only effective for very low-level bacterial contamination. Fermentation performance as well as yeast viability and vitality are often positively influenced by acid washing, though it depends on the yeast strain employed. For each litre of thick yeast slurry, 3% food-grade phosphoric acid is added until the pH drops to 2.0–2.1. The pH of the acid washing solution is determined through titration. To minimise the effect of the acid on the yeast cells, the acid and the slurry should be kept at a low temperature (< 5 °C). A contact time of 4–6 h is customary; recirculating with a pump or stirring with a magnetic stir bar enhances the effect. After the elapsed time, the yeast is washed to remove the acid either in a yeast funnel (mentioned above under yeast washing) or in a cylindroconical yeast tank.

Contact with the acid does, in fact, harm the yeast as it removes minerals and nutrients. Acid washing tends to weaken bottom-fermenting yeast more than top-fermenting yeast, so the pitching rate should be increased accordingly. The response to acid washing varies from strain to strain. Healthier cells are less impacted by acid washing. Care should be taken to carry out this procedure in a precise manner as excessive exposure to strong acid will dramatically and negatively affect cell vitality and fermentation performance. In general, acid washing yeast can cause a reduction in cell vitality, viability, fermentation rates and the degree of attenuation. It may also bring about changes in yeast attributes such as flocculation behaviour. Acid washing does not eliminate wild yeast. Acid washing yeast that has already been stressed, e.g. in high-gravity fermentations, should be avoided. Yeast cells in slurries containing alcohol are more likely to die when exposed to acid. The presence of alcohol acts synergistically with pH, elevating cell death.

However, the benefits of acid washing yeast outweigh the disadvantages since beer-spoiling bacteria are not able to survive in a strongly acidic environment. Acid-washed yeast should be pitched immediately and not stored.

Procedure for washing yeast:

1. Collect a representative sample of the yeast slurry in a beaker and note the volume.
2. Fill a burette with food-grade phosphoric acid and note the volume.
3. Measure the pH and slowly add acid to the slurry, swirling to mix.
4. Continue adding acid until the pH reaches 2.0–2.1.

5. Read the volume of acid remaining in the burette and subtract from the original volume to determine how much acid was used.
6. Using the sample volume and the acid volume, determine how much acid is needed for the volume of yeast to be pitched.
7. Add the required volume of acid to the yeast slurry to be pitched and stir for no longer than two hours.

Literature and further reading

Hutzler, H., Zarnkow, M., Hans, S., Stretz, D., Meier-Dörnberg, T., Methner, Y., Schneiderbanger, H., Jacob, F., *New Yeasts – New Beers*. Brewing and Beverage Industry International, 03-2020, 16–23

Narziss, L. *Abriss der Bierbrauerei*. Wiley-VCH Verlag GmbH & Co., 2017

Simpson, W., Hammond, J. *The Response of Brewing Yeasts to Acid Washing*. J. Inst. Brew., Vol. 95, pp. 347–354, September-October, 1989

| Other microorganisms

For some beer styles, non-*Saccharomyces* yeast or bacteria may be employed. Although beers brewed with mixed microorganisms have gained in popularity, their practical application can be challenging and may require more time to produce satisfactory results. Brewers should attempt mixed microbial fermentations, especially with 'wild' cultures, only after careful consideration, because without a separate building and equipment (tanks, hoses, fittings, etc.) designated specifically for that purpose, the inevitable result is almost always microbial contamination on the brewing yeast side of production.

Kveik

This term does not actually refer to bacteria or wild yeast but rather to a group of domesticated strains of brewing yeast clustered in the far north of Europe. Kveik comprises strains of *Saccharomyces cerevisiae* that have been isolated from cultures of mixed microbes largely originating in Scandinavia, primarily in Norway. The mixed culture has been used for centuries to brew what is known as farmhouse ale, which represents any of the beers produced by the rural populations for personal or local consumption according to traditional brewing practices. Unlike kveik, farmhouse ale is not limited to Scandinavia but is found throughout Europe north of the Alps.

Kveik is generally highly flocculent, ferments rapidly and relatively cleanly at higher temperatures (30–40 °C) and produces esters but few phenolic compounds or off-flavours. Each strain has its own mixture of fermentation by-products with aromas ranging from citrus, peach and stone fruit to doughy and even sulphurous and lager-like. Fermenting beer near human body temperature may be very attractive to bacterial beer spoilers who like the warmer temperatures. Therefore, the vitality of the yeast should be high and the pitching rate sufficient to keep them at bay. The duration of primary fermentation is short, very often between 24 and 36 h.

Strains of this yeast can also be gently dried into flakes, making storage of the yeast over longer periods very practical without having to maintain a liquid culture. Reportedly, if dried carefully, kveik yeast can also be kept for a considerable period and subsequently resuscitated in wort. Some smaller breweries, especially those just starting out, have less control over temperature on the cold side or likewise have very limited volumetric capacity to ferment and mature beer. As many brewers who produce saison have also found, kveik may be a solution to such problems. It provides brewers with the opportunity to develop beers that one can produce rather more quickly but are nevertheless tasty. The term 'craft' when used in conjunction with brewing is a big tent and is now quite multifaceted. In some circles, it has come to mean taking time and going to great effort to meticulously brew beer, allowing it to mature gradually over months or even years, while in other circles it has come to mean, "How quickly can I produce a big, flavourful IPA?" Though kveik stems from indigenous Scandinavian farmhouse traditions, it has offered those brewing the latter a means to ferment cleanly and very quickly well above 30 °C, since the yeast generates fruity esters that drinkers of top-fermented beers relish and also gets the job done in half the time.

Table 5: A selection of the properties of kveik yeast

A selection of kveik's properties	
Alcohol tolerance	13–16%
Phenolic off-flavours	none
Attenuation	75–85%
Flocculation	highly flocculent
Primary fermentation temperature	30–43 °C
Ester production	fruity aromas

These properties can vary substantially from strain to strain.

Brettanomyces

To first allay any confusion, readers may have seen this genus of yeast referred to as *Dekkera*. Fungi are strange creatures and sometimes defy taxonomic classification because they might have been isolated in their asexual form and then subsequently be found to sporulate. *Dekkera* is used for this genus in its sporulating form, meaning that *Dekkera* refers to the ascospore-forming or the sexual teleomorphic counterpart of *Brettanomyces*. The anamorphic form, *Brettanomyces*, undergoes asexual budding and is the one brewers normally deal with. The same taxonomy applies to the genus of yeast commonly found in some wild fermentations, especially those involving fruit: anamorph: *Kloeckera apiculata*, teleomorph: *Hanseniaspora uvarum*.

Brettanomyces strains are well-known for producing fruity, horsey and barnyard or peppery and cinnamon-like aromas. However, they can impart undesirable aromas to beer, like Band-Aid or burnt wood. Those familiar with certain types of Belgian beer may have already experienced the flavour and aroma nuances *Brettanomyces* can produce. *Brettanomyces* can achieve high levels of attenuation because the yeast can ferment sugars called dextrins, which *Saccharomyces* cannot. Microbial populations involved in most sour beer fermentations seem to work symbiotically or in succession, such as *Brettanomyces* in conjunction with *Pediococcus*. *Brettanomyces* can 'clean up' after *Pediococcus*, smoothing out edges and digesting any 'slime' or 'ropiness' the bacteria create.

A little over 200 million years ago during the Triassic, when the ancestors of all modern mammals including humans, were largely represented by small, shrew-like creatures, the genera *Brettanomyces* and *Saccharomyces* diverged to follow discrete evolutionary paths. Since then, *Brettanomyces* species have adapted to habitats exhibiting the following environmental stresses: high concentrations of ethanol, a low pH, low oxygen and little to no readily fermentable nitrogen and carbon sources. This is a good description of beer highly attenuated by a mix of microorganisms after several months in the maturation tank/barrel. *Brettanomyces* possesses a high resistance to osmotic stress and produces a very unique set of flavours in beer. Those species that are considered wine spoilers can eat the cellobiose in the wood of barrels; however, the species used in brewing generally do not, though they do ferment a broader range of sugars than *Saccharomyces*.

Refer to the section on barrel maturation below.

Figure 62: Many brewers are exploring alternative fermentation methods. The image is a montage of the visible manifestations of various kinds of alternative and less conventional brewing and wild yeast strains during fermentation. *Photos by Karen Fortmann of White Labs*

Bacteria

'Sour is the new hoppy,' has been a phrase common in some craft beer circles for a while now. Those aspiring to delve into the complexity that mixed microorganisms can provide their beers may want to devote themselves solely to this pursuit or, as mentioned, otherwise keep their more conventional, yeast-fermented beers entirely separate from their products fermented with other microorganisms. Once bacteria have been introduced into a production facility, even briefly, they are difficult to get rid of.

Those without the capital to build two separate breweries have a number of alternatives. They can sour their wort on the hot side, which greatly reduces the risk of infection on the cold side. If the mixed microbes are inoculated on the cold side and conventional beers and beers with mixed microbes are to be produced at a brewery, then two separate cold-side production areas are required. The cast-out wort can be split into two streams and either pitched with or exposed to the relevant microorganisms. In either case, the wort should be handled in a completely separate facility (coolship or foeder/barrel cellar) away from the conventional beer. The cold-side equipment, including hoses, tanks, gaskets, barrels, etc., should stay in one facility or other and never be moved back and forth.

There are a variety of bacteria naturally occurring on malt that are employed in the production of acidulated malt and in 'kettle souring' in the brewhouse. *L. brevis* and *Pediococcus damnosus* are two microorganisms common in sour beers. Beers brewed with these bacteria, usually in conjunction with *Saccharomyces* and *Brettanomyces*, can produce complex, flavourful beers, if they are given sufficient time to do so.

If one wishes to brew sour beer rather quickly and to more simply create a reproducible and pleasantly drinkable product, it is more expedient to inoculate wort with *Lactobacillus amylolyticus*, which is also a species of lactic acid bacteria present on barley malt. With regard to souring beer on the hot side, why is inoculating wort and fermenting it with pure cultures of this single species advantageous over allowing a microbial free-for-all with the bacteria native to barley malt?

L. amylolyticus thrives at 52 °C, and at that relatively high temperature, many other microorganisms, which may produce off-flavours, are eliminated. Therefore, *L. amylolyticus* cultures can be cultivated without difficulty, that is, as long as some CO_2 is present or otherwise bubbled through the fermentation vessel to discourage respirative yeast. This bacterial species establishes itself quickly and dominates in wort. As lactic acid bacteria go, they can tolerate acid well, producing high concentrations of L(+)-lactic acid from fermenting malt sugars, dextrins and starch. Though some species produce other fermentation by-products, lactic acid is what sour beer brewers desire most from these bacteria. Fermentation by-products, some of which can be quite unpleasant in sour beers, are not produced by this homofermentative species, meaning that they do not generate off-flavours, such as diacetyl (or worse). *L. amylolyticus* bacteria are not beer spoilers because they are sensitive to hops and do not grow below 30 °C. Since they are hop-sensitive, *L. amylolyticus* bacteria have to be cultivated in first wort diluted to an original gravity of approximately 12%. However, *L. amylolyticus* is not suitable for fermentation on the cold side, in barrels or foeders, because they prefer temperatures higher than are generally present in a cellar and, as mentioned, cannot tolerate hops. For this reason, German brewers use *L. amylolyticus* to create nutrient-rich natural lactic acid from first wort (*Sauergut*).

Other species of lactic acid bacteria encountered on the cold side of the brewing process are normally viewed as beer spoilers, but if given enough time, some of them can be employed to create complex, flavourful, pleasantly tart beers. However, once they are in a brewery, they are there to stay, so caution and restraint are recommended. Refer to the section on barrel fermentation and ageing.

Spontaneous fermentation

A Belgian lambic-style spontaneous fermentation process, meaning one in which wort is inoculated with 'wild' airborne and wood-dwelling microorganisms, is hit-and-miss at best without extensive experience in brewing, fermentation and blending (refer to the section on fermentation and maturation in barrels below). The process requires an environment able to foster the development of the proper mix of microorganisms and a brewing process that selects and caters to their needs. Though some are airborne, like enterobacteria, or drip into the wort from the surrounding structure above the coolship, such as wild yeasts, most of these microorganisms are harboured in the wooden barrels necessary for the production process. Brewers must therefore learn something about cooperage and take on the responsibility of maintaining a significant collection of wooden barrels (refer to the section on barrels below). Lambic-based beers are subtle masterpieces of the brewer's art when done well, but they take time. At least three years under the proper conditions are needed to produce a mature lambic that will then usually be blended with younger beer and subsequently bottle conditioned. Or one-year old lambic can be mixed with cherries or other fruits and left to mature as well.

A note of caution

Brewers must be vigilant in keeping two separate sets of equipment on hand downstream from the brewhouse, if the brewery is not devoted solely to fermentation either with *Saccharomyces* brewing yeast or with mixed microbes. Contamination of pure *Saccharomyces* yeast strains is inevitable unless strict separation is maintained. Otherwise this will result in contamination of the brewery's conventional beers by beer-spoiling microorganisms. For example, even cleaning a used wine or beer barrel or other such vessel in close proximity to the fermentation area for conventional production can lead to contamination by microorganisms that will subsequently be very difficult to eliminate from the process.

Literature and further reading

Back, W., Gastl, M., Krottenthaler, M., Narziss, L., and Zarnkow, M., *Brewing Techniques in Practice*. Fachverlag Hans Carl, 2019

Garshol, L., *Historical Brewing Techniques: The Lost Art of Farmhouse Brewing*. Brewers Publications, 2020

McGreger, C., McGreger, N. *Bacteria, Brueghel, Barrels, Blending and Brett* (Parts 1–5). Brauwelt International II–VI, 2018

White, C., Zainasheff, J., *Yeast: The Practical Guide to Beer Fermentation*. Brewers Publications, 2010

THE BREWING PROCESS

Overview

Properly performing the steps in the brewing process will help ensure that the quality and the drinkability of the beer are high and that the beer has a decent shelf life.

Almost all breweries perform the same processes. How they carry out these steps can vary according to the beer style, i.e. the malt/adjuncts in the grist on the hot side and the microorganisms employed on the cold side. Though some of the steps below may be excluded, they generally occur as follows:

1. milling
2. mashing
3. separation of mash solids
4. wort boiling
5. separation of wort solids
6. chilling, aeration
7. fermentation
8. maturation, conditioning
9. filtration
10. filling, packaging

In figure 63 depicting possible brewhouse vessels, the line from the roller mill to the whirlpool represents a modern, conventional Central European four-vessel brewhouse (the whirlpool is not counted). Above this line, a mash vessel is shown, which can be inserted into the process to replace both the mash tun and mash kettle below it, while the rest of the process remains the same. Underneath the lauter tun is a mash filter, an alternative to a lauter tun. One line below the mash filter, a traditional ale brewery is depicted, with a wooden mash-lauter tun replacing the following at the top: the mash tun, mash kettle and lauter tun. Rather than using a whirlpool, some traditional British breweries have a hopback, which functions similarly to a lauter tun but is designed to filter out the wort solids with the addition of a bed of fresh, whole hops. The bed filters out the hot break material and the spent hops added during the boil. This has the further benefit of infusing the wort with aromatic hop oils.

THE 'HOT SIDE'

The diagramme below depicts the 'hot side' of the process as it is generally carried out in smaller breweries:

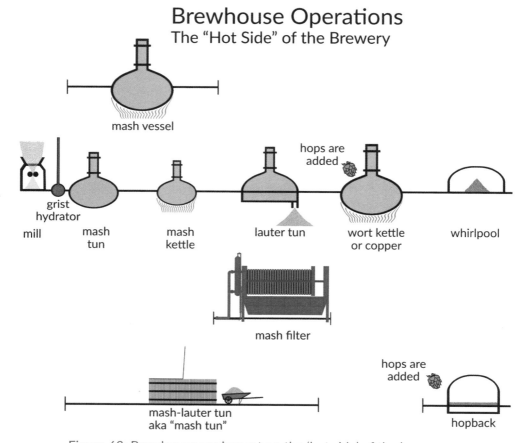

Figure 63: Brewhouse equipment on the 'hot side' of the brewery

Sizing a brewhouse

In order to know what dimensions a brewhouse should be, one must first determine the expected annual production volume of the brewery. One has to figure (conservatively) the expected annual sales volume of beer using market data and then apply some simple mathematics. For example, if the desired annual output of the brewery is approximately

6,000 hl and there are around 250 workdays per year not counting weekends, then the following would be true:

average daily beer production = 6,000 hl ÷ 250 d = 24 hl ≈ 25 hl per day

The 'brew length' refers to the volume of cast-out wort produced per batch in a brewhouse. Of course, there are losses on the cold side, so the wort volume produced on the hot side must be higher, and beer sales are not constant over the year. It would be advantageous not to size the brewhouse for the peak production volume, such as for the months June to August in the Northern Hemisphere, but to the expected routine brew length, because shifts can be added during periods of increased production. Otherwise, the oversized equipment will remain unused many days of the year. This is an unwarranted extra investment that could be saved or spent elsewhere.

In order to reduce capital investment, one could install a smaller brewhouse (in the example above, equipment to produce 20 hl of cast-out wort) and plan on incorporating supplementary shifts (double brew days or add Saturday shifts) throughout the year, where necessary. This would reduce the initial financial outlay. Furthermore, rather than purchasing a larger brewhouse, the number of times a brewhouse can produce a batch of wort per day can be increased by installing additional vessels; for instance, a wort collection vessel can be added at a later date, when production increases. This vessel captures the wort from the lauter tun or mash filter, rather than it being run off directly into the wort kettle, thus allowing faster turnaround in the brewhouse.

If a brewhouse is to be automated, in order to justify the significant cost associated with automation, it would be prudent to plan on brewing around six batches of wort per day.

The types of beers to be brewed at a production facility determines the type of brewhouse that should be installed. The more 'flexible' the brewhouse is, the more types of beer one can brew; likewise, the more control one has over the parameters and the more efficient the process. For this reason, a combined mash-lauter tun is not recommended, i.e. the mash vessel should at least be separate from the lauter tun.

Some brewers working at a small scale, such as craft brewers producing a wide range of beers, may have unconventional requirements for their brewhouses. For instance, brewers may routinely produce beers with a high original gravity (e.g. 16 °P), which would require a larger mash vessel and lauter tun. Those wishing to add more hop pellets than is customary either in the wort kettle or the whirlpool may require a larger whirlpool. Additions of whole hops in a modern brewhouse makes separation of the hops after the boil difficult, as whirlpools were designed for the use of pellets (hop powder). Aside from a means for separating out the hot break material, whole hops necessitate some sort of filter, like a hop jack, since a whirlpool is less suitable for handling whole hops. Refer to the section on hot break separation below.

| Milling

Criteria

The malt is crushed between rollers of a mill or pulverised in a hammer mill in order to make the starch and other compounds inside of the kernels accessible to the malt's own enzymes. The mill and the milling process affect the downstream processes with regard to their efficiency as well as the ease and rapidity by which they proceed. The distance between the rollers should be set according to the following criteria:

- the type of mill
- the type of malt
- the grist composition
- the brewing equipment
- the mash method

The type of mill: A dry mill is common in smaller breweries. These crush the grain prior to the grist coming into contact with water. Some mills incorporate a conditioning step in which the kernels are moistened with lukewarm water, which increases the elasticity of the husks. In wet mills, mashing commences when the strike liquor mixes with the malt while milling takes place.

The type of malt: British pale malt is more highly modified and thus is milled slightly more coarsely, while pilsner malt should be milled more finely. Of course, this depends on the other factors as well.

The grist composition: A suitable grist composition will result in a more uniform and permeable grain bed which allows the wort to run off at the proper speed. Destruction of the husks also releases certain undesirable compounds into the wort which later have a negative impact on the beer. If the grist comes out of the mill too fine, the husks may also be destroyed. This effectively eliminates their capacity to form a filter in the grain bed. The grist composition not only affects the wort separation process in the brewhouse, it also determines extract yield. A mash filter allows the malt to be milled much more finely, even with a hammer mill, because the husks do not form a filter bed as they do in a lauter tun.

The brewing equipment: A mash-lauter tun with no agitator or heating jackets requires a coarser setting for the mill, while malt milled for a heatable mash vessel or vessels with an agitator and a separate lauter vessel can be milled at a finer setting. Mash filters are now dimensioned so that smaller breweries can utilise them as well.

The mash method: Pale malt for a single temperature infusion will be milled more coarsely than pilsner malt for use with decoction mashing, which is also due to the equipment utilised in each process.

Safety

Dust removal and containment

Milling equipment itself can be hazardous, due to the rollers used to crush the malt and other moving parts, but danger can also arise from the dust generated through the process. Though the grain crushing process used in brewing does not produce the level of dust that a flour mill does, one has no choice but to contend with it, since it is nevertheless dry and can be combustible. Most two-roller malt mills are actually not capable of producing particles small enough to be considered explosive and are marked as such, usually with a metal stamp. However, keeping the milling area clear of dust should nonetheless be a routine exercise in every brewery.

The following measures, if implemented correctly, should be sufficient to warrant the safety of the milling area:

- **Containment:** The room housing the mill should be separate from the rest of the production area, not only because the dust is a potential fire hazard but also because it can carry microorganisms from the milling area to other parts of the brewery.
- **Dust removal:** The mill must be enclosed yet properly ventilated. The room should be vented to the outside so that the dust does not accumulate in the air. It is inevitable that dust will build up in the room. This simply must be removed at the end of every workday and thus should be on a checklist of the day's tasks. Some breweries are equipped with dust collectors, which are connected to the mill and are able to vacuum up the dust, transporting it out of the milling area and depositing it in a drum outside, which should also be emptied at the end of every brew day. The dust can be disposed of with the spent grain, hot break material and other organic waste.
- **Suppression:** One would need to ensure that the manufacturer of the milling equipment meets all of the legal safety requirements for one's region or state. An explosion-proof motor is a sensible precaution as well as any other measures that avoid the creation of sparks and thus any chance of igniting the grain dust. All the electrical wiring in the room housing the mill, any equipment installed for dust removal should not create sparks that could ignite dust.

Respiratory risks

Inhalation of malt dust may cause an adverse reaction in susceptible personnel, especially those already suffering from asthma or similar respiratory issues. Milling can thus expose brewery personnel to respiratory hazards. Either the exposure to dust must be reduced through ventilation equipment or suitable masks must be made available to the personnel involved in milling or both. An independent regulatory body can be contracted to determine whether the level of exposure is permissible or not. If the exposure is below the permissible limit, suitable masks should nevertheless be supplied by the brewery, but their usage would then be voluntary.

Silos

The storage of base malt in silos is standard for all but the smallest of breweries. Besides the dangers of climbing atop a tall structure, such a massive amount of grain presents a potential risk for anyone who might fall into the silo and be engulfed in grain, perhaps during the processing of filling, inspecting or emptying the silo. Fall protection usually by means of a shock-absorbing or self-retracting lanyard of a fixed length is recommended for any work performed above a large volume of grain. Personnel are advised never to work alone under such circumstances. Suspension trauma relief straps are also highly recommended.

A note on gluten

Cereal grains are important sources of protein for the people of the world, and those without health issues related to their consumption benefit greatly from ingesting them as part of a healthy diet. However, though they are exceedingly rare, certain health conditions can arise from consuming the proteins found in cereals; these conditions include coeliac disease, wheat allergies, and non-coeliac gluten sensitivity.

- **Coeliac disease** is a rare but very serious auto-immune disease, characterised by the lining of the small intestine becoming inflamed when it comes into contact with certain proteins. As a result, the immune system attacks its own intestinal tissue, leading to degeneration of the villi that line the small intestine. This damage, if severe enough, results in malabsorption of nutrients and therefore malnutrition and perhaps even cancer.
- **Wheat allergy** causes the production of antibodies that induce an immune response when the proteins found in wheat are ingested. Symptoms can vary widely, from very mild to as serious as anaphylaxis.
- **Non-coeliac gluten sensitivity** describes a condition in which certain proteins cause symptoms in individuals who have tested negative for coeliac disease and wheat allergy. These symptoms improve after foods containing these proteins are removed from the diet.

Gluten is found in, among other foods, grains and grain products, like bread, pasta and beer. All varieties of wheat including spelt, einkorn and kamut, as well as triticale, rye, barley and oats contain gluten. Common brewing cereals contain gluten peptides in the following forms:

- barley: hordein
- wheat: gliadin
- rye: secalin
- oats: avenin

There are cereal grains, from which beer can be produced, that do not contain gluten, including corn (maize), millet, sorghum and rice. Gluten-free pseudocereals, such as amaranth, buckwheat and quinoa, can also be used in this capacity.

Brewers can offer beers for those wishing to reduce but not eliminate the amount of gluten in their diets by cleaning the mill and conveyors. They can also add enzymes to break down the gluten on the cold side of the brewery. However, it is impossible to eliminate trace amounts of gluten in the brewing and dispensing equipment to the extent that those suffering from coeliac disease will not experience an auto-immune response to the beer. Thus, a completely separate production facility and packaging area dedicated exclusively to gluten-free products are essential to brew gluten-free beer. Specialised training plus regular inspections by the relevant governmental agencies may be obligatory in gluten-free beer production depending on the regulations in one's country or region.

Concerning the other raw materials in brewing, neither water nor hops contain gluten; however, yeast is typically propagated using a medium containing gluten. Therefore, brewers must either propagate their own yeast or find a trusted vendor who can certify that the yeast they supply is produced in a certified gluten-free environment.

In the European Union Member States, the Commission Implementing Regulation (EU) No 828/2014 lays down harmonised requirements for the provision of information to consumers on the absence or reduced presence of gluten in food and sets out the conditions under which foods may be labelled as 'gluten-free' or 'very-low gluten'. A beer can be labelled 'gluten-free' if it contains no more than 20 mg/kg of gluten (less than 20 ppm) and it can be labelled 'very-low gluten' if it contains no more than 100 mg/kg of gluten (less than 100 ppm of gluten).

Brewers wishing to produce gluten-reduced or gluten-free beers should consult the laws governing such products in their own state or territory.

Gluten in brewpubs and retail outlets

Unfortunately, coeliac disease and gluten sensitivity are becoming more frequent. Those producing beer on premises in a brewpub or at a brewery tasting room must be aware that when milling barley or wheat malt, the malt dust can be dispersed through the air to such an extent that coeliac disease sufferers will come into contact with the grain dust. Especially of concern are the breweries located in shopping centres and other communal areas, where people may not be aware that a brewery is present. It is therefore advisable to install a dust removal system, if one is concerned about customers potentially coming into contact with gluten. Prospective employees must be informed of the fact that anywhere in a brewpub, gluten may be present in the air and dust.

When setting up a dispensing line for gluten-free beer, all components of the line, e.g. hoses, gaskets, O-rings, must be new and should remain dedicated to serving gluten-free beer. Dispensing personnel and servers also need to receive training concerning the proper handling of gluten-free products and respect regulations regarding sharing allergen information with consumers.

Cleaning and destoning the malt

Before milling the grain, it is wise to install a destoner and a dust removal system before the malt reaches the mill. It is surprising how many malt-sized stones and how much dust can be cleaned from the malt. Eliminating the stones will help preserve the rollers in the mill. Figure 64 shows stones removed from the malt at a small brewery.

Figure 64: Stones removed from malt

Setting the mill

The most common types of mills installed in smaller breweries are two and three-roller dry mills, although conditioned and wet milling do find application in them as well. In sole consideration of grist quality, disregarding cost or other factors, six-roller mills are the best and are the most common dry mills in the industry. The throughput and efficiency of a mill are determined by the length and number of the rollers, their diameter and the speed they turn. The gap setting and thus the friction between the malt and the rollers themselves also play a role. The more rollers a mill has, the higher the throughput of the mill, and generally speaking, the finer the grist is milled, the more efficient the extraction. The surface of the rollers (the degree of fluting) can affect this process by increasing or decreasing the amount of friction.

The grist for a traditional British-style mash-lauter tun with a deep grain bed requires coarser mill settings than the grist for a lauter tun with a comparatively shallow grain bed. The following roller settings can be employed with the mills presented in the table below:

Table 6: Roller settings for mills

Mill	Distance between the rollers [mm]		
	First set	Second set	Third set
Two-roller, dry	0.6–1.4	--	--
Two-roller, wet	0.4	--	--
Three and four-roller	1.3–1.6	0.4–0.7	--
Five and six-roller, dry	1.6–2.0	0.7–1.1	0.2– 0.4
Five and six-roller, conditioning	1.4–1.9	0.5–1.0	0.2–0.4
Five and six-roller, mash filter	1.0–1.4	0.4–0.6	0.1–0.3

Source: Vogelpohl, H. *Brauereianlagen.* Vorlesungsskriptum, Wissenschaftszentrum Weihenstephan, 2005

As mentioned above, a hammer mill can also be employed in conjunction with a mash filter.

Evaluating the grist

The malt should be visually examined every time it is milled. The time required for milling should not vary drastically. Ideally, the rollers should press the endosperm out of the husks, leaving it intact for the subsequent lautering process. Depending upon the type of mill and the brewing process, this may not be entirely the case, but a satisfactory compromise can be achieved. For instance, 100 g of the husk fraction in a lauter tun grist should fill a volume of approximately 750 ml to ensure that the husks provide an adequate filter bed. In fact, a rapid method for evaluating the grist is to mill malt at a particular roller setting and then weigh out 100 g of a representative sample. Place the malt in a beaker and then read the volume of the grist on the gradations on the wall of the beaker. Compare the volume of 100 g of whole malt kernels to the volume of 100 g of grist – the greater the difference, the finer the grind.

Comparing different brewing procedures, in traditional British-style brewing, with a mash-lauter tun and a high bed depth, the malt cannot be milled as finely. On the other hand, the malt is more highly modified, so its constituents more readily dissolve in the mash liquor. The malt kernels are cracked and less finely ground to allow for run-off of the deep grain bed, and ultimately, the efficiency is thus not as high, even with the greater level of modification.

In traditional Central European brewing, the malt is milled more finely, in part, due to the less modified malt, requiring that the grain bed be quite shallow by comparison. The efficiency is higher; however, the lauter tun has to be much wider to create a greater surface area. Of course, in a mash filter, the grist is very fine, and the efficiency very high. The time required to complete the process is also relatively short.

Refer to the section on wort separation below.

The simplest method for determining proper mill function is to manually examine the grist. Take a handful of grist and look at it closely. The kernels should be broken into pieces and be separated from the husks. The husks should largely be intact but mostly empty, free of barley endosperm. How finely one should mill the malt is, of course, governed by how the brewery is equipped to separate the mash solids from the wort.

Though the brewhouse equipment determines how finely malt should be milled, when the sieving is complete, the results should more or less resemble the photo (fig. 66) of grist milled for a lauter tun:

Figure 65: Barley malt grist
milled for a lauter tun
Photo: *Lance Snow*

Figure 66: Grist fractions of malt milled for a lauter tun
Photo: *Wolfgang Lindell*

Grist Fractions and Brewhouse Equipment

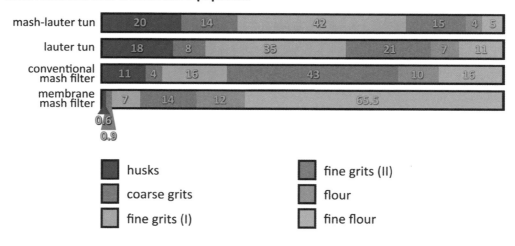

■ husks	■ fine grits (II)
■ coarse grits	■ flour
■ fine grits (I)	■ fine flour

Figure 67: Grist fractions and brewhouse equipment

Figure 67 provides some guidance concerning the approximate targets for each kind of wort separation system. The numbers represent percentages of each type of grist fraction exiting the mill, from the husks to the grits and flour:

Brewers should invest in regular servicing of their mills. This will ensure that the mill settings are correct and that the grist fractions are optimised for their brewing methods.

The benefits of optimised milling are summarised in figure 68. The arrows illustrate how milling affects other processes downstream throughout beer production, all the way to the finished beer:

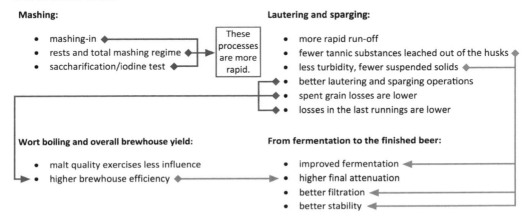

Figure 68: The benefits of optimised milling (Source: Miedaner, H. *Technologische Betriebsüberwachung und Qualitätsoptimierung.* Vorlesungsskriptum, Wissenschaftszentrum Weihenstephan, 1999)

A note on husks

There are mills that are designed to separate the husks so that they do not enter the finer grits/flour rollers, thus remaining more intact for lautering. Husk separation also produces beers with a finer bitterness. This would be an option to consider for breweries dedicated to brewing pilsners or similar beers. Once the endosperms have been milled out of the husks, they are separated in a set of sieves from the rest of the grist so that their undesirable constituents are less intensely extracted during mashing, particularly in a decoction regime. The husks can be inserted into the process at a later point, such as in the lauter tun, so that they can still perform their indispensable role in forming the filter bed. This process can remove astringency and creates finer, more subtle flavour characteristics in paler, more delicate beers.

For breweries with modern mash filters capable of separating the wort from the mash solids without any of the husks, the husks can be completely removed in the mill and any starch adhering to them can then be mechanically recovered. This results in a concentrated grist fraction free of the insoluble, polyphenol-rich husks. The 'void' (2 to 5%) in the malt bill can be filled with more malt or other ingredients, contributing extract to the brewing process. The wort concentration is higher, thus effectively increasing brewhouse capacity and likewise saving energy.

Also worthy of consideration concerning husks would be in the usage of roasted barley in stouts and other darker beers. Dehusked barley imparts a milder, less astringent roastiness to darker beers. The roasted barley does not need to be mashed, since the enzymes and extract play no role in conversion; thus, milling it separately and adding it to the lauter tun can prevent conveying any unpleasant acridity into the finished beer.

| Mashing

The goal of mashing is to break down the starch in the crushed endosperm of the malted barley to such an extent that brewing yeast finds it fermentable. Barley is composed of 55 to 65% starch, and maltsters and brewers want to extract as much of it as possible with as little waste as possible. The starch of the barley is like the juice of the vintner's grape, but starch is simply too large, complex and tightly wound for yeast to consume it, unlike grape juice. The task of breaking the starch down falls to maltsters and brewers.

Criteria

The mashing regime is determined by the following criteria:

- the degree of modification and gelatinisation temperature of the malt
- the brewing equipment
- the beer style

The type of malt: see above; the more highly modified the malt, the less intense the mashing regime. If the gelatinisation temperature of the malt is high, a portion of the mash may need to be heated to unlock the starch in the kernel and make it accessible to the malt enzymes (decoction).

The brewing equipment: the vessels and how they are equipped determines what processes can take place in the brewhouse.

The beer style: the mashing regime is partially determined by the origin of the beer style and thus the malts used, flavour profile, etc.

Equipment

Mashing can occur in a variety of ways using a number of different vessels.

Mash tun: a vessel in which the strike liquor (the hot brewing water) is thoroughly mixed with the grist. A grist hydrator or a wet mill could be positioned immediately upstream from this vessel, where the crushed malt would be mixed with the brewing liquor. These vessels are usually not equipped with heating of any kind.

Mash-lauter tun (mash-conversion vessel): these vessels are common in Britain. As a rule, they cannot be heated and are often simply referred to as a 'mash tun'. They may still be made of wood but can be constructed from metal. They are equipped with a false bottom, which though it is not optimal, saves space, since a lauter vessel is redundant. In some Belgian variations on this vessel, an agitator is installed in the vessel.

Mash kettle: this vessel is direct-fired or heated indirectly with steam or hot water and is where a portion of the mash can be heated or boiled. It is generally smaller than the mash tun. In Central European decoction mashing and in Belgian turbid mashing, this is where a portion of the mash is heated.

Figure 69: A traditional brewhouse for brewing lager beer

Mash vessel: this is the general term for a direct-fired or jacketed vessel with the capacity not only to hold but to also precisely heat the entire mash. These vessels are most often used where step infusion mashing is carried out.

Both a **mash vessel** and a **mash kettle** require agitators and fine temperature control. The placement, accuracy and reactivity of the temperature probe is key to controlling the mashing process; thus, it should regularly be calibrated.

A traditional brewhouse for brewing lager beer is pictured in figure 69.

The purpose of mashing

Some reading this may ask, "Why go to all the trouble of malting and mashing? Is it not possible to brew beer with raw (unmalted) grain?" It is possible, and yet, it requires that the work of malting and mashing be carried out by exogenous enzymes added in the brewhouse. Even the ancient Mesopotamian, Egyptian and Celtic brewers understood that malted grain – at least a relatively large proportion of it in the grist – was necessary for making beer. Though these ancient peoples knew nothing of the enzymes in grain and the fact that yeasts are microorganisms, they realised that without malt and a sourdough culture, it was not possible to make good beer of a consistent quality. Brewers of one of Europe's oldest beer styles, lambic, for instance, understand that by adding 40% unmalted wheat to the grist, they will feed the mix of microorganisms whose presence they wish to encourage in their spontaneously-fermented, long-maturing beers (the wheat they use also has a low gelatinisation temperature). The larger polysaccharide and protein molecules from the wheat endosperm feed a succession of microorganisms over several years. Normally, however, brewers would not add that much unmalted grain to their grists but rather quite a bit less, usually to improve foam, body and/or mouthfeel, e.g. oats in dry stout or chit malt in pilsner.

100 % malt

0 % malt

raw grain*
(*or* poor mashing techniques)

well-modified malt
(+ good mashing techniques)

favours brewing yeast due to degraded starch and proteins

favours bacteria due to long starch and protein chains

*Raw grain includes chit malt.

Figure 70: Percentage of malt versus raw grain and how they favour different microorganisms

Ultimately, the job of the maltster and brewer is to deliver small molecules, which serve as nutrients for the brewing yeast so that they can metabolise these nutrients into carbon dioxide and alcohol along with some agreeable fermentation by-products. This is the case for most every beer style. By favouring brewing yeast with the appropriate malted grains and brewhouse techniques (as well as pitching a sufficient number of healthy cells), even a less careful brewer can ordinarily make a beer free of off-flavours resulting from microbial contamination, since the yeast will dominate the substrate, thus hindering the growth of other microorganisms. In conventional brewing, if the maltster has done his/her job and mashing is carried out properly, the wort – the aqueous solution containing the substances obtained from the malt – should contain enough fermentable extract for brewing yeast to produce beer.

Principal parameters

Brewers must be very mindful of the following during mashing:

- **Temperature**

  Enzymes can be rapidly denatured above certain temperatures whereas their activity is optimal at others, thus while mashing in and when heating the mash, brewers must be vigilant that the mash is homogenously mixed and never heated too quickly.

- **pH**

  The acidity of the mash must be adjusted to find a happy medium for all the enzymes essential to the processes that occur during mashing, primarily during starch conversion and protein degradation.

- **Mash concentration**

  This is expressed as the grist to liquor ratio [a mass comparison]:

  a thick mash → 1:2.5 to 1:3

  a thin mash → 1:4.5 to 1:6

For instance, a thick mash at a ratio of 1:2.5 for 2000 kg of grist would require 5000 kg (litres) of brewing liquor.

- **Hot-side aeration**

  Keeping oxygen uptake to an absolute minimum on the hot side makes for more pleasantly flavourful, stable beers, since oxygen is more reactive at higher temperatures and damages the molecules brewers want to preserve. Moreover, during mashing, the enzymes are very sensitive to the presence of oxygen and will become compromised in their efficacy. (For more on the topic of oxygen refer to the section on beer and food safety addressing oxygen uptake of beer.)

Why is the temperature of the mash important?

The enzymatic processes crucial to the mashing process break down the proteins, starch and other substances in the mash. They are, of course, biological in nature; thus, they are deactivated or denatured by heat. For this reason, brewers must be constantly aware of the temperature of the mash and whether heat is evenly distributed throughout. Hot spots will denature enzymes in those portions of the mash that become too warm.

Enzymes not only have temperatures at which they can be denatured, some lower or higher than others, but they also have temperature optima at which they work most efficiently and effectively.

Concerning the temperature optimum, the concept refers to the equilibrium reached between an increase in the rate of the reaction and the decline in the rate through denaturation. As the temperature increases, the enzymatic activity reaches a peak. This is the optimum. Above that temperature the rate of denaturation increases. Some enzymes are more thermally stable than others; however, at the temperature optimum, few enzymes last more than 20 minutes under the conditions in the mash; thus, a rest extending beyond this time is usually superfluous.

Why is the mash pH important?

The concentration of H^+ ions, meaning the acidity or the pH value of the medium, most favourable for the activity of the enzyme is referred to as the pH optimum.

As discussed below in the section on single temperature infusion mashing, if a brewer is targeting only the two major amylolytic enzymes (α- and β-amylase) in highly modified malt, a pH of 5.6 would be advantageous, since proteolysis was extensive during malting. However, if a mash consists of grist from less modified malt, finding a happy medium among the other enzymes contributing to the extract would ultimately be beneficial, even though lowering the pH to 5.4 will slow the pace of starch conversion due to the higher pH optimum of α-amylase. On the other hand, the activity of the peptidases (carboxypeptidases, endopeptidases) is enhanced, causing many more proteins to enter the mash, most especially the concentration of FAN. Even the polyphenol content increases, while the β-glucan content drops slightly.

Some substances derived from the malt or the minerals in the water increase the buffering capacity of the mash and therefore the wort. By lowering the mash pH, the buffering capacity is reduced, facilitating a cleaner pH drop during fermentation. Acidulated malt at 3 to 6% of the grain bill also serves this purpose well. Lactic acid bacteria native to barley are cultivated on the surface of malt. The lactic acid lowers the pH of the mash. Lactic acid can also be purchased or produced in the brewery with hop-sensitive lactic acid bacteria and diluted first wort.

Why is the grist to liquor ratio important?

The grist to liquor ratio and enzymatic activity

If the mash is too thick, the enzymes, especially the amylolytic enzymes, cannot access their intended substrate or their activity is substantially slowed. Nevertheless, in a thicker mash, the enzymes are denatured more slowly, and their activity is sustained for a longer time. Therefore, a happy medium has to be reached with regard to the accessibility of the substrate and denaturation. This generally corresponds to a grist to liquor ratio of 1:3 to 1:4. With a British-style mash, there is no agitation, and the mash is held at a single temperature. For this reason, a thicker mash and a longer rest are possible. If performing a step infusion or decoction mash, a thinner grist to liquor ratio is recommended, because this facilitates agitation and the dispersal of heat through the mash.

The grist to liquor ratio and pH

The thicker the grist to liquor ratio, the lower the mash pH. Of course, this is also determined by the water chemistry. As mentioned, 100% pilsner malt grist mashed in distilled water at a grist to liquor ratio of 1:4 produces lauter wort with a pH of around 5.8. Brewing liquor must contain some minerals, or the yeast will lack essential nutrients, negatively affecting the beer quality; there will be a hollow character in its appeal to the drinker. These minerals, however, alter the pH of the mash. Not only that, but the grist to liquor ratio also affects the pH, since the thicker the mash is, the lower the mash pH. For instance, at a grist to liquor ratio of 1:2.5 with a mash pH of 5.4, if the mash is diluted to 1:5, the pH will rise to pH 5.7. This is only logical since the brewing liquor has a higher pH.

The grist to liquor ratio and wort and beer quality

Decoction mashing will result in some water escaping as vapour, which must be taken into account when planning the mashing regime. From brew to brew, the grist to liquor ratio in the mash and the volume of sparge liquor in the lauter tun should remain consistent as this relationship affects the nature of the finished beer. A mash that is too thick necessitates more sparging, which in turn may mean more undesirable, harsh tasting substances will be rinsed out of the grain bed. This is especially noticeable in pale beers, like pilsner, pale ale, *Weissbier*, blonde ale, etc.

Fermentable extract

The majority of the extract produced during mashing consists of maltose, a sugar composed of two glucose molecules. The remainder of the extract is composed of fructose, glucose, sucrose (glucose + fructose) and maltotriose, a sugar consisting of three glucose units.

Glucose

Glucose is the most abundant monosaccharide (single unit sugar) on the planet. There are other monosaccharides, but plants frequently use glucose to make their carbohydrates by connecting glucose molecules in chains using a variety of different bonds. For this reason, yeast cells as well as other microorganisms prefer glucose to other sugars. Yeast take these molecules apart during fermentation, which is where the alcohol and CO_2 in beer come from.

Glucose is the building block of α and β-glucans. α-Glucans are made of chains of glucose bound together by an α-glycosidic bond, hence their name. The bonds are primarily in 1,4 and 1,6 configurations.

Maltose and maltotriose

Brewing yeast, like almost all living creatures, prefers molecules made of glucose joined by α-1,4 bonds, if they are not too long. If a compound is made of two glucose molecules bound with an α-1,4 bond, it is called maltose. This disaccharide is the most abundant degradation product of saccharification. Brewing yeast prefers maltose but, of course, also consumes single glucose molecules. Three glucose molecules joined by two α-1,4 bonds create maltotriose, the largest sugar yeast cells can consume.

Unfermentable extract

The molecules with α-1,6 bonds are called dextrins and are not absorbed and metabolised by yeast, but they are nevertheless useful, as they contribute to the mouthfeel of beer. These α-1,6 bonds provide the branches in the amylopectin molecule derived from malt starch and can be targeted during mashing (refer to the information on enzymes below) but in doing so, brewers must realise that although the degree of attenuation will be higher, their beer may seem slightly thinner with regard to mouthfeel and body. However, proteins as well as pentosans and hemicelluloses impart body and head retention to beer.

The compounds known as β-glucans are bound together by another type of bond, β-type glycosidic bonds. Yeast cannot consume glucose bound together like this, so they leave it alone. The β-glucans, primarily the remnants of cellular support structures, have to be broken down by other enzymes, such as β-glucan solubilase and β-glucanase. The endosperm's support structures should be degraded during malting because if β-glucans are present in large quantities, they can disrupt the brewing process by slowing or halting lautering, filtration, etc.

Enzymes

Starch conversion

During malting and mashing, maltsters and brewers exploit the barley's own natural enzymatic capacity for catalysing the chemical degradation of the complex molecules stored in the kernel. Modification (the proteolytic and cytolytic degradation of the endosperm) in modern malthouses is executed in such a way that brewers largely need only focus on the amylolytic processes involved in starch degradation. This occurs in the mash and is referred to as conversion.

Mashing refers to the practice of steeping grist in warm brewing liquor in order to allow the tightly packed starch in the malted barley kernels to become susceptible to physical and chemical degradation through the processes of gelatinisation, liquefaction, saccharification and solubilisation. The subsequent steps of lautering and sparging involve rinsing out this soluble extract from the husks and other solid residues. The essential step of converting the long glucose chains in the starch into small molecules (sugars) is catalysed by enzymes. In addition, other important compounds, like proteins, are broken down to their component parts, and minerals are liberated as well. These are especially important for nourishing the yeast while they ferment the sugars to CO_2 and alcohol.

The enzymes listed below are involved in starch degradation:

- α-amylase
- β-amylase
- maltase
- limit dextrinase
- invertase (saccharase, sucrase)

The significance of gelatinisation

A small portion of the starch granules may have been degraded during the malting process, and during milling, an even smaller portion may have been mechanically crushed. Therefore, below the gelatinisation temperature, these granules can be enzymatically degraded in the mash. Otherwise, the vast majority of the starch must first be hydrolysed above the gelatinisation temperature for the enzymes to do their work. Of the enzymes involved in starch conversion, the two most important ones in the mash are α-amylase and β-amylase. These are the only two that exhibit substantial activity above the normal gelatinisation temperature of the starch in malting barley. The gelatinisation point in malting barley is around 60 °C, generally varying between 58 °C and 62 °C or even higher. Maltsters cannot influence the gelatinisation temperature of malt to any significant degree. Refer to the section on gelatinisation for a more detailed description of what happens in the endosperm.

β-Amylase

The temperature and pH optima for the enzyme β-amylase are 60–65 °C and 5.4–5.6, respectively. One can, however, see in figure 71 below that β-amylase is still quite active down to at least 5.2. This enzyme approaches starch from the outside and works its way inwards. It attacks only one part of the long glucose chains, the 'non-reducing ends' of the chains as they are known, thereby breaking off maltose, a two-glucose sugar, one that is small enough for yeast to consume. When it reaches an α-1,6 bond, part of the branching chain of amylopectin, β-amylase stops and does not continue down that particular chain of glucose molecules. In other words, the α-1,6 bond halts the β-amylase, causing it to find other non-reducing ends to engage. The enzyme is active below its temperature optimum but with ungelatinised starch there is little it can do. It is only capable of snipping off maltose from the non-reducing ends of straight chains of amylose, since the amylopectin molecules are wound up tightly and are thus inaccessible. β-Amylase is quite quickly denatured even within its optimum range. At 65 °C after only 10 minutes, over half of its enzymatic capacity is compromised. In a more concentrated mash (approx. 1:2.5–3), the enzyme will survive longer than in a thin mash (1:4), but above 70 °C, it is completely inactivated. Nonetheless, β-amylase cannot accomplish the work of starch conversion alone. If a brewer were wanting to reduce the degree of attenuation in a particular beer, curtailing the β-amylase rest within the framework of the mashing regime would do it.

α-Amylase

The enzyme α-amylase attacks starch from inside, breaking off long chains that allow β-amylase to keep working by exposing more non-reducing ends, unless the temperature is too high or too much time has elapsed, and β-amylase activity has dropped off. α-Amylase functions best between 70–75 °C within a pH range of 5.6–5.8 (though at a lower pH it remains active – see figure 71) and is denatured above 80 °C. The enzyme breaks apart amylopectin, causing the viscosity of the mash to decline rapidly.

Pieces consisting of around 6–7 glucose units are snipped off by the α-amylase. These pieces continue to be enzymatically degraded until the amylose and amylopectin have been converted to simple sugars, like glucose, maltose and maltotriose, including the branching pieces, known as dextrins. Though its temperature optimum is higher, α-amylase tolerates a slightly more acidic mash relatively well. When the iodine reaction is negative, starch conversion is complete.

Other enzymes

There are other enzymes involved in starch conversion, but their activity is not as extensive as that of α-amylase and β-amylase. Limit dextrinase, maltase, and invertase contribute only slightly to the degradation processes taking place during mashing for a variety of reasons. These are summarised below:

- Their temperature and pH optima fall outside those common in brewing.
- They are denatured at temperatures below the gelatinisation point.
- In the case of limit dextrinase, there are compounds in malt that can inhibit the function of this de-branching enzyme.

However, if a brewer decides to perform a more intense mashing regime and will be mashing in at a low temperature, then these enzymes may come into play to at least a small degree.

Limit dextrinase

Not only is the temperature optimum for limit dextrinase activity usually below the gelatinisation point but, as mentioned, there are compounds in the malt that inhibit limit dextrinase from functioning at its full potential. Limit dextrinase is primarily of interest to whiskey manufacturers as it increases fermentability. This enzyme is often ignored by brewers; however, it has a role to play especially in the fermentability of high adjunct worts.

Maltase

This enzyme splits off a single glucose from the non-reducing end of the starch molecule, and shows a higher affinity for shorter chains, but the enzyme has the highest affinity for maltose. The pH optimum of the enzyme, at 6.0, is slightly above the normal pH of the mash. The temperature optimum lies between 35 °C and 45 °C. However, the activity of this enzyme is negligible, since a relatively high concentration of maltose must first be present in the mash for maltase to work. Targeting this enzyme would require a special mashing regime.

Invertase

Invertase, otherwise known as saccharase or sucrase, splits sucrose into its component sugars, that is, glucose and fructose. Its temperature and pH optima are 50 °C and 5.5 but between temperatures 62 and 67 °C some activity is evident as well.

The pH and temperature optima of the amylolytic processes

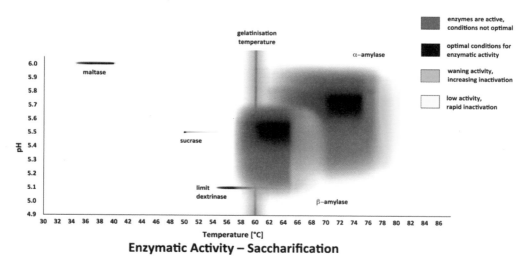

Figure 71: The enzymes involved in saccharification during mashing

What is happening on a molecular level to the starch?

Once starch gelatinisation has taken place, the long α-glucan chains of amylose and amylopectin (fig. 72) are exposed to the enzymes in the aqueous milieu of the mash, where they can be converted to smaller molecules.

Figure 72: Long α-glucan chains of amylose and amylopectin

If little to no limit dextrinase activity occurs, which is often the case, then α- and β-amylase face starch containing α-1,6 bonds. Given that a suitable rest is chosen and both enzymes can work in unison for a few minutes, the starch is broken down as depicted in figure 73.

As it works its way up the molecule, the β-amylase is halted in its degradation of a single glucose chain by an α-1,6 bond. However, the α-amylase can break up the starch even more into pieces four to ten glucose units in length. This provides the β-amylase with more molecules to attack from the non-reducing ends. These smaller glucose chains are known as oligo-saccharides.

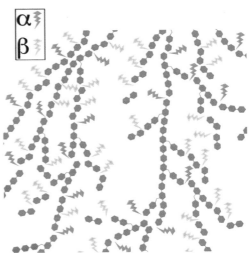

Figure 73: The enzymes α- and β-amylase degrading starch containing α-1,6 bonds

If the mash-in temperature is around 55 °C, and the mash is slowly heated up to the gelatinisation point, then some limit dextrinase (LD) activity may occur, especially if the grist to liquor ratio is not too thin. With limit dextrinase activity, the α-1,6 bonds are broken at the branching points of the amylopectin, resulting in long glucose chains linked by α-1,4 bonds, as depicted in figure 74.

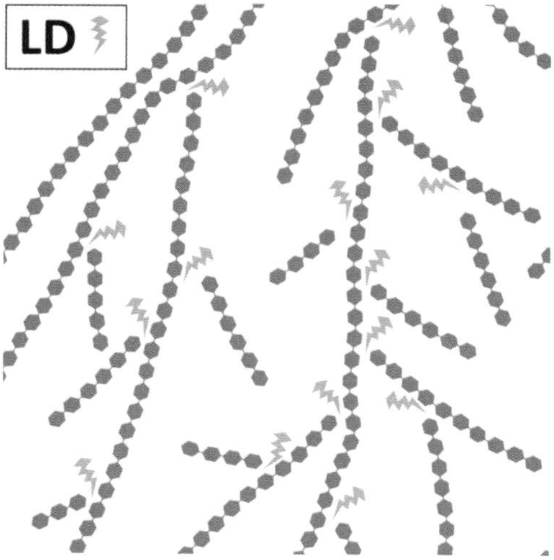

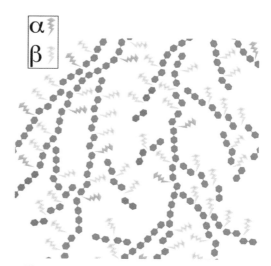

Figure 74: The enzyme limit dextrinase breaking α-1,6 bonds

These chains can be more effectively converted to glucose, maltose and malto-triose. Therefore, the final attenuation of the beer will be higher, meaning that more of the starch degradation products will be consumed by the yeast and during fermentation, more alcohol and carbon dioxide will be produced. Because there are fewer α-1,6 bonds, which normally stop the β-amylase activity, the enzyme can break off maltose molecules from the non-reducing ends of the chains. If a suitable mashing regime is chosen, as mentioned above, then the starch is broken down as depicted in figure 75.

Figure 75: The enzyme limit dextrinase breaking α-1,6 bonds

The products of starch conversion

The combined activity of α- und β-amylase during saccharification creates maltose, comprising approximately 45% of the starch degradation products, while some larger pieces of starch remain. Maltotriose comprises the smallest portion (~12%). Maltose and maltotriose consist of two and three glucose molecules, respectively, bound together with α-1,4 bonds. Thus, fermentable single glucose molecules, maltose and maltotriose as well as unfermentable limit dextrins are the starch degradation products found in a converted mash (refer to the iodine test).

Dextrins are remnants of the branching points of the amylopectin, contain an α-1,6 bond and cannot be metabolised by brewing yeast but can contribute to the body of beer. They are small enough that they do not react with iodine.

Figure 76: The products of starch conversion

Figure 77: Oligosaccharides

If mashing is not implemented properly, the starch may be converted overwhelmingly to oligosaccharides, those glucose chains larger than maltotriose linked by α-1,4 bonds (fig. 77). The final attenuation is low, and the drinkability will also be unsatisfactory. These oligosaccharides are impossible for yeast to consume but other microorganisms can. Bacteria will find a nutrient-rich substrate if they make their way into the beer. This increases the infection pressure on the beer due not only to the higher nutrient level but also to the lower alcohol content and higher pH.

Proteolysis

Why is it vital that some protein degradation occurs during malting and mashing? Both the yeast and the foam/body of the beer require it; however, yeast cells need tiny amino acids, while the foam and body of the beer are enhanced by larger peptides and proteins. Therefore, some degradation must happen during malting and mashing to feed the yeast, but not too much, or the beer will have no head and leave an empty impression.

Depending upon the level of modification (refer to the section on understanding a malt analysis), there are proteins in various stages of degradation in malt. More than once, the authors have encountered confusion concerning the protein content and the level of protein modification in the popular literature, where one finds statements that falsely indicate that the percentage of protein in the malt serves as an indicator for whether a brewer needs to perform a protein rest during mashing. The percentage of protein in the malt does not, in fact, determine whether a protein rest is required, but rather it is the degree of protein modification, characterised by the Kolbach index, soluble protein, free amino nitrogen, Hartong VZ 45 °C, among others. Of course, a certain amount of FAN is needed for the yeast to reproduce well, to generate the desired range of fermentation by-products and for fermentation to proceed smoothly and swiftly. If, however, there is too much FAN in the wort, this can interfere with fermentation and once fermentation is over, some will still remain in the beer. This threatens the microbiological stability of the beer by increasing the infection pressure.

If malt has been highly modified (Kolbach index ≥ 42%), like traditional British malt, a protein rest offers no advantage and will be detrimental to the beer. On the other hand, if the malt is less modified (Kolbach index ≤ 35%) or wheat malt is present in the grist, a protein rest would be advisable. A protein rest is less useful with some unmalted adjuncts, such as wheat and oats, but it may help to a small degree.

The enzymes that break down proteins during mashing work from the inside out or from the outside in, similar to α- and β-amylase. The exopeptidases attack peptides from the outside in, but the conditions under which most of them perform best are not usually found in a brewer's mash: they generally prefer an alkaline milieu (pH 7–10, no activity < 6). The only set of exopeptidases that are active in the mash are four carboxypeptidases.

The carboxypeptidases are responsible for approximately 80% of the amino acids liberated during mashing due to their higher resistance to heat. As figure 78 shows, they are relatively thermostable, especially compared to the other relevant proteolytic enzymes, the endopeptidases.

The endopeptidases are proteolytic enzymes that work from the inside out. The temperature optima of these oxygen-sensitive enzymes fall between approx. 40 and 50 °C. The endopeptidases break large proteinaceous molecules down to low molecular weight compounds. Thus, under favourable conditions, they produce a large amount of low molecular weight compounds, among them amino acids. Should wort be lacking in amino acids and other proteins, it would be beneficial to modify the mashing regime to facilitate endopeptidase activity.

Other proteolytic enzymes, the aminopeptidases and dipeptidases, are present in the mash and their temperature optima fall between 40–45 °C, but due to their pH optima (7.2 and 8.2, respectively), they exhibit little activity in the mash.

Figure 78 shows the combined optima of the carboxypeptidases and the endopeptidases, the two most relevant sets of enzymes involved in protein degradation, as well as the temperature range of 45–55 °C most favourable in fostering their activity. At 50 °C, the activity of the combined proteolytic enzymes reaches a peak under the conditions in the mash. As one can see, a low mash-in temperature with a slow rise through the above temperature range or a 15–30 min rest at 50 °C within that range will increase the total protein in the wort including the free amino nitrogen (FAN). Though assimilable proteins are central to the health of yeast, some types of malt are already so highly modified that they contain enough soluble nitrogen that a protein rest during mashing is not required. Too much protein degradation manifests itself in the finished beer in a lack of foam formation and head retention as well as in a weak body and thin mouthfeel, because middle and high molecular weight proteins are responsible for these attributes in the finished beer.

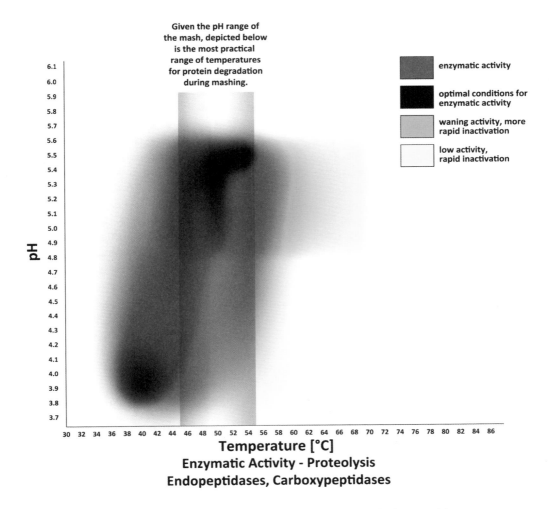

Figure 78: The enzymes involved in proteolysis during mashing

The closer the pH of the mash is to 5.0, the greater the proteolytic activity. Nevertheless, this is not really possible given the fact that the amylolytic activity would be impaired. Yet, this does draw attention to the necessity of treating the brewing liquor, as carbonate hardness will hinder the activity of the proteolytic enzymes. Additionally, due to their extreme sensitivity to oxygen, oxygen uptake during mashing should be kept to a minimum to ensure that proteolytic activity occurs as desired.

Weissbier yeast strains are famous for generating a clove-like aroma (attributable to 4-vinyl guaiacol and 4-vinyl phenol). During fermentation, the generation of these two aroma compounds, among others, can be influenced by mashing in at a low temperature and including a protein rest. This releases more ferulic acid into the mash, which is used by the yeast to create the compounds responsible for the clove-like aroma.

Cytolysis

The cell walls and other structural components of the endosperm are composed largely of glucose molecules in chains connected to each other by β-type glycosidic bonds (refer to the section on starch above). These must be dissolved with a different set of enzymes than the other polysaccharides joined by α-type glycosidic bonds, such as are found in starch. Normally, breaking these structures down to a sufficient level to allow mashing to be conducted is the responsibility of the maltster. However, the degradation of these substances (hemicelluloses and pentosans) continues in the mash.

Though one rarely encounters it nowadays, if malt is undermodified, then a β-glucan solubilase mashing regime can help increase the extract yield. This involves mashing in thick (35 °C, pH unadjusted) and separating ⅓ or more of the mash to be heated to 65 °C for around 25 min. This allows the β-glucan solubilase to break off soluble, high molecular weight β-glucans. Cold liquor is added to the separated and heated mash before it is added back to the main mash, so that the total mash reaches 45 °C when mixed together. This allows the endo-β-1,4 glucanases to then degrade the high molecular weight β-glucans.

Phosphorolysis

The phosphatase enzymes (optima: 50–53 °C, ± 5.0) increase the buffering capacity of the wort. In doing so, sometimes the pH does not drop far enough during fermentation. When the final attenuation is reached, with some yeast strains, the pH of the beer may still be above 4.5. This can increase the likelihood of microbial contamination. Mashing in at a higher temperature (62 °C), such as with the *hoch-kurz* mash method will inhibit this enzymatic transformation of the phosphates.

Summary

The following table provides an overview of the temperature optima for the various enzymes active during mashing. The figure of the thermometer to the left of the table shows the maximum range within which normal mashing regimes take place. In the table, the enzymes with the lowest temperature optima are at the bottom. Going up the table, the temperature optima increase, finally finishing at the top with mashing out, the highest temperature reached during mashing unless a decoction mash is employed:

Table 7: Temperature optima of the enzymes present in the mash

78°C ►

35°C ►

Temperature	Enzymes	Notes
≥ 95 °C	decoction of a portion of the mash (thermal, non-enzymatic)	thermal digestion → greater access to starch in less modified malt; Maillard reaction products, enzymes denatured
78 °C	mash out	lowers viscosity α-amylase continues to function
70–75 °C	α-amylase (pH 5.6–5.8)	**amylolysis** saccharification; degradation of starch from inside product: oligosaccharides, 'dextrinisation rest'
62–65 °C	β-glucan-solubilase (pH 6.8)	**cytolysis** β-glucans are released from their matrices product: high molecular weight β-glucans (soluble)
60–65 °C	β-amylase (pH 5.4–5.6)	**amylolysis** saccharification; degradation of starch from reducing ends product: maltose, hence the name 'maltose rest'
approx. 60 °C	starch gelatinisation (thermal, non-enzymatic)	unwinding of the starch helices necessary pre-requisite for saccharification
55–65 °C	lipases (pH 6.8–7.0)	**lipolysis** triglycerides, lipids degraded products: fatty acids and glycerin
50–53 °C	phosphatases (pH 5.0)	**phosphorolysis** degradation of organically bound phosphates product: inorganic phosphates
45–55 °C	lipoxygenase (pH 6.5–7.0)	**lipolysis** degradation of long chain fatty acids
45–50 °C	endo-peptidase (pH 3.9–5.5) carboxypeptidase (pH 4.8–5.6)	**proteolysis** degradation of proteins an increase in peptides and free amino nitrogen
35–45 °C	endo-1,4-β-glucanase (pH 4.5–4.8) exo-β-glucanase (pH 4.5)	**cytolysis** pre-solubilisation of the grist degradation of gum substances products: low molecular weight β-glucans, glucose

The pH of the mash should fall between 5.3 and 5.6 to promote the malt's own enzymes to bring about starch conversion. For those wanting to create a sour beer, fermentation by brewing yeast will be sluggish if the concentration of acid is too high, i.e. below a pH of 4.0. This sluggishness will increase amid other rapidly mounting difficulties below 3.5.

Common methods

Single temperature infusion

A method employed with well-modified malt for making British-style ales. Even with highly modified malt, the brewhouse efficiency is comparatively low. Infusion is generally carried out in a mash-lauter tun. The *strike liquor* is the water that is combined with the grist when mashing in. It is heated to a specific temperature, which will bring the mash, after thorough yet gentle stirring, to the saccharification temperature (fig. 79).

Taking into account the pH and temperature optima of the enzymes involved in starch conversion as well as the gelatinisation point common in malting barley, if a simple single step infusion mashing regime is to be carried out – whether for style considerations or due to equipment limitations – a pH between 5.4 and 5.6 and temperatures between 63 °C and 68 °C would be desirable (fig. 80). In an English-style isothermal 65 °C mash (versus multi-step or decoction), saccharification is more rapid between 5.3 and 5.6. However, under the conditions of an isothermal mash at this temperature, the optimal pH may be somewhat lower, since the amount of extract produced in the mash peaks at between 5.2 and 5.4.

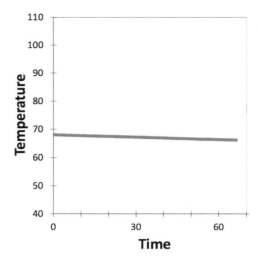

Figure 79: Single temperature infusion mashing

In this case, a thicker mash (approx. 1:1.25–1.3) would protect the enzymes, particularly the β-amylase. Since the level of protein modification in the malt used for this kind of mashing regime is quite advanced, the lower temperature and pH optima of the enzymes involved in protein degradation are of little concern.

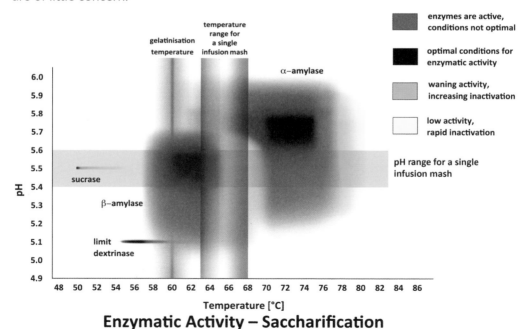

Enzymatic Activity – Saccharification

Figure 80: Temperature and pH ranges commonly used in single step infusion mashing

Finding a 'sweet spot' – or a 'dry spot'

Between 60 °C and 70 °C, the amount of maltose created in the mash wanes as the temperature rises, since the β-amylase activity more rapidly drops off. Above 65 °C, it is very swiftly inactivated. Some fleeting activity may still be present above 65 °C but not much. This is the reason a thicker mash is recommended for higher mash temperatures, since this helps preserve the enzymes, though if the mash is too thick the enzymes cannot reach the substrate.

Conversely, as the temperature rises, the concentration of oligosaccharides increases in the mash over 65 °C, as the α-amylase activity increases. The key with a single step infusion mash is to have enough β-amylase activity that the oligosaccharides sliced off of the amylopectin by the α-amylase can be broken into as many maltose molecules as possible before the β-amylase is denatured. This allows both of the principal enzymes in starch conversion to contribute to the process.

Thus, a mash temperature of between 63 °C and 65 °C will create a drier beer than a mash temperature of around 68 °C, or one even closer to the α-amylase optimum. As the mash temperature approaches the α-amylase optimum, the finished beer will tend to possess a more complex sweetness. The oligosaccharides also tend to contribute to the mouthfeel, but the infection pressure on these beers will also be greater.

This kind of precision in measuring temperature necessitates not only careful, low oxygen agitation but regular calibration of the devices that measure temperature and pH in the brewhouse.

Stepped mashing

Both step infusion and decoction mashing allow the enzymes to enter the aqueous solution of the mash well below their temperature optima. This gentler process results in fewer of the enzymes experiencing heat damage, and thus more of them are available and active when the mash reaches their respective temperature optima, though with modern enzyme-rich malt this is rarely an issue. Step infusion is performed in a vessel with precise temperature control and an effective agitator that does not whip air into the mash. Rests at the temperature

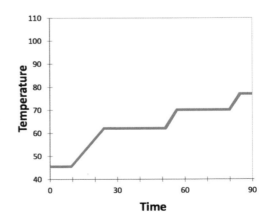

Figure 81: Step infusion mashing

optima for the various enzymes (proteolytic, amylolytic) start anywhere from around the 30s (°C) to the low 70s (°C), though a mash-in temperature below 45 °C is rare. Step infusion is common around the world, as the process greatly increases the efficiency over single-temperature infusion and is less energy-intensive than decoction.

Compared to a beer brewed using a decoction mashing regime, since the mash is not boiled, the Maillard reactions add less colour to the wort, due to less melanoidin formation. Moreover, the beers are softer and more neutral since there is less extraction of the compounds present in the husks.

The combined optima of all the relevant amylolytic and proteolytic enzymes are depicted in figure 82. Given that the enzyme α-amylase is so critical to saccharification, and its pH optimum is higher than the other enzymes relevant in the mashing process, it is imperative that the pH not be dropped too low through mash acidification.

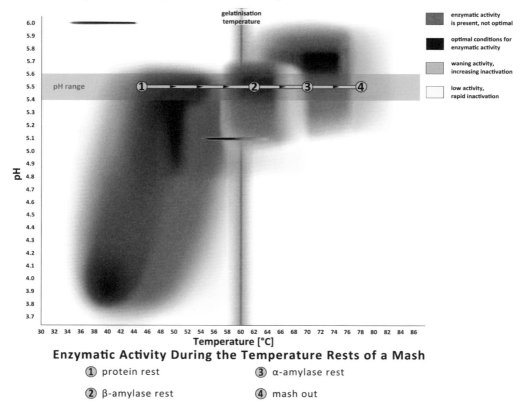

Enzymatic Activity During the Temperature Rests of a Mash

① protein rest ③ α-amylase rest
② β-amylase rest ④ mash out

Figure 82: Enzymatic activity with temperatures and pH optima in a step infusion mash

As depicted in figure 82, for saccharification to occur in a multi-step mashing regime involving a protein rest, the mash pH should still remain high enough that it does not inhibit α-amylase activity. Therefore, even with a protein rest, a pH within the range shown above, approximately 5.4 to 5.6, is recommended for the mash.

If mashing in at a low temperature, the malt required for the process of step infusion should not be as highly modified as British malt; otherwise too much of the high molecular weight protein necessary for body and foam would be broken down to their smaller constituents during the protein rest. Refer to the section on malt analysis for more information.

The grist to liquor ratio should be around 1:4 (but no higher), unless the heating steps up to each temperature rest are to be achieved by adding hot brewing liquor (not optimal). In a mash vessel with steam jackets or some other form of heating, the mash should be heated no more rapidly than 1 °C/min under agitation. With dry mills and more traditional brewhouse equipment, a grist to liquor ratio of 1:4 is common, while in more modern breweries with conditioned or wet milling and less total evaporation in their wort kettles, a grist to liquor ratio of 1:3.3 is the norm.

Decoction methods

These mashing regimes require a mash tun and a mash kettle or a similar arrangement allowing a portion of the mash to be heated entirely separate from the main or rest mash.

Why decoction?

Brewers around the world have been known to pronounce decoction a mere fetish of Central European brewers or beer purists who want to uphold traditional brewing practices simply for their own sake. There is a biochemical basis for these mashing regimes, but the malt has to have been produced with the process in mind. Or, on the other hand, it could simply be that malt quality requires decoction to obtain enough extract from the malt.

Central European brewers who still traditionally employ decoction – with the proper malt – find the following aspects to be positive in utilising this mashing regime:

- The starch in the decoction mash is gelatinised, and thus it is digested and available to the β-amylase (see below).
- The higher final attenuation markedly increases drinkability.
- Though their formation, if excessive, can negatively influence the finished beer, Maillard products do impart character. One undesirable result of the Maillard reactions, the Strecker aldehydes, are volatilised and driven out in the wort kettle.
- The flavour stability is enhanced if the oxidases, such as the lipoxygenases, among others, are denatured in the decoction mash.
- The proteolytic enzymes are also eliminated in the decoction mash, which can be positive for foam (an increased concentration of higher molecular weight proteins).
- Modern malt is well-fortified with enzymes, and thus a decoction or two will not denature so many of them that the mash will not convert.

Decoction for more β-glucan and starch degradation

With less highly modified malt, it would be imperative to mash in below the temperature optima of the enzymes one hopes to employ for the degradation of β-glucans, protein and/or starch and then raise the temperature to meet each one respectively in accordance with the information in the malt analysis. Separating a decoction mash and heating it to the boiling point, or close to it, is particularly advantageous when the heated mash is returned to the main mash, and the temperature is raised to the β-amylase optimum, since this makes starch available to the β-amylase that it would otherwise not have access to. Upon reviewing the roles of the two major enzymes involved in saccharification, α- and β-amylase, many brewers come to the realisation that mashing would be more efficient if α-amylase could work from within the amylopectin *first* to scatter it into much smaller pieces. By doing so, this would then provide oligosaccharides for the β-amylase enzymes to attack, so they could go to work cleaving off maltose. With decoction, this is actually possible, at least to some extent. By contrast, in infusion mashing, the β-amylase enzymes have been or are rapidly becoming denatured by the time the α-amylase enzymes reach their optimum and are breaching the large amylopectin molecules. Thus, to some extent, β-amylase misses out on slicing maltose off the ends of the many starch fragments made available by the α-amylase. Though all of the enzymes are denatured in the boiled portion of the mash, the β-amylase remaining in the main mash is ready to attack the oligosaccharides sliced off by α-amylase in the decoction mash. Similarly, the starch exposed through the thermal digestion of decoction is bared to the enzymes as well.

Energy consumption and other considerations

Similar to a step infusion mash, in heating the mash during decoction, the temperature should rise no more rapidly than approximately 1 °C per minute under agitation. The heated portion of the decoction mash does not necessarily have to be boiled, merely heated to 90–95 °C or so under agitation and held for the duration of the decoction to allow digestion of the starch. Breweries equipped with vessels capable of decoction mashing can also perform turbid mashing for lambic production or other more difficult mashing procedures to produce a variety of beers with a wide range of raw materials, e.g. from undermodified and/or unmalted grains. Despite the added expense, brewhouse equipment capable of performing a wide variety of mashing procedures provides flexibility and fosters creativity, allowing brewers to order small, custom-made batches of craft malt for whatever beer style they may want to brew from whatever period in history.

Mixing and mashing

In order to hit the correct rest temperatures when performing a decoction mash (this does not account for the temperature of the copper or stainless vessel itself), the following formula can be used:

$$V_{DM} = V_{TM} \times \frac{T_{TM,\ target} - T_{TM,\ start}}{T_{DM,\ target} - T_{DM,\ start}}$$

V = volume   T = temperature   DM = decoction mash   TM = total mash

An example of how the temperatures and volume are plugged into a formula to yield the volume of the decoction mash:

$$V_{DM} = 25 \text{ hl} \times \frac{62°C - 45°C}{95°C - 45°C} = 8.5 \text{ hl}$$

95 °C is used because the decoction mash cools slightly before it can be mixed back into the main mash.

Hoch-kurz decoction

The decoction procedure depicted below is known as a *hoch-kurz* mashing regime (from German for 'high-short'), since the mash-in temperature is higher and the process shorter. By gently heating the mash altogether and not separating a portion for decoction, this regime can be performed as a step infusion mash as well. It is best carried out at a pH between 5.4 and 5.5. By mashing in at the temperature of the maltose rest, the endopeptidase activity is restricted, thereby increasing the percentage of high molecular weight proteins in the wort. However, a sufficient concentration of FAN must be available for the yeast. Though somewhat inhibited, the carboxypeptidases should provide enough FAN, if the protein content of the malt is ≤ 10.8% and the Kolbach index is ≥ 39–40%.

The malt should be over 85% friable with fewer than 2% completely glassy kernels. The coarse-fine extract difference should be less than 1.8% and the viscosity sufficiently low (< 1.50 mPa·s). Otherwise, rather than a *hoch-kurz* mashing regime, a more intense procedure with a protein rest would be prudent.

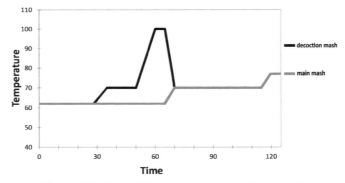

Figure 83: A *hoch-kurz* single decoction mash

The benefits of a *hoch-kurz* mash with the appropriate malt is evidenced by a rapid drop in the pH during fermentation, since the low phosphatase activity reduces the buffering capacity of the wort, as well as superior head retention and mouthfeel in the finished beer. By avoiding the lipoxygenase optimum (45 °C), fewer of the products of fatty acid oxidation, such as carbonyl compounds, are present in the beer, greatly improving the flavour stability. Lowering the pH of the mash down to 5.1 also helps keep lipoxygenase activity low. With the high mash-in temperature and the rest at 62 °C, the cytolytic modification in the malt must be sufficient, since β-glucans are released by the enzyme β-glucan solubilase at that temperature and virtually no β-glucans are broken down during *hoch-kurz* mashing process. This could potentially result in delays at the filter.

Double decoction

A double decoction mash schedule similar to that depicted in figure 84 is suitable for brewing Bohemian and German lagers. A decoction mash can be especially practical if malt is less modified (like Bohemian malt) or otherwise slightly undermodified.

The lower two rests (50 °C, 62 °C) of the first decoction mash can be omitted, if this is deemed advantageous for the particular malt in use, i.e. if it is more highly modified or already contains enough soluble nitrogen.

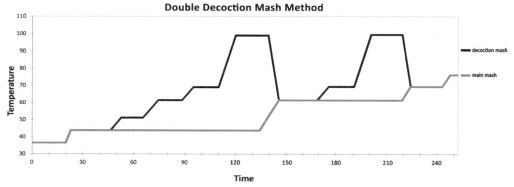

Figure 84: A double decoction mash

Mashing commences with a grist to liquor ratio of 1:4. Czech brewers would mash in low and likely raise the temperature at the lower end to 45 °C by slowly adding brewing liquor heated to 80–100 °C. This is known as 'scalding' and the dilution at this stage must be taken into consideration when calculating the volume of the strike liquor. In this case, the grist to liquor ratio when mashing in would be closer to 1:3 to 1:3.5 depending upon the amount of dilution.

The decoction mashes are drawn at ⅓ the total mash volume and are thick, at approximately 1:2.2–2.5. In heating the decoction mashes, careful heating and agitation are imperative for two main reasons. Firstly, rests in which the enzymes are expected to convert starch to sugars or proteins to amino acids occur in the mash kettle. Secondly, even though the mashes are to be boiled or at least heated close to boiling, brewers would be well advised to avoid as much thermal stress as possible during mashing, as the resultant compounds do not age in the packaged beer gracefully.

In returning the decoction mash back to the main mash, brewers must take care not to pump the heated, thick portion from the mash kettle back into the mash tun too rapidly or without sufficient agitation in the mash tun, in order to protect the enzymes in the main mash.

The gelatinisation temperature of the starch in malt is higher than the optimum temperature for β-amylase (maltose rest, approx. 62 °C), this mash schedule may be employed to expose the starch to the appropriate enzymes, since ungelatinised starch will not convert in the mash very well at all. In utilising malt with a high gelatinisation temperature, one can also eliminate the second decoction and only perform the first, in order to save time and energy.

An alternative to step infusion and/or decoction

A procedure known as *Aufgussverfahren* in German involves only heating the brewing liquor and not the mash itself. It is similar, but for this reason, different from a step infusion mash. It was especially common in the breweries of the past when only one metal vessel was capable of withstanding the heat of a flame. With a direct-fired vessel, heating only the brewing liquor will lead to fewer Maillard products being formed.

The strike liquor for mashing in is a blend of cold and hot liquor. The process of mashing in is carried out thick with the strike liquor at the appropriate temperature, for instance, so that the mash reaches 62 °C. After the β-amylase rest is complete, more brewing liquor is poured over the mash slowly under agitation to raise the temperature to 72 °C, so that the grist to liquor ratio is approximately 1:4 or a bit higher.

Selecting a mashing regime

Breweries equipped with the vessels necessary to carry out more complex forms of mashing are traditionally found in Central Europe but are gaining popularity in smaller breweries. The only drawback of such a brewhouse is that they are quite a bit more expensive. Many smaller operations start with the basic equipment for ale production merely because it not only requires fewer and less expensive brewhouse vessels but also less time and cellar capacity.

Mashing adjuncts

Without adding exogenous enzymes, a maximum of 40% maize (corn) or rice should be added or 20% raw barley or wheat (exception: lambic). It is crucial that the gelatinisation temperature be close to that of the malt, otherwise a separate mash cooker is necessary to first gelatinise the adjunct mash prior to mixing it with the malt mash. Six-rowed malt or malt with a higher protein content can be employed for this purpose with adjuncts containing less protein. The adjunct mash needs liquor to gelatinise as well. A grist to liquor ratio for the adjunct mash of 1:4–5 and for the malt mash of 1:2.5–3 is recommended to obtain a first wort similar to that of an all-malt mash. An iodine test can be performed to monitor conversion of the whole mash by the malt enzymes.

Quality control points: mashing

- brewhouse equipment
- malt/grist quality
- grain bill (malt, adjuncts)
- mash liquor quality
- grist to liquor ratio
- suitable mashing regime
- pH and temperature
- starch conversion (iodine test)
- minimise oxygen uptake/hot-side aeration

Separation of the mash solids from the wort

Lautering and sparging

During this process, the solid parts of the grain are separated from the sweet liquid run-off. In smaller breweries, this ordinarily takes place in a mash-lauter tun or a lauter tun. Both types of vessels possess a false bottom, a sieve-like floor positioned above the bottom of the vessel upon which the mash solids rest and form a filter bed. Drains at the bottom of the vessel lead to a grant or underback where the rate of the run-off can be controlled/monitored. This sweet liquid is now known as wort. From there, the wort is directed to the wort kettle or an intermediate storage vessel, where the wort obtained from rinsing the grain bed with hot brewing liquor is collected.

How well the protein degradation during malting and mashing was carried out can be observed by how quickly the grain bed settles out and the wort level forms above it after short recirculation. Of course, it is imperative that no channels develop in the grain bed, otherwise rinsing the extract from much of the bed will be impossible. If this is the case, i.e. that the run-off contains very little extract, or the run-off becomes too slow, cutting the bed and then recirculating until the run-off is relatively clear are recommended. The lipids in turbid run-off provide reactants for oxidation reactions also involving Maillard products which in turn result in ageing compounds (refer to the section on the Maillard reactions below). The time required for lautering, the turbidity of the run-off and the measures taken over the course of the lautering and sparging processes, such as cutting the bed, should be monitored and recorded for each batch of wort produced. Higher bed depths make it difficult to thoroughly rinse the grain bed and result in lower values for brewhouse efficiency. Specific lauter floor loading for the various types of mills is presented in table 8:

Table 8: The type of mill and specific lauter floor loading

Type of mill	Specific lauter floor loading	Bed depth
dry mill	165–175 kg/m^2	29–32 cm
conditioned milling	175–185 kg/m^2	32–33 cm
wet mill	225–235 kg/m^2	39–41 cm
hammer mill (membrane filter)	55 kg/m^2	3–4 cm

The lauter tun false bottom consists of pieces which can be taken out so they can be thoroughly cleaned, but should, nevertheless, fit very snugly together to prevent grain solids from passing through. A modern lauter floor is composed of stainless steel and should be far enough above the bottom of the vessel that suction on the grain bed does not occur. The openings in the lauter floor are long and thin, usually 0.7 mm wide on top and 3–4 mm on the underside. The openings in the lauter floor may be cut in the metal itself, or it can be composed of wedge wire with supports underneath. They possess an open area between 6 and 25%. This percentage, however, does not determine how quickly run-off will be, since it only supports the actual filter bed, which are the grain husks. The spaces on the floor can nevertheless become clogged with beer stone, if they are not cleaned regularly.

In order to ensure that air does not interfere with the run-off of the wort and to reduce hot-side aeration, it is recommended that 'underletting' be carried out, which is to fill the space under the false bottom with 75–80 °C brewing liquor, prior to transferring the mash to the lauter tun. Also advisable for this reason, the sparge liquor should be gently sprayed over the grain bed before the level falls below the surface. If the brewery is equipped to do so, deaerating the sparge liquor is recommended in order to reduce hot-side aeration.

The collection points underneath the false bottom normally each capture wort draining from an area amounting to around 1 m² of the grain bed. As lautering proceeds and the sparge liquor dilutes the run-off, the pH of the run-off rises. The higher pH, which rises by 0.3 to 0.6, results in extraction of less desirable compounds in the grain bed. Over-extraction of the husks compromises the flavour stability of the beer. The phenolic compounds in oversparged wort can be harshly bitter. The pH of the run-off should not rise above 5.8 to 6.0, depending upon the types of malt/grain in the grain bill.

There are two general approaches to lautering :

1. Continuous sparging: The more common and, from the standpoint of wort quality, more advantageous method is to recirculate until the wort is quite clear. Once lautering commences, the liquid level over the bed begins to drop. When the level is close to but not below the top of the grain bed, sparge liquor is evenly sprinkled over the surface. Sparging continues until the desired volume is obtained. Craft brewers have new-fangled terms for this: 'German sparging' or 'fly sparging'.

2. Parti-gyle sparging: This practice was more common when gradations in the quality of beer were sold at different prices, for instance, the first wort would be drained into one wort kettle and brewed into a higher quality, more expensive beer. The bed was then sparged and that wort was collected in a second kettle and sold as a cheaper beer of lesser quality, and so on. This is impractical and usually carried out when producing a higher gravity beer brewed only with the first wort, e.g. a Scottish style 'wee heavy'. In order to prevent wastage, the bed is sparged and a 'small beer' is produced from the sparged wort. Craft brewers, likewise, often refer to this method as 'English sparging' or 'batch sparging'.

To prevent what German brewers call a *Blausud*, or wort collected in the kettle that tests positive for the presence of starch with iodine, it is best not to completely deactivate the α-amylase until the wort boils. Therefore, sparge liquor should be heated to around 80 °C, because once an enzyme has been deactivated, there's no bringing it back.

Mash filters

A mash filter can also be employed at this stage. Mash filters are more common in larger breweries, where numerous batches of wort are brewed per day and a higher, more consistent yield is required; however, they are gaining in popularity in smaller breweries as well. The process of separating the mash solids from the wort is not only carried out more swiftly but also more efficiently, so that brewers can greatly increase their production volumes. The initial investment in a mash filter would be worthwhile for breweries producing upwards of 10 or more batches of wort per day. A mash filter may be useful in smaller breweries where high gravity brewing is practiced or beers with a higher original gravity are brewed, since a mash filter is more efficient at higher gravities than a lauter tun, in part, because the grist can be milled more finely. Where brewhouse space is limited, they may also be of interest.

Mash filters are similar in appearance and to a certain extent, in function, to a sheet filter for beer. They are less sensitive to fluctuations in quality than more traditional methods.

Mash filters can generally be divided into the older, conventional filters and the more modern ones: membrane filters and high-pressure filter presses. The malt can, in this case, be milled with a roller mill, a hammer mill, or a submerged disc mill, depending upon the mash filter. Coarser grist is utilised in the conventional ones, while the modern ones require extremely fine grist (refer to milling above).

Some modern mash filters are capable of separating the wort from the mash solids with none of the husks remaining. The husks can therefore be completely removed in the mill and any starch adhering to them is capable of being mechanically recovered. This results in a concentrated grist fraction free of the insoluble, polyphenol-rich husks. The 'void' (2 to 5% of the total malt bill) can be filled with more malt or other ingredients, thus contributing extract to the brewing process. The wort concentration is higher, effectively increasing the brewhouse capacity. This saves energy and eliminates some of the less pleasant flavours contributed by the husks in more delicate beers.

If nitrogen or carbon dioxide are used to purge and pressurise the mash filter, oxygen uptake is very low. The more finely milled malt is rinsed under pressure with the solid material being retained on a set of filters.

The mash solids form a vertical 'grain bed' 3 to 7 cm thick against the filter material, which were made of cotton fabric earlier and now consist of polypropylene or other plastic polymers. Filter membranes consist of thermoplastic elastomers (TPE), which are used to press the mash solids against the polypropylene filter sheets. Some filters combine the two by interspersing membranes between the filter sheets in the plate.

Once a conventional mash filter has been prepared and purged, the process steps run as follows:

- The mash is pumped into all the chambers.
- The solids form a vertical layer that is 6 to 7 cm thick.
- The first wort is collected.
- Sparging begins and the sparged wort is collected.

- The spent grain is removed.
- The operating pressure normally rises to no more than 0.3 bar.

With a membrane filter, the process is slightly different:

- The chambers are filled with the mash.
- The operating pressure at this stage is between 0.2 and 0.5 bar.
- The solids form a 4 cm vertical layer between the filter sheets and the membranes.
- The first wort is collected.
- Once the line into the filter for the mash has been rinsed, the initial compression is carried out at around 0.7 bar.
- The solids are compressed to approximately 3 cm.
- Sparging occurs in two phases:
    1. The filter is filled with sparge liquor until the chambers are full.
    2. Sparge liquor then flows through the filter until the gravity of the wort flowing out of the filter drops to a set limit or the desired volume of wort is collected, and sparging is halted.
- The final compression occurs at approximately 1.5 bar to press the last runnings out of the solids.
- The spent grain is removed.

Spent grain

The spent grain or brewer's grain are removed from the brewhouse and are usually transported to farms for use as animal feed. Spent grain is also finding application as a raw material in biogas production plants.

Quality control points: solids separation (lautering and sparging or filtration)

- gravity
- pH and temperature
- clarity
- colour
- aroma/flavour
- minimise oxygen uptake/hot-side aeration
- run-off rate

| Wort boiling

The three factors to consider during the wort boiling process are temperature, time and movement. In virtually every small brewery, wort boiling is carried out at atmospheric pressure, though some systems boil above and below ambient pressure. Heat energy is most often supplied indirectly either by steam or pressurised hot water, though direct heating is not unheard of. Heat is necessary to bring about the changes required during wort boiling but excessive heat is detrimental to wort quality. If the wort is heated effectively yet gently and evaporation is good, the boil can be kept to an hour. Breweries in the past boiled for longer, in part, due to poor evaporation. A small wort kettle is generally heated on the sides and at the bottom. As wort kettles grow in size, due to the surface area (x^2) increasing at lesser rate than the volume (x^3), in order to satisfactorily boil the wort, either an internal or external calandria must be integrated into the wort boiling system. However, in most smaller breweries, a calandria is not necessary to heat the wort to boiling and maintain the temperature at the boiling point. Heat recovery systems are common in most modern breweries. The heat from the vapours rising from the boiling wort can be recovered with a vapour compressor or a vapour condenser.

Why do brewers boil their wort at all, since it requires a great deal of energy to heat aqueous liquids? Though some alternatives to wort boiling have been developed, given all that must be achieved by the process, they are not entirely practical, and in any case, one rarely finds them in smaller breweries. The duration of the boil is determined by the beer style as well by the philosophy of the brewer. The boil usually lasts 60 to 90 min.

Brewers boil the wort for a variety of reasons, all of them important to the finished beer:

1. The application of heat sterilises the wort, thus eliminating all of the microorganisms derived from the malt and any other source.
2. Undesirable, volatile substances, must be driven out, such as DMS and some Maillard products.
3. In order to adjust the gravity, the wort is concentrated through evaporation.
4. Protein-polyphenol compounds ('hot break material') are precipitated.
5. The wort becomes slightly darker through the formation of colour and aroma compounds.
6. All of the malt enzymes are denatured and thereby inactivated.
7. The α-acids in the hops have to be isomerised which makes them soluble in the aqueous solution of the wort.

The brewer adds hops at different time points in the boiling process to impart both bitterness and hop aroma to the beer. The higher the temperature of the wort, the more rapidly the isomerisation of the α-acids occurs. Likewise, the longer the hops boil in the wort, usually about an hour for the bittering hops, the more α-acids will be isomerised and dissolved in the wort. By comparing the mass of the hops and the percentage of α-acids they contain in the bittering addition (usually expressed in mg/l or g/hl) and the concentration of α-acids in the finished beer (IBU), one can establish what the brewery's hop yield is. If a brewer is curious about the specifics of the hop yield, such as how well the brewhouse extracts the α-acids and also where losses occur, such as in the whirlpool or on the cold side, he/she can take several samples (e.g. cast-out wort, chilled wort, green beer, filtered beer) and have them tested for bittering units (mg/l of α-acids).

As the wort boils, the EBC bittering units increase more quickly than does the iso-α-acid content because the analysis method for EBC bittering units measures a wider range of the bitter substances from the hops, while methods that measure the iso-α-acids, detect only those and nothing else. Most of the other bitter substances dissolve in the wort more rapidly than the isomerisation process of the α-acids can occur. Thus, if the boil is cut short or a substantial amount of the hops are added later in the boil, these two analyses will yield considerably different values. Furthermore, dividing the hop additions so that they occur three or more times during the boil (rather than a single bittering addition at the beginning and a single aroma addition at the end) will have a positive effect on the flavour stability as well as the quality of the bitterness. Of course, the iso-α-acid yield will be lower for the later additions.

Hops can be added towards the end of the boil, so that the volatile substances in the hops do not evaporate and disappear up the stack with the other vapours. The quantity and α-acid content of the hops as well as the hop yield determine the number of bittering units in the finished beer.

As mentioned, the polyphenol content of the hops is crucial to beer quality. When hopping in the brewhouse, choosing hops with low cohumulone levels, a high polyphenol to α-acid ratio and a high amount of auxiliary bitter substances will impart a more pleasant bitterness to the beer and increase its flavour stability. Furthermore, beers brewed with high carbonate liquors become harsh when high concentrations of hop bittering substances are added during the boil. Paler, stronger beers brewed in liquor that allows high hop rates, especially those acidified properly in the brewhouse, can bear bittering substances well with little to no harshness. The better the husks are preserved during milling, even to the point of separation, will also contribute to a finer bitterness (refer to bitterness below under sensory analysis.) It is no accident that the first 'global' beers, i.e. pale ale followed by pilsner, were produced with 100% lightly kilned barley malt (fewer Maillard products) and the appropriate brewing liquor (no harsh, lingering aftertaste in the finished beer). High hop additions protected these beers to some degree over long land and sea transport routes. Other beers shipped longer distances depended upon acids derived from darker or roasted grains and/or microorganisms in addition to hops.

Wort acidification generally benefits the overall fermentation process, increasing the degree of attenuation, produces milder, paler, more drinkable beers while also improving the flavour stability and head retention. However, regardless of the kind of acidification, either with diluted first wort fermented with lactic acid bacteria (*Sauergut*) or some kind of acid, it is best to do so in the final ten minutes of the wort boiling process. In doing so, hop isomerisation is more effective, protein coagulation is not excessive (the pH optimum for protein coagulation is 5.2) and less DMS is cleaved from *S*-methylmethionine (SMM), otherwise known as DMS precursor (DMS-P). The wort should be acidified to reach a pH of approximately 5.1. The pH of the finished beer should nevertheless not fall below 4.2 for an all-malt beer not kettle-soured or fermented with mixed microbes.

The extract in the wort can be measured using a variety of instruments: a hydrometer, refractometer or an oscillating U-tube density measuring device.

Among British brewers, the wort kettle is still referred to as the copper, even though most are now made of stainless steel.

It was once deemed beneficial to the quality of the wort to allow air to flow through the open doors of the wort kettle during the boil. Due to the modern emphasis on oxygen-free boiling, this is no longer the case. If possible, it would be better to avoid or at least hinder excessive airflow into the kettle. This aids in preventing the formation of the carbonyls involved in ageing.

Copper finings

The finings added to the boiling wort to aid in the precipitation of protein are not made of copper but are used in the copper, i.e. the wort kettle. The most common finings are known as Irish moss and prepared from dried marine algae, which contain carrageenan, a polysaccharide comprising galactose chains interspersed with sulphate groups. Its chemical composition means that it is negatively charged. Silica gel can be used in the place of Irish moss; however, the finings known as isinglass, a derivative of the proteinaceous swim bladders of fish, are not employed at this stage but rather to clarify beer in the cask or conditioning tank.

Copper finings encourage the sedimentation rate of the hot break material, but too much causes the finished beer to leave the drinker with an empty impression. Thus, it is best to dose them at a rate so that the clarity of the chilled wort improves to an acceptable level with the least amount of finings. Empirical optimisation of the ideal level of copper finings for a brewery's wort therefore involves determining the effect the finings have on the chilled wort.

Wort that is too clear, i.e. devoid of virtually all turbidity, has been dosed with too much finings. There may not be a sufficient concentration of FAN in the wort for the yeast.

| Brewhouse work and the bitterness of beer

- Pale malts allow for larger additions of bittering hops.
- More intact husks/husk separation produces finer, less astringent bitterness in the finished beer.
- Soft brewing liquor produces a finer bitterness and allows for a larger addition of bittering hops.
- An intense boil and more time increase the isomerisation rate.
- A finer bitterness is produced by mashing less intensely.
- A normal hop yield, i.e. degree of utilisation, for whole hops and pellets is usually around 25 % to 35 % and depends not only on hot side but also cold side operations.

- Acidifying the wort at the end of the boil rather than at the beginning, increases the hop yield.
- Proper brewhouse work (brewing liquor treatment, malt bill, milling, mashing, acidification, lautering, sparging, boiling) produces less harshly bitter beers.
- Hops possessing low cohumulone levels, a high polyphenol to α-acid ratio and a high amount of auxiliary bitter substances tend to impart a more pleasant bitterness and increase the flavour stability.
- Adding hops late in the boiling process or in the whirlpool conserves a portion of the volatile hop oils in the finished beer.

Quality control points: wort boiling

- target gravity
- duration of the boil
- intensity of the boil
- undesirable, volatile substances are driven out
- sterilisation of the wort, elimination of microbial contaminants
- denaturation of malt enzymes
- formation of hot break material for subsequent precipitation
- pH
- clarity
- colour
- aroma/flavour
- isomerisation of hop bitter acids
- minimise oxygen uptake/hot-side aeration

Hot and cold break material

Hot break material form large flocs during a vigorous wort boil, but if the boil is not sufficiently intense or, on the other hand, if the shearing forces are too great, for instance in some calandria, the hot break material may form finer flocs, which do not precipitate well. Cold break material only forms fine flocs, which first appear in chilled wort and normally amount to about 20% of the hot break material. Both consist of proteins, while cold break contains more polyphenols and carbohydrates. The vast majority of the lipids are removed from the wort with the hot break material and spent hops. Too much hot and/or cold break material carried over into the wort can negatively influence the finished beer by either clinging to the yeast and making the assimilation of nutrients and thus fermentation needlessly difficult (off-flavours) or may survive fermentation and end up in the packaged beer. Regardless of how the hot break material is removed, it must be done fairly effectively; however, fine filtration is not desirable at this stage either, as a slight amount of hot break material and about one-third of the cold break material provides the yeast with vital nutrients (long-chain fatty acids, zinc).

Hot break separation

This generally occurs in a whirlpool. The wort enters the whirlpool tangentially at 3–5 m/s, causing the solids formed during boiling and the spent hops (added as pellets) to amass in the middle of the vessel through the action of centripetal motion. In 1926, Einstein solved the mystery, the so-called 'tea leaf paradox'. Given that swinging a ball in a circle on a rope around a central point causes the ball to fly away from that point, one would expect the same in a teacup. Einstein was able to describe the reason tea leaves do not gather at the bottom of a teacup on the outside but rather in the centre. This also explains why the hot break material and spent hops are forced into the centre of a whirlpool as depicted in figure 85 by the motion of the wort entering the vessel tangentially. Whirlpools function best when the height to diameter ratio is 1:1– 1:5. The most common ratio is 1:3 because it is most favourable for the sedimentation of the hot break material. One way to judge

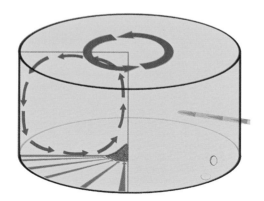

Figure 85: The teacup effect

Figure 86: The difference in suspended solids between the whirlpool inlet and outlet

the efficacy of a whirlpool is to measure the change in the suspended solids in the wort entering and exiting the whirlpool. Though this is done instrumentally in larger breweries, this can also be done visually with samples viewed in a graduated cylinder.

Brewers producing the heavily hopped pale ales popular in some craft beer markets may reach the capacity threshold of a standard-sized whirlpool. For this reason, some hoppy ale brewers purchase oversized whirlpools. With less heavily hopped beer styles, a standard-sized whirlpool is sufficient.

The combination of the whirlpool and plate wort chiller serve as a means for hot break and spent pelletised hop removal followed by chilling to pitching temperature. Two pumps are required to simultaneously bring about flow in both directions. The whirlpool first came into fashion when hops were dried and ground into powder (and subsequently pelletised), which is a relatively modern process. Therefore, other forms of hot break/ spent hop separation were utilised when whole hops were the norm, and these devices have become popular in smaller modern breweries for a variety of reasons (see below). Some brewers add hops at this stage to impart hop aroma to the wort. Whirlpools do not function well with whole leaf hops, so it is recommended that whirlpool additions consist of pelletised hops. Very little isomerisation occurs, but there is enough that the bitterness will increase slightly.

Avoiding off-flavours

Hot break removal must be done effectively enough that the material does not coat the yeast and compromise fermentation in addition to causing off-flavours in the finished beer.

A major issue during this stage of brewing is the accumulation of dimethyl sulphide (DMS) in the wort. A derivative of the essential amino acid methionine, the molecule, S-methylmethionine, (SMM) also known as DMS precursor (DMS-P), is cleaved by the heat of the boiling wort to produce DMS. The DMS is then driven out by the force of the vapour rising from the boiling wort in the kettle. Even though the vast majority of the DMS evaporates during the boil, a substantial amount of the SMM or DMS-P remains in the wort. After the boil is finished, the DMS-P continues to be cleaved, forming DMS while the wort remains hot but does not boil. Since no vapour is rising out of the wort, the free DMS, as it is known, remains in the wort. This would not be a problem if the human sensory apparatus were not so sensitive to it. For this reason, the hot break material and hop residues must be separated from the wort quickly, so that chilling can commence. For this reason, though a whirlpool rest is recommended to allow the wort solids to settle and form a cone in the centre, the wort should not be left in the whirlpool any longer than necessary. A general rule of thumb would be from the end of boiling to the end of wort chilling to permit an absolute maximum of 100 min. Wort chilling itself should require no longer than 40 minutes.

The concentration of the free DMS in the chilled wort should be no more than around 100 micrograms per litre (μg/l or parts per billion, ppb) – in some beer styles even less, approx. 70 μg/l, because the sensory threshold for DMS is so low in humans. Thus, DMS should be lower – around 40–50 μg/l – in the wort exiting the whirlpool.

Refer to the section on sulphurous compounds in beer for more information.

Aside from the unwanted wort volatiles, if the wort in the whirlpool cools to 80 °C or below, the cone of hot break material and spent hops may not form well, or if already formed, it may disintegrate. Therefore, the time required for good separation of hot break material to occur (cone formation) should be recorded on the brewhouse log sheet.

Traditional methods employed with whole hops

Hop jack and coolship

At the time when whole hops were the norm, a combination of two pieces of equipment was employed for removing the hops and the hot break material as well as some of the cold break. A metal filter, referred to as a 'hop jack' or simply as a 'cage' in Britain or as a *montejus à houblon* or *Hopfenseiher* on mainland Europe, was installed immediately upstream from the coolship. The hop jack filtered the spent whole hops, while the coolship, a shallow vessel (max. 10–12 cm wort depth) was designed to allow the hot break material and some of the cold break to settle out rapidly. These were both prevalent well into the early 20th century. The hop jack/coolship combination (the drawing in figure 88 depicts both) was advantageous for keeping DMS in the wort at a level below the flavour threshold, as the vessel was so shallow and the wort surface so broad that the amount of evaporation and thus cooling was huge. Therefore, any DMS split off of DMS-P was still driven out. With this amount of evaporation, the wort cooled to temperatures below which DMS was formed at a significant rate. A traditional coolship was dimensioned so that the temperature dropped to around 70 °C quite rapidly during the brewing season, i.e. autumn, winter and spring. The authors have spoken to Bavarian brewers of an older generation who have stated that the coolship let the wort *ausstinken*, in other words, the coolship as employed at that time allowed the undesirable volatiles in the wort to evaporate with the vapour as it billowed into the air and out the louvred windows above the coolship, i.e. literally to 'stink out'. Unless the wintry chill permitted, before vapour stopped rising from the wort in the coolship, the wort would have ordinarily been dropped by gravity through a Baudelot cooler, which was employed not only to chill the wort with ice water to the desired pitching temperature (traditionally 6 °C for bottom-fermenting yeast) but would have also aerated the wort. Part of the problem with subsequent solutions to this stage in the process, such as the whirlpool, is that DMS accumulation in the wort and more of the cold break remains in the wort prior to chilling (approximately one-third is desired for yeast nutrition). If the room housing the coolship is properly designed (airflow, drippage, etc.) and kept clean, it represents an elegant solution to this stage in the process but is difficult to use with significant amounts of pelletised hops. Studies conducted in the late 19th century indicate that microbial con-

Figure 87: A traditional coolship in Bavaria

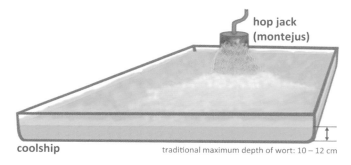

Figure 88: A coolship with a filter for whole hops

tamination with the use of coolships was very low as a result of the billowing evaporation and, in fact, usually occurred due to the presence of biofilms between the wort chiller and the yeast pitching/fermentation tank.

Hopback

The hopback was favoured by the brewers in Britain and Ireland, which served the purpose of not only removing the hot break material and perhaps some of the cold break but also of generously infusing the wort with hop essential oils. Whole hops formed a layer in a vessel with a false bottom or filter and the hot break material was retained on their prodigious surface area, similar to a lauter tun but with fresh hop cones instead of grain husks. Some breweries were equipped without a vessel dedicated for this purpose, that is, a hopback as such was not present. Rather, during the time the wort was boiling, the mash-lauter tun was emptied and filled with a layer of whole hops in order to serve double duty as a hopback. Upon leaving the hopback, the wort passed through some sort of cooling vessel or chilling device, prior to pitching.

For modern brewers on a tight budget utilising the lauter tun as a hopback, i.e. as a means to remove hot break material and spent hops as well as to infuse the wort with hop oils, might be practical. Given the vessel occupancy in the brewhouse, this will limit the number of batches that can be brewed per day. More hot-side aeration may also occur with a hopback or similar method of filtration.

Re-interpretation by craft breweries

In modern craft brewing, hopbacks and coolships have experienced a renaissance. A novel yet very widespread resurgence has taken place in smaller breweries, though the modern interpretations differ in their function from the original devices.

The craft hopback

A craft hopback now only serves to infuse wort with essential oils, as most breweries are equipped with whirlpools to remove hot break material and spent hops because they use pellets or extract in their wort kettles. Figure 89 shows the spent whole hops in a modern hopback. It is also possible to construct a hopback that allows infusion of the wort with hop pellets.

Figure 89: A craft hopback

Devices similar to craft hopbacks in their design have evolved and been moved downstream. These devices allow intensive contact between whole hops or pellets and wort or green beer – not on the hot side but on the cold side (refer to hopping on the cold side below).

The craft coolship

Craft brewers have also resurrected coolships and frequently place them downstream from the whirlpool. Historically, these two vessels would never have been installed in conjunction with one another, as it would have been counterintuitive, since they largely serve the same function. Nowadays, craft brewers employ the coolship's broad surface area to inoculate wort with microorganisms borne on air, vapour and drippage. This practice evolved out of an amalgam of Belgian lambic production, where the hop jack/coolship combination is still found, and contemporary craft brewing. However, many craft coolships, with their greater depth and smaller surface area, belie the original function of a coolship and more often resemble open fermentation vessels. Thus, some manufacturers of craft coolships seem unfamiliar with the physico-chemical changes occurring in the wort at this stage, or they would design them accordingly, i.e. shallow (max. wort depth 15 cm) with a very large surface area. This would also facilitate greater levels of inoculation with airborne microorganisms.

Evaporation after hot break separation

Some modern breweries, even relatively small ones, have installed equipment in the brewhouse that allows some evaporation of volatile compounds to occur downstream from the whirlpool. These devices vaporise the DMS and other undesirable wort volatiles formed in the wort during hot break separation. Of course, with a coolship, this would have been unnecessary, so this is a relatively modern problem – one only experienced by breweries since the adoption of pelletised hops and whirlpools. A wide variety of options are available for doing so. Some strip the wort using steam; others use the residual heat from the whirlpool to do so in a thin film, while still others do so in thin film evaporators under a vacuum. Figure 90 shows a type of thin film evaporator that operates below atmospheric pressure.

Figure 90: A thin film evaporator

A note on hot-side aeration

Hot-side aeration of the mash and/or the wort brings with it a number of disadvantages. When the wort is hot, oxygen quickly reacts chemically with compounds in the wort, such as carbohydrates, proteinaceous compounds, polyphenols and bittering substances.

Starch conversion and other enzymatic reactions can be impaired. Additionally, lautering slows, the extract efficiency suffers, and the wort darkens. During wort production in the presence of oxygen, Maillard products can develop into staling compounds. The oxidation of the longer chain fatty acids, which are the result of lipid degradation during mashing (especially linoleic acid and linolenic acid). Downstream in the process, these are further oxidised to carbonyls, which emerge as ageing compounds in the finished beer (refer to the section on the primary challenges to good beer in trade). The bitterness of the wort and thus the finished beer may be diminished or affected in an otherwise negative manner, such as becoming harsh or unpleasant. Overall, the resulting beer will lack a satisfactory flavour stability and will often exhibit off-flavours. (Refer to the section on the beer and basic food safety and on the staling of beer.)

Shearing forces

Through cavitation in a brewhouse pump, in unfavourable conditions during the wort boiling process or if the hot wort is centrifuged, the shearing forces acting upon the hot mash or wort can result in off-flavours, most commonly those reminiscent of cooked onions.

> **Quality control points: cast-out wort**
>
> - target gravity
> - pH
> - clarity
> - colour
> - aroma/flavour
> - bittering units
> - minimise oxygen uptake/hot-side aeration
> - DMS (indicator for undesirable wort volatiles)
> - hot break separation (efficacy, duration)

Literature and further reading

Back, W., Gastl, M., Krottenthaler, M., Narziss, L., and Zarnkow, M., *Brewing Techniques in Practice*. Fachverlag Hans Carl, 2019

Briggs, D., Boulton, C., Brookes, P., Stevens, R., *Brewing Science and Practice*. Woodhead Publishing Ltd., Cambridge, UK, 2004

Forster, K., Rittenauer, M. *Neues Application Center für die Malz- und Bierbranche*. Brauwelt Nr. 23, Fachverlag Hans Carl, 2020

Narziss, L. *Abriss der Bierbrauerei*. Wiley-VCH Verlag GmbH & Co., 2017

Narziss, L., Back, W., *Die Bierbrauerei, Band 2: Die Technologie der Würzebereitung*. 8. Auflage, Wiley-VCH Verlag GmbH & Co., 2009

Sacher, B., Becker, T., *Some Reflections on Mashing* (Parts 1 and 2). Brauwelt International, nos. 5 and 6, Fachverlag Hans Carl, 2016

Schneider, J., Krottenthaler, M., Back, W., Weisser, H., *Study on the Membrane Filtration of Mash with Particular Respect to the Quality of Wort and Beer*. Journal of the Institute of Brewing, 111(4), 380–387, 2005

Schwill-Miedaner, A. *Verfahrenstechnik im Brauprozess*. Fachverlag Hans Carl, 2011

Sovrano, S., Buiatti, S., Anese, M. *Influence of malt browning degree on lipoxygenase activity*. Food Chemistry 99 (2006) 711–717

Zhuang, S., Shetty, R., Hansen, M., Fromberg, A., Hansen, P., Hobley, T., *Brewing with 100% unmalted grains: barley, wheat, oat and rye*. Eur Food Res Technology, Springer-Verlag Berlin Heidelberg, 2016

For turbid mashing: McGreger, C., McGreger, N. *Beers of the World – Lambic*. Brauwelt International V 2019

THE 'COLD SIDE'

The diagramme below depicts the 'cold side' of the process as it is generally carried out in smaller breweries:

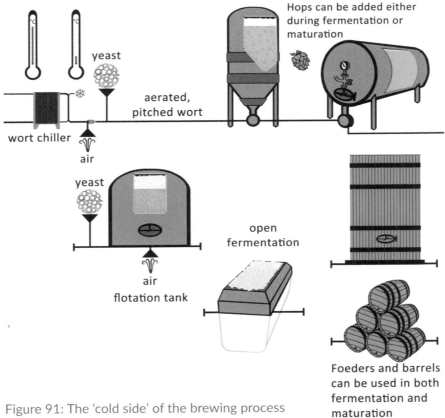

Figure 91: The 'cold side' of the brewing process

Wort chilling and aeration

The wort must be chilled at this stage because brewing yeast cells prefer wort close to room temperature or cooler. If the wort is too warm, it can reduce the vitality of the yeast or even kill them. When the wort is chilled, much of the energy that went into boiling it can also be recovered for later usage. Wort chillers are generally counterflow plate heat exchangers and can be divided into two general types: singe-stage and multi-stage. The coolant flowing in the opposite direction of the wort in a single-stage heat exchanger is normally brewing liquor, which is heated up for the next batch of beer. A single-stage chiller in a temperate climate or with cool ambient water is usually sufficient to chill wort for top fermentation. In a multi-stage heat exchanger, there are usually only two stages, water at ambient temperatures and refrigerated food-grade glycol. This kind of system allows brewers, for example, in warmer climates to chill the wort to lager brewing temperatures (6 to 9 °C). By dividing the chiller into two stages, some energy savings are still possible through heat recovery and likewise less glycol has to be chilled for the process to be effective. The type of glycol used in brewing is food-grade propylene glycol. Ethylene glycol (antifreeze), on the other hand, is toxic and should never be utilised anywhere it might come into contact with the product.

In breweries where brewing occurs less frequently than once per day, another type of coolant can be employed, for instance, process water. This water still must be drinking water quality, since any leaks between the plates will result in contamination of the wort.

Upon cooling to below about 80 °C, one has to worry about microbial contamination. Wort bacteria (short rods) can be present in the chiller, aeration apparatus or other equipment and piping where wort is present. Lactic acid bacteria may also be present in biofilm or poorly maintained equipment and piping. They may be latent but can travel to the fermentation vessel with the wort and reproduce in there once anaerobic conditions exist. (Refer to the section on cleaning and hygienic design).

Aeration and oxygenation

Oxygenation merely refers to the introduction of oxygen into a system. Immediately after the wort is chilled in the brewhouse, it is aerated. Because the air contains oxygen, the wort is oxygenated, meaning that oxygen physically enters the stream of wort coming out of the heat exchanger.

The lower temperature, the better oxygen physically dissolves in wort, and the less likely it is to chemically react with the compounds in the wort. Cold aeration of the wort until 5 to 10 mg/l of oxygen are dissolved in it is necessary for the yeast. Their cells need oxygen to undergo budding, meaning asexual reproduction. In order to reproduce, more cell membranes must be generated which requires oxygen (refer to the section on propagating and harvesting yeast). If the yeast cells do not receive enough oxygen, there will not be enough cells in suspension and the beer will be poorly attenuated, fermentation will stretch on for a long time, the beer will be full of undesirable compounds and exhibit off-flavours. The yeast will also not be healthy enough to harvest and repitch either. (For more on the topic of oxygen refer to the section on beer and food safety addressing oxygen uptake of beer.)

For small to medium-sized breweries, it is generally not advisable to use pure oxygen to provide yeast with the oxygen they need but rather sterile air. One exception would be in high gravity beer production (refer to the section on oxidation – chemical reactions with oxygen).

Table 9: 12% wort aerated to the point of saturation at the following temperatures contains these concentrations of oxygen (Source: Narziss, L. *Abriß der Bierbrauerei.* Wiley Verlag):

Temperature [°C]:	5	10	15	20
Oxygen [mg O_2/l]:	10.4	9.3	8.3	7.4

Sintered metal stones and Venturi tubes

Though they are quite common in small breweries, sintered metal 'stones' (fig. 92) for wort aeration are less recommended than Venturi tubes, as they are almost impossible to clean and can thus harbour beer spoilers.

Figure 92: A sintered metal aeration stone

Aerating the wort with a Venturi tube is more hygienic, since a Venturi tube can be more thoroughly cleaned. Even though the flow rate is much faster through a Venturi tube, the air is nevertheless well mixed with the chilled wort. The picture in figure 93 shows a Venturi tube in its housing in the brewhouse.

Figure 93: A Venturi tube

Figure 94 provides a schematic representation of a cross-section of a Venturi tube and the operating principle in wort aeration:

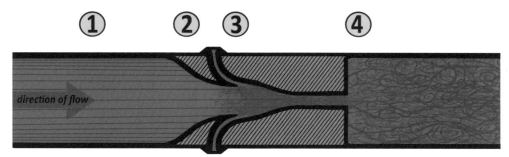

Figure 94: A drawing of a Venturi tube

① The flow through the tube is usually laminar in the inlet, up to the point where the flow is restricted.

② The narrowing of the tube increases the velocity of the wort flowing through the tube, thus lowering the pressure. This, in turn, pulls the air into the wort.

③ This section of the tube is called the throat. Sterile air enters the tube where the flow becomes turbulent. As the tube narrows further, the flow rate increases after the air enters the wort.

④ This section of the tube is the diffuser. The tube opens abruptly, slowing the velocity again, causing turbulent flow, which results in rapid and thorough mixing of the air and wort.

Testing the hygienic conditions at the chiller

Forced wort test

A simple, inexpensive method for monitoring the cleanliness on the hot side of the process is the forced wort test. Before pitching the yeast, collect a sample of chilled wort in a sterile container (a pre-sterilised bag or jar with a screw cap). Place the sample in a warm place and observe for signs of infection (gas bubbles, foam, cloudiness) over several days.

Interpreting the results

If any of these signs occur after one day, this indicates a serious contamination. Measures must be taken immediately to thoroughly clean the heat exchanger and the hoses/lines conveying the chilled wort. Should signs of contamination first appear after several days, this means the contamination is not as severe but cleaning measures must still be taken. The more rapidly the wort sample changes, the greater the effect on the beer. If seven days have passed with no change to the sample, it can be assumed that the cleaning regimen is effective.

Quality control points: chilling the wort

- gravity
- pH
- pitching temperature
- clarity
- colour
- aroma/flavour
- bittering units
- microbiological status (wild yeast, beer spoilers)
- DMS (indicator for undesirable wort volatiles)
- aeration (method, amount, hygiene)

| Yeast pitching

At this point, the selected strain of yeast at the proper cell count enters the production process. The wort should be aerated to a level sufficient to supply the yeast with oxygen. However, after the yeast is pitched through to packaging, the wort and beer need to remain as oxygen-free as possible.

Pitching rate

Factors affecting the pitching rate:

- strain
- yeast viability
- fermentation temperature
- flocculation characteristics
- fermentation capacity
- yeast handling prior to pitching
- desired flavour profile
- wort composition
- gravity of the wort

Pitching incorrect amounts of yeast, both underpitching and overpitching, may well result in off-flavours.

- A **low pitching rate** can result in extended lag times and more yeast repro-duction. Not enough yeast cells means that not all of the sugar will be fermented in the wort (a lower degree of attenuation). Extremely low pitching rates may also cause stuck fermentations.
- A **high pitching rate** can create isolated hot spots in the cone, filtration problems and possible haze issues once the beer has been bottled.

Yeast cell count

By aerating the wort, the yeast cells are provided with oxygen, which they utilise for biosynthesising cell wall components necessary for reproduction through budding. By reproducing in this way, the yeast doubles or triples the number of cells in the wort, for instance, bottom-fermenting yeast cells will increase their numbers from around 10 to 20 million to up to 60 million cells per ml. This occurs before fermentation begins. If yeast does not have enough FAN, trace amounts of certain minerals, most especially zinc, among other nutrients, reproduction and fermentation will be unsatisfactory. Commercially available yeast nutrients can supply the reproducing and fermenting cells with these and other essentials.

Determining how much yeast to pitch

The amount of dry yeast to be pitched for a specified volume of wort is listed on the packets of dry yeast. The same applies for ready-to-pitch yeast. When working with cropped yeast in the brewery, the simplest method of figuring out how much yeast to add is based on weight. The solids in a yeast slurry must somehow be isolated and weighed, which requires additional preparation such as centrifugation or wet solids measurement. However, with access to a microscope, using a haemocytometer to determine yeast cell count is an inexpensive and fairly accurate method for obtaining yeast cell counts. (Refer to the section below to find out how to properly use a haemocytometer.)

Pitching rates vary from brewery to brewery. A general rule of thumb is one million cells per ml per degree Plato, depending upon the yeast strain and physiological condition. Yeast suppliers will also provide recommendations for pitching rates for individual strains.

There are brewers who pitch yeast according to its appearance. They attempt to harvest the healthiest yeast. This would correspond to thick, white, creamy, fresh smelling, yeast slurry that is neither slimy nor dark in colour. This slurry is subsequently used for fermenting the next batch of wort. Experienced brewers also know that by pitching approximately one litre per hectolitre of thick yeast slurry, this will amount to 10 to 20 million cells per ml in the pitched wort. If it is a bit thinner, they pitch more.

Pitching yeast can be done more consistently and accurately by counting the cells beforehand. Some top-fermenting strains require less, while some bottom-fermenting yeast may require more.

Table 10: Yeast cell counts in pitched wort

Yeast	Cell count
Top-fermenting	8–12 million per ml
Bottom-fermenting	10–18 million per ml
Brettanomyces spp.	400,000 to 500,000 per ml

Pitching the yeast into chilled wort

Yeast can be added manually to the fermentation tanks, blended with wort prior to addition in a dedicated vessel or dosed directly into the stream of chilled wort during transfer from the brewhouse to the tank. Most automated dosing of yeast is controlled by meters which measure the turbidity. Regardless of how the yeast is pitched, care should be taken not to allow the yeast to become infected with microbial contaminants.

Since cropped yeast will contain compounds derived from hops and malt, it is advisable to harvest yeast from a less hopped, paler batch of beer to pitch into darker beers and not the other way around. Yeast which has fermented strong beers should not be repitched, as its vitality has been compromised due to the presence of high concentrations of alcohol.

Bottom-fermenting yeast is normally repitched five to seven times, while top-fermenting can be repitched numerous times as long as the yeast remains vital with a high fermentative capacity.

The viability and vitality of yeast

These two terms concern the health of the yeast cells.

Viability refers to the status of a yeast cell: dead or alive. Active cells are colourless while dead cells stain. Viability yields no information regarding fermentation performance or metabolic activity.

The number of dead yeast cells being added to the wort during pitching should be kept to a minimum as this causes quality problems due to

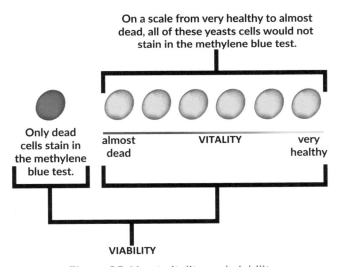

Figure 95: Yeast vitality and viability

haze formation, as well as negatively affecting flavour stability. The methylene blue test is relatively simple to carry out and can be used to gauge yeast viability. There are tests with other stains available as well. Dead cells or unhealthy cells, which are prone to undergo autolysis, have a negative influence on the finished beer, affecting the flavour, the shelf life and the foam.

Vitality determines whether the yeast will be able to perform the tasks brewers set forth for them in the fermentation vessel. Vitality is an expression of metabolic activity and varies along a continuum (fig. 95). Though it is often taken for granted, healthy yeast is critical in the production of good beer. There is no rapid method for measuring vitality. Though measuring the intracellular pH is used, the method still cannot predict performance. The most reliable method thus far for determining the fermentative capacity of yeast is to actually ferment wort with it.

Pressure versus shearing forces

Though yeast can withstand a significant amount of pressure, they do not tolerate shearing forces or axial distension very well (fig. 96). Therefore, a brewer should avoid subjecting yeast to these forces to the greatest extent possible.

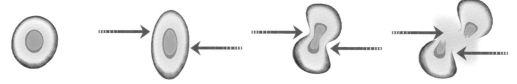

Figure 96: Shearing forces acting on yeast

How does one avoid damaging levels of shearing forces when handling yeast? With variable frequency pumps, the flow rate can be slowed to reduce the forces acting on yeast cells. Piping and equipment with sharp edges on their surfaces or rapid changes in diameter can pull and push yeast in every direction. Designing or acquiring equipment better suited to handling yeast gently is recommended. Aeration nozzles and static mixers can also increase these forces on yeast to the point that they are harmful.

Collecting samples for yeast cell counts

Sample collection to determine a yeast cell count is relatively straightforward. As only the number of yeast cells is of interest here, aseptic technique is not necessary. For samples not analysed within one hour, copper sulphate is added to halt yeast multiplication.

Materials: a 100 ml sample flask and a wash bottle containing 70% ethanol or methanol by volume, 3% (by volume) aqueous copper sulphate solution.

1. Collect the sample from any kind of sampling device. Pre-sterilisation is normally not necessary, but rinse with alcohol afterwards.
2. If sampling from a fermentation tank, prior to sampling, allow enough beer to flow to ensure that the sample is representative of the contents of the fermentation vessel.
3. Store the sample at a maximum temperature of 10 °C and analyse within one hour after collection.
4. The sample may be preserved for up to 48 hours by adding 5 ml of the copper sulphate solution to the 100 ml sample flask before or after sampling.

Refer to the section on microbiology and laboratory techniques for more information about counting cells with a haemocytometer as well as aseptic technique for collecting yeast sample to test for microbial contaminants.

Counting yeast cells with a haemocytometer

A quality control programme at a brewery of any size requires a microscope – even homebrewers use them nowadays. Examining yeast regularly with a microscope endows brewers with valuable experience. They learn to recognise the health status or the vitality of their yeast, and healthy yeast are the only ones that make good beer. So, brewers need to become conscious of the needs of their yeast and how to indulge their every whim.

A haemocytometer or cell counting chamber can be used to determine the number of cells in a defined volume of propagated yeast or harvested yeast. Knowing how many cells are present per ml allows the brewer to decide how much yeast slurry to pitch.

In figure 97, this particular haemocytometer consists of nine large squares, each of which measures 1 × 1 mm. The central square contains 25 smaller squares, each at 0.2 × 0.2 mm, and in turn, each of those is divided into 16 even smaller squares, measuring 0.05 × 0.05 mm.

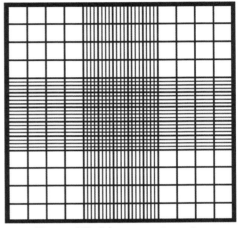

Figure 97: A haemocytometer

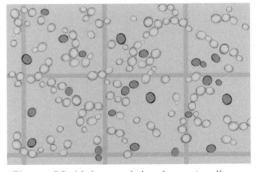

Figure 98: Living and dead yeast cells on a haemocytometer

Equipment

Methylene blue solution (1%), microscope with a 40x objective, haemocytometer slide and cover slip, graduated pipette, container such as a graduated cylinder.

Sample preparation

1. Collect several ml of yeast slurry. Make the necessary dilutions so that the number of yeast cells are able to be counted on the grids marked on the slide. Keep a record of the dilutions as this will be needed later in the calculation.

2. Usually a dilution will have to be made, so start by mixing 1 ml of yeast with 9 ml of water (1:10 dilution) if a lower concentration of cells is expected or 1 ml of yeast with 99 ml of water (1:100 dilution). Use a graduated pipette to measure the yeast slurry and the water used for dilution.
3. Once the yeast slurry has been diluted, add the methylene blue solution drop by drop until the slurry is an intense blue, swirling the slurry until the colour remains the same. Let stand for one minute.
4. Place the cover slip on the side and then using a pipette, transfer a small volume of the diluted yeast slurry to one of the chambers on the slide according to the manufacturer's instructions.
5. Adjust the slide using the platform so that the square in the centre is visible. It should consist of multiple smaller squares with gridlines.
6. Count the number of cells in five of the squares according to the manufacturer's instructions.
7. Using the cell count and the dilutions performed, calculate the concentration of yeast cells according to the manufacturer's instructions. Calculate the pitching rate based on the cell count in the yeast slurry.

Refer to EBC Method 3.1.1.1 Haemocytometry.

Phenolic off-flavour (POF) test

This test can be performed on yeast to find out whether they react positively or negatively to generating volatile phenolic compounds. Most lager yeast are negative. Top-fermenting Belgian and Bavarian *Weissbier Saccharomyces cerevisiae* strains, *Brettanomyces* species and many wild yeasts are positive (refer to the section on barrel maturation with *Brettanomyces* above). For instance, if the following hydroxycinnamic acids are converted to these volatile phenolic compounds, then the yeast is POF-positive:

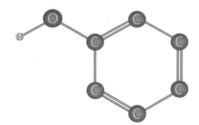

Figure 99: The fundamental structure of phenolic compounds

Table 11: Phenolic compounds and flavour descriptors

Hydroxycinnamic acids	Phenolic compounds	Descriptors
ferulic acid	4-vinyl guaiacol (4-VG)	clove-like, spicy
p-coumaric acid	4-vinyl phenol (4-VP)	medicinal
cinnamic acid	4-vinyl styrene (4-VS)	styrofoam-like
caffeic acid	4-vinyl catechol (4-VC)	plastic, bitter, smoky

Refer to EBC Method 2.3.9.5 Phenolic Off Flavour (POF).

Literature and further reading

Back, W., Gastl, M., Krottenthaler, M., Narziss, L., and Zarnkow, M., *Brewing Techniques in Practice*. Fachverlag Hans Carl, 2019

Hill, A. (ed.), *Brewing Microbiology*. Woodhead Publishing Ltd., Cambridge, UK, 2015

| Fermentation

Fermentation is carried out by yeast. The two most prominent types of microorganisms in brewing – whether they are unwanted or not – are yeasts and lactic acid bacteria. Once the yeast has consumed the oxygen in the wort, under the anaerobic conditions they utilise two main metabolic pathways alcoholic and lactic fermentation. Lactic acid bacteria prefer to absorb glucose degrade it to pyruvic acid or pyruvate, excreting lactic acid and perhaps other fermentation by-products. We do the same thing when we have unfit muscles. If our muscles do not receive enough oxygen, they have to undergo lactic acid fermentation. Sore muscles are the result.

However, ethanol fermentation is the step in the brewing process in which the yeast converts the available sugars in the wort to

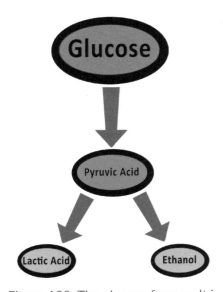

Figure 100: The glucose from malt is first degraded to pyruvate and is either fermented to ethanol or lactic acid depending upon the type of metabolic pathway present in the microorganisms

pyruvate. These wort sugars consist mostly of glucose molecules. The yeast metabolises the pyruvate and excrete ethanol and CO_2 into the wort as well as other fermentation by-products. Maltose consists of two glucose. The yeast takes each glucose in the maltose molecule and breaks it down chemically to extract energy from it. As the yeast does so, over time, the wort becomes beer. The yeast also creates aroma and flavour compounds as by-products.

Fermentation and its outcome can be controlled by adjusting the pitching rate, the temperature and the concentrations of fermentable extract and oxygen in the wort. The required temperatures during this stage are determined by the particular type of yeast and the optimal conditions for fermentation and maturation of the wort and green beer. Primary fermentation lasts anywhere from several days to up to several weeks, depending on the yeast strain selected, wort composition and the conditions during fermentation.

What should happen during fermentation?

- The yeast cell count increases, then declines.
- The gravity and the pH of the wort drops.
- Ethanol, CO_2 and by-products, such as esters and diacetyl, are produced.

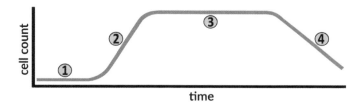

Figure 101: Yeast activity is divided into discrete phases

Yeast activity is divided into discrete phases (fig. 101):

① **Lag or adaptive phase:** The yeast cells adapt to their environment; oxygen is consumed and falls to undetectable levels, while fatty acids are taken up as well in preparation for reproduction. The cell count remains constant and thus outwardly no activity is apparent during this phase. This phase lasts 12 to 24 h.

② **Logarithmic phase:** Reproductive growth occurs as the yeast rapidly consumes sugar, proteins and other nutrients. The concentration of free amino nitrogen and pH decline rapidly as fermentation commences. Aromatic and flavour compounds present in the finished beer are formed during reproduction. Pitching more cells per ml thus reduces the amount of these aroma and flavour compounds.

③ **Stationary phase:** Cell division slows or stops when the nutrients in the wort drop to a point that they are limiting to yeast growth. The yeast cell count in the wort reaches its maximum and any remaining sugars and amino acids are consumed. The yeast cells prepare for a period of scarcity by changing their physiology. Flocculation begins (the cells form clusters and sediment out). The yeast cells 'hope' that the nutrients will again increase. By altering their physiology to avoid starvation and storing energy (as glycogen), they await further developments.

 Dormant phase: Loss of cell viability due to ageing and an increase in the ethanol concentration. The number of cells per ml decreases rapidly. To be avoided is yeast autolysis, when the yeast releases proteinases and glucanases producing unwelcome compounds in the beer.

Autolysis is dependent upon environmental factors, such as temperature, ethanol concentration, pH and osmotic pressure. Autolysis products comprise low molecular weight compounds among them fatty acids and high molecular weight cell wall material, like glucans. The low molecular weight compounds negatively affect beer flavour and appearance, while the compounds derived from the cell walls produce turbidity. Proper yeast handling and maintaining good practice during fermentation and maturation should prevent autolysis affecting the flavour and quality of the beer.

By monitoring physical conditions such as pH, temperature, cell count and gravity, brewers can gather insight into what is going on the fermentation tank. As fermentation progresses, the gravity and pH should decrease, while ethanol, carbon dioxide and fermentation by-products are formed.

Should a brewer be working with open fermentation vessels, through direct observation of the top of the fermenting wort, a brewer can tell what is happening under the surface of the foam.

Stages of fermentation

Additional sediment of hot break material can be removed from the fermentation vessel approximately 12 hours after transfer from the whirlpool.

Generally speaking, once the yeast is pitched, the following occurs, more or less, depending upon a variety of factors (strain, vitality, temperature, etc.):

- The dissolved oxygen is rapidly taken up by the yeast.
- The yeast cells multiply.
- The yeast consume all of the simple wort sugars.
- The yeast release substances that lower the pH.
- Ethanol and carbon dioxide are produced through fermentation.
- Substances that impart flavour – whether good or undesirable – such as esters, higher alcohols, diacetyl, sulphurous compounds, etc., are created by the yeast.

Attenuation

As the yeast turns the extract into ethanol, carbon dioxide and various other compounds and the gravity drops, the wort changes into beer. This process is known as attenuation.

As fermentation progresses, brewers measure the gravity and record it. These values are plotted against other data such as pH, temperature and time. In order to understand not only how fermentation is progressing, the apparent attenuation of the green beer can be calculated using the following equation. It is termed 'apparent' because of the presence of ethanol. The real attenuation can be measured in a laboratory or approximated by multiplying the apparent attenuation by a factor of 0.81 to compensate for the less dense ethanol.

$$\text{apparent attenuation [\%]} = \frac{\text{original gravity [°P]} - \text{apparent residual extract [°P]}}{\text{original gravity [°P]}} \times 100$$

$$\text{real attenuation [\%]} = \text{apparent attenuation [\%]} \times 0.81$$

The final attenuation a beer reaches at the end of fermentation also aids in assessing how well the brewhouse work was carried out, assuming that the malt quality remained consistent.

It is rumoured that to increase the body of a beer, the attenuation can be halted by a practice known as 'crashing', meaning to cool fermenting beer rapidly so that the yeast drop out of suspension. Not only is this detrimental to yeast quality, but this claim has no validity. Halting fermentation prematurely results in the following:

- The infection pressure on the beer increases.
- The risk is higher that bottles will explode on the shelf (even if flash-pasteurised, due to an infection with over-attenuating yeast or other spoilage microorganisms).
- The drinkability is lower due to the residual fermentable extract.

Forced fermentation test

The final attenuation of a particular batch of pitched wort can be determined rather quickly by performing this simple test. With access to a magnetic stir plate and a heat source, it is possible to expedite the fermentation process in a laboratory setting. Gravity readings are taken regularly until the values remain constant. For more information on measuring the limit of attenuation, refer to EBC analyses 8.6.1 and 8.6.2.

Microbiological testing

Approximately 24 h after pitching yeast and approximately one week after pitching, the beer should be tested for the following (refer to the section on microbiological analysis below):

- anaerobic microorganisms
- aerobic microorganisms
- *Saccharomyces* wild yeasts
- non-*Saccharomyces* wild yeasts

Tank geometry

Open fermentation vessels

Fermentation can occur in open or closed vessels. Open vessels are the more traditional of the two. The brewers who employ them usually claim that their beers taste better because they are able to skim the hop resin stipples (fig. 107) and any leftover hot and cold break material off the top of the foam. They also find that during fermentation undesirable, volatile compounds are able to more easily escape into the atmosphere. Brewers are also able to observe the surface of the fermenting wort and green beer and look for any anomalies that might be visually recognisable. Of course, with open vessels, brewers must be concerned with airflow into the fermentation cellar, the general quality of the air and the removal of carbon dioxide. The carbon dioxide from open fermentation cannot be captured for recovery.

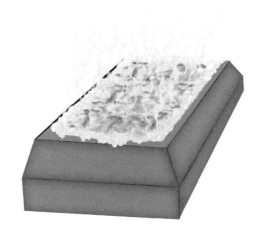

Figure 102: An open fermentation vessel

Closed, cylindroconical vessels

Modern vessels generally possess a maximum diameter to height ratio of 1:2 to 1:2.5 not including the headspace. This is gentler on the yeast with regard to pressure and temperature in the cone. The fermentation is more generally advantageous; for instance, the esters are finer, and the yeast excrete fewer proteinases, which are detrimental, especially for unpasteurised beer. The yeast harvested from the bottom of the cone for repitching are white in colour and are also much healthier. A cylindroconical tank (CCT) should not exceed 12 metres from the bottom of the cone to the maximum level of the liquid at the top. This is probably not an issue for smaller breweries. Above the liquid level, a minimum of 20% to 25% headspace should be added to the height of the tank to allow for expansion and foam formation during fermentation. The angle of the cone at the bottom of the tank is usually 60–75°, an angle which does not allow yeast to easily adhere to the inside wall but rather to collect at the bottom in order to facilitate its removal. Fifty years ago, cylindroconical tanks, known colloquially as 'pencils', were constructed to be much higher, with a diameter to height ratio of 1:3.5 or even 1:5. These are not as common anymore. However, for performing pressurised fermentation, a ratio of 1:3.5 or 4 is customary. The greater the ratio of the height to the diameter, the more headspace a CCT requires.

The turbulent column of gas within the tank facilitates greater contact between yeast and the substrate (wort). The spectrum of fermentation by-products is different due to the geometry of the tank. There are fewer higher alcohols and esters and other volatiles present in the finished beer. Cylindroconical fermentation vessels therefore produce more neutral beers. The pitching and fermentation temperatures, of course, also play a role. The movement of the fermenting wort within a tank is illustrated in figure 104. During primary fermentation in CCTs, especially those over 10 m tall, allowing the fermentation temperature to rise (for bottom fermentation to 11 or 12 °C, for ale yeast fermentation to the low 20s) can help ensure optimal yeast reproduction and a stronger, more homogeneous convection. This can prevent stratification within the tank. The concentrations of fermentation by-products, i.e. higher alcohols and esters, are usually no higher due to the tank geometry than during cooler fermentation in horizontal tanks. The rapidly rising column of carbon dioxide bubbles in a cylindroconical tank causes 'washing' of the substrate to occur. Some of the concentrations of volatiles in the fermenting beer are influenced by this. However, fewer bitter substances derived from the hops are lost in closed, vertical cylindroconical tanks.

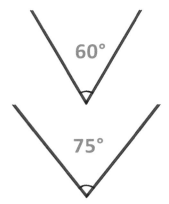

Figure 103: Angles on the cone of a CCT

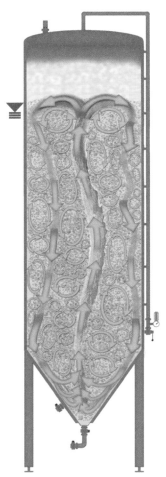

Figure 104: Circulation in a CCT

Closed, horizontal vessels

Horizontal fermentation vessels are not as commonplace in smaller breweries because harvesting yeast is more challenging, and the vessels are not as easy to CIP. With regard to the fermentation by-products, the opposite is true in horizontal vessels concerning the rising bubbles during fermentation The column of rising bubbles is not as narrowly focussed and thus less dramatic in its effects. The substrate (wort) does not move around as much in horizontal tanks, and thus the yeast cells do not constantly come into contact with the substrate. For this reason, the yeast ferments the wort differently and more higher alcohols and esters are produced during fermentation. The finished beer from these tanks will also contain more volatiles since fewer are washed out. The resultant beers are less neutral in flavour.

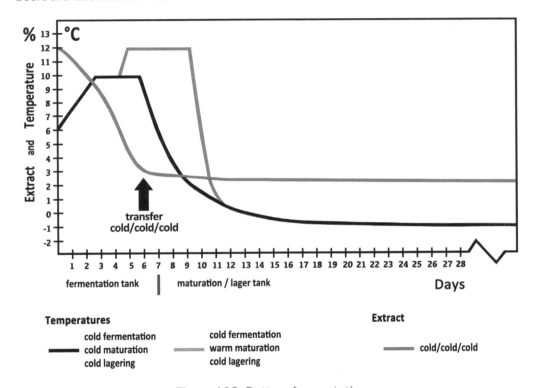

Figure 105: Bottom fermentation

Stages of bottom fermentation

- foam blanket formation
- young kräusen/low kräusen
- high kräusen/formation of cauliflower stippled heads
- brown kräusen/hop resin stipples
- post-kräusen/collapsing foam blanket

Foam blanket formation and low kräusen

After pitching the yeast, anywhere from six to 36 hours may pass before any activity is observed. Low kräusen is marked by a ring of foam on the surface of the wort close to the centre. This stage is reached when the gravity reading has dropped by about one-half degree Plato, the pH is considerably lower, and the temperature has begun to increase. A sample collected at this stage will have a lot of yeast cells in suspension and appear almost milky. Bubbles of CO_2 should be visible rising to the top.

Kräusen stages

Mounds of foam in the form of 'cauliflower heads' rise on the surface of the wort around 24 to 48 hours after the yeast is pitched. These are referred to as the kräusen stages of fermentation.

As fermentation progresses, the 'high kräusen' state is reached. The greatest yeast activity is present at high kräusen. Bubbles of CO_2 released by the yeast rise to the surface of the wort, forming 'cauliflower' or 'rocky heads'. These peaks become less dense and separate, turning a cream colour. This takes place about two to four days into fermentation. During this stage, the temperature should be regulated (cooled) to remain at the optimum temperature for the yeast strain. The fermenting wort should smell and taste as expected. It should not be sour or exhibit atypical aromas and the fermentation should be vigorous.

Figure 106: Kräusen, the meringue-like head typical of Central European bottom fermentation

As the carbon dioxide bubbles rise, they push the hop resins to the top of the foam. Of course, they can also be skimmed off from open fermentation vessels, which is why some traditional Central European brewers still continue to practise open fermentation, as they feel the hop bitterness is 'nobler' when the resins are skimmed from the foam.

Fermentation continues to slow until the foam starts to collapse. In a cylindroconical fermentation tank, even if cone cooling is present, any yeast that has settled on the bottom should be removed from the green beer. This should be done often, as autolysis can occur quite quickly.

Figure 107: Brown kräusen or hop resin stipples
Photo: *Chip McElroy*

If the green beer is to be transferred to a maturation tank, this would be the time to do so.

Post-kräusen

The yeast should be flocculating well and settling out to form a compact layer of sediment. This stage of fermentation is reached when the majority of the sugars have been consumed by the yeast and there is an obvious decrease in the rate of fermentation. Also referred to as the post-kräusen stage, the yeast continues to convert the remaining sugars into ethanol and CO_2. As the nutrients become depleted and the alcohol level increases, the yeast start to flocculate and sediment out. As the fermentation rate slows, the foam head will begin to fall due to less CO_2 being liberated from the wort, leaving a foam ring on the wall of the tank. The gravity should level out. The beer may be transferred when the gravity readings have only decreased by 0.5 °P within a 24-hour period. The beer can now be transferred to the conditioning or maturation tank. The gravity should be around 1–2 °P above that expected in the finished beer.

Top-fermenting yeast strains continue to ferment at 17–24 °C.

Bottom-fermenting yeast prefer temperatures of 4–5 °C at this stage.

- The fermentation rate slows considerably.
- Some changes occur in the flavour profile through yeast activity or through stripping with CO_2.
- Diacetyl is converted by the yeast; temperatures can be elevated slightly to speed up diacetyl reduction (1–2 days).
- Yeast flocculates and sediments out resulting in a beer that is clear and bright.
- Final gravity is achieved.

The contents of the tank should be cooled when the apparent gravity is approximately half of the original gravity. The temperature should be reduced slowly by no more than 1–1.5 °C per day. Rapid cooling may result shock the yeast, damage viability, hindering fermentation and producing off-flavours.

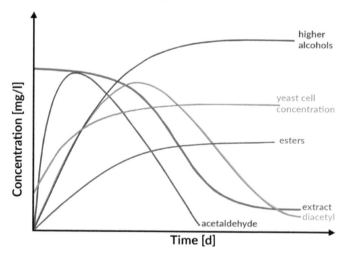

Figure 108: The concentration of fermentation by-products over primary fermentation and maturation; this graph is only intended to show the relative concentrations of relevant fermentation by-products as fermentation and maturation progress

Stages of top fermentation

Prior to the advent of lager beer, top fermentation in breweries with a strain of *Saccharomyces cerevisiae* was much more widespread than it is now. Nevertheless, traditional styles, such as English ale, Belgian ale, stouts and porters, *Weissbier*, *Kölsch*, *Altbier* and *Gose*, among others, remind us of the formerly ubiquitous presence of top-fermented beers. These beers are often pleasantly fruity and floral or even phenolic in some cases due to the high concentrations of fermentation by-products. Among craft brewers, top-fermented beers are popular because of their quick turnaround, and the fact that they can be brewed on less equipment, requiring less capital investment. Traditional open vessels take advantage of the fact that top fermentation occurs in two general stages: first, any residual break material, hop resins and insoluble polyphenol-protein colloids rise to the surface and can be removed. Secondly, the yeast rises to the surface (fig. 110) and can be harvested in the 'barm' or yeasty froth that crowns the green beer. The fermentation vessels for *Weissbier* are furnished with a slight depression on one portion of the lip at the top of the tank. The yeast in the barm froths over and down a yeast chute, called a *Schnabel* ("bill" or "beak") where it then drops into a yeast collection vessel below. Normally, top-fermenting yeast should remain in suspension; that is, it should not flocculate out or rise to the surface, until final attenuation is reached. In Yorkshire, however, the highly flocculent yeast common in breweries there has to be 'roused' by means of recirculation, so that it remains in suspension.

As mentioned, due to the higher temperatures, top fermentation occurs at much faster rate than bottom fermentation, but the rise and fall of the head of foam is similar. Of course, there is one exception: The heaving froth on top of the fermenting wort is teeming with yeast if it is a true top-fermenting strain.

In just a few hours after pitching, activity is present on the surface of the wort. The foam blanket rises, forms a thick crown and falls away quite quickly. Usually towards the end of the third day, the green beer contains approximately 3.0–3.5% extract. If fermentation occurs in an open vessel, at this point, the green beer is often transferred to a sealed maturation tank. After two to three weeks at a temperatures ranging from 1 °C to 4 °C, final attenuation is reached with approx. 1.8–2.0% residual extract remaining. This provides enough CO_2 to create a refreshingly lively beer. As with bottom-fermented beer, the pH of the finished beer should reach 4.3 to 4.4. The process is depicted in figure 109.

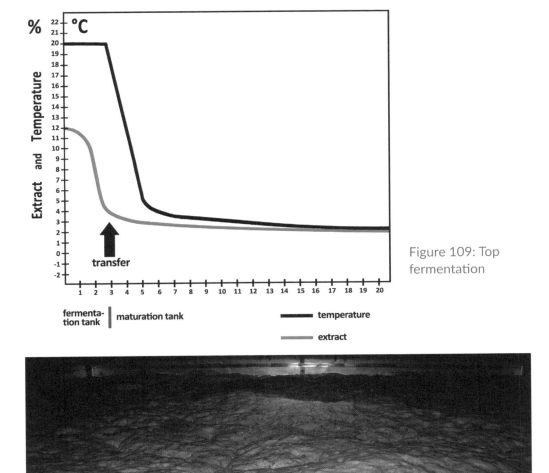

Figure 109: Top fermentation

Figure 110: Yeasty froth or 'barm' during the true top fermentation of British ale

Addressing common fermentation problems

Yeast is slow to start fermenting the wort

- Chill the wort rapidly to pitching temperature. Since wort is full of nutrients for a variety of microorganisms, it is very important to rapidly chill the wort to the pitching temperature. This allows the yeast to start fermentation and the relatively low temperature keeps competitor microorganisms at bay.
- Chill the wort to the optimal temperature for the yeast strain being pitched. At higher temperatures, yeast becomes stressed and off-flavours may result. Alternatively, if the temperature is too low, then yeast can sediment out, leaving the wort unfermented.
- The physiological condition of the yeast is important. Yeast viability should be at 95% or higher.
- Aerate properly and consistently.
- If dry yeast or a packaged culture is used, a starter is helpful to allow the yeast to adapt to wort. Take care to rehydrate dry yeast according to the manufacturer's instructions.
- Ensure that the amount of yeast pitched is correct by determining the cell count and calculating the volume of yeast slurry to pitch.

Stuck fermentations

If the extract concentration of the wort ceases to further decrease during fermentation and is still nowhere near final attenuation, this is known as a stuck fermentation. A possible remedy for this problem would be to add fermenting wort at high kräusen to the green beer with a stuck fermentation. The fermenting wort should exhibit an attenuation level of 20–25% and be equal to approx. 8–12% of the green beer volume.

Monitoring key fermentation parameters is advisable, in order to determine why the fermentation has stalled, namely:

- extract concentration
- temperature
- wort composition and the grain bill
- yeast cell count and volume of the pitched yeast
- flocculation behaviour of individual yeast strains
- microbial contamination

Flavour stability and fermentation

What measures can be taken to increase flavour stability during fermentation?

- Fastidious cleaning in the fermentation cellar (work area, tanks, piping) keeps any beer-spoilage microorganisms at bay.
- Cold maturation or conditioning befitting the yeast strain and beer style produces clear, stable, flavourful beers (refer to the section below).
- Yeast should not be exposed to extremely high pressure or shearing forces.
- Avoiding oxygen uptake on the entire cold side should be a top priority.
- The yeast should be provided with sufficient free amino nitrogen (but not too much).
- Pure, viable, vital yeast:
  - produces flavourful beers.
  - outcompetes any microorganisms that may be in the wort.
  - reaches a final attenuation close to the limit of attenuation, since any residual fermentable sugar increases the infection pressure on beer.
  - brings about a precipitous pH drop, which ensures that the finished beer will possess a pH value no higher than 4.5.

Quality control points: primary fermentation

- gravity/alcohol content
- fermentation rate
- pH and temperature
- yeast (viability, vitality, cells in suspension, flocculation)
- microbiological status (wild yeast, beer spoilers)
- visual inspection
- aroma/flavour
- vicinal diketones (VDK) and other green beer congeners below the flavour threshold
- minimising oxygen uptake
- techniques (method, hygiene)
- tank geometry

Conditioning/maturation

Depending upon the type of beer being produced, maturation can last anywhere from a few days to a several months. Ale brewers refer to this stage as conditioning, while Central European brewers speak of maturation and lagering. In both cases, the temperature of the green beer is lowered gradually to the optimal maturation temperature for the particular yeast strain. Maturation brings about a more well-rounded, mellow, less 'green' flavour and aroma to the beer.

As time passes, beer clarity improves as the yeast cells continue to flocculate and form a layer of sediment at the bottom of the fermentation vessel. Haze-forming proteins precipitate out and are removed from the beer. A key goal of maturation is that yeast cells eliminate the unpleasant flavour compounds that are responsible for the typical 'green beer' bouquet. Vicinal diketones (VDKs) serve as indicators for the progress of maturation, since they are fundamental to 'green beer aroma'. Diacetyl is the most prominent among them primarily because it has the lowest sensory threshold of all the VDKs. Diacetyl should decrease to a concentration at or below the sensory threshold, depending on the beer style. Maturation is finished when the beer has the desired flavour and aroma profile and final attenuation has been reached.

Conditioning is only carried out a few days to a few weeks for top-fermented styles, while bottom-fermented beer may be matured for weeks or even months. Beer clarification can also be achieved through the addition of finings. Follow supplier instructions on dosage and technique. (Refer to the section on clarification below.)

The foam stability is affected by the conditions under which the beer is matured. Beer stored above 2–4 °C, especially with excessive yeast in suspension, will result in poor foam stability. The green beer transferred from the fermentation tank can be centrifuged prior to transferring it to the maturation tank if the yeast have not flocculated and sedimented out well. A device for transferring and blending beer is depicted in figure 111. At warmer maturation temperatures, yeast are more apt to excrete glycerides and medium chain fatty acids (chains 6–12 carbons long), which are not conducive to foam

Figure 111: A device for transferring and blending beer

formation and head retention. One advantage of maturation with mixed microbes is that the C6–C10 fatty acids can undergo esterification, which can impart a pleasant fruitiness to the beer (refer to the section on barrel ageing). If the temperature or the cell count is too high, yeast can also undergo autolysis, which can ruin the flavour of the beer.

Of course, oxygen must be kept out of the beer to the greatest extent possible, so it is paramount for the quality of the finished beer to quietly and gently rack the green beer into the purged maturation tank, if it is to be transferred to another tank.

During maturation, beer can reach a point where its overall impression is one of pleasant, well-rounded synergy (refer to the section on drinkability). By contrast, some beers may never develop to that extent or are simply not given sufficient time to do so. Others attain it and through poor filtration, filling and/or storage practices lose it again. Among those aspects of the beer that change for the better during maturation, the bitterness should arrive at a point – whether it is strong or weak – that it either quickly or slowly fades on the palate. Bitterness that persists and does not diminish over time, especially with an astringent character, is undesirable in any beer.

Hopping on the cold side

Dry hopping is normally carried out at this stage, though some craft brewers prefer to do it earlier, especially those who brew hazy IPA, since little conditioning is required for that particular beer style and the hops apparently contain certain hexoses, which impart unique flavours to those beers. Particular care should be taken when dry hopping, to avoid any introduction of oxygen, as it is only detrimental to beer at this – and at any – stage. Mesh bags containing dry hops should be purged with carbon dioxide or nitrogen gas to exclude as much oxygen as possible from the hops prior to placing them in maturation tanks. Hopping on the cold side also causes the pH of the green beer to rise, which is actually undesirable from the perspective of microbiological and flavour stability. Therefore, this must be taken into consideration when dry hopping.

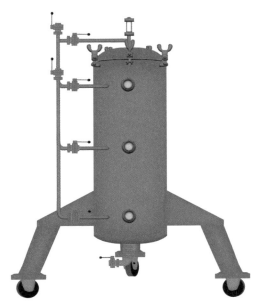

Figure 112: A device for hopping beer on the cold side

Craft brewers employ a variety of methods and devices to impart hop aroma to beer. Some breweries use a small tank, in which they create a slurry of pellets and de-aerated, sterile chilled brewing liquor. Larger, specially built tanks are equipped with an agitator and are designed to eliminate air (purgeable, therefore, more hygienic and lower oxygen). This can be transferred to the maturation tank ahead of the green beer. The dilution should be minimal but would need to be taken into account in the brewhouse. After a day or two, the spent hops are drawn off the bottom of the cone daily until they have mostly been removed from the tank. The beer may have to be centrifuged at the end of maturation.

The dry hopping devices are known variously as hop rockets, hop cannons, hop torpedoes and hop guns, some of which they have constructed themselves. They share a common purpose and design: to inject hop essential oils into beer over a short time period with fewer hops. Some are even automated. These devices allow heavily dry hopped beers to be brewed in large-scale production. By circulating green beer through a bed of hops or pushing hop pellets into tanks full of green beer, these devices provide an alternative to dry hopping with a net or by other means. Oxygen uptake would need to be strenuously avoided when running beer through such a device, meaning they have to be thoroughly and carefully purged with inert gas. Hops are expensive and these methods require fewer hops than conventional dry hopping methods. If pellets are to be pushed into a tank, hard corners should be avoided, if possible. The piping should be more similar to the piping found in facilities where, for instance, bulk grain is moved around pneumatically with wider diameters and long, gentle 90° curves. Pellets should be pushed with as little pressure as possible into a tank.

'Hop creep'

Hop additions on the cold side can cause something colloquially known as 'hop creep', which results in the production of more alcohol and CO_2 in the dry hopped beer, if the yeast is still active.

Research into this phenomenon has revealed that hops actually contain amylases that can hydrolyse certain carbohydrates ordinarily unable to be metabolised by yeast. Hops, as it turns out, are a source of minute quantities of fermentable sugar, which can also be metabolised by any yeast still active and in suspension in the dry hopped beer. The cell count of the yeast in suspension and the temperature of the dry hopped beer play a role in the extent of the 'hop creep'. Thus, the fermentable extract in the malt is not the only source of extract, though hops do not contain very much.

Results include over-carbonation and/or gushing in bottle conditioned beer; thus, 'hop creep' may be a safety hazard.

Diacetyl in beer

As fermentation begins to slow, brewers monitor the diacetyl level to get some idea of a beer's maturity, because diacetyl serves as an indicator substance for a host of aroma compounds found in maturing beer. Young beer or 'green beer' as it is known, contains perceptible levels of diacetyl, most prominent among the green beer aroma compounds due to its low sensory threshold and characteristic buttery, butterscotch flavour/aroma. Diacetyl, otherwise known as the VDK 2,3-butanedione, is generally unwelcome in most beers, though at levels right at the sensory threshold it can add fullness or a rounded maltiness to beer, as evinced by some Bohemian pilsners. Yeast must be in suspension for the green beer flavour to disappear entirely. Yeast that flocculate early and 'don't finish the job' so to speak, can produce beer with undesirable levels of diacetyl and other green beer aroma compounds. Reduction of diacetyl is, in fact, one of the primary objectives of the traditional lagering of bottom-fermented beers. When maturing beer was stored in ice cellars, fine temperature control was not possible. After transferring the beer to barrels in the cellar, diacetyl reduction was fairly slow going since temperatures dropped gently over time to near or below freezing. Cellarmen allowed the beer, therefore, to rest for eight to 12 weeks after fermentation was finished to give the yeast enough time to digest the green beer aroma compounds and to establish the subtly fine character of an extensively lagered beer. Nowadays, each fermentation/maturation tank often has its own temperature control, and thus a so-called 'diacetyl rest' can be carried out.

This involves allowing the green beer to warm up slightly towards the end of fermentation, thus increasing the rapidity with which yeast eliminate the diacetyl. As top-fermenting yeast are already working at higher temperatures, simply permitting the temperature to remain at the same level is sufficient to bring about the same result.

Puzzled brewers have been known to ask: "Why is there no diacetyl in my beer during maturation, but it's in my beer after filtering and packaging?"

Diacetyl is not created directly by yeast. Rather, yeast generate another compound (α-acetolactate) that turns into diacetyl entirely outside of the cell without the help of yeast (through oxidative decarboxylation). Once this has occurred, however, the yeast cells absorb and metabolise the diacetyl, releasing another compound (acetoin) that, in turn, is assimilated and degraded by yeast as well.

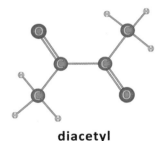

diacetyl

Figure 113: A molecule of diacetyl

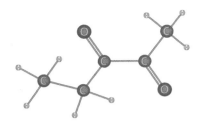

2,3-pentandione

Figure 114: A molecule of 2,3-pentanedione

Both diacetyl and a related compound 2,3-pentanedione, known collectively as vicinal diketones (VDKs) have low flavour thresholds. Yeast create intermediate compounds that turn into diacetyl and 2,3-pentanedione over the course of synthesizing amino acids (valine, leucine, isoleucine).

Diacetyl is reduced first to acetoin and then to 2,3 butanediol; both are characterised by descriptors such as sweet, buttery, creamy, dairy, fatty and fruity, but their flavour thresholds in beer are higher, so they largely remain undetected, though they may affect the overall sensorial impression of the beer in a synergistic manner.

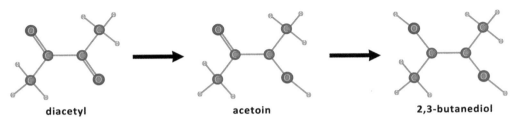

diacetyl   acetoin   2,3-butanediol

Figure 115: The molecules diacetyl, acetoin and 2,3 butanediol

The only reason diacetyl is an issue in beer, is because the human olfactory apparatus is so sensitive to it. Diacetyl can be detected in some light lager beers at approximately 0.05 ppm, and 2,3-pentanedione at a threshold about 10 times higher. As mentioned, diacetyl is reminiscent of butter or butterscotch, while 2,3-pentanedione is cloying, honey-like but can also be buttery and creamy. Both are eliminated by yeast through a 'diacetyl rest'. The compounds finally released into the beer is 2,3-butanediol and 2,3-pentanediol. These two 'diones' need to be reduced to their respective 'diols' by yeast. Why? Because the 'diols' have a much higher flavour threshold than the 'diones'.

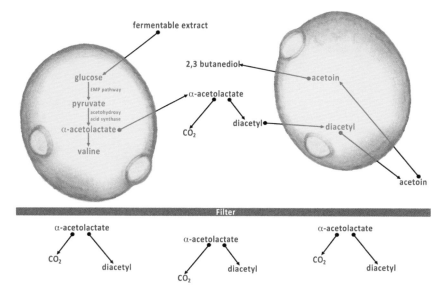

Figure 116: Valine biosynthesis in yeast and diacetyl reduction during maturation versus in filtered beer

Once the yeast has removed itself from the beer through flocculation or been removed through filtration, it is not present to enzymatically degrade the diacetyl to 2,3-butanediol. Therefore, diacetyl remains in the beer above the sensory threshold.

In order to bring diacetyl down to manageable levels in bottom-fermented beers by the end of maturation, brewers should keep the following in mind:

- **Free amino nitrogen:** Supplying yeast cells with enough FAN so that they do not need to synthesise substantial quantities of amino acids (primarily valine) may help in reducing the total amount of diacetyl generated during fermentation.
- **Zinc:** This mineral is essential for the overall good health of the yeast.
- **pH:** The pH of the wort and green beer during fermentation and maturation should not be too high.
- **Living, vital cells:** The living to dead ratio of cells should be as high as possible, and the yeast should possess a high vitality.

- **Cell count:** There needs to be a sufficient number of cells during maturation to eliminate the diacetyl in the green beer.
- **Strain selection:** Some yeast strains produce more diacetyl than others independent of the conditions during fermentation and maturation.
- **Temperature:** A diacetyl rest – allowing the temperature to rise slightly at the end of fermentation – will cause the yeast to eliminate diacetyl more quickly. Cooling the green beer down to maturation temperatures too rapidly or too early stresses the yeast as well, and this can cause them to settle out prematurely.
- **Aeration:** By aerating the yeast, the cells receive sufficient amounts of oxygen which reduces the generation of diacetyl.

Forced diacetyl testing

For those seeking a simple method for checking diacetyl levels in beer, a sample of beer (sealed) can be placed in a water bath at a temperature of 60–70 °C for approximately 20 minutes. Allow the beer to cool to room temperature, remove the lid and smell it for the presence of diacetyl. The method of simply allowing the beer to warm up to room temperature without heating does not always deliver reliable results.

Cylindroconical tanks

Most modern fermentation and maturation tanks are cylindroconical in shape. The cone is designed to allow yeast and suspended solids to sediment out to a central outlet at the bottom of the vessel. Cylindroconical tanks should <u>always</u> be equipped with cone cooling in order to better control the temperature during fermentation and maturation. In the examples below (fig. 117), the coolant in the tank on the left is maintaining a fermentation temperature tank of around 9 °C (the temperature probe is on the left side of the tank at the top of the cone). Due to the density of water, keeping beer cool during maturation is almost impossible without a jacket in the cone. Water, and thus wort and beer, are densest at 4 °C; therefore, even though the cooling jackets on the cylindrical part of the tank have a temperature of around 0 °C, the beer in the cone is around 4 °C.

With a cooling jacket in the cone, the situation pictured in figure 118 is rectified and the maturing beer can be cooled to the proper maturation temperature.

However, even with a jacket in the cone, sedimented yeast should be frequently drawn off the bottom to avoid unpleasant aromas and flavours. The yeast at the base of the cone produces heat (fig. 118), which accelerates degradation processes through the enzymes present in the dead cells. The temperature probe may read 0 °C, but the temperature at the bottom of the cone, where yeast cells are undergoing enzymatic degradation, is much higher (6 °C or even higher). As mentioned above, this degradation process is known as autolysis and produces characteristic off-flavours in the finished beer. After primary fermentation has peaked, it is essential that the yeast settled out at the bottom of the cone be regularly purged from the tank.

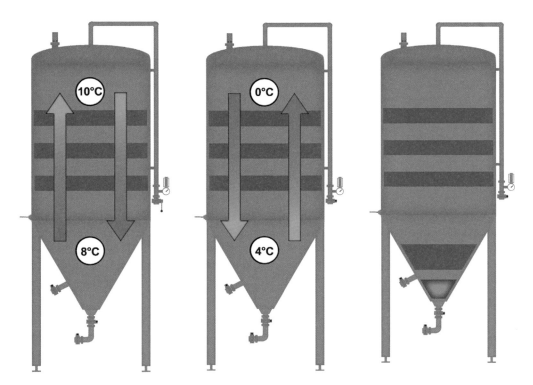

Figure 117: Changes to the density of beer during fermentation and maturation in CCTs

Figure 118: The base of the cone in a CCT where autolysis may occur under adverse conditions

pH

The pH of the finished beer should be less than 4.5, preferably between 4.2–4.3. If souring is performed in the brewhouse in the production of sour beers, dropping the pH to a low value prior to fermentation is not advisable. A pH of < 3.5 may be detrimental to yeast.

Temperature

Top-fermenting strains prefer temperatures of 17–24 °C, although some strains, like saison yeast or kveik, may perform better at slightly higher temperatures (up to 28 °C or even higher). Too high, and phenolic odours and other off-flavours will become evident, making the beer unpalatable.

Bottom-fermenting strains ('lager yeast') function at lower temperatures (8–14 °C).

Sulphurous compounds in beer

Thiols are also known as mercaptans and possess an -SH group bound to an organic molecule. They are found in beer and can be positive or negative. Thiols can be detected easily due to their low sensory threshold. Thiols are fermentation by-products and contribute to the fruity aroma and flavour of some white wines. Other thiols are derived from malt and hops. The thiols in hops, though poorly understood, contribute to the fruity nuances in hop essential oils.

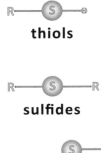

Figure 119: Sulphurous compounds in beer

Table 12: Sulphurous compounds and their flavour descriptors

Sulphurous compound	Descriptor
4-mercapto-4-methylpentan-2-one (4MMP)	*Ribes*, blackcurrant
3-mercaptohexan-1-ol (3MH)	rhubarb, citrus, exotic fruit
3-mercaptohexyl acetate (3MHA)	passionfruit, guava

There are other thiols, often grouped under the umbrella term for the off-flavour 'mercaptans', that possess unpleasant sulphurous odours like raw sewage, cat box, garlic, onions, rotten eggs, cabbage or natural gas. These can also be fermentation by-products or derived from malt or hops, but some of the worst offenders are encountered when yeast undergoes autolysis.

Dimethyl sulphide

As discussed above, though the primary source for DMS in beer is on the hot side in the brewhouse, DMS can be formed through the enzymatic reduction of dimethyl sulphoxide (DMSO) and during the Maillard reactions through a combination of glucose and with sulphurous amino acids. The arrows in figure 121 indicate the relative amounts of DMS produced through these reactions.

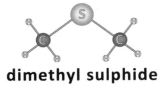

Figure 120: Dimethyl sulphide (DMS)

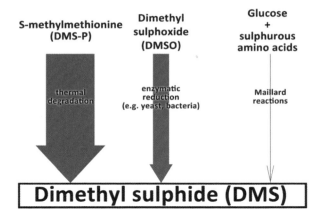

Figure 121: Sources for DMS in beer

Lightstruck beer

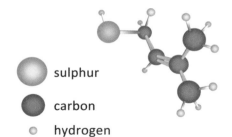

3-methyl-2-butene-1-thiol

sulphur

carbon

hydrogen

Figure 122: 3-methyl-2-butene-1-thiol

One particular thiol is especially prevalent in packaged beer and the bane of anyone wanting to bottle their beer in clear or green glass. The reason beer should be stored in a dark place, is that clear and green glass bottles provide no protection against exposure to light, especially at ultraviolet wavelengths which are the most damaging. However, even in brown bottles UV rays can alter a beer's composition. The only bottles capable of fully blocking UV are manufactured with a protective coating. Though numerous chemical reactions deleterious to the aroma and flavour of beer occur through exposure to UV light, the most noticeable are the ones that arise in conjunction with a certain group of hop-derived compounds. Light at the blue end of the visible spectrum and beyond it in the ultraviolet at wavelengths ranging from 350 to 500 nm changes isohumulones to 3-methyl-2-butene-1-thiol (MBT) in the presence of sulphurous compounds and riboflavin (vitamin B2), which acts as a photosensitiser. A diagramme of an MBT molecule is pictured in figure 122 and is one of the thiols present in the secretions of American skunks (fig. 123), hence the name 'skunked' for lightstruck beer. For those who have never been to the Americas and smelled the scent of a skunk, the odour of these small mammals' secretions exhibits a distinctively sulphurous note accompanied by other unpleasant volatile compounds. Sometimes, those unfamiliar with this odour confuse 'catty' with 'skunky'. It is apparent upon smelling the scent of skunk why it works as a defence mechanism for these animals and why anything approaching this odour would be undesirable in beer. MBT also has a very low odour detection threshold in beer (30 ng/l or ppt).

Apparently, two other compounds with an odour very similar to MBT have been discovered in beer as well, are also products of photodegradation and likewise contribute to the 'skunked' beer aroma. This reaction can occur rapidly enough that over the course of drinking a litre of beer from a clear glass mug on a sunny day in a beer garden, this off-flavour will be perceptible in the beer before one can finish it. Thus, beer should not be placed in the sun, even in brown bottles. Tetrahydro-iso-α-acids and hexahydro-iso-α-acids, otherwise known as 'tetra' and 'hexa' hop products, have been created to improve the light stability of beer by removing the double bonds on their side chains through hydrogenation. These hop products allow breweries to continue to use clear and green glass bottles with some level of impunity, though they do not prevent the other kinds of damage to beer brought about by UV radiation.

Figure 123: Lightstruck or 'skunky' beer

Sulphur dioxide

Raw materials, brewhouse processes, fermentation by-products, and additives, such as the reductones from the Maillard reactions (see below), phenolic compounds, vitamins, like vitamin C in fruit or in ascorbic acid additions prior to filling, serve as antioxidants capable of capturing oxygen. They

Figure 124: Sulphur dioxide (SO_2)

also prevent or otherwise hinder reactions with free radicals. Among these reducing agents is sulphur dioxide (SO_2), which is produced during fermentation in the synthesis of sulphurous amino acids. It is present in beer in a bound or free form. In the bound form, SO_2 can be tied to various organic molecules, such as carbonyl compounds. SO_2 is oxidised to form sulphate. Therefore, employing yeast which produces SO_2 during fermentation is beneficial for the flavour stability of one's finished beer. SO_2 in concentrations around 10 mg/l (or higher) have been shown to increase the flavour stability of beer.

Hydrogen sulphide

A number of bacteria reduce inorganic sulphate to sulphide in order to meet their needs for sulphur, since it is a key element, along with carbon, hydrogen, nitrogen, oxygen and phosphorous, for life on the planet. Bacteria belonging to the genus *Zymomonas*, such as *Z. mobilis*, employ this metabolic pathway, which results in the creation of hydrogen sulphide (H_2S) gas. (Refer to the section on beer-spoiling bacteria below.) This volatile compound imparts an extremely unpleasant odour to the beer, reminiscent of rotten eggs, sewers and swamps.

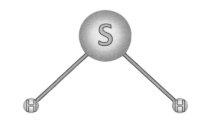

Figure 125: Hydrogen sulphide (H_2S)

Fermentation, maturation and ageing in barrels

How are wooden barrels used in the brewing industry?

Beer all over Europe has been stored in wooden barrels and casks for millennia, but these vessels were made of very dense wood or were more often pitched, meaning they were covered in hot tree resin that dried when cooled to effectively separate the beer from the wood. This kept the yeasts in the wood, which are practically impossible to completely eliminate from barrels, away from the beer.

Not all mixed microbial fermentations are the same. Some are conventional, i.e. with *Saccharomyces* species of brewing yeast, and are only performed by a mix of microbes during maturation. Others are mixed yet inoculated with a slurry of known microbes. While still others are fermented and/or matured with microbes that exist in the ambient environment, primarily those in the wood of barrels or foeders. A rare, yet traditional process, which has experienced a revival in recent years, originated in Belgium and involves fermentation and/or maturation with the microbial communities living in the wood of barrels. After the essence of the wine or spirit has been extracted from the barrel, the naked oak is still good at harbouring microorganisms. This is a tradition dating back centuries. Barrels contain or are seeded with wild microbial communities, which quickly adapt, perish or evolve into a unique set of 'house' microorganisms. These organisms ferment the wort racked into the barrel at temperatures ranging from close to freezing to the low twenties (°C), depending upon the location and whether the cellar is heated/cooled. Alternatively, the wort can first be fermented in stainless steel tanks, and subsequently, the green beer is matured in wood, preferably. The temperature requirements can vary during maturation as well, depending upon whether or not additional wort, sugar or fermenting green beer is added, which would require fermentation temperatures until maturation commences. In cellars without climate control, lactic acid bacteria flourish in the summer, while yeast better tolerate the cooler temperatures. Lambic fermentation, which solely depends upon ambient microorganisms, lasts approximately two to three years in barrels and can generally be divided into four stages.

Table 13: The four general stages of spontaneous fermentation

The four general stages of spontaneous fermentation as it occurs in lambic production		
1.	Enterobacteria	Several types of acid are produced (lactic, acetic, succinic acid). The pH drops by 0.5 rapidly. By the end of the first month, alcohol eliminates the enterobacteria in suspension.
2.	Yeasts	*Debaryomyces hansenii*, common in dairy and meat products, will readily metabolise lactic acid but not sugars commonly found in wort. *Hanseniaspora uvarum* consumes proteins from unmodified grains (clarity); *Saccharomyces cerevisiae* produce most of the ethanol and ale-like esters; casks begin fobbing.
3.	Lactic and acetic acid bacteria	Further acidification is crucial for character; exopolysaccharides (EPS) are formed (ropiness), eliminated later by *Brettanomyces* species.
4.	Yeasts	*Brettanomyces* species *bruxellensis* and *lambicus* 'clean up' and attenuate the beer; no dextrins remain (thin body); synthesis of aromatic, fruity, 'winey' esters; likewise an increase in 'goaty' fatty acids, which should remain low. Attenuation by *Brettanomyces* is higher in the presence of *Pediococcus*.

Lambic fermentation and maturation proceeds as presented in figure 126. One inoculated with higher cell counts of yeast and bacteria would follow a similar pattern. It might not take as long, but the successive waves of microorganisms nevertheless do take some time:

These practices are currently being enthusiastically explored by craft brewers and some have yielded excellent results, including those with beers matured on local fruit.

Newly constructed or acquired wooden vessels can be inoculated with a 'soup' from a tried-and-true vessel or by purchasing a mix of microorganisms to create such a soup. If a barrel or foeder has produced good beers, then some of the fermenting liquid or the lees from that vessel can be used to inoculate a new one. This may require several 'seedings'. In acquiring used barrels, careful inspection, including smelling the inside through the bung hole, is advisable. Barrels with unpleasant odours should be avoided.

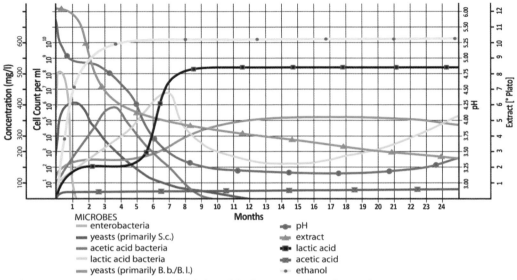

Figure 126: Lambic fermentation dynamics

Smaller barrels or barrels made of more porous wood allow higher rates of micro-oxygenation. One way to reduce micro-oxygenation is to simply leave the pellicle formed by the microorganisms on the surface of the beer intact, but this does not prevent the microorganisms under the pellicle from accessing any oxygen in the headspace. Naturally, the pellicle makes it impossible to sample the beer from above. However, by drilling a small hole in the head of the barrel and plugging it with a stainless steel nail, small samples can be taken from the barrel without disturbing the pellicle on top.

For this reason, the type of wood and the size of the barrel, at least in part, can determine what fermentation by-products *Brettanomyces* species produce. Some *Brettanomyces* species seem to be uniquely suited – perhaps even adapted – for life in oaken barrels. These yeast species tend to work very slowly over many months. In lambic fermentation, *Brettanomyces* does not attain peak cell counts per millilitre until about the eight-month mark. The *Brettanomyces* strains in lambic can flourish under aerobic and anaerobic conditions, a characteristic consistent with their capacity for forming a pellicle on the surface of beer inside the barrel. Brewers of sour beers generally avoid disturbing the pellicle, as it serves to protect the beer, since the acetic acid bacteria in the barrel oxidise sugars and ethanol to produce acetic acid during fermentation.

The influence of *Brettanomyces* on beer during maturation varies on a spectrum from sweet pineapple aromas (usually in younger beers) to those often described as horsey and barnyard or peppery, herbal, clove and cinnamon-like (in those aged somewhat longer). However, aromas that are much less favourable can arise, especially when beer is matured too long. These are musty and mouldy or are reminiscent of Band-Aid, burnt wood, antiseptic or even mothballs. Though they can develop during fermentation, new oak barrels and smoke-tainted raw materials can also be the source for unpleasant smelling volatile phenols.

One reason *Brettanomyces* are used in the maturation of beer is because they can consume dextrins, further protecting the beer from microbial contamination and increasing the flavour stability. This is most effective if the original gravity of the wort is above 14.5 °P. *Brettanomyces* strains can flourish under aerobic and anaerobic conditions. In the presence of higher oxygen concentrations, *Brettanomyces* generates more acetic acid (the acid in vinegar) and less alcohol, whereas the opposite is true with lower concentrations of oxygen.

Brettanomyces bruxellensis is the predominant species in Brussels, while *Brettanomyces lambicus* can also be found further afield around the Pajottenland, homeland of lambic. *B. lambicus* ferments lambic, Flanders red and *Oud Bruin*, while *B. bruxellensis* produces an earthy, horse blanket aroma and, for example, performs the bottle conditioning in the famous Trappist ale Orval. They probably belong to the same species and are different strains.

Apparently, *B. anomalus* has been isolated in stouts from Ireland and elsewhere in the British Isles. Its influence on beer has been described as delicate and slightly fruity (pineapple). *B. claussenii* creates more subtle aromas and flavours than other species, though it is most likely a strain of *B. anomalus*. In the past, beers brewed with dark malts and hard water, such as London-brewed porter, which were not conducive to higher hop rates and were transported on the high seas, seemed to have been preserved by a few genera of lactic acid bacteria and *Brettanomyces* (primarily *B. claussenii*).

Brettanomyces exhibits a range of metabolic activity crucial in producing their unique flavour profile. The enzymes, α-glucosidase, β-glucosidase, esterase and vinylphenol reductase play an important role during maturation. *Brettanomyces* species are among the yeast that bring about the high levels of attenuation typically found in lambic and other beers brewed with it, because this yeast exhibits *α*-glucosidase activity, which enables it to hydrolyse wort dextrins.

β-Glucosidase is an enzyme capable of degrading the disaccharide cellobiose, a carbohydrate resulting from the toasting of the oaken staves. Researchers have not been able to culture any *Brettanomyces* species living in lambic barrels capable of hydrolysing cellobiose, meaning that they do not possess the enzyme β-glucosidase, as the wine-spoiling species do.

B. custersii has shown a propensity for hydrolysing glycosidically-bound compounds derived from hops, which

Table 14: Phenolic compounds produced by *Brettanomyces* yeast and their aroma descriptors

Volatile phenols	Descriptor
4-ethyl catechol	phenolic, medicinal
4-ethyl guaiacol	spicy, clove-like
4-ethyl phenol	medicinal, horse blanket
4-vinyl guaiacol	clove-like
4-vinyl phenol	phenolic, medicinal

contribute to the flavour of the matured beer. Likewise, the glycosidase activity has been implicated in freeing flavour-active compounds present in cherries crucial to the flavour profile of Belgian kriek.

The esterase activity produces ethyl esters (e.g. ethyl acetate and ethyl lactate) and hydrolyses the acetate esters (e.g. isoamyl acetate and phenethyl acetate). *Brettanomyces* can better hydrolyse acetate esters than non-acetate esters; thus, the ester balance is skewed in beers matured by these yeasts.

The vinylphenol reductase activity produces the vinyl phenolic compounds that are characteristic of beers matured with *Brettanomyces* (refer to the POF test below). Some of these phenolic compounds and their aromas are presented just above.

Moreover, some *Brettanomyces* species share a relationship with lactic acid bacteria. Evidence indicates that there may be a relationship between *Brettanomyces* and *Pediococcus*, in which they require one another's presence for mixed microbial fermentations to be successful. 'Ropiness' can be attributable to *Pediococcus damnosus* var. *viscosus*. This phenomenon occurs in 'sick' beers when long, stringy threads of exopolysaccharides (e.g. dextrans, levans) are formed by bacteria. Other microbes known to cause ropiness are species belonging to *Acetobacter*, *Leuconostoc* and *Lactococcus*. Ropiness is extremely unpleasant in terms of mouthfeel, but the flavour and aroma of the beer remain unaffected by it. *Brettanomyces* may be able to consume or otherwise break down the polypeptides associated with ropiness. Another advantage of this relationship is that *Brettanomyces* can eliminate the diacetyl produced by *Pediococcus*.

Experience among brewers who employ mixed microbes has shown that once they are established in barrels or other wooden vessels like foeders, they are usually quite stable.

Wine and spirits barrels

Barrels have become almost ubiquitous in craft brewing for a variety of reasons. Rather than buying new barrels, breweries often prefer retired wine or spirits barrels, because they impart a new dimension to the character of the beer, unachievable in any other way. Racking beer into barrels so that they become infused with the essence of the previous occupant, such as allowing an imperial stout to age for several months in a bourbon barrel, is a practice without precedence, solely invented by craft brewers. Ageing in previously occupied barrels can involve secondary fermentation but wine and spirits barrels are generally employed simply to transfer the flavours and aromas of the previous occupant to the beer.

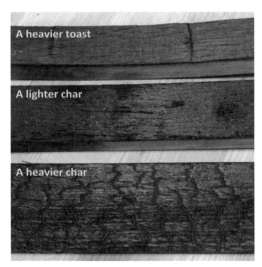

Figure 127: Toasted and charred barrels staves
Photo: *Yuseff Cherney*

One important aspect of barrel maturation is the slow, constant diffusion of oxygen through the pores of the wood, known as natural microoxygenation. Though oxygen is the brewer's enemy, craft brewers produce high gravity beer, ferment it in a tank and then mature it in barrels, similar to wine and spirits, like whiskey. These beverages spend time in barrels because the flavour of the wood is integral to their character. Some wines are aged in toasted barrels, in order to bring about desirable changes in colour, structure and aroma. The complexity and stability of some wines benefit from compounds derived from oak. The same is true for spirits. 'Brown liquors' are the spirits produced by ageing on wood, and these include scotch, bourbon, rye whiskey, brandy (such as cognac), añejo, tequila and rum. Generally speaking, wine barrels are toasted, and spirits barrels are charred. Figure 127 depicts various levels of toasting and charring. This, of course, will have an effect on the aroma and flavour of the beer stored in the barrel.

What does the charring contribute to the sensory profile of these beverages? Flavours derived from the wood include terpenes and lactones. Yeast alter compounds extracted from the wood to produce terpenes, which are characterised as 'tea' and 'tobacco'. Terpenes are familiar to brewers because they are prominent in hops. Lactones are derived from the lipids in the wood. The gamma-lactones are found in sweet and creamy foods, such as in bread, peaches, coconut, roasted nuts and butter. White wine and whiskey drinkers know them well. The compound cis-β-methyl-γ-octalactone has been

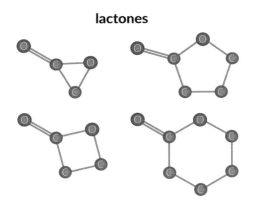

lactones

Figure 128: Various lactones

dubbed the 'whiskey lactone' since it is prominent in the nose of oak aged spirits. The following compounds have also been identified in beer aged in whiskey barrels by means of gas chromatography: 4-hydroxy-2-butanone, 2-acetylfuran, butyrolactone, 2,3-butandiol and decanoic acid. By charring the oak, spicy notes and those reminiscent of cloves, coal tar and smoke are created. Slow oxidation of the beverage in the barrel eliminates off-aromas, such as rubbery odours. The astringent tannins derived from the wood become oxidised, producing alluring fragrances. For barrel-ageing without fermentation or maturation with microbes, some brewers prefer extreme fluctuations in temperature while others tend towards the opposite. The level of humidity is also a crucial factor, since more humidity means that less moisture will be evaporated from the barrel and vice versa. The physical changes are understood, and these factors ultimately come down to the brewer's philosophy and the transformations the brewers wish to bring about in their barrel-aged products.

Brewers have been experimenting with oenological methods for barrel-aged beers, such as techniques involving fractional blending (inspired by the 'solera' method) or *sur lie*. Fractional blending allows brewers to set up continuous sour beer production. Like some vintners, brewers of beers with more acidity and perhaps late fruit additions are choosing to mature their beers for longer periods on yeast lees with occasional stirring, i.e. the *sur lie* technique. Though yeast undergo autolysis, the results are considered desirable because of the beer's enhanced body (creamier, richer) along with its increased complexity and depth of flavour (fruit, wood, hazelnut). However, as with autolysis during fermentation, this technique can also give rise to unpleasant sulphurous compounds (hydrogen sulphide, thiols (mercaptans) and fatty acids (old yeast, meaty). Thus, it may be prudent with most beers to mature only with the yeast in suspension.

Table 15 provides some examples for pairing beers with used wine and spirits barrels:

Beer	Barrel
red fruit beers, Belgian ale, sour beers	red wine
pale bock, wheat beer, pale *Weizenbock*, saison	white wine, tequila
barley wine, dark bock	rum
Scotch ale, old ale, dark bock	whiskey, bourbon
dark fruit beers, dark *Weizenbock*, stout, porter	whiskey, bourbon, port or brandy

Wine barrels tend to pair well with sour beers, while spirits barrels are better suited for more conventionally fermented beers, though this is not always the case. Beers with a higher ABV tend to be those set aside for barrel ageing. Some have an ABV as low as 6%, but most are around 8–9% ABV.

Finding suitable barrels

A good nose is the best tool for selecting barrels. One has to think about what problems a barrel might cause in the brewery.

Checklist for acquiring retired barrels:

1. Are the barrels tightly sealed? Barrels that are not bunged, that is, those not sealed with closures, may need to be avoided.
2. Unbung the barrel and smell it. Are there any off-odours?
3. How long has the barrel been empty?
4. What was the previous occupant?
5. Have they been sulphured?
6. Where were the barrels stored? Inside or outside?
7. Look outside and inside for cracks or any other fatal flaws. Are any of the staves, cants and hoops damaged?
8. Check for pests, like wood-boring insects, mice, etc.
9. One should also be wary of low-priced barrels.

It is best to use freshly emptied wine or spirits barrels. Barrels newly drained of their spirits usually do not require cleaning due to the sterilising effects of the concentrated alcohol. A freshly emptied barrel that has been rinsed with hot water and can subsequently pass the 'smell test' can usually be filled right away with no further cleaning. A barrel empty for over two months or so has to be cleaned following the same procedures one would employ for new barrels, that is, hot rinsing (80 °C) followed by ozone or a solution of ⅔ to ⅓ sodium metabisulphite and citric acid (pH ≈ 3.2). Cleaners and sanitisers for barrels have to be food grade. There are other more extreme cleaning procedures for barrels, like steam or sodium percarbonate, but for small breweries these may require too much effort. The sodium metabisulphite and citric acid solution can sit in the barrels while they are empty to inhibit microbial contamination. Making a stronger solution is not recommended as it may taint the beverage stored in it.

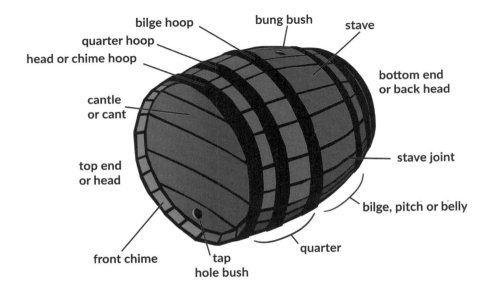

Figure 129: Parts of a barrel

Blending beers fermented, matured and aged in barrels

This is purely sensory and requires extensive experience, so brewers must practice often to maintain the skill (refer to the section sensory analysis below). Since each barrel contains its own microcosm of microbes, when blending to create a beer to package for sale, brewers should keep in mind that blending is about a quest for balance. This practice is not only applicable with barrel-aged beers; blending is a valuable tool because it allows brewers to smooth out any rough edges.

Literature and further reading

Cantwell, D., Bouckaert, P., *Wood & Beer – A Brewer's Guide*. Brewers' Publications, 2016

De Keersmaecker, J.; *The Mystery of Lambic*. Scientific American, August 1996

Guinard, J.; Lambic. Brewers Publications, 1990

McGreger, C., McGreger, N. *Beers of the World – Lambic*. Brauwelt International V 2019

McGreger, C., McGreger, N., *Bacteria, Brueghel, Barrels, Blending and Brett* (Parts 1–5) Brauwelt International II–VI, 2018

McGreger, C., McGreger, N., *Barrels of Beer – A New Perspective on an Old Craft* (Parts 1–5). Brauwelt International III, 2016 – I, 2017

O'Neill, P. *Cellarmanship*. Campaign for Real Ale Ltd, 5th edition, 2010

Steensels, J., Daenen L., Malcorps, P., Derdelinckx, G., Verachtert, H., Verstrepen, K., *Brettanomyces yeasts—From spoilage organisms to valuable contributors to industrial fermentations*. International Journal of Food Microbiology 206 (2015) 24–38

Winter, I.; *Investigations of Possible Location Dependence of Unique Microflora in Lambic Beer*. School of Life Sciences, Heriot Watt, 2013–2014

Quality control points: maturation

- gravity/attenuation/alcohol content
- temperature
- pH
- yeast (flocculation, sedimentation, removal)
- microbiological status (wild yeast, beer spoilers)
- carbonation
- dissolved oxygen
- visual inspection
- aroma/flavour
- bittering units
- VDK and other green beer congeners below the flavour threshold
- minimise oxygen uptake (tank transfer, dry hopping)
- tank geometry

CLARIFICATION

In order to obtain clear or 'bright' beer as it is known, a variety of processes are at a brewer's disposal. Clarification is defined as the removal from suspension of particulate matter, yeast and other compounds associated with turbidity through aggregation and sedimentation, centrifugation, filtration or other means.

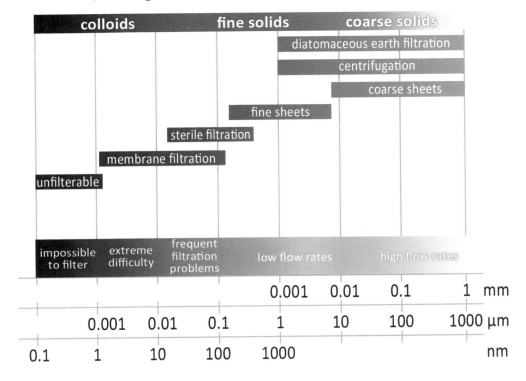

Figure 130: Filtration and pore sizes

Maturation/Conditioning

This requires patience and temperatures close to freezing (refer to the section on maturation under the brewing process). A maturation tank is usually horizontal so that the sediment does not need to travel far in the beer to settle out.

The sedimentation rate is roughly equivalent to the square of the particle size, meaning that a particle 10 times the size of another particle will fall to the bottom of the tank 100 times faster. This is the reason that in some breweries finings are added prior to packaging their beer. The finings are positively and negatively charged and attract the particles suspended in the beer whether they are yeast, proteins, polyphenols, etc.

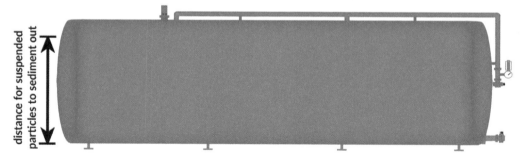

Figure 131: A horizontal maturation tank

Centrifugation

Centrifuges, also known as separators, can be installed between the fermentation and maturation tanks to reduce the yeast in suspension. This reduces the yeast cell count in the green beer, thus lowering the risk of autolysis in the maturation tank. Any fining agents and the particulate matter adhering to them can also be removed from the beer with a centrifuge. Nowadays, centrifuges are even equipped with optical sensors that can measure the turbidity, allowing brewers to adjust it to a fairly precise value.

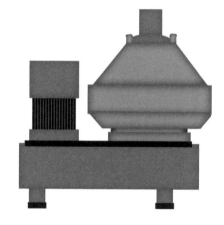

Figure 132: A centrifuge

Centrifuges are finding application in small craft breweries where hop-heavy, slightly hazy beers are produced. Less hop oil is lost compared to filtration with diatomaceous earth, and beer losses are lower as well. Craft brewers find the overall sensory impression of their beers to be more satisfactory when centrifuged. Diatomaceous earth is an excellent filter aid for some beers – those that are less infused with hop oils. Given that centrifuges are less expensive to operate and the flow rates are more rapid than diatomaceous earth filtration, many craft breweries are choosing this form of clarification over others.

However, in craft breweries producing beers that need to be bright, such as a pilsner, conventional filtration immediately downstream from a centrifuge is also practical because with a great deal of the particulate matter eliminated, the length of time a filter can remain in operation can be extended. This cuts the amount of filter aids needed, and also reduces beer losses. Beer can even be recovered from surplus yeast with a centrifuge.

Filtration

The objectives of filtration are to clarify the beer in order to make it more visually appealing and to reduce the amount of yeast in suspension as well as perhaps some of the bacteria. A variety of filters for application in breweries exist; for instance, horizontal or vertical leaf filters, candle filters, crossflow filters or plate filters perhaps used in conjunction with various filter aids.

The pressure in a filter must always be over the saturation pressure of the CO_2 in the beer. Of course, the pressure increases as filtration continues, since the pores become smaller. As the pressure increases so do the particles in the filtrate that might have remained adsorbed to the filter channels (see below). Thus, when the pressure reaches a high enough level that the turbidity of the beer begins to drop, then it is time to lower the volume of beer passing through the filter/increase the amount of filter aid per volume of beer – or simply start over again, if necessary.

If the temperature is allowed to rise from the maturation tank to the filter, the particles one wishes to remove through filtration can dissolve in the beer again. For this reason, some breweries set up a heat exchanger between the maturation tanks and the filter to keep the temperature of the beer low. This is especially applicable with bottom-fermented beers, which are lagered at sub-zero temperatures.

Types of filtration

The following figures depict the types of filtration commonly found in breweries.

Surface filtration

As the name implies, particles are only retained at the surface of a filter (e.g. sieving, fig. 133). When the particle size distribution is relatively uniform and the amount of solids in the feed is relatively low, such as downstream from a diatomaceous earth filter, surface filtration, like membrane filtration, is possible. Surface filtration requires a large surface area and is generally more expensive than depth filtration.

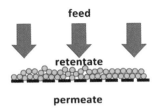

Figure 133: Surface filtration

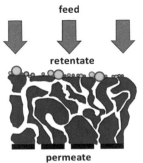

particles trapped on the surface of the filter bed

Figure 134: Particles trapped on the surface in depth filtration

Surface filtration can also occur with depth filtration, for instance during powder filtration. Particulate matter is retained on the surface (fig. 134).

Depth filtration

Depth filtration through entrapment

This occurs when particulate matter becomes wedged in a channel of the filter bed due to its size. The effective diameter of these particles is larger than a measurement would indicate due to Brownian motion.

Depth filtration through adsorption

Small particles will adhere to the sides of the pores in a filter bed by means of adsorption. One example of such particles in beer are the proteins that enhance the foam and mouthfeel but can also cause non-microbiological haze in packaged beer. In this case, neither too much nor too little should be removed.

Brewery filters

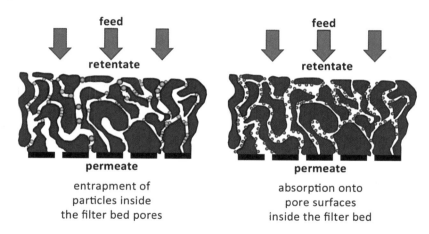

entrapment of
particles inside
the filter bed pores

Figure 135: Depth filtration
through entrapment

absorption onto
pore surfaces
inside the filter bed

Figure 136: Depth filtration
through adsorption

Plate filters

These filters can be used as the only means of filtration but are commonly employed downstream from another filter, since their flow rates are quite slow. If this is the case, the plate filter is referred to as the secondary or polishing filter, which removes the finer particles after the coarser ones are retained by the primary filter. Sheets, made of cellulose, cotton, glass or synthetic fibres, are sandwiched between plates which act as supports.

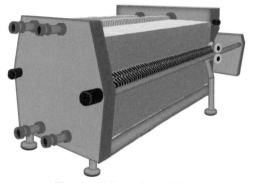

Figure 137: A sheet filter

Filter sheets are usually 3 to 4 mm thick and thus depth filtration is possible within the sheets. They can be single or two-stage (coarse and polish filtration). Plate filters can also be utilised in pre-coat filtration or be impregnated with substances that attract charged particles similar to how finings function.

Membrane filtration

The beer must be filtered prior to undergoing membrane filtration in order to eliminate coarser solids upstream from the membrane filter. Even so, being a type of surface filtration, filtering beer in this way can be difficult and expensive as the membranes often become fouled and must be cleaned. For microbiological stability, a pore size of ca. 0.45 μm is required to eliminate yeast and most beer spoilers, though the beer is not actually 'sterile' in a strict sense. Membrane filtration at this pore size or smaller is sometimes referred to as cold pasteurisation. Key constituents contributing to the sensorial impression of the beer are retained on the membrane in the process. Therefore, the overall impression of the beer may suffer but the thermal stress from tunnel pasteurisation can be avoided.

Pre-coat powder filtration

The most relevant filter aid used in powder filters for beer clarification is diatomaceous earth (the microscopic silica shells of algae), though others are available e.g. perlite, silica gel, cellulose, PVPP. Perlite (aluminium silicate), like diatomaceous earth, exhibits a large surface area; however, it is not created by single-celled algae but by volcanic processes. Both silica gel and PVPP (polyvinylpolypyrrolidone) target colloidal stability. Silica gel eliminates proteins in the beer, while PVPP, which can be washed with a hot solution of caustic and reused, removes polyphenols from the beer.

Even though filter manufacturers are attempting to move away from the use of diatomaceous earth for health and safety concerns as well as due to issues with disposal, a viable alternative has as yet been elusive. Prior to this or any filter aid being dosed into

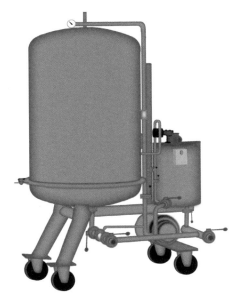

Figure 138: A horizontal leaf filter

and suspended in the beer, personnel should wear personal protective equipment, most especially a proper mask. The reason that alternatives to diatomaceous earth have not been generally adopted is that as a filter aid, it brings with it significant advantages:

- Due to its very high surface area (convoluted shells of tiny marine algae) and composition (silica does not dissolve in beer), it is highly effective and practical as a filter aid for beer.
- Diatomaceous earth is relatively inexpensive.
- The flow rate remains reasonably stable during the filtration process.

Powder filters are available with wire mesh supports arranged as horizontal or vertical leaf filters, as candle filters or, as mentioned, as plate filters in which the powder is supported by a sheet rather than a leaf or candle.

As exemplified by a diatomaceous earth filter, in order to facilitate depth filtration, the following is generally implemented in pre-coat powder filtration:

1. **Slurry**: A certain amount of the filter aid is thoroughly suspended in a given volume of beer or deaerated cold liquor in the mixing vessel next to the pressure vessel on the filter.
2. **Pre-coat**: A thin layer of the filter aid is evenly distributed across the leaves or septa within the pressure vessel of the filter. One can use a different grade of filter aid for pre-coating a filter prior to beginning the body feed.
3. **Body feed**: This refers to the in-line dosing of the filter aid in the beer. The amount dosed into the beer is dependent upon the grade of the filter aid and the turbidity level of the beer.

How the production process affects filtration

Poorly modified malt (β-glucans) and inadequate milling and mashing (low gelatinisation and starch solubility, positive iodine test) can produce wort that will be difficult to filter later. Excessive shearing forces throughout the entire process upstream from the filter can also negatively affect the filterability of beer.

Healthy yeast is crucial to producing filterable beer. Unhealthy yeast can contribute to problems during filtration if they are stressed (low cell count, high gravity wort, high fermentation temperatures). Stressed yeast or yeast undergoing autolysis may excrete compounds that hinder the filtration of beer. Glycogen is an energy storage compound made by yeast and is similar to amylopectin. It cannot be removed through filtration and can cause turbidity.

Vulnerabilities

As mentioned, one of the most important aspects in any part of cellaring, which includes the clarification of beer, is that oxygen should be kept out of the beer to the greatest extent possible. If de-aerated water is available, this would be ideal for purging the filter. Carbon dioxide or nitrogen gas can also be used. Keeping oxygen out of the beer prevents the oxidation of compounds in the beer but is also of great significance with regard to its microbiological stability.

Though the beer at this point should have a relatively low pH (≤ 4.5), contains alcohol and soluble bitter substances from the hops and is also mostly free of oxygen, the strictest care must be taken to keep microorganisms away from it. Some beer spoilers can create polysaccharides and generate slime which can block a filter at very low concentrations.

Approximately 5 to 6% of the volume of the beer will be lost during filtration.

| Pasteurisation

Beer is more stable than wort solely due to the simple sugars and other small molecules in it having been consumed by microorganisms which have pushed the air out of the substrate and lowered the pH with their fermentation by-products. Consuming the compounds in the wort and releasing metabolic products, in effect, turning the wort into beer, makes the liquid less appealing to yeast and bacteria or other microorganisms. However, in the microbial world, enemies lurk in every nook and cranny, even in the air. Beer can be further microbiologically stabilised by heating it to ensure that any microorganisms present have been killed prior to or after packaging. Breweries pasteurise with different purposes in mind. Some who may be sending their beer abroad or are transporting their beer under more arduous conditions need to tunnel pasteurise to be on the safe side, after the beer has been bottled. Others, who are confident in the hygienic condition of their filling line, want to perform a prophylactic treatment to ensure adequate stability for regional distribution with a flash pasteuriser.

The degree to which a beverage is heated is expressed in pasteurisation units.

A pasteurisation unit corresponds to heating a beverage to 60 °C and holding it at that temperature for 1 minute. Putting this into an equation one can express pasteurisation units as follows, where t is time and T is temperature:

$$PU = t \times 1.393^{(T - 60)}$$

Some beverages require heating to a higher level of pasteurisation units than others. Low-alcohol, non-alcoholic beers, beer-based beverages and soft drinks would need to be heated to a higher temperature, i.e. to an increased number of pasteurisation units, since the protective properties of normal beer, those discussed above, are lessened or almost non-existent in these beverages.

Typical minimum and maximum levels of pasteurisation for general beer styles are presented in table 16:

Table 16: Beer styles and pasteurisation units

Beer	PU min	PU max
pale and dark lager	15	25
ales and stouts	20	35
low-alcohol beer	40	60
non-alcoholic beer	80	120

Flash pasteurisation

A plate heat exchanger capable of withstanding the saturation pressure of the CO_2 in the beer at pasteurisation temperatures, normally between 68 °C and 72 °C, can be used during a process called flash pasteurisation. For a beer that contains 5.5 g of CO_2 per litre, a saturation pressure of 8.5 bar overpressure is required (fig. 141). Of course, the heat exchanger must be able to withstand pressures 4 to 5 bar above the maximum pressure required. One advantage of this process is that it has no negative effects on the beer's flavour profile, because the duration of the pasteurisation step is very short. The beer is heated only briefly, for just a few seconds. Another great advantage of flash pasteurisation is the energy efficiency of the process. The beer coming out of the cellar chills the beer leaving the pasteuriser at a very high efficiency (mid to high 90s [%]), so the heat exchanger does not have to heat the beer very much. One disadvantage of this method is that there is a chance that beer spoilers can contaminate the beer between the flash pasteuriser and the packaging process. Therefore, from the flash pasteuriser to the packaged beer, the brewery personnel must work very hygienically and carefully monitor this portion of the process carefully for any microbiological anomalies, i.e. not only for the presence of obligate, potential and indirect beer spoilers but also in the indicator microorganisms.

Brewers have been known to use a flash pasteuriser to neutralise the yeast still in suspension prior to pitching new yeast in wort or sugar for bottle conditioning. It would be better to filter this older yeast out prior to pitching new yeast, because older yeast cells, when pasteurised in beer can produce off-flavours. If a beer is not to be bottle conditioned, one method for prolonging the aroma and flavour of fresh yeast in a beer style, like Bavarian *Weissbier*, which would benefit from this, is to filter the beer, pitch fresh, vital yeast (often injected in-line) and then flash pasteurise the beer to neutralise the yeast. This creates a more stable beer which retains the aroma of fresh yeast for longer.

Tunnel and chamber pasteurisation

Pasteurising beer after it has been filled is advantageous from the standpoint of microbiological safety, since any microorganisms entering the beer up to and including filling will be killed in the packaged beer. Of course, the bottles must be able to withstand the pressure of the beer being heated to the necessary temperatures. Pasteurising beer after packaging does have a considerable effect on the flavour profile of the beer, one that is generally considered to be quite negative (Maillard products, ageing compounds), since the packaged beer cannot be heated quickly (bottle breakage) and must be subjected to a long heating and cooling process. It is not very energy efficient either. For example, to reach a temperature of 67 °C, bottles would be heated for 20 to 25 min to 67 °C with hot water, held at that temperature for 20 min to ensure that all of the beer in the bottle reaches that temperature, and then cooled for 20 to 25 min to around 25 °C.

Chamber pasteurisation is suitable for smaller runs of bottles, for instance, 600 to 800 bottles at once. Hot air, hot water or a water-steam mixture heats the bottles in a sealed chamber. The duration of the process would be similar to tunnel pasteurisation.

Literature and further reading

Filtration and Stabilisation – EBC Manual of Good Practice. European Brewery Convention and Fachverlag Hans Carl, Nürnberg (2019). ISBN 978-3-418-00856-1

Beer Pasteurisation – EBC Manual of Good Practice. European Brewery Convention and Fachverlag Hans Carl, 1995

Back, W., Gastl, M., Krottenthaler, M., Narziss, L., and Zarnkow, M., *Brewing Techniques in Practice.* Fachverlag Hans Carl GmbH, 2019

Basarova, G., Savel, J., Basar, P., Lejsek, T., *The Comprehensive Guide to Brewing from Raw Material to Packaging.* Fachverlag Hans Carl GmbH, 2017

Narziss, L. *Abriss der Bierbrauerei.* Wiley-VCH Verlag GmbH & Co., 2017

Goldammer, T., *The Brewer's Handbook: The Complete Book to Brewing Beer.* Apex Publishers, 2008

Bright beer

After filtration, beer can be stored in bright beer tanks until packaging. Carbonation can take place in-line between the filter or maturation tank and the bright beer tank or by placing the tank under pressure. Some brewers carbonate the beer directly in the tank using a carbonation stone made of sintered metal or porous stone. The carbon dioxide is forced through the stone to create fine bubbles into the beer. After successful carbonation, the beer can be packaged and sent to the warehouse. The temperature in the bright beer tank is close to 0 °C to allow carbon dioxide to go into solution. Since this is the last step in the production process before packaging and the last opportunity to undertake adjustments, multiple measurements and analyses are carried out to ensure that the beer is in compliance with specifications.

Determining the carbonation level of beer

Carbon dioxide is one of the reasons beer is refreshing. Beer with too little CO_2 is flat-tasting, lacklustre and unappealing, even in styles which are known for being less carbonated. CO_2 also contributes to mouthfeel, aroma and flavour. The appearance of a beer with no CO_2 is uninviting. Every style of beer has a certain amount of carbon dioxide dissolved in it due to the process of fermentation, though some beer styles contain more than others. Before taking a sip, if a stable head of finely latticed foam is on the beer (given that this is appropriate for the style), such as in figure 139, this already conveys a positive impression about the quality of the beer to the drinker.

Carbon dioxide is measured according to weight/volume or weight/weight, that is, in g/l or g/kg, which are the same for all practical purposes, or as a weight percentage, i.e. g/100 g.

Carbon dioxide is also measured by volume/volume. A volume is the amount of CO_2 that will fill a given vessel with one atmosphere of pressure at 20 °C. The conversion factor for volumes per litre to grams per litre is 1.96:

Figure 139: A stable head of finely latticed foam

$$1 \text{ vol/l} = 1.96 \text{ g/l of } CO_2$$

The levels of carbonation for various beer styles varies according to tradition, the brewing and fermentation processes, how the beer is served, among other factors. Beer styles and their customary carbonation levels are provided in table 17:

Table 17: Carbonation levels for selected beer styles

General guideline	grams per litre		volumes	
Carbonation according to beer style	min	max	min	max
European lager	4.3	5.3	2.2	2.7
British cask ale	2.4	3.5	1.2	1.8
Belgian ale	3.7	4.7	1.9	2.4
North American ale and lager	4.9	5.1	2.5	2.6
lambic (lower), gueuze (higher)	6.5	9.0	3.3	4.6
kriek, framboise/frambozenbier (fruit lambic)	5.9	8.8	3.0	4.5
porters and stouts (on draught)	2.9	4.3	1.5	2.2
porters and stouts (bottled)	3.3	4.5	1.7	2.3
Weissbier (Southern German wheat beer)	6.5	8.8	3.3	4.5

Carbonation levels can be measured using a number of devices, such as an optical measuring device or one using a piston. The device shown on the following page optically measures both dissolved CO_2 and O_2.

If none of these devices are at hand, the temperature and pressure on a tank can be used to estimate the dissolved carbon dioxide. The concentration of CO_2 in solution increases with increasing pressure and decreasing temperature. The dissolved CO_2 is also dependent upon the composition of the beer. The 'saturation pressure' simply

refers to the pressure at which the gaseous carbon dioxide above the beer and the carbon dioxide dissolved in the beer are in equilibrium.

Simple slide rules or applications for smart phones/computers can provide the same information.

Although the saturation pressure is also dependent upon the composition of the beer, this graph should provide a relatively accurate guide to carbonation.

An example of how different beers compare concerning their levels of carbonation and the amount of pressure required for them to be at equilibrium at their respective serving temperatures is provided in figure 142.

Figure 140: A device for optically measuring dissolved CO_2 and O_2

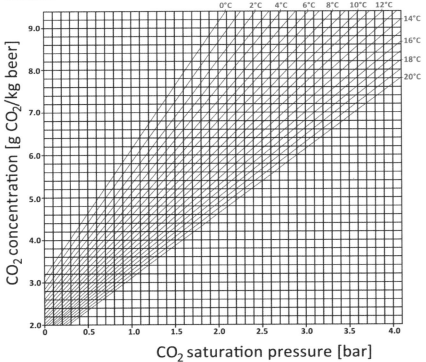

CO_2 saturation pressure [bar] above atmospheric pressure

Figure 141: CO_2 concentration and saturation pressure at various temperatures

- *Ungespundetes* served directly from the lager tank (0°C) at atmospheric pressure
- **Hand-pulled British ale served at 12°C with 0.3 bar of head pressure on the cask**
- **European lager dispensed at a temperature of 8°C at a pressure of almost 1.3 bar**
- ***Weissbier* dispensed at a temperature of 8°C at slightly over 2.2 bar**

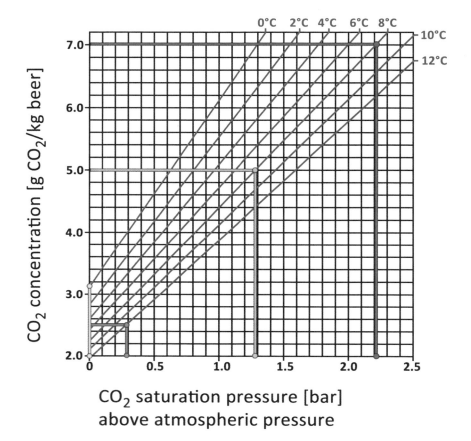

Figure 142: Examples of CO_2 concentrations and saturation pressures in various beer styles

The saturation pressures depicted above do not include the friction and pressure losses between the keg and the tap of the dispensing system.

| Brewery gases

Carbon dioxide

By and large, the yeast cells consume the dissolved oxygen in wort before they commence fermentation. Shortly after pitching, the oxygen level begins to drop, and once it is depleted, fermentation begins in earnest. The yeast produces carbon dioxide which saturates and percolates up through the wort as it turns into beer. This not only drives out oxygen, creating an anaerobic environment, but also serves to lower the pH, impacting enzymatic activity and the cell membranes of microorganisms. At atmospheric pressure, *Saccharomyces* species are fairly tolerant of carbon dioxide.

If yeast is fermenting wort at a rapid rate, and CO_2 is constantly escaping the liquid across its surface, then very little air will come into contact with the wort/green beer (see aeration and oxidation below). As this slows down, it becomes imperative that the beer be protected from air ingress. When air enters a tank, it is inevitable that it will diffuse throughout the entire tank, meaning that some mixing of the oxygen and the CO_2 will occur, and where the oxygen meets the gas-liquid interface, it will dissolve in the beer.

The idea that carbon dioxide forms a protective layer over the top of beer during maturation is therefore not completely representative of reality. Similarly, when purging a tank from the bottom, the air is not completely pushed out the top of the tank. These are oversimplifications of what actually occurs. Distinct strata of pure gases never form. The CO_2 will always contain some air. Only by imitating fermentation with the steady stream of CO_2 released from the lower portion of a tank, can a protective layer be maintained. This is impractical and unwarranted if brewers are careful. Other steps can be taken to prevent or otherwise eliminate any air ingress on the cold side of the brewing process.

Natural and artificial carbonation

Central European brewers usually retain the carbon dioxide already in solution from fermentation and the maturing beer because their tanks are designed to hold pressure. English speakers say 'bunging' but Americans have also adopted the German term for this and added '-ing' to it to create their own word 'spunding'. Aside from being less expensive and less wasteful, the quality of the carbonation, liveliness, foam formation and head retention is superior when the beer is 'naturally' carbonated, especially for long tank-matured lagers. An advantage of spunding is that there is always positive pressure on the beer, which aids in keeping air out (and thus oxygen and any microbes in the air).

Generally speaking, to properly and consistently carry out spunding, the tank must be sealed at precisely the same gravity every time or the green beer should be allowed to reach final attenuation and then a precise amount of wort + yeast or actively fermenting wort should be added in the high kräusen stage. A general rule of thumb is that the volume of fermenting wort should be calculated to amount to 15% of the volume of the green beer. Figure 143 shows an older lager tank with 0.5 bar of pressure on it at approximately 0 °C, meaning that the beer has around 4.6 g/l of carbonation.

Tanks manufactured to withstand some overpressure should meet all local and regional requirements. It is a frequent practice among US craft brewers to perform in-line or tank carbonation with CO_2 diffusers in the form of ceramic or sintered metal 'stones' or using membranes. This is due to the general lack or affordability of ASME (American Society of Mechanical Engineers) approved fermentation/maturation vessels available to craft brewers (rated to 2 bar). Pressure vessels in the US must meet the requirements of the ASME Boiler and Pressure Vessel Code (BPVC), and many other countries have adopted these same standards (refer to the link below).

Figure 143: A maturation tank with 0.5 bar of head pressure on it.

Carbonating in a bright tank is quite simple and straightforward but is slower than in-line carbonation. This method of carbonation is also not as efficient, as some CO_2 escapes through the pressure relief valve and thus is more apt to push out desirable volatile aroma compounds derived from fermentation and dry hopping. If carried out too hastily or incorrectly, it can even knock CO_2 out of solution. Carbonation devices in bright tanks require particularly careful cleaning and sanitising.

In-line carbonation is performed in a device made for this purpose. Older methods include a length of pipe and a sintered metal stone. These are less efficient and less hygienic than modern in-line membrane injectors, which can be purchased as a mobile unit. In-line injectors push the CO_2 through a membrane creating extremely tiny bubbles which dissolve immediately at the proper temperature. This is very efficient and does not waste CO_2. Thus, desirable volatile aroma compounds are not lost to the atmosphere. Modern in-line carbonation devices do not require sintered metal stones or other equipment and are therefore much more hygienic. They are also designed for cleaning-in-place without the need to dismantle.

Conditioning after packaging

Beers are frequently bottle conditioned, or as the Belgians put it 'refermented in the bottle'. The term 'conditioning' refers to the chemical and physical changes that occur in the tank or in the packaged beer through microbiological means, usually by *Saccharomyces* yeast or sometimes by *Brettanomyces*. Examples include Belgian and English ales as well as *Weissbier*. Bavarian *Weissbier* is conditioned with an admixture of *Speise* (yeast in wort in the log phase at high kräusen) in bottles and kegs for two to three weeks at temperatures ranging from 8 to 20 °C. English ale is routinely cask conditioned but is also bottle conditioned. Lager beer is, of course, matured in tanks for four to 12 weeks or even longer and then bottled and so is not bottle conditioned in the traditional sense. Lambic and gueuze are mixed with wort and refermented in the bottle over at least one summer and usually through cooler seasons. Lambic beer cellar temperatures usually vary from just above 0 °C to the low 20s °C over the year. This seasonal fluctuation is as important to the bottle conditioning of lambic-based beers as it is to lambic fermentation. The lactic acid bacteria flourish in the summer, while the yeast can better tolerate cooler temperatures. Other types of beer matured with mixed microbes will undergo similar processes. One sometimes hears the word used in this context: 'the condition of the beer'. The 'condition' in this case refers to the level of carbonation in the beer.

A second fermentation can be induced in the beer after final attenuation is reached by adding sugar or fermentable extract to the beer. As mentioned above, brewing yeast (*S. cerevisiae or S. pastorianus*) generates approximately 0.46 g of carbon dioxide for 1 g of fermentable extract. This does not apply to super-attenuating yeast like *Brettanomyces* species, *Saccharomyces cerevisiae* var. *diastaticus* or wild yeast, which can ferment dextrins and oligosaccharides. If they are in the beer, less wort or *Speise* should be used. However, if inverted sugar syrup, sucrose or dextrose is added to bottle condition the beer, it would be the same amount, since there are no dextrins and oligosaccharides in these sugars.

To cask condition, enough residual extract can be left in the beer when it is racked for this purpose. Priming with sugar syrup (refer to the section on sugar above) was common practice in British ales several decades ago but is not as widespread now. Some experienced drinkers of cask conditioned ale are not as pleased with the lack of a second fermentation in the cask, as they feel the beer exhibits more liveliness and, in their minds, has a more appealing flavour if the publican induces a second fermentation in the cellar.

To bottle condition, it is generally best to first allow beer to mature and reach final attenuation. Brewers use priming sugar, cast-out wort, first wort, top-fermented and/or bottom-fermented green beer in the log phase (high kräusen) and many different types of yeast.

Explosions and gushing

If too much sugar is added, gushing will occur or in extreme cases bottles might even explode. However, gushing can also be caused by setting the spunding pressure too high, fungal contamination (e.g. *Fusarium*) on the malt, calcium oxalate (mitigated by lagering at low temperatures) and a number of other factors can play a role, such as the shape and inner surface of the bottle, surfactant residues in bottles, isohumulones and heavy metals, among others.

Cellaring beer in bottles like wine

Storage in a cool cellar or similar space away from light is ordinarily only meant to preserve a beer's flavour for as long as possible. The vast majority of beers simply do not improve with age. However, a few bottled beers are capable of withstanding the ravages of age for a very long time when stored properly – some even improve over time. Furthermore, ageing most certainly cannot improve bad beer, because novel flavours and aromas are not so much created during cellaring as some of them simply fade away while others become more conspicuous.

Which beers under what conditions?

Though many different types of beer are bottle conditioned (usually top-fermented beers), not every beer style is conducive to being laid down in the bottle like wine. Beers that have been bottle pasteurised are not meant to be cellared because the microbes are dead in them. A flash-pasteurised beer can be inoculated with fresh microbes immediately prior to bottling given that some residual extract remains in it, or sugar, wort, *Speise* or fruit can be added. As a rule, the original gravity of the wort should be around 15 °P or above so that cellaring imparts a vinous quality to the beer during maturation. Obviously, no sunlight should reach the bottles. Cool generally means between 4 °C and 7 °C. Bottled beers should only lie on their sides if they are corked (some, like gueuze, are corked then capped), otherwise, they should be stored upright.

Carbon dioxide recovery systems

Given that the beverage industry in some regions has recently suffered from shortages of food-grade carbon dioxide and the fact that large volumes of this very gas escape to the atmosphere during fermentation, these systems are now considered to be much more practical than they have been in the past. These systems range in size and can recover carbon dioxide at a rate of 20–10,000 kg/h. They are connected to a brewery's fermentation tanks and consist of a foam separator, a collection device like a balloon, a gas washer, a compressor, an activated carbon filter, a stripper, a drier, a refrigeration unit, a storage tank and an evaporator. Modern systems clean the carbon dioxide so effectively that the purity of the gas is well above 99.95%. There is a lower annual production threshold for the amortisation of these systems, but it continues to drop, as manufacturers are increasingly reacting to the needs of smaller breweries.

| Nitrogen

Generation and uses in the brewery

The use of the diatomic molecule (N_2) in the form of a gas has a number of applications in brewing. Because it comprises almost 80% of the air we breathe, nitrogen is abundant in the atmosphere and is able to be isolated relatively easily from the other molecules floating around with it. Nitrogen can be used to purge tanks or even brewhouse vessels of oxygen and/or carbon dioxide. Using CO_2 for this purpose can be expensive. Food-grade nitrogen gas can be purchased, like carbon dioxide, in bottles. Generating it on-site, however, ensures that food-grade nitrogen is readily available any time it is needed. Nitrogen generation has become affordable for smaller breweries and can be quite advantageous and implemented quite easily. It is less expensive in the long run (than purchasing it and using CO_2 to purge tanks and lines), and there is a ready supply always available on-site. Brewers are finding nitrogen useful in isobarometric filling lines as well.

Nitrogen generators help in removing the oxygen molecules. This is done using a couple of different methods downstream from the brewery's oil-free air compressor, where food-grade air is generated. The two methods employed for this are known as pressure swing adsorption and membrane nitrogen generation.

For all practical purposes, nitrogen gas is inert, because the triple bond between two nitrogen molecules is extremely strong. Nitrogen is much, much less soluble in water, and thus beer, than carbon dioxide. In nature, lightning can separate the bond of molecular nitrogen in the air, but bacteria are almost always necessary to accomplish this in a process known as 'nitrogen fixation'. If a brewery has that much electricity being discharged in the air or these kinds of bacteria living in the beer, then drastic measures are required indeed.

Refer to the section on dispensing with nitrogen below.

| Compressed air

Another method for pushing beer through dispensing lines is to use compressed air. This, of course, never comes into contact with the beer, because there is a liner inside of a tank separating the two of them. Tanks designed to house these liners and an air compressor capable of generating food-grade, oil-free, odourless air pressure are the prerequisites for serving beer in this manner. Horizontal and vertical tanks are available, generally in 500 to 1000 litre volumes. Prior to filling the tank with beer, the liner is inserted into the tank. Advantages of these systems include the fact that the gases used to push the beer do not dissolve in the beer and the tanks are relatively easy to clean, since the beer never comes into contact with the tank's surface. One disadvantage is that the liners are single use and must be disposed of in an environmentally responsible manner.

Quality control points: bright beer

- gravity/attenuation/alcohol content
- pH and temperature
- yeast (flocculation, sedimentation, removal)
- microbiological status (wild yeast, beer spoilers)
- carbonation
- dissolved oxygen
- visual inspection (colour, turbidity)
- aroma/flavour
- VDK and other green beer congeners below the flavour threshold
- bittering units
- clarification techniques (method, hygiene)
- filterability and its effect on flavour stability
- minimise oxygen uptake (purge filters of oxygen)

Literature and further reading

ASME BPVC: www.asme.org/wwwasmeorg/media/resourcefiles/shop/certification%20&%20accreditation/bpv-certification/bpvc2019_brochure.pdf

Berninger, M., *Stickstoff als Alternative zu Kohlendioxid*. Brauwelt no. 46–47, 2018

Vogeser, G., S. diastaticus: *geliebt und gefürchtet*. Brauwelt no. 10, pp. 270–273, 2020, Fachverlag Hans Carl

PACKAGED BEER

After all laboratory tests have been run and the beer has been evaluated sensorially, the decision is made to package the beer if the beer is in specification. Beer is commonly filled in kegs, casks, cans and bottles. The beer can be flash pasteurised on the way to the filler or tunnel pasteurised after packaging in the bottle. During packaging, closures, can seams and crown caps should be monitored for proper application. Various laboratory tests are conducted to determine the chemical, microbiological and sensory status of the beer. At this point, it is recommended that one or more reference samples be collected and stored in an archive. There, they are regularly monitored for any change in physical appearance such as sediment formation, neck rings, etc. Samples should be kept in the archive until the end of the published shelf life has been reached.

Beer packaged in any form should have a best before date printed on it. Some breweries print the date the beer was filled on the packaging as well. Packaged products which are not properly labelled are not permitted to be sold on the market.

Once the beer has been packaged, it should be moved to the storage area at the brewery. This storage area should be cooled to between 5 and 6 °C.

The following microbiological analyses should be carried out on the packaged beer (refer to the section on microbiological analysis below):

- anaerobic microorganisms
- aerobic microorganisms
- *Saccharomyces* wild yeasts
- non-*Saccharomyces* wild yeasts

A note on PET as packaging material for beer

Bottled beer, especially that which is packaged in PET bottles, is also susceptible to damage by UV light. Beer bottled and kegged in PET, particularly the bottles featuring only a monolayer barrier, do not provide adequate protection against gas migration. Suitable multilayer bottles with the proper coating can prevent both problems from occurring to some extent.

Kegs

The kegs themselves should be visually inspected for damage to the kegs and their fittings. When in doubt the keg should be emptied of any remaining beer and pressure, then taken apart and inspected. The temperature and pressure at the individual cleaning, sanitising and filling steps on the kegging line should be monitored and recorded on a regular basis. This involves the concentrations of the cleaning and sanitising solutions as well as the rinse water (pH or conductivity). Oxygen uptake should, of course, be kept to an absolute minimum as with every step in the process.

Microbiologically speaking, evaluating the status of the filling unit itself and the surrounding environment (refer to swab tests and ambient air tests in the appendix) on a regular basis would be shrewd. If steam is employed, obviously, the kegs must be completely cooled prior to being filled with beer (fobbing, oxidation, Maillard product formation). The outside of the keg, particularly the valve, should be rinsed and free of any beer or cleaning chemicals. As mentioned in the section on water, cleaning solutions with a high chloride content can cause corrosion.

Single-use kegs

Single-use kegs are on the rise as an alternative to conventional deposit kegs. The basic problem with plastic kegs is the material they consist of, its permeability to gases and its environmental impact. Oxygen and other gases are able to pass through the barrier layers. Furthermore, plastic kegs cannot withstand changes in pressure and temperature very well. There are, in fact, stainless steel single-use kegs designed to be filled on conventional kegging lines, to be sent out to customers and not returned. They are not as environmentally unfriendly as they sound, since stainless steel is expensive, and it is highly unlikely these kegs will go unrecycled, regardless of the country to which they are sent. As opposed to plastic kegs, single-use stainless steel kegs possess intrinsic value once they are emptied.

Bottles and cans

Although most would agree that beer tastes better on tap or on hand pull, beer drinkers purchase most of their beer in bottles and cans; this was the case even before the onset of the coronavirus pandemic. Filling lines are by far the most expensive equipment in breweries and are likewise costly to operate and maintain but are often necessary due to this tendency among beer drinkers, i.e. that many would rather drink their beer at home than in a public house or cafe. The quality of both of these types of containers, the fill levels and oxygen uptake as well as hygiene, cleanliness and microbiology are the primary concerns.

Container quality

Bottles are usually brown to protect the beer as much as possible from UV light (refer to the section on lightstruck beer). They can be returnable or non-returnable. Cans, or tins as they are sometimes known, have a bad reputation among older consumers, but due to advances in canning and material technology, cans have become a very attractive way to package beer, since cans protect quite well against both light and oxygen ingress.

Brewers must make enquiries into the local and regional laws regulating beverage filling and packaging and observe them carefully to ensure their products face no difficulties on the market. Modern bottling lines automatically check the empty bottles and the full ones. For smaller breweries, where investment in an entirely new bottling line is out of the question, a less expensive alternative is available in the form of a single module that performs a complete bottle inspection. These modules do not take up very much space and can be installed in conjunction with and integrated into most existing bottling lines. They can be customised to perform the full range of empty and full bottle inspections. Bottle inspectors on the empty side are a necessary part of a filling line because any bottles containing liquids or soil prior to filling have to be rejected. Empty bottles can be visually monitored for defects. On some older bottling lines at smaller breweries, both the empty and full bottles are passed in front of a light field for visual inspection. This is not optimal and can fatigue the filling personnel's eyes not to mention their minds before very long, requiring that station to be occupied by all personnel in turn for short periods. Common defects in bottles include chipped or broken bottles and glass fragments in the bottles. The glass may be folded, blistered, contain 'stones' (unmelted glass or foreign material), or be flawed in some other way, e.g. the glass is too thin or thick. Glass threads or spikes stretching from one side of the inner wall to another may be present. The sealing surface, i.e. where the crown cap meets the bottle, may be chipped, split, torn, rough, uneven, askew or otherwise non-uniform, making properly capping the bottle impossible.

Refer to EBC method 11.12 Visual Assessment (Defects List) of Glass Bottles

Modular equipment and inspectors are available for canning lines as well, in which case they perform an inspection of the entire inner wall of the empty cans, including the condition of the flange, and also expedite setting the seamer correctly so that the can is sealed properly. Relatively inexpensive inspectors for performing seam checks on the full cans are also available.

Prior to filling, disposable containers have to be rinsed, while returnable ones must be washed. Rinsers can be purchased as stand-alone devices or be integrated into the packaging line. Returnable bottles, of course, have to be sorted and cleaned by the brewery prior to filling. Washers for returnable bottles are quite large and can be one-end or two-end. If the bottle washing machines are one-end, the dirty bottles enter at the bottom and exit at the top. The more hygienic – and more expensive – alternative are the two-end machines, which separate the two streams of bottles at either end of the bottle washer. These machines are massive and require a great deal of maintenance as well as chemical and microbiological monitoring. Consult the manufacturer's specifications for operations, cleaning and maintenance.

Filling and packaging

Bottles

Full bottle inspectors determine whether the bottle has been properly filled, scans for floating particles on the side or at the bottom and whether the cap is crimped on correctly. Affordable modular label and packaging inspectors are also available.

uncrimped

crimped

Figure 144: A crown cap – uncrimped and crimped

Crown caps should be visually inspected quite frequently over the day. This not only entails the obvious, whether the crowns are centred and crimped correctly onto the bottles, but to what extent the crown caps are crimped. Spot checks can be performed with a crimp gauge, which is merely a piece of metal with very precisely measured holes drilled into it. The holes on a crimp gauge are placed over the crown closure, and with only the force of gravity, it should either fall past or become stuck on the crimped cap. Most crimp gauges have holes labelled GO and NO GO, which indicate whether a cap is insufficiently, sufficiently or excessively tight. In the example given in figure 146, the two centre holes are labelled GO and represent the minimum and maximum allowable tolerances for a properly crimped cap. The two outer holes are marked NO GO and indicate that caps are not crimped well enough or are crimped too tightly. The skirt diameter of the crimped cap are standardised according to the types of bottles and crown cap one is employing. Figure 146 represents one example of a crimp gauge:

diameter of a properly crimped crown cap

Figure 145: Crown cap diameter

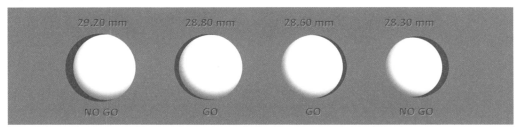

Figure 146: A crown cap crimp gauge

Refer to EBC method 11.30 Bottle Seal Integrity Determination.

For spot checks and regular monitoring of the filling line, templates are available for common bottle types. Filled bottle samples are normally pulled from the line and checked from each filling element on the filler. The template (fig. 147) is for returnable Central European NRW 500 ml bottles. The upper and lower limits for tolerance of fill levels are printed on the template. These are also used to ensure that the full bottle inspector has been calibrated and is functioning properly.

Refer to the EBC method 11.3.2 Net Contents of Bottles as Measuring Containers (Non-Destructive Template Method).

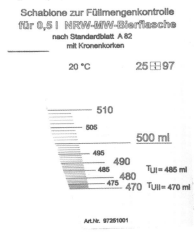

Figure 147: A template for manually measuring fill levels in 500 ml NRW bottles

Cans

The lengths and thicknesses of the seam depicted in figure 148 should fall within certain specifications. Sometimes the body hook or the end hook can be too short, causing the can to leak or be unable to withstand the pressure of the beer when warmed to room

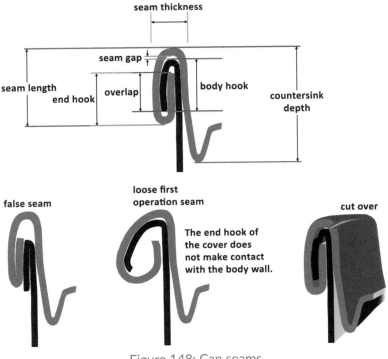

Figure 148: Can seams

temperature. The false seam in figure 148 may lead to a knocked down flange which will be immediately visible. A cut over occurs when the cover becomes fractured at the top. The cover can also develop a sharp surface on the inside radius, which is known as a sharp seam. Other problems include drooping, wrinkling, pleating, puckering and the formation of spurs along the seam. Therefore, the seaming process and full cans must be carefully monitored.

Refer to EBC method 11.21 Can Seam Evaluation and specifications from equipment manufacturers for operating and critical parameters as well as parameters for weekly inspections.

Inspectors

If a brewery's primary business is done in bottled or canned beer, inspectors save a great deal of stress, time and effort. However, even with bottle and can inspectors, the personnel in charge of filling should regularly – every hour to half-hour, depending on the line – perform cap/seam checks on bottle/can runs, labelling, fill levels, date stamps, etc. Headspace readings should be performed regularly as well, at least on every run.

Modern equipment for inspecting bottles and cans has become much more affordable over the past few years. Fill weights of cans were monitored in the past, but with modern technology, x-rays, gamma rays and inductive sensors are employed to check fill levels and the filled cans' inner pressure.

All of these data should be recorded and entered into a spreadsheet or other data monitoring system that allows the data to be graphed.

Labelling and dating

Local regulations should be checked to ensure the mandatory information are provided according to legal requirements.

Oxygen uptake

The oxygen content of the packaged beer depends on a variety of factors, such as the oxygen in the beer prior to filling, the oxygen picked up in the filling process and the amount in the headspace after packaging. In order to understand where oxygen might be entering the process, if possible, it would be advantageous to measure the dissolved oxygen in the beer at several points in the process, such as in the bright beer tank, in the manifold and in shaken and unshaken bottles or cans. This will allow filling personnel to locate where leaks or other sources of oxygen ingress might be.

Dissolved oxygen represents the amount in the liquid, while oxygen in the headspace is the amount above the beer. The oxygen in the headspace will eventually react with the packaged beer. Thus, if measuring dissolved oxygen in a bottle or can, it is best to shake the can or bottle prior to the measurement. Though one should quickly cap or seam after filling, it is nevertheless important to induce foaming immediately prior to doing so, for the purpose of driving out a large portion of the oxygen in the headspace. Even by flooding the receptacle containing the crown caps with CO_2 or N_2, some oxygen uptake can be prevented. The seal in a crown cap on bottles is not impervious to air and will also allow CO_2 to escape. Over a six-month period, approximately 1.5 mg/l of oxygen will enter the headspace of the bottle (slightly less if the cap is furnished with an oxygen-absorbing seal). This oxygen will eventually react with the beer, resulting in off-flavours associate with oxidation. Pry-off crown caps are more effective at providing an oxygen barrier than are twist-off crown caps or swing top closures.

Refer to the section on oxygen on the cold side below for more information.

Microbiology

Why is the filling area such a critical area from a microbiological standpoint? During packaging, the beer can become infected through secondary contamination. In the filling area, biofilms readily develop and spread quickly without vigilant hygiene and cleaning. The rotating components can become contaminated and continue recontaminating everything they touch, while also being difficult to inspect and to clean. The personnel bring in microbial contaminants as does the air flowing through the filling area. There is beer covering a portion of the equipment, and the temperature and humidity in the filling area are conducive to microbial growth. Returnable containers and bottle washers present a further challenge to hygiene, especially if the airflow is unfavourable.

In order to keep biofilm formation to an absolute minimum the following is recommended:

- The filler should be cleaned after every workday. Foaming detergents followed by a sanitiser after rinsing are advantageous in this area.
- The filling line (star wheels, heads, capper, etc.) and the associated equipment should be sprayed down with hot water (approx. 85 °C) every 2 to 4 h for 2 min – and not as a fine mist but with a wide solid stream of water. This avoids a precipitous temperature drop before the water can come into contact with the equipment.
- The filler should be subjected to routine deep cleaning and maintenance at least once per week (components taken apart and cleaned, gaskets checked, etc.)
- All parts of the filler and associated equipment should be hygienically designed and easily accessible for cleaning.

- Any dead-ends or recesses can be sprayed with 70% ethanol at the end of the workday.
- At the end of the workday, after the cleaning regimen is complete, the floor should be thoroughly cleaned and disinfected.
- The number of screws, nuts, bolts, recesses, etc. on the equipment should be kept to a minimum.
- Anti-microbial additives are available for chain lubricants, i.e. for lubricating those moving parts that do not have a chance of coming into contact with beer.
- Equipment surfaces should be smooth, i.e. the level of roughness should be low.
- Foam, composite material, etc. should be avoided.
- Personnel must be made aware of the necessary hygienic practices for the filling area.
- Airflow from less hygienic areas should be avoided. A HEPA filter for the air flowing into the filling area is recommended. Even some smaller breweries are now creating clean rooms for their filling equipment.

Refer to the sections below on biofilm formation and microbiological sample collection.

Quality control points: packaged beer

- gravity/attenuation/alcohol content
- pH and temperature
- yeast (flocculation, sedimentation, removal)
- microbiological status (wild yeast, beer spoilers)
- carbonation
- visual inspection (colour, turbidity)
- aroma/flavour
- VDK and other green beer congeners below the flavour threshold
- bittering units
- minimising oxygen uptake (dissolved oxygen monitoring in packaged beer)
- filling and packaging (method, inspection/monitoring, hygiene)

BEER AND BASIC FOOD SAFETY

It is imperative that a brewer be familiar with the parameters of the brewing process and the properties they bring about in beer. The brewer is responsible for monitoring production in order to guarantee that these properties are in the final product. They are essential to brewing high quality beer with a reasonable level of stability (flavour, colloidal, foam).

There are, however, extremely heat-resistant, spore-forming pathogenic strains among wort bacteria (*Bacillus* and *Clostridium*), which can enter the process through the raw materials (malt, yeast). Some can survive the mashing and wort boiling processes. They can lie dormant and proliferate when wort is not handled properly, i.e. not promptly chilled, pitched and fermented. They are the reason that proper cleaning, especially on the cold side, is of such consequence (refer to the section on cleaning). Fortunately, due to the properties outlined below, pathogenic microorganisms cannot grow in beer produced correctly using conventional methods.

Figure 149 shows the means available to brewers to protect their beer from spoilage. These properties are inherent to beer and have made it safe to drink for centuries. They protect it from infection by undesirable microorganisms and can be influenced in the brewing process as depicted. The infection pressure of a particular beer describes how likely its inherent properties are to collectively inhibit or invite microbial contamination and growth.

The inherent protective properties of beer

All of the properties discussed here will vary from beer to beer; however, for a beer to be stable and safe to drink, brewers must be aware of these properties and manipulate them so that they work in a synergistic manner. For instance, if a beer is relatively low in hops (but not lacking them entirely), such as *Weissbier*, the other properties, that is, nutrient content, brewhouse work, ethanol content and pH will need to be adjusted to compensate.

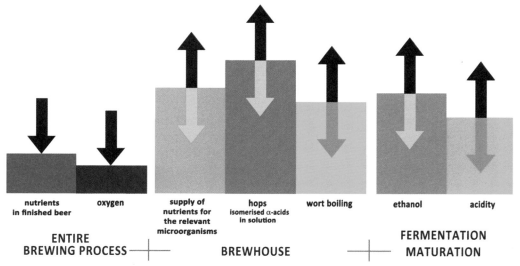

These two properties of beer should be low regardless of the style and have to be controlled from the beginning to the end of the process; they are only detrimental in their effects on beer.

Maltsters create malt that can be processed by competent brewers to produce wort full of the compounds that favour the desired microorganisms, i.e. strains of brewing yeast, so that undesirable micro-organisms have little chance in competition with them.

These two properties, isomerisation of hop bitter acids and wort boiling, are determined in the brewhouse; most all brewers boil their wort, but among some craft brewers it has become fashionable not to do so. Completely omitting this step is not devoid of risk.

Though the amount of ethanol and acidity are determined by the nutrients available to the microorganisms in the wort, these two properties are created during fermentation and serve to protect the beer from undesirable microorganisms.

| nutrients in finished beer | oxygen | supply of nutrients for the relevant microorganisms | hops isomerised α-acids in solution | wort boiling | ethanol | acidity |

ENTIRE BREWING PROCESS —|— **BREWHOUSE** —|— **FERMENTATION MATURATION**

Figure 149: The inherent, protective properties of beer and how they can be adjusted to improve flavour stability

A scarcity of nutrients

The degree of attenuation at the end of fermentation is of interest for brewers, not only because they want to ensure that the wort sugars have been converted to ethanol and carbon dioxide but also with regard to flavour stability and the likelihood that the beer will become infected if some fermentable sugars remain. *Saccharomyces* species are capable of consuming sugars rapidly, effectively starving other microorganisms in the wort.

There is a misconception among some brewers who believe that slowing attenuation towards the end of fermentation through reducing the temperature in the fermentation vessel and finally putting a stop to it slightly early increases the mouthfeel of the finished beer. This is not true and also negatively affects the flavour. If a beer is not fully attenuated, then the infection pressure increases on the beer and the flavour stability suffers. Nutrients, such as proteins and sugars increase the infection pressure of beer by making it susceptible to microbial attack.

This can also lead to issues with the packaged beer. If residual sugars are available and some yeast or other microorganisms are present in unpasteurised beer, cans and bottles can explode on the shelf. For this reason, rapid chilling, or 'crashing' as it is known in some circles, of the beer towards the end of fermentation should be avoided. The yeast needed for maturation may react negatively to the brisk change in temperature and not sufficiently condition the beer afterwards. Besides, even if this is not the case with a particular strain, the yeast can nevertheless react negatively and excrete undesirable substances in the beer due to the temperature shock, ultimately affecting beer flavour and stability.

Oxygen

Low oxygen environment

Yeast produce carbon dioxide during fermentation, creating a low oxygen environment in the beer. It is best throughout the cold side of the process to keep it that way by de-aerating brewing liquor and keeping the oxygen uptake as low as possible.

Some compounds in the beer are very sensitive to oxidation. To avoid off-flavours and rapid ageing of the beer, keep air out at every point in the process. The maximum acceptable concentrations of oxygen in the finished beer are ≤ 0.05 ppm, although ≤ 0.03 ppm would be preferable.

Harmful chemical reactions

Oxygen is also a cellular poison for all life on the planet – including yeast. Wort aeration immediately after chilling is the one and only point where air is permitted to enter the process, otherwise oxygen is considered the brewer's worst enemy. (Refer to the section on wort aeration in the brewing process.) For this reason, it is not advisable to use pure oxygen to oxygenate yeast but rather sterile air, as too much dissolved oxygen may have substantial deleterious effects for fermentation and the flavour stability of the finished beer because it will chemically react with the substances in the wort. When using pure oxygen, it is easy to overdo it. Since air is only ⅕ oxygen, wort saturated with air is much less susceptible to oxidation and hence to forming ageing compounds. Some breweries have even resorted to aerating their propagated yeast and not their wort. The only reason one should consider using pure oxygen is in the production of high gravity beers. If this is the case, it should still be dosed in-line very prudently.

Of course, dissolved oxygen, only refers to the oxygen finding its way into the process on the cold side of production, which may or may not eventually oxidise the beer, depending upon how long it takes for the packaged beer to be consumed. If the beer after packaging is kept in a cold, dark place this can slow these reactions. This is the reason supermarket displays outdoors or at ambient temperature next to large windows is very harmful for packaged, especially bottled, beer.

Oxidation is usually mentioned in conjunction with reduction in chemistry. Oxidation and reduction are chemical reactions that are complementary because they involve an exchange of electrons between molecules. Oxidation occurs when a molecule loses electrons during a reaction, and reduction is the opposite. The chemical reaction of oxidation can produce harmful free radicals, and antioxidants are chemical compounds that inhibit their creation. Oxidation reactions make beer and most other foods taste 'old'. This is the reason some brewers add ascorbic acid to their packaged beer. Refer to a chemistry textbook on redox reactions for more information.

Refer to the section below on beer-spoiling microorganisms for information on *Pectinatus* and *Megasphaera*, two genera of bacteria that live in low-oxygen environments.

A note on hot-side aeration

Hot-side aeration of the mash and/or the wort brings with it a number of disadvantages. When the wort is hot, oxygen chemically reacts quickly with compounds in the wort, such as carbohydrates, proteinaceous compounds, polyphenols and bittering substances, immediately undergoing a broad range of reactions. Starch conversion and other enzymatic reactions can be impaired. Additionally, lautering slows, the extract yield suffers, and the wort colour darkens. The bitterness of the wort may be diminished or affected in an otherwise negative manner, such as becoming harsh or unpleasant. The resulting beer will lack satisfactory flavour stability and will often exhibit off-flavours. Oxidation in the brewhouse leads to elevated levels of the following compounds: 2-pentanone, 2-methylbutanal, 3-methylbutanal, 2-heptanone, 2-furfural and heptanal (refer to the section on sensory analysis below).

Dissolved oxygen and total package oxygen

It is very helpful to measure dissolved oxygen where practical on the cold side of production because this enables brewers to establish where the oxygen may be entering the process, allowing them to rectify the situation. Letting air into the production process is easy, while removing it is impossible for all practical purposes.

As with carbon dioxide, the lower the temperature, the higher the oxygen solubility in wort; however, oxygen is less reactive at low temperatures. Thus, dissolved oxygen is affected by the temperature, pressure and amount of oxygen in the beer already.

The oxygen readings should be done at the following points in the process:

- immediately upstream from the filter
- in the bright tank
- the manifold on the filler
- in the packaged beer

Points where oxygen may be getting into the cold side of the process:

1. when transferring
2. unpurged hoses, tiny leaks, bad gaskets (if beer leaks, air gets in)
3. rinse/purge water has not been sufficiently degassed
4. filtration (insufficient purging, air ingress)
5. improper procedures during artificial carbonation
6. impure gas during purging/carbonation
7. long disruptions/faulty procedures on the filling line
8. the filler is not sufficiently foaming the beer
9. faulty capping/seaming on the filling line

For testing in packaged beer, a CO_2/O_2 meter allows highly accurate measurements in the laboratory.

In performing oxygen measurements, total package oxygen includes the dissolved oxygen and the oxygen in the headspace. Thus, to get an idea of the total package oxygen when measuring dissolved oxygen, the bottle or can should be shaken. There are, of course, devices designed to measure the oxygen in the headspace. The total package oxygen of a freshly filled beer should be 0.06 to 0.08 mg/l or less. Modern filling lines keep the total oxygen in the beer below 0.1 mg/l, given that the beer entering the filling line already contains around 0.02 mg/l normally. During filling approximately 0.02 mg/l is picked up, and the oxygen in the headspace amounts to 0.06 mg/l or less. Even on older lines, during the filling process itself, the oxygen uptake in the beer should be no more than 0.03 mg/l, while in the headspace above the beer, the oxygen content should be less than 0.15 mg/l. Altogether, the total oxygen in the beer and the headspace should not exceed 0.25 mg/l. Oxygen uptake during the filling of cans is slightly higher. If all the proper safeguards are taken with a modern canning line, however, the maximum total oxygen content in cans should be comparable to that of bottles.

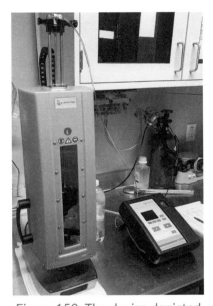

Figure 150: The device depicted above samples directly from the package and determines not only the CO_2 content but the alcohol content, original gravity, density and O_2 content as well. Other measurements are also possible with such devices, including pH, turbidity and colour.

Hops

As discussed in the section on raw materials and wort boiling, hops are the most common beer ingredient since they impart soluble bacteriostatic compounds to the beer when they are boiled in the wort. Besides providing a pleasant bitterness to balance the malty sweetness derived from the grain, hops can inhibit cell function in some bacteria in an acidic solution. The iso α-acids derived from hops – especially given the synergy between wort pH and the acids from hops – are an effective deterrent against many Gram-positive microorganisms, primarily lactic acid bacteria but most notably against pathogens.

Wort boiling

In the distant past, beer was commonly created without boiling the wort. This beer was almost always consumed very quickly, but even then, very often the mash was heated to such an extent that it was more or less pasteurised anyway. A relatively modern beer, *Berliner Weisse* is one example of a beer style produced without boiling the wort, but the wort is normally held at approximately 80 °C for some time. The primary problem with not boiling the wort at all or even pasteurising it at 80 °C is two-fold: first, the wort is not sterilised. Harmful microorganisms are not removed. Second, hop isomerisation does not occur to any extent, meaning that the iso α-acids are not dissolved in the wort. Not only are the microorganisms, which arrived on the raw materials, air, equipment, brewery workers, etc., left to their own devices, there was also neither heat applied nor any iso α-acids dissolved in the wort to inhibit the growth of the less desirable ones. Thus, the valuable bacteriostatic properties of hops cannot protect the beer. Refer to the section on hops below.

Alcohol content

Ethanol provides a barrier to infection in beer by eliminating bacteria. The majority of brewing yeast strains have the capacity to produce up to 10–15% ethanol by volume. However, there are many factors which influence the production of ethanol and the tolerance yeast have for it, including temperature, pH, dissolved oxygen and the presence of organic acids.

Acidity

The pH scale represents the negative of the base 10 logarithm of the activity of the hydrogen ion. The more H^+ ions there are in a liquid, the more acidic it is.

Measures can be taken to warrant that the brewing liquor and the mash/wort fall within the proper range.

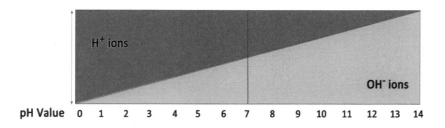

Figure 151: The logarithmic scale of pH is shown linearly in this diagramme.

It is essential that the wort be at the proper pH prior to pitching the yeast, so that when the yeast enters the wort, through the process of fermentation the beer reaches a pH of 4.5 or lower.

As mentioned, by promptly pitching sufficient numbers of viable and vital yeast cells, other microorganisms stand little chance of gaining a toehold in wort. The pH of beer is one of the reasons that pathogenic microorganisms cannot be found in relevant numbers in it (fig. 152). Refer to the sections on brewing liquor treatment, mashing and wort boiling as well as fermentation and maturation for more detail regarding the pH at various stages in the brewing process. Table 18 represents a general rule of thumb for the prevention of microbial contamination in the finished beer.

Table 18: A general rule of thumb for ensuring that the pH in the finished beer is sufficiently low to prevent the growth of the vast majority of foodborne microorganisms.

General rule of thumb	
brewing liquor	≈ 6.5
mash/wort	≈ 5.5
beer	≤ 4.5

Yeast cells – and, if applicable, other microorganisms – in wort generate various organic acids as products or by-products of the biochemical pathways being carried out during fermentation. As fermentation progresses, the pH of the wort drops; in fact, beer brewed with mixed microorganisms generally reaches a lower pH than those brewed with a single strain of *Saccharomyces*.

Refer to the section on beer spoilage microorganisms below.

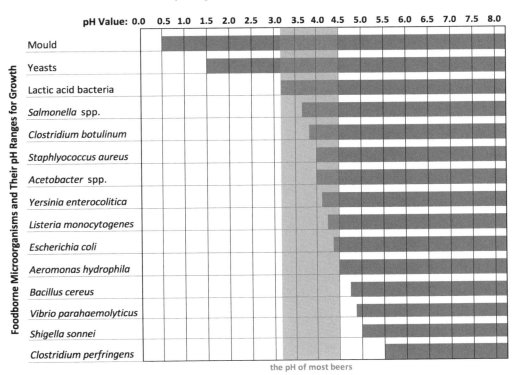

Figure 152: Foodborne microorganisms and their pH ranges for growth

| Traditional approaches

All beers were at one time drunk as fresh as possible, some without being fermented for more than a few hours. Keeping beer alive, i.e. with active microbes, for instance, through a short period of conditioning, and then drinking it quickly (e.g. British ale, *Altbier*, *Weissbier*, *Gose*, etc.), has been the most common strategy throughout history. This works very well as long as everything along the production chain falls into place at the appropriate time. As brewers honed their skills over the last 400 years and developed

Spontaneously-fermented lambic	Pale, bottom-fermented beer
Malted barley + unmalted wheat	100% malted barley
Intense mashing exposes starch and yet much of it enters the production process relatively intact (especially the starch from the wheat).	Malting and intense mashing exposes starch and breaks most of it down to molecules yeast can metabolise.
Nutrients: very high attenuation through long fermentation and maturation with mixed microorganisms ("mashing" is carried out, in part, by microorganisms in the cellar over a long period); virtually no nutrients remain in lambic that bacteria or yeast can exploit under the conditions present in the matured beer.	Nutrients: high attenuation coupled with selection of cold-tolerant microorganisms (pure lager yeast cultures). Compounds unable to be degraded in the mash and metabolised by brewer's yeast remain, e.g. dextrins, which can be exploited by other microorganisms – **only** if they can tolerate the conditions present in the matured beer.
Alcohol content, approx. ~ 5% ABV	Alcohol content, approx. ≥ 5% ABV
Ambient cellar temperatures (10–15 °C, though with seasonal variation, which is critical, throughout fermentation, maturation and bottle conditioning	Cold fermentation (8–10 °C and maturation (-1–1 °C) in ice-chilled cellars; beer remains near freezing until served; few microorganisms can flourish under such conditions. The beer is kept cold until it is consumed.
Low hop rate: ageing hops results in fewer iso α-acids, but other constituents are relevant, (e.g. polyphenols); low iso α-acids allow the necessary bacteria to flourish	High hop rate (coupled with especially soft water) creates a pleasant, noble bitterness while also protecting the beer with a relatively high concentration of iso a-acids.
Low oxygen environment	Low oxygen environment
Final pH: 3.2–3.8, perhaps with the addition of sour cherries (polyphenol-rich, acidic)	Final pH below 4.5 Normal pH: 4.2–4.5

more selective methods, they also created strategies for keeping beer drinkable for extended periods. Refer to the box featuring two traditional methods for increasing flavour stability prior to the development of modern practices, such as refrigeration, fine filtration, stabilisation, etc. Both lambic and lager production developed in climate zones where an interface between beer brewing and viniculture was present. Consequently, these production methods may owe some of their innovation a few hundred years ago to a cross-pollination of ideas between the two. Note that in each example below, the beer is highly attenuated and once maturation commences is protected from further spoilage by other barriers to infection. All of these stresses on potential spoilage microorganisms ultimately act in unison, and therefore they have a greater synergistic impact. This is the reason that brewers should learn to manage these processes, so that they can create barriers to microbial infection. In doing so, brewers will foster conditions under which quality control is much simpler, thus requiring less effort on their part.

Assessing beer safety – examples

Drawing on the information presented above, the brewer is in a position to assess the beer from the standpoint of both safety and stability. If a particular beer were to be exposed to beer spoilers, would they be able to gain a foothold and multiply?

Example 1: An extreme instance would be a lightly hopped, non-alcoholic beer produced by halting the fermentation process. If the concentration of iso α-acids is low and there is no more than 0.5% alcohol by volume, two of the important hindrances to microbial growth have been removed. For a precise definition of what constitutes a non-alcoholic beer, brewers should consult the respective federal and local regulations. With halted fermentation, there is a high concentration of simple sugars left in solution, and the pH of the beer is somewhat higher than normal, perhaps 4.8. Since so many of these properties are lacking, beer spoilers would probably multiply easily. A number of beer spoilers, including the bacteria belonging to the genera *Megasphaera* and *Pectinatus*, would find this beer attractive. Thus, the nature of this particular beer would require additional safeguards to compensate for the lack of protection, such as pasteurisation in the bottle or, along with a very strict and careful cleaning regimen in the packaging area, flash pasteurisation.

Similarly, some brewers are experimenting with omitting the wort boiling step. This may, if combined with other factors, make the beer much more susceptible to contamination by undesirable microorganisms. By excluding the wort boiling step, one not only eliminates the thermal annihilation of any microorganisms in the wort from the brewhouse processes but also negates the protection and stabilising effects afforded the beer by boiling hops in the wort (iso α-acids, polyphenols, etc.).

Example 2: Another extreme instance might be a highly-attenuated double IPA with 7% ABV, made from a multi-step mash, with a pH of 4.1 and 65 IBU of bitterness. This set of properties working synergistically serves to make this beer much safer and more stable than the lightly hopped, non-alcoholic beer presented in example 1. The high concentration of iso α-acids dissolved in the beer is protective against most Gram-positive bacteria, such as those belonging to the genera *Bacillus* and *Staphylococcus*, though certain species of *Lactobacillus* and *Pediococcus*, i.e. beer spoilers, can still persist in the beer. However, the wort was boiled, and the pH is relatively low, which eliminated the microbes up to wort chilling and serves to discourage the growth of any that may have entered the process downstream from fermentation. This further lowers the infection pressure on the beer. Moreover, due to the high level of attenuation, there are few nutrients left in the beer (no simple sugars or amino acids), unless the contaminating microbes can ferment dextrins or residual oligosaccharides (e.g. wild yeast). Finally, the beer is made even less attractive by the high ethanol concentration. Most beer spoilers would even find this beer daunting.

By consciously controlling and adjusting the properties inherent to beer through the production process, a brewer is not only able to safeguard that his/her beer is safe to drink but can greatly enhance the flavour stability as well. If one of these properties is not what it should be or is almost completely absent, others must compensate for it; for instance, if very few or no hops are boiled in the wort, the acidity, ethanol content and the microorganisms involved in fermentation are more critical in protecting against beer spoilers and even food-borne pathogens. A perfect example of this type of compensation is evident in beers fermented with mixed microorganisms, such as lambic or kriek. Although both beers hardly contain isomerised α-acids derived from the aged hops, they are somewhat more acidic than typical ales and lagers. They have also been very highly attenuated by the mix of microorganisms fermenting them, leaving next to no nutritive substances for other microorganisms to consume. From a bacterial standpoint they are inhospitable deserts. In addition, the sour cherries in the kriek add both polyphenols and acidity which serve to preserve and protect the beer.

In conclusion, all of the properties in the figures above should be actively monitored and controlled to produce safe, stable beers.

Improving flavour stability in production

As long as the beer is at the brewery, measures can be taken to improve and maintain flavour stability. In the brewing process, the following practices can positively impact flavour stability:

- minimising oxygen uptake in every step of the production process from raw materials to the packaged beer by purging filter aids and tanks with carbon dioxide and using de-aerated water to push beer in pipes
- achieving good wort clarity during lautering with a low solids content without over-extraction of the husks

- restricting the action of enzymes and oxidation reactions that decrease flavour stability
- eliminating undesirable wort compounds without excessive thermal stress
- pitching yeast with a high level of vitality and strong reducing capacity
- generating higher levels of SO_2 in beer or adding antioxidants
- processing and filling beer so that the positive elements of the flavour profile are retained
- protect packaged beer in the warehouse from exposure to heat and sunlight

It is important to keep in mind that ordinarily a best before date on a bottle or can of beer is not a gauge for how long a beer's flavour will remain at an optimal level but rather how long the turbidity is predicted to remain in the same state as when the beer left the brewery. The best before date does not serve as an estimate for predicting when the quality of the flavour will deteriorate to a point that the beer is no longer at its peak. Otherwise, it would be much shorter. Of course, as mentioned above, both the turbidity and the flavour stability of packaged beer are highly influenced by the conditions under which the beer is stored.

SENSORY ANALYSIS

The human sensory apparatus

Of course, the two senses most associated with evaluating beer are smell and taste but the other senses, particularly the visual and the tactile play a significant role. Perhaps listening to the foam collapse or the bubbles popping on the surface might at times be compelling, but aural input is rarely taken into consideration when judging beer.

- **Nose:** In most people, the olfactory bulb can differentiate an astonishing number of volatile compounds.
- **Tongue:** Salty, sweet, bitter, sour and umami are distinguished by the clusters of bulbous nerve endings on the tongue (taste buds).
- **Eyes:** Visual examination is of great importance in the overall evaluation of beer.
- **Tactile:** Other sensations in the mouth and on the face are provided primarily by the trigeminal nerve. This nerve is part of the trigeminal somatosensory system.

When humans drink beer, their sensory inputs are combined to form their overall impression of the beer. Though these inputs synergistically affect one another, they can be divided as follows:

- **Olfactory:** a wide variety of aromas and flavours
- **Gustatory:** salty, sour, sweet, bitter and umami (savoury)
- **Trigeminal:** tactile, texture, e.g. hot, cold, the tingling sensation of acid, the fizz of carbonation, etc.
- **Visual:** appearance, e.g. colour, clarity, foam formation and head retention, etc.

Flavour perception is an amalgamation of multiple sensory inputs. Flavour scientists describe 'flavour' as the sum of inputs from somatosensation, gustation, and olfaction. What particular organ detects a certain sensation and provides which specific inputs is not normally comprehended by those who do not endeavour to understand the sensory analysis of foods. For instance, the appearance of a bright yellow lemon, the sourness on the tongue, the tingling detected by the haptic system and the essential oils and other aromas detected by the olfactory bulb all combine in the brain almost instantly to characterise the overall sensory impression of the fruit. However, it is possible for tasters to differentiate between them, especially when they practice how to distinguish certain sensory characteristics.

Volatile compounds emanating from beer reach the olfactory bulb through the nostrils when a person sniffs the beer, and through the mouth, when a person drinks it. When sniffing a beer, the 'aromas' reach the olfactory bulb through what is called 'orthonasal olfaction'. But when a person drinks a beer, what the olfactory bulb perceives is referred to as 'retronasal olfaction' because it travels behind the soft palate and then up to the olfactory bulb. Consequently, retronasal perception generally occurs when beer is in the drinker's mouth; thus, it is often referred to as 'taste'. For this reason, retronasal olfaction is frequently confused with taste. To those in the field of sensory analysis, this is known as 'smell–taste confusion'. Gustatory and retronasal perception are fundamentally different. However, the orthonasal and retronasal perception of odours are also different.

The five basic types of gustatory perception are salty, sour, sweet, bitter and umami (savoury). Contrary to popular belief, the five basic receptors, which detect different tastes, are not localised on specific zones of the tongue's surface. Texture (mouthfeel, tanginess, carbonation, etc.) and other sensations are detected by the trigeminal somatosensory system, which is crucial in chemosensation and in a person's overall sensory perception of beer.

Of the above types of sensory evaluation, only laboratory analysis of beer is superior to visual assessments. The laboratories of larger breweries are usually equipped with the appropriate devices to visually test beer (colour, haze, etc.).

Ultimately, a group of humans has to judge whether a beer will be acceptable to other humans, since beer is meant to please those equipped with human sensory apparatus. Humans are highly sensitive to certain compounds, down to parts per billion or even less, while we do not detect other substances very well at all. By judging and thus generally knowing what is acceptable to most of beer drinkers, sensory analysis supplements other types of analyses to provide a more complete picture of the final product as well as the influences of specific aspects of the various production processes. Sometimes laboratory testing produces either unsatisfactory results or none at all, and sensory analysis is all the feedback a brewing team has to fall back on, especially in smaller breweries with limited laboratory facilities.

Given that careful procedures are followed, sensory data can be recorded and statistically analysed. To obtain reliable results, the panel of tasters should be trained, become certified and be subjected to frequent testing. Fortunately, procedures for sensory testing are standardised at an international level. This aids brewers around the world in their ultimate goal of producing results from sensory testing which are accurate, objective and reproducible.

Bitterness can be evaluated by a sensory panel that is familiar with the product specifications. This should be sufficient for small breweries lacking specialised equipment for this analysis or funds for outsourcing.

Sensory analysis is inexpensive and useful but difficult to implement with an inexperienced panel.

Assembling a panel

People can be generally classified into three categories concerning their olfactory and gustatory faculties. With regard to the sensory perception of foods and beverages, there are three categories of people: super-tasters, tasters and non-tasters. Super-tasters possess more fungiform papillae, a type of taste bud on the tongue. Around 35% of women are super-tasters while only around 15% of men can be classified as such. Super-tasters are generally more sensitive to substances with a bitter flavour than tasters and, for this reason, may be overly sensitive to the hop bitterness in beer. Tasters can be roughly characterised as follows:

- Supertasters experience a sensation derived from a certain substance, such as diacetyl or bitter flavours, with a higher than average intensity. Though they may not know how to express it yet, they can detect the substance in question at very low concentrations.
- Others are able to obtain a good overall impression of a particular beer and with the proper training can express specific aspects of what they are sensing but do not have a supertaster's abilities.
- There are others who simply seem to enjoy having a beer with friends but can't say much more about it than that. Individuals in this group will have difficulty contributing to a sensory panel.

Selecting candidates

- They should be willing and able to devote the necessary time to training their sensory abilities.
- They should be available to regularly participate in scheduled tastings and have permission from their superiors to attend tasting sessions.
- Their participation should be voluntary.
- They should be reasonably healthy and not suffer from major health problems or alcohol addiction.

So, how does one go about gaining experience and maintaining one's skills as a taster?

First, no one excels at every aspect of sensory analysis. For this reason, it is best to assemble a panel, gathering those with average to above average olfactory and gustatory perception with perhaps a supertaster or two. Sensory analysis takes advantage of the fact that the human brain builds strong associations with flavours and aromas to produce what is known as gustatory imagery. The authors attended a blind tasting years ago where a participant stated afterwards that one aspect of a beer reminded him of 'something that comes in a glass jar! It's maybe a bit earthy, a little salty and slightly sour....pickled black olives!'

Thus, detecting aromas and flavours is half the battle. Finding standard descriptors and identifiers is just as important. There are resources to help those interested in honing their sensory skills in addition to learning how to express what they smell, taste and feel.

By practicing frequently and regularly. Like language skills or anything else, one's ability to sensorially evaluate raw materials as well as intermediate and final products withers on the vine when not maintained.

The basic flavours can be practiced using the following substances at these concentrations:

Table 19: Reference substances for basic flavours

Flavour	Reference substance	Concentration [g/l]
sweet	sucrose	6.0
sour	citric acid	0.4
salty	sodium chloride	1.3
bitter	isohumulone	0.012
umami	monosodium glutamate	0.5
astringent	γ-aminobutyric acid	0.051

Source: Norm DIN 10961, *Schulung von Prüfpersonen für sensorische Prüfungen*, 1996.

Kits are available for practicing common beer off-aromas/off-flavours. Sensory analysis kits, though expensive, are convenient and easy to use. The flavour standards in these kits are dosed into training samples so the samples are adulterated with these substances. In this way, the panellists can learn to identify off-flavours and off-aromas in water, beer, etc.

Each panellist should receive on-going training in the identification of off-flavours and should be tested regularly in order to evaluate the sensitivity of his/her palate. The results of the tests should be documented, and the panellist's performance monitored over time for any fluctuations in their abilities. The objectives of the training should be as follows:

- Learn sensory techniques: sniffing, sipping, holding in one's mouth.
- Improve sensitivity: learn to distinguish sensory impressions, to recognise differences and to determine threshold values.
- Hone one's ability to evaluate the product's (beer) characteristics.
- Learn the lexicon of aromas and flavours and how to identify them.

For sensory panels tasked with making the final decision on releasing a beer for distribution, a sample should be prepared which is distinctly out of specification for the brand. This will test the conviction and willingness of the panel to prevent a substandard beer from being released and ensure that they are acting in the best interest of the brewery.

Training panellists and brewery personnel to avoid production errors

Add a small amount of cleaning agent or sanitiser (1 ml to 100 ml of beer) to a beer sample and cover the sample with parafilm to prevent anyone from drinking it. Puncture the parafilm so that participants can sniff the adulterated sample, making it clear that they are not to taste it. Dispose of the sample immediately afterwards. The participants should describe their impression of the off-aroma in the beer.

Dilute a beer sample with brewing liquor (10 ml in 100 ml) in order to educate the brewery personnel concerning how errors in production can result in dilution of the beer during blending or by pushing the beer with brewing liquor. Compare the diluted sample with an undiluted one for aroma, flavour (bitterness) and mouthfeel (body).

A simple method for training brewery personnel to detect diacetyl involves collecting a sample of actively fermenting wort from a fermentation vessel and heating it. Transfer the sample to an aroma-neutral container with a lid that is capable of immersion and place it in a water bath at 60 °C for 1 h. The container should be filled half full and the lid should be firmly sealed onto the container. Fill another identical container with a sample of packaged beer and subject it to the same treatment. The heat will volatilise the diacetyl in solution causing it to accumulate in the airspace above the surface of the liquid. After 1 h remove the lids on both containers and immediately smell both samples, comparing the aromas and noting any differences. Samples with diacetyl will smell of butter, buttered popcorn or butterscotch, while those without diacetyl will not, though they will smell like boiled beer.

Collect a yeast sample and transfer it to an aroma-neutral container with a lid and place the sample in a warm area for 12 h. Compare the sensory impression of a fresh yeast sample with that of the sample subjected to 12 h in a warm environment. This should improve the sensitivity among brewery personnel regarding the appearance and aroma of fresh pitching yeast.

Brewery personnel should be made aware of whom they need to consult if they have any doubts about the sensory nature of raw materials or intermediate and final products.

The above training exercises were adapted from information found in the book: Pellettieri, M., *Quality Management: Essential Management for Breweries*. Brewers Association, 2015.

| How to set up a tasting room

Ideally, a tasting room should be designed to facilitate sensory analysis under defined conditions while restricting any factors which could influence the panellists.

Samples should be prepared for sensory analysis in an area isolated from the tasting room but located in close proximity to it, if possible. External influences such as odours, noise or interruptions should be held to a minimum. The atmosphere in the tasting room should be climate-controlled at a temperature comfortable for the panellists. The colour scheme, furnishings and lighting should be neutral. To minimise distractions during tastings, booths or cubicles may be employed. An area should be designated for group tastings and discussion.

Equipment and materials:

- clean, standardised tasting glasses
- trays to distribute samples among panellists
- evaluation forms, writing utensils, a computer for data entry
- a white board or flip chart
- a designated dishwasher for cleaning glassware
- a sink for rinsing out glassware and washing hands
- a bucket to discard samples
- pure standards for training panellists to detect specific compounds in beer

| Conducting a tasting

Our senses are sharper in the morning, between 10:00 and 11:00, so schedule tastings then if possible. It is best to wait at least 30 minutes after eating or smoking to evaluate beers in a tasting.

As mentioned, the tasting room should be quiet and free from any external odours, if space and resources allow.

If multiple beers are to be evaluated, sipping water and eating white bread between samples helps to neutralise the taste buds.

Clearly communicate the objectives of the tasting to the participants. Allow participants enough time to taste and record their impressions. Discussion should begin after everyone has had a chance to evaluate the beer.

Use the same glass form/design for tasting all the beers similar in style. The glassware should be clean and free of any fat or soap residues. Beer should be tasted in order of intensity, from less to more.

Beer should normally be sampled at 10–12 °C, and no more than 10 samples should be analysed per sitting. The duration should be no longer than 30 min.

Participants should be encouraged to use all of their senses when evaluating the beer:

- **Hear:** opening the beer and pouring it into a glass
- **See:** colour, clarity or turbidity, perlage (effervescence), foam consistency
- **Smell:** aroma, undesirable odours, overall intensity, balance
- **Taste:** flavour, off-flavours, bitterness, aftertaste, overall intensity, balance
- **Touch:** mouthfeel, body, astringency

| Assessing beer

Beer can be evaluated within the framework of the following:

Flavour stability: The panel tastes beers with the purpose of detecting changes in them as they age. Ageing can be carried out either naturally or artificially. The panel evaluates how aspects of ageing become evident over time and e.g. how decreasing oxygen uptake from the brewhouse to the filling line affects the beer.

Microbial contamination: This is caused by unwanted yeast or bacteria, e.g. should the concentration of diacetyl be unusually high in a batch of beer, it is almost certainly not from the yeast but rather contamination by lactic acid bacteria, such as *Pediococcus*.

Tainted ingredients: This can be the result of raw materials or processing aids that have been corrupted in some way or are less than pure, e.g. chlorinated water or tainted diatomaceous earth.

Errors in production: Incorrect or improper raw materials, processing aids or production processes can result in bad beer. Rarely do novel products created in this way result in good beer, e.g. pilsner malt vs. pale malt or different mashing or fermentation schedules, etc.

Product consistency: Between batches, differences can be found as well as their probable root causes, e.g. two lots of pale malt were different or two brewers are following slightly different procedures.

Refer to the section on evaluation sheets below.

Sensory analysis in the brewery

In the not so distant past, the brewer supervised the brewing process, moved through the areas of the brewery every day and monitored progress without the benefit of sophisticated measuring devices. There were no staff members tasked with taking samples to perform analyses as part of quality assurance. Much of the progress in beer production could be seen, smelled, tasted or touched. Yeast was propagated or re-pitched and beer in the maturation cellar was tasted and assessed sensorially. Although today's brewers have access to much more technology, for the most part, they are still able to use the methods of the past – their five senses – to carefully monitor beer during the production process.

Sensory analysis is a crucial part of a quality control programme. It is also very cost-effective, given that the human sensory apparatus is more sensitive than a gas chromatograph or other expensive laboratory devices, especially when coupled with other members in a panel of trained tasters.

In addition to the visual inspection and evaluation of raw materials described earlier in the book, the following methods allow for additional quality control as well as insight into the nuances of the flavour and aroma characteristics of raw materials. Throughout the brewery, it is important to sensorially evaluate how the process is developing – this even applies to detecting if the temperature is too high or low at a particular point in the process. As mentioned, consistency is important in brewing, especially for flagship beers brewed on a regular basis. If off-flavours are entering the production process, sensory analysis allows brewers to localise where and how they are coming into it. Experienced brewers often come to rely more on their five senses than laboratory devices and technology:

- **raw materials:** brewing liquor after treatment, malt, hops and pitching yeast
- **intermediate products and processing aids:** cast-out wort, fermenting wort, maturing beer, filter aids, stabilisation agents
- **finished products:** beer in the maturation tank, beer off the filter, beer from the bright tank, archived beer, packaged beer from the filling line and from the market (shelf life)

Raw materials

Sensory analysis of raw materials is useful for evaluating their quality and potential impact on the finished beer. These analyses are not part of the visual inspection and are not as widespread or standardised as those for beer.

Sensory analysis of brewing liquor

After treatment, the brewing liquor should be completely neutral, odourless, tasteless, colourless, free of any evolving gases and clear.

Examples of contaminants in water and their odour/taste references include the following. This list is not exhaustive:

Table 20: The aromas and flavours of selected substances in brewing liquor

Substance	Aroma/flavour	Source
benzaldehyde	sweet almonds	natural sources, industrial processes
geosmin	earthy, algal	Gram-positive bacteria, cyanobacteria
chlorine	swimming pool	water treatment
D-limonene	citrus	citrus fruit
trimethylamine	rotten fish, ammonia-like	decomposing plants and animals
dimethyl disulphide	decaying vegetation	decay of grass in drinking water reservoirs
dimethyl trisulphide	septic aroma	decay of vegetation
hydrogen sulphide	rotten eggs	anaerobic bacteria
salty	chloride ions, sulphates	geologic formations, agriculture, urban run-off
chlorophenols	medicinal	water treatment

An activated carbon filter, in addition to more advanced treatment methods, would be useful if such compounds were present as contaminants.

Malt sensory hot steep method

This method entails the extraction of malt flavours and aromas from malt kernels using distilled water under application of heat. This method is an excellent tool for evaluating malt quality and consistency in the brewery.

- The malt (55 g) is milled in a coffee grinder reserved for this purpose for 30 seconds to a flour-like consistency.
- Weigh out 50 g of malt flour and transfer to an insulated flask.
- Pour 400 ml of distilled water at 65 °C into the flask and seal.
- Mix the contents thoroughly by shaking for 20 seconds.
- Wait 15 min; swirl the flask to resuspend the contents, and then pour the contents into a funnel lined with fluted filter paper or a coffee filter.
- Collect the first 100 ml of filtrate in a beaker and return it to the flask to rinse out any grist particles.
- Pour the remaining liquid into the filter.
- Collect all the filtrate in the beaker (approx. 300 ml in 30 to 45 minutes).
- Perform a sensory evaluation within 4 h of filtration.

For more information on how to sensorially evaluate the liquid extracted from the malt refer to the ASBC Hot Steep Malt Evaluation Method, which includes a base malt flavour map and a standardised base malt lexicon.

Hop tea sensory method

This method involves the extraction of hop flavour and aroma compounds using water at ambient temperature. It allows brewers to become familiar with the individual flavour and aroma characteristics of a particular hop variety. Obviously, the hops will be expressed in beer differently; however, this method enables brewers to form general opinions about the hops they are using.

- Weigh out 10 g of hop pellets or 12 g of whole hops.
- Mill the hops in a coffee grinder reserved for this purpose until a fine powder is obtained (10 to 15 seconds for pellets, 20 seconds for whole hops).
- Place the hop powder in a glass French coffee press reserved for this purpose together with a magnetic stir bar (if available).
- Add 0.5 litres of water at 21 °C.
- Insert the plunger and press it down to a height slightly below the surface of the liquid.
- Place the French press on the stir plate and set the mixing speed at 40%.
- Allow the liquid to mix for 20 minutes. Alternatively, swirl the solution frequently for 1 h.

- After the elapsed time, remove the French press from the plate and depress the plunger to the bottom.
- Pour the hop solution into a clear tasting glass and sensorially evaluate.

The spider diagramme for hop aroma included above in the raw materials section on hops is useful for comparing two similar beers or two beers brewed with the same wort but different late hopping regimes. The spider diagrammes highlight how different the olfactory impressions of late-hopped beers can be.

Yeast

Developing a sense of how to judge healthy yeast by its appearance, odours and flavours is an important skill for brewers. It is also worthwhile to be able to distinguish the aromas of top-fermenting and bottom-fermenting yeast.

Refer to the section on raw materials about yeast for information on sensory analysis. As mentioned above, the sensory impression of fresh yeast and yeast subjected to warm temperatures for 12 h can be compared to train brewery personnel concerning the characteristics of pitchable yeast.

| Testing

Discriminative testing

Discriminative tests allow brewers to find out whether a perceptible sensory difference exists between two different beers. The data obtained from such tests allow for statistical analysis of the results to determine if the difference is indeed perceptible or the participants' choices were merely a matter of chance. Discriminative tests establish if there is a statistically significant difference between two products according to blind tasting results, and for this reason, the number of tasters should be as large as possible. The following tests are commonly employed for this kind of sensory analysis.

- paired comparison
- triangle test
- tetrad test
- duo-trio test
- two-out-of-five test
- ranking test
- different from control test

Of the above tests, the tetrad test is reported to be the most efficient and accurate, especially for smaller groups of participants. The data gained from these tests are unbiased and useful for ferreting out the effects of changes to raw materials, production processes, processing aids, storage conditions and packaging. Thus, they are a practical tool for making informed decisions.

By conducting a blind test, this means that the participant is unaware what the sample is, while a double-blind test refers to one in which neither the participant nor the proctor of the test knows the identity of the samples. A double-blind test eliminates any subconscious bias the person conducting the test might project.

Refer to the EBC analyses 13.6–13.9 for more on these discriminative tests.

Sensory threshold testing

A number of the tests listed above can be employed for this purpose. This establishes the participant's sensitivity to a given substance by comparing concentrations. The ranking test is often used to establish at what concentration a participant can detect a substance by ranking samples in their order of intensity. The samples would be prepared beforehand with steadily rising concentrations of a substance, e.g. diacetyl.

A test that is practical in this regard is the so-called 'different from control test'. Participants are presented with a control and a sample containing a certain concentration of the substance in question. Increasing concentrations of the substance are compared to the control sample. The control can be given in both cups if desired, in order to test for a false positive. Performing the sensory threshold test in this way can help avoid palate fatigue.

Evaluative testing

Tasters conducting this kind of testing usually do so within the framework of quality control and need to have had a great deal of ongoing practice to do it well. Not everyone is equipped with the same sensory toolbox – some have a large and varied set of tools while others are only able to detect the most fundamental aromas and flavours. Everyone can be trained to utilise and improve upon what they have been endowed with. Practice is key but also internalising a deep well of accurate descriptors and linking them to sensory stimuli is imperative. Having them at one's disposal is important for describing the olfactory and gustatory impressions of beer. The faults one generally encounters in beer should also become linked to points in the production process and ways in which these faults can be rectified.

For more information on these tests and how to conduct them, refer to the sources listed below.

Table 21 provides recommendations for the level of sensory analysis training for members of the sensory panel and the facilities available to them according to brewery output.

Table 21: Types of recommended sensory training and brewery size

	<1,000 hl	1,000 to 5,000 hl	5,000 to 10,000 hl	10,000 to 30,000 hl	> 30,000 hl
Sensory training for sensory panel general training (a brewery's brands)	★ ★ ★	★ ★ ★	★ ★ ★	★ ★ ★	★ ★ ★
sensory training for sensory panel discriminative testing	★ ★	★ ★ ★	★ ★ ★	★ ★ ★	★ ★ ★
sensory training for sensory panel sensory threshold testing	★	★ ★	★ ★ ★	★ ★ ★	★ ★ ★
sensory training for sensory panel evaluative testing	★	★ ★	★ ★ ★	★ ★ ★	★ ★ ★
sensory training dedicated tasting room	★	★ ★	★ ★	★ ★ ★	★ ★ ★

★ ★ ★	★ ★	★
essential	recommended	beneficial

The lexicon

There are many flavour and aroma compounds in beer and through their synergistic intermixing, their number multiplies exponentially. However, one quite often encounters some very common flavours and aromas in beer. The tables at the back of the book provide a mere sampling of some of them. Note that not all are pleasant or desirable. Though off-aromas and off-flavours may be unpleasant, it is useful to become familiar with them so one can understand for quality control purposes how and why they enter the production process.

| Drinkability

Asserting that a beer has a high drinkability means much more than to imply it is merely 'potable', i.e. 'fit for drinking, drinkable', or 'thirst-quenching'. After draining a beer, if a drinker is compelled to immediately request another from the server, this is a sign that the brewer understands balance and the subtle art of brewing. This kind of beer would be deemed to have a high level of drinkability. Given that brewers want to sell their beer, drinkability is a good trait for a beer to possess. Likewise, this term should not be confused with a descriptor like 'acceptable' which implies that a beer is adequate, yet unexceptional.

Craft beer and drinkability

Across the British Isles and Europe, where most of the beers that have inspired craft brewers are produced, one can find highly drinkable beers that induce happy customers to repeatedly order 'just one more'. And yet, thirsty patrons in tasting rooms, bars and restaurants often come across beers that possess no faults, are not at all unpleasant and are quite palatable. But they lack a high level of drinkability. A first beer does not necessarily lead to a second or a third. Seasoned beer enthusiasts are regularly faced with beers fitting this description brewed by enthusiastic brewers who know how to mill malt, turn valves, add hops and pitch yeast – and can generally brew good beer. Nevertheless, they have yet to master the craft of brewing highly drinkable beer. Many beers from the 'new wave' of craft brewing are flavourful, experimental in nature and challenging; it is true that they are almost never boring. Brewing a beer with a high level of drinkability is, however, more difficult to achieve, in part because it is also harder to define than other attributes of beer, such as bitterness or sourness. This is one aspect of those Old World traditions that can perhaps still serve as a source of inspiration for the 'new wave' of craft brewers.

Harmony, subtlety and balance should be afforded the deference they deserve. One can experience this when enjoying a fine British ale, Flanders red, lambic, *Weissbier*, *Helles* or pilsner, among others. The constant invention of beer styles and a revolving door of novel ingredients are not marks of quality *per se*, though they do trigger innovation. Brewers cultivate nuanced skill by honing their abilities through brewing 'naked' beers – those with just a few ingredients, that is, with no overwhelming flavours and aromas capable of hiding faults. This certainly does not mean that the beers have to be middling or run-of-the mill – quite the opposite, they should possess an exceptional drinkability. More than a few craft brewers focus more heavily on ingredients at the expense of developing an appreciation and understanding for the contributions of the brewing process.

What contributes to a beer's drinkability?

The sensory aspects of drinkability are generally considered to be the most important, such as the aroma, flavour, texture and temperature of the beer. However, not to be dismissed are also cognitive and physiological effects of the beer on the drinker. A beer will almost certainly possess a low level of drinkability, if it is considered by those tasting the

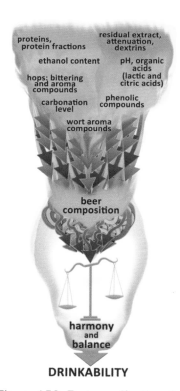

Figure 153: Factors affecting the sensory aspects of drinkability

beer to be satiating, or thick and filling. It has been shown that, generally speaking, as the sensation of satiety increases, the desire to drink another beer decreases. Aside from this, a beer's serving temperature, carbonation level and appearance (clarity, foam formation, head retention) – even the shape of the glass – also play a role in how a beer's drinkability is perceived.

The 'sensory effect', as it is called, is not the only factor affecting drinkability. Further influences, mostly out of the hands of the brewer, can be summarised as 'presentation' and 'what a person eats'. The former, i.e. how a beer is perceived by a drinker at the restaurant or bar as well as in marketing and in advertising, falls under the umbrella term 'cognitive effects' in the literature, because the brain plays a role in the perception even before the drinker takes a sip. Other psychological factors can be classified under this rubric. The latter refers to whether the person is eating or has eaten, what the person has eaten and whether the person is drinking on an already full stomach, etc. These factors are encapsulated under the 'ingestive effect.' Factors related to these comprise the nutrients one has taken in and their absorption by the alimentary canal into the bloodstream and the influence they have over brain function. These substances include ethanol, glucose and amino acids. This aspect of drinkability is designated as the 'post-absorptive effect'. The interplay of all of these effects with regard to drinkability can be imagined as they are depicted in figure 154.

Figure 154: Drinkability and the various effects influencing it

The factors a brewer does have control over are as follows:

- **Brewing liquor**: treat it properly according to the beer style.
- **Malt quality control**: refer to the section on malt above.
- **Adjunct usage**: this may change aspects of the drinkability of some styles, like pilsner.
- **Mashing regime**: select one that is appropriate for the style, and within the style guidelines, one that will maximise the final attenuation (refer to the section on mashing).
- **Boil**: intensity, time, hot break (refer to the section on wort boiling).
- **Hops**: whole or type 90 pellets of noble, unfertilised hops for lagers or more traditional low-alpha British varieties for ales impart a finer bitterness than high alpha varieties with fewer auxiliary bitter substances and polyphenols (refer to the section on hops above).
- **Yeast strain**: especially important are viability, vitality and achieving a high final attenuation.
- **Conditions during fermentation**: aeration, yeast cell count, temperature, pH drop, rapidity, etc. (refer to fermentation above).

- **Maturation**: long conditioning/maturation at low temperatures is valuable, regardless of – but appropriate for – the beer style. The practice of *aufkräusening* is beneficial, too, if appropriate for the beer (refer to the section on maturation above).
- **Tank geometry**: a tank's geometry is partially responsible for the fermentation by-products in the beer and its clarity (refer to the section on tank geometry above).

Drinkability is still nevertheless a somewhat nebulous concept, even though a beer exhibiting a high level of drinkability may be plainly apparent to seasoned beer enthusiasts. Therefore, no objective analyses for determining drinkability have as yet been developed.

Literature and further reading

Brauer, J., Lenzini, J., *Fermentability ratios, attenuation scores and drinkability*. Brauwelt international 2021/I pp. *38-41* Fachverlag Hans Carl

Gastl, M., Hanke, S., Back, W., *"Drinkability" – Ausgewogenheit und Harmonie der Inhaltsstoffe sowie Anreiz zum Weitertrinken*. Brauwelt no. 45 pp. 1316–1322, 2007

Mattos, R., Moretti, R. *Beer Drinkability—A Review*. MBAA TQ vol. 42, no. 1, pp. 13–15, 2005

MEBAK, *Sensory Analysis*. MEBAK (publisher), 2014

Narziss, L. *Abriss der Bierbrauerei*. Wiley-VCH Verlag GmbH & Co., 2017

The reference books listed in the back of this book also provide information for those wishing to learn more about how the malting and brewing processes contribute to the overall quality and drinkability of beer.

Evaluation sheets

Most sensory evaluations of beer are subdivided as follows:

Aroma: The volatile compounds detected by orthonasal perception vary widely in humans, but regardless of their combined effect, the overall aroma of the beer must be attractive to the drinker.

Flavour: This is a combination of what the drinker senses on the tongue and retronasally as well. It should be neither overbearing nor lacking. As mentioned above, flavour is a fusion of smell, taste and other sensations.

Mouthfeel: The body cannot be thin, mouthcoating or contribute to a feeling of being satiated. It should normally be none of those but rather should be agreeably full. As stated above, detection of a beer's texture is primarily attributable to the trigeminal somatosensory system.

Bitterness: The bitterness should be fine and crisp, not harsh or astringent and should not persist long after the beer is swallowed (refer to the section on hop bitterness).

Bitterness is not only derived from hops in beer but other processes in the brewhouse and in fermentation as well. The images in figure 155 can aid in determining the kind of bitterness perceived in beer. These different descriptors and their accompanying graphs are meant to aid in the characterisation of the bitterness within the first 10 to 15 seconds of sampling a beer.

Liveliness: This contributes largely to an impression of freshness in beer and involves not only fine CO_2 bubbles but also the acid balance of the beer.

Balance/harmony: The synergy of the flavours and aromas from the malt, hops, fermentation and other flavours as well as the mouthfeel and liveliness should form an agreeable overall impression.

Acidity: Particularly important for sour beers, the mixture of organic acids should be pleasant; it is measured primarily as titratable acidity.

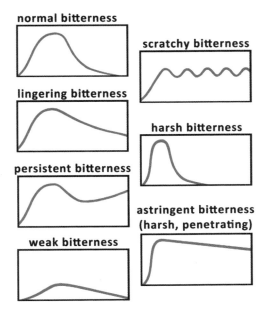

Figure 155: Visual representations of the kinds of bitterness typical in beer
Source: Hopsteiner Simon H. Steiner, Hopfen, GmbH

Aftertaste: The aftertaste emerges after beer has been swallowed. If it lingers too long or becomes objectionable, this does not promote drinkability. This attribute can be grouped with flavour (as in the example below) or it can be a separate attribute, perhaps one that is not weighted as heavily as the others.

A number of evaluation sheets have been developed for carrying out tastings in a consistent and practical manner. After determining which sheet to employ for assessing a brewery's beers, the same sheet should continue to be used, if possible. If the same panel conducts the tastings using a single sheet for evaluating a brewery's beers and these records are kept over time, especially concerning a brewery's main brands, then any variation in the beers will become apparent, especially if these data are tracked in a graphable spreadsheet. The panel at the brewery may decide that certain attributes should be weighted more heavily than others. For instance, the scores for aroma, flavour, quality of bitterness and drinkability can be given twice the weight of body, liveliness and aftertaste (a separate category in this case). The tasting panel must decide what attributes are most important for the brewery.

Name:	Beer:
Date:	

Refer to the descriptors in the appendix, under "Aroma descriptors for hops" and in figure 156 for terms to more precisely define the attributes of the beer and the quality of the bitterness under the column heading "Descriptors".

Attribute	Scale	Descriptors	Score
Aroma	5 excellent, very true to style 4 good, true to style 3 minor fault, not quite true to style 2 fault, not true to style 1 extreme fault		
Flavour Aftertaste	5 excellent, very true to style 4 good, true to style 3 minor fault, not quite true to style 2 fault, not true to style 1 extreme fault		
Body Mouthfeel	5 very suitable, very true to style 4 suitable, true to style 3 minor fault, not quite true to style 2 fault, not true to style 1 extreme fault		
Liveliness	5 very lively, very true to style 4 lively, true to style 3 slightly flat, not quite true to style 2 flat, not true to style 1 extremely flat		
Quality of bitterness	5 very fine 4 fine 3 moderately fine 2 harsh 1 harsh, penetrating, astringent		
Overall impression Drinkability	5 excellent drinkability 4 suitable drinkability 3 moderate drinkability 2 lacking drinkability 1 completely uninviting		

If evaluating a sour beer, this category can be added.

Acidity	5 extremely refreshing, mellow, tart 4 pleasantly tart, quite refreshing 3 tangy, slightly penetrating 2 quite dry, penetrating, unpleasant 1 biting, astringent, very unpleasant		

TOTAL	

Additional notes

Figure 156: A general evaluation sheet for beer; an addendum for sour beer is included under the standard attributes

Since many breweries produce beers with significant additions of bittering, flavour and aroma hops, an evaluation sheet has been devised for judging these kinds of beers:

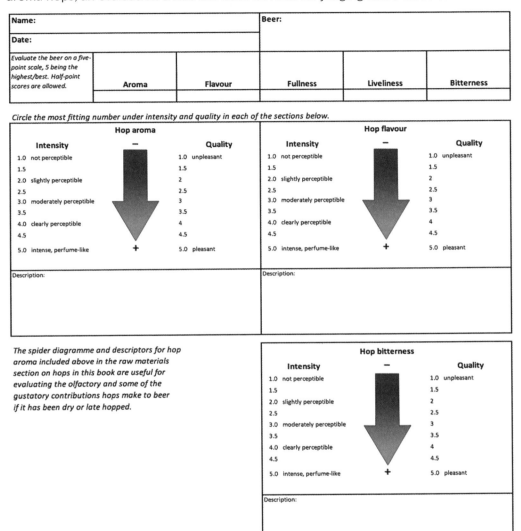

Figure 157: An evaluation sheet for highly hopped beers

Literature and further reading

The source for the above evaluation sheets as well as other information in this section: Mitteleuropäische Brautechnische Analysenkommission (MEBAK), *Sensory Analysis*. MEBAK (publisher), 2014

Rogers, L. (ed.), *Discrimination Testing in Sensory Science: A Practical Handbook*. Woodhead Publishing Ltd., Cambridge, UK, 2017

The colour of wort and beer

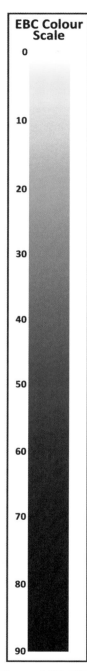

Figure 158: EBC colour scale

Where does beer get its colour? Primarily from the different types of malt used in the grain bill. The colour in malt comes from chemical reactions known as non-enzymatic browning, that is, the Maillard reactions and caramelisation. Non-enzymatic browning reactions are dependent upon many factors, including temperature, water activity, pH, moisture content and chemical composition.

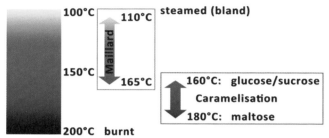

Figure 159: Temperature, the Maillard reactions and caramelisation

On a side note, enzymatic browning may be of interest for brewers who have ventured into the realm of fruit beers, as the darker colour of dried fruit, such as is present in raisins, is derived from this type of browning.

The reactions in the complex processes associated with non-enzymatic browning primarily occur during kilning in the malting process. Brewhouse operations also increase the colour of the wort primarily through the Maillard reactions, especially if the vessels are direct-fired. During fermentation the colour of the wort lightens slightly.

Table 22: Beer colour

Beer colour	EBC units
very light	2 – 3
straw	4 – 5
pale	6 – 8
gold	9 – 11
light amber	12 – 14
amber	15 – 17
medium amber	18 – 19
copper/garnet	20 – 24
light brown	25 – 29
reddish brown/chestnut brown	30 – 34
dark brown	35 – 48
very dark	49 – 78
completely black	79+

Judging colour must be done with either a comparator or even more accurately with a spectrophotometer. The scale is only included here to provide approximate values for the colour of wort and beer and was adapted from the EBC scale. Table 22 provides descriptions of beer colour and an approximation of the corresponding EBC units.

The Maillard reactions

From the touch of radiant gold in a pilsner down to the deep reddish black of a stout, the Maillard reactions are responsible for the colour of beer. However, they also greatly influence the aroma and flavour of beer.

These reactions are too complex to delve into here; however, those interested in learning more about them should consult the texts on food chemistry in the reading list in the back of the book. The Maillard reactions occur with the reducing sugars and proteins, peptides, amines or amino acids present in foods as reactants. The most common reducing sugars involved in the reactions are glucose, fructose and maltose. In order to briefly outline what occurs in overview, the raw materials and some of the products of the reactions are highlighted here. Aldoses and ketoses are simple sugars with an aldehyde group and a ketone group, respectively. Reducing sugars are those with a free aldehyde or free ketone group that can act as reducing agents. These are combined with amino

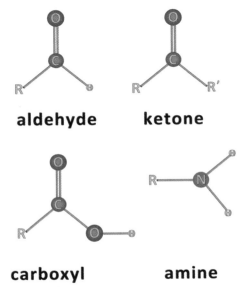

Figure 160: Functional groups common among Maillard products

acids under the application of heat. Of course, amino acids are the building blocks of proteins, which contain an amine and a carboxyl functional group. The 19 amino acids and various reducing sugars produce a whole host of compounds which provide hundreds of flavours and a wide array of colours to foods we enjoy. The concentration of amino acids drops in malt and wort as the Maillard reactions increase.

Products of the Maillard reactions are both negative and positive for the finished beer. The Maillard reactions can occur very slowly at relatively low temperatures but become much more rapid at around 140 °C and continue up to around 165 °C.

Within the framework of these reactions high molecular weight melanoidins are formed. These impart a brown pigment to the malt and wort, contain nitrogen and exhibit various levels of solubility in aqueous solutions.

Maillard reactions and lipid oxidation

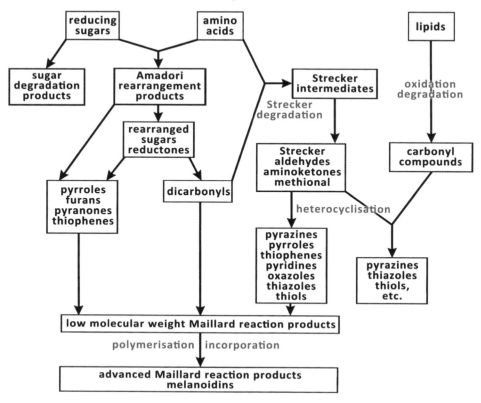

Figure 161: The Maillard reactions and lipid oxidation

Melanoidins also increase the antioxidant activity. In the brewhouse, some of the products of Maillard reactions cause more coagulable nitrogen to precipitate. For this reason, there is less coagulable nitrogen in chilled dark wort, which could have repercussions for yeast nutrition. However, the olfactory contribution of the melanoidins can also be negative; for instance, those derived from the amino acid proline are very bitter.

If the mash or wort is exposed to excessive thermal stress in the brewhouse, such as in a direct-fired mash or wort kettle, this can produce off-aromas in the beer. If the malt is overmodified and there is too much FAN in the wort or when oxygen reacts with the wort or beer, Strecker aldehydes can form during storage. This is one reason that one should be careful of hot-side aeration and use carbon dioxide, nitrogen or deaerated water to purge tanks and other equipment. The non-enzymatic oxidation of polyphenols also contributes to the increase in colour.

Malt has already undergone the various reactions which cause the colour to increase in it, due to the withering and curing processes. 3-Methylbutanal is an important contributor to the malty aroma of darker malt and the pleasant sweetness of darker beers (refer to table 23 below).

3-Methylbutanal and 2-isopropyl-5-methyl-2-hexenal are two volatile compounds that increase gradually with malt colour and are present in the Congress wort, while the Maillard products furfural and 5-methylfurfural increase exponentially as malt colour intensifies. Hexanal is one compound that decreases with increasing malt colour. It is derived from the lipid linoleic acid and is found in green and pale malts but to a lesser extent in darker malts. This is one of the lipid degradation products that is involved in reactions with Maillard products (refer to the list of flavour and aroma descriptors in table 24).

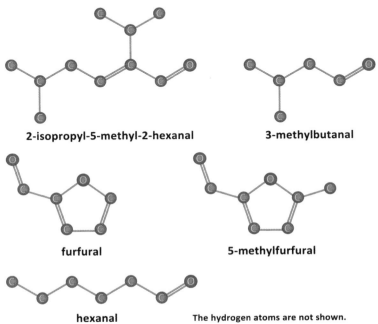

2-isopropyl-5-methyl-2-hexanal   **3-methylbutanal**

furfural   **5-methylfurfural**

hexanal   **The hydrogen atoms are not shown.**

Figure 162: Aldehydes affected by an increase in malt colour

A wide range of intermediate products are also created. Some are stable, while some are not. The degradation of the carbonyls results in, among other molecules, hetero-cyclic compounds. Carbonyls also react with aldol condensation products and other aldehydes. These reaction products are present in every type of malt.

Reductones are compounds, as the name suggests, that act as reducing agents and thus serve as antioxidants in beer. They increase in the wort as the colour increases.

More highly modified and kilned malts provide greater concentrations of reactants for the Maillard reactions, and thus the wort colour increases as the degree of modification of the malt in the grain bill increases. If the increase in colour is too great, the beer will be unpleasantly bitter.

Many volatile compounds arise, yielding an extremely wide range of aromas, some of them desirable, some of them not. This is one of the important roles of wort boiling, to apply enough heat to the wort to bring about the evaporation of these volatile compounds. The aromas present in malt kilned to various levels add character to beer. However, Maillard products in beer pasteurised after bottling are involved, for example, in chemical reactions that accelerate the rate at which ageing compounds increase to above their respective sensory thresholds, especially in the presence of oxygen.

A process known as the Strecker degradation of amino acids involves de-aminating and decarboxylating amino acids to produce aldehydes and aminoketones. These products are responsible for strong aromas and flavours.

Table 23: Amino acids, their corresponding Strecker aldehydes
and their sensory impressions

Amino acids	Strecker aldehydes	Aromas/flavours
methionine	methional	vegetal aroma, mashed potatoes, associated with staling and autolysed yeast as well as non-alcoholic or low-alcohol beers
phenylalanine	phenyl-acetaldehyde	green, floral, honey-like, sweet, rose, green, grassy, hyacinths, bread, baked cereal; associated with ageing
valine	2-methylpropanal	green, overripe fruit, wet cereal, straw, cocoa
leucine	3-methylbutanal	malty, fruity, toasted bread, baked cereal, cocoa
isoleucine	2-methylbutanal	fruity, sweet, roasted, cocoa
alanine	acetaldehyde	pungent, fruity, green apple, cider, solvent, paint thinner

Aldehydes can be positive and, for instance, impart a 'malty' character to beer, but they can also be negative, especially over time as the beer ages. The Strecker degradation of amino acids to aldehydes is where many off-flavours associated with non-enzymatic browning originate. How the flavours and aromas of the following aldehydes – and for that matter any of the substances in beer – are perceived depends upon a wide variety of factors including which compounds are present with them.

The other products of the Maillard reactions further combine with those from Strecker degradation to create strong flavour compounds known as heterocyclic compounds, such as pyrazines, pyrroles, oxazoles, thiophenes, pyrones and thiazoles (fig. 163). These heterocyclic compounds – chemical ring structures with other elements in addition to carbon in their rings – are the products of these reactions. Amino acids and sugars can produce them both with and without lipids. The heterocyclic compounds are desirable in dark malt and create a wide range of aromas in beer. They are numerous and can be reminiscent of freshly baked bread, browned potatoes, sautéed mushrooms, green wood, popcorn, cocoa, pralines, toffee, nuts or coffee and impart pleasantly roasted notes. The concentration of heterocyclic compounds increases as the duration of the boil increases, especially at higher temperatures. Therefore, beers produced from wort boiled longer and/or at higher temperatures exhibit more of the pronounced aroma notes outlined above. They can also, in part, be boiled off in the brewhouse. If wort brewed with dark malt undergoes additional thermal stress, this can manifest itself as burnt or cooked off-aromas in the finished beer.

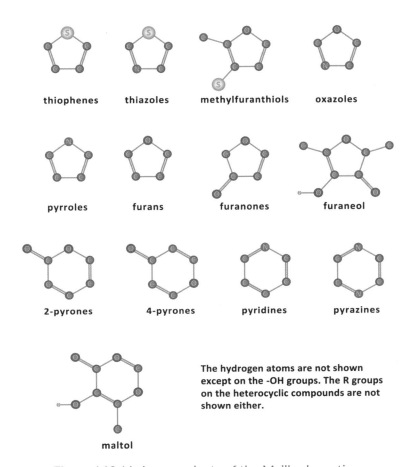

thiophenes   thiazoles   methylfuranthiols   oxazoles

pyrroles   furans   furanones   furaneol

2-pyrones   4-pyrones   pyridines   pyrazines

maltol

The hydrogen atoms are not shown
except on the -OH groups. The R groups
on the heterocyclic compounds are not
shown either.

Figure 163: Various products of the Maillard reactions

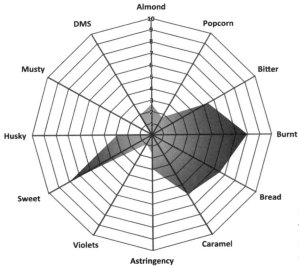

Figure 164: The flavours associated
with the Maillard reactions as the
reactions advance, and the colour of
the malt/beer increases

The aroma of the crust on freshly baked rye bread and the aroma of a fresh *Dunkles* are very similar, for the same reasons. The olfactory threshold for these substances can be as high as 10 ppm and as low as 0.002 ppb. As the colour of malt increases, the flavour and aroma impressions move from malty, nutty, bread and biscuit-like to burnt, bitter, astringent, coffee and chocolate-like. Overuse of specialty malts results in beer that is excessively caramel-like, roasty or simply burnt and unpleasantly bitter tasting.

Darker speciality malts contain many intermediate compounds from the Maillard reactions. As the heterocyclic compounds containing oxygen and nitrogen increase, this is associated with intensification of 'dark malt flavours'. The caramel-like flavours stem, in part, from the heterocyclic compounds containing oxygen, while the more burnt notes are derived from those containing nitrogen. The toasted malt flavour is partially attributable to maltol. In roasted barley and malt, there are few intermediates from the Maillard reactions remaining. This could be due to pyrolysis (see caramelisation), advanced polymerisation and evaporation or a depletion of the substrates available for the Maillard reactions, or all of the above. The only compounds that seem to increase along the whole colour scale are pyrazines and pyrazine derivates.

Caramelisation

These reactions also occur under application of heat but only involve sugars. In wort, the sugars that are caramelised are mainly maltose with some glucose, fructose and sucrose.

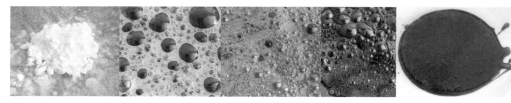

Figure 165: The colour of powdered sugar heated on a stovetop as caramelisation progresses

The caramelisation process (shown above with powdered sugar on a stovetop) involves the pyrolysis of sugar in which condensation, isomerisation, dehydration and fragmentation reactions occur and unsaturated polymers are formed, which lend colour to the caramelised sugar. The reaction is slowest at a neutral pH. It increases both at higher and lower pH values. A large number of compounds are formed in these reactions, many of which are still poorly understood. Some of the compounds responsible for the nutty, roasty, more complex sweetness of caramelised sugar are listed in table 24.

Table 24: Products of caramelisation and their sensory impressions

Compounds	Aromas/flavours
diacetyl	butter, butterscotch
esters	fruity
lactones	rum-like
furans	nutty
maltol	toasted notes
acetic acid	sour

Because caramelisation occurs at higher temperatures, the products of caramelisation are most relevant in specialty malts and in certain types of brewing sugars. With higher levels of thermal stress, such as with a direct-fired mash or wort kettle, the products of caramelisation can increase in brewhouse operations.

Thermal stress

If the brewhouse process is too extreme with regard to exposure of the mash and wort to heat, the beer will exhibit evidence of thermal stress in the form of lower flavour stability. Good maltsters understand how to produce malt with less thermal stress (e.g. curing at higher temperatures at shorter intervals), but brewhouse operations can also contribute a fair amount as well.

Undue thermal stress on beer either through the brewing or malting processes is undesirable. It can have olfactory repercussions which are immediately obvious, or off-aromas and off-flavours can develop over time as the packaged beer ages (refer to the section on forced ageing above). Many of the products of thermal stress are indicators for diminishing flavour stability.

Thermal stress increases the non-enzymatic browning of the wort (Maillard and caramelisation reactions) and is not only manifest in darker worts but also in fouling. The compounds serving as indicators for thermal stress are as follows: 2-furfural, 5-methylfurfural, ethyl nicotinate, γ-nonalactone.

Reducing thermal stress in the brewhouse can be implemented as follows:

- Decoction mashes can be held close to the boiling point and not boiled.
- The duration of the boil should only be as long as necessary to accomplish the objectives under the section on wort boiling.
- The whirlpool rest should be kept as short as possible (also to reduce the amount of DMS in the wort).
- Calandria should be equipped with pumps to initiate the circulation of the wort in order to reduce fouling.

As discussed above, the fouling on brewhouse equipment, especially on calandria, must be removed as part of the brewhouse cleaning regimen.

Thermal stress can be assessed with analysis methods using thiobarbituric acid and aniline. The thiobarbituric acid index (TBI) measures the products of the Maillard reactions and other organic compounds, and the aniline number (AN) provides a quantitative determination of 2-furfural. The TBI is primarily employed to evaluate the thermal stress in malt and wort, though it can be utilised for beer as well, while the AN assesses thermal stress and ageing in pale beers. The AN increases over time and more rapidly at higher temperatures.

PRIMARY CHALLENGES TO GOOD BEER IN TRADE

Beer becoming stale as it ages is a major quality issue for the brewing industry. The two primary mechanisms responsible for the staling of beer are lipid oxidation and the Maillard reactions. Lipid oxidation accounts for the emergence of (E)-2-nonenal, the notorious 'cardboard' aroma in stale beer. Its olfactory threshold is unfortunately very low at 0.035 ppb. Among other factors, the staling of beer involves certain carbonyl compounds, such as aldehydes, which develop during storage. As long as they are below their respective flavour thresholds, the beer will taste fresh, but after the carbonyl compounds (fig. 166) exceed these thresholds, they are often perceived as off-flavours. Maillard products react with oxygen to cause staling of the beer during storage. The formation of aldehydes and the Strecker degradation of amino acids are two of the numerous pathways in

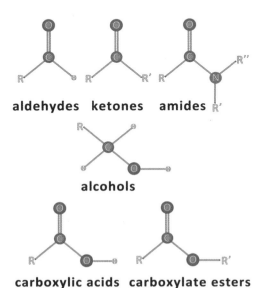

Figure 166: The functional groups of carbonyl compounds associated with beer ageing (plus alcohols)

the Maillard reactions (refer to the section on the Maillard reactions). Compounds derived from hops also degrade to create off-flavours (e.g. lactones, ketones and ethyl esters). Heavy metals along with oxidative enzymes, such as lipoxygenase, and activated oxygen from enzymatic reactions are also detrimental to beer quality.

However, the raw materials, processes on the hot and cold side and some additives also function as antioxidants. Phenolic compounds from the malt and hops, the melanoidins from the Maillard reactions as well as sulphur dioxide from fermentation are among the compounds that increase the flavour stability of beer by serving as antioxidants.

The interactions of all of these compounds in addition to outside influences (e.g. temperature, storage conditions, ageing, etc.) play a role in how well a beer survives after leaving the brewery. Flavour stability is thus one of the major challenges facing breweries today.

Issues with the stability of packaged beer:

- Temperature: beer should be kept cold.
- Exposure to light: beer should be stored in a dark place.
- Transport: agitation should be avoided to the greatest extent possible.
- Exposure to air: oxygen reacts with compounds in beer to rapidly bring about ageing.
- Hygienic conditions: the storage area should be clean.

Signs of problems with physical (colloidal) stability:

- haze formation
- presence of gels
- precipitation of particles

Signs of microbial contamination:

- off-flavours and off-aromas
- souring
- overcarbonation and gushing
- strong haze
- presence of films, gels or particulates

Signs of problems with flavour stability:

- The colour and clarity change.
- The beer exhibits little to no foam formation or head retention.
- There are noticeable off-flavours and off-aromas.
- The body is thin and lacking.

Forced ageing of beer

Forced ageing is a means by which brewers can accelerate the ageing in their beer in order to predict relatively quickly how the beer will change over its shelf life. The beer is subjected to adverse, extreme conditions, and in a laboratory, the turbidity is measured. While the beer is being subjected to these adverse conditions, the length of time it takes for the haze to increase by a certain degree is measured (> 2 EBC formazine units). This time period is then multiplied by a conversion factor, in order to estimate its shelf life.

However, even without laboratory equipment, the ageing processes in beer can be accelerated to determine how the beer will fare over its shelf life. After subjecting a set of bottles over different periods to these unfavourable conditions and accelerating the ageing process, sensory analysis of the beer can be carried out to gain insight into its resistance to ageing. The brewery's beers and others from the market can be compared in this regard.

A set of bottles from the filler is set aside and treated as follows:

- untreated beer: 24 h at 40 °C and 24 h at 0 °C
- stabilised beer: 24 h at 60 °C and 24 h at 0 °C

If possible, forced ageing occurs more effectively when the bottles or cans are placed on a shaker or are agitated in some way for several hours as part of the process. This cycle is repeated until changes in the clarity, flavour and aroma are perceptible. Forced ageing allows comparisons to be made with beers stored normally (under refrigeration, un-agitated in the dark). The differences can be entered into a database, which can provide some insight into the expected shelf life of a particular beer. A form or spreadsheet can be created that facilitates a direct comparison of the recorded sensory and analytical data for a single batch of packaged beer, with some bottles or cans being stored normally and with others being set aside for forced ageing.

Table 25: Degree of staling and sensory characteristics

Degree of staling	Flavour characteristics
fresh	clean and crisp (dependent upon beer style)
slightly stale beer	increased sweetness, *Ribes*, cardboard and papery notes; decreased bitterness; estery character
stale beer	increased bread-like character; decline in body
very stale beer	honey-like flavour
extremely stale beer	sherry-like flavour

Source: Boccorh, R., Paterson, A. *Variations in flavour stability in lager beers.* Poster, 2002

Storage conditions

As the graph in figure 167 indicates, the warmer beer is stored, the more quickly it will develop signs of ageing. Even if beers are meant to be laid down, they need to be treated well; that is, they need to be stored properly in a cool and dark place.

Beers that are to undergo bottle or cask conditioning still need to be kept relatively cool. Of course, the temperature will depend upon the yeast used for conditioning.

As most beer ages, predictable changes in the flavour and aroma occur over time. These changes can be accelerated by storing packaged beer in a warm room as well as shaking or jostling it repeatedly. *Ribes* is the genus name of plants producing berries like blackcurrants and gooseberries. As packaged beer ages, it reaches a certain point at which this aroma increases rapidly and then peaks over time. It also diminishes quite quickly as well. This aroma is sometimes also described as 'catty' and 'tomato

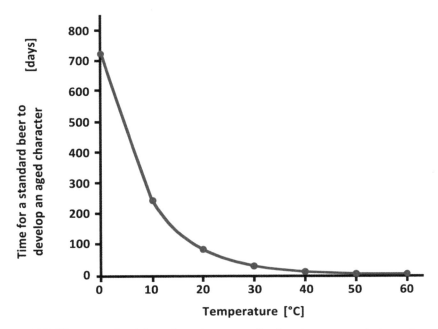

Figure 167: Time required for a beer to generally develop an aged character as a function of temperature;
Source: Bamforth, C., and Lentini, A. *The flavor instability of beer (Beer: A Quality Perspective)*, Burlington, MA : Academic, 85–109, 2009

leaves'. The beer acquires a honey-like aroma and a sweet, toffee-like flavour over time, which becomes sherry-like. This is accompanied by the pleasant bitterness of the hops fading perceptibly. Later in the ageing process, packaged beer develops an aroma reminiscent of wet cardboard as well. None of these changes are, of course, favourable. For this reason, beer should be stored in a cool, dark place and consumed as fresh as possible, unless it is one of the rare beers that can benefit from ageing (refer to the section on bottle conditioning below).

Literature and further reading

Coghe, S., Martens, E., D'Hollander, H., Dirinck, P., Delvaux, F. *Sensory and Instrumental Flavour Analysis of Wort Brewed with Dark Specialty Malts*. J. Inst. Brew. 110(2), 94–103, 2004

Dalgliesh, C. E., *Flavour stability*. Proceedings of the European Brewery Convention Congress, 623–659, 1977

Lehnhardt, F., Becker, T., Gastl, M., *Flavor stability assessment of lager beer: what we can learn by comparing established methods. Eur Food Res Technol* 246, 1105–1118 (2020)

Morales, F., van Boekel M., A study on advanced *Maillard Reaction in heated casein/sugar solutions: color formation*. Int'l Dairy Journal 8, 907–915, 1998

Whitfield, F.B., Mottram, D.S. *Volatiles from Interactions of Maillard Reactions and Lipids*. Critical Reviews in Food Science and Nutrition, 31(1/2):l—58, 1992

Beer ex works

Field quality

Unless a brewery only sells its beer out of a tasting room or is a brewpub where the beer remains in-house in tanks until it reaches the customer, then the brewery should have personnel trained in assessing and troubleshooting the field quality of the beer. They should be able to correct any errors in how the beer is being stored, remedy problems with dispensing at bars and restaurants, train bar staff about how to clean dispensing lines, if necessary, and educate gastronomy staff on how to pour and present the brewery's beers.

Sound advice to those handling packaged beer is to imagine they are handling milk. If it were treated like milk, though beer is not nearly as delicate, a lot of the damage done to beer outside the brewery would be eliminated. If it were always kept cool and out of the sun and drunk relatively fresh (first in/first out) within a few weeks of packaging, brewers, consumers and everyone in between would be a lot happier. This applies to pasteurised beer as well. Even beers that are meant to be aged in bottles need to remain in a dark, cool place, like a cellar.

Dispensing systems

Practical hygiene

Good beer can become bad beer in poorly maintained dispensing equipment. Obviously, due to the reasons mentioned above, any exposure of the beer to the air would be detrimental and should be avoided.

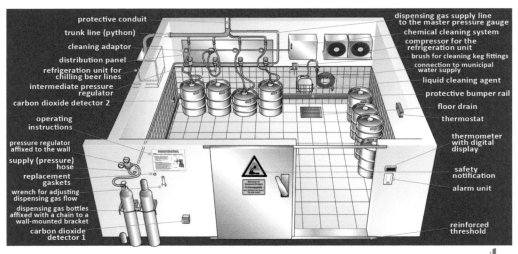

Used with the kind permission of the Deutscher Brauer Bund e.V.

Die deutschen Brauer
Deutscher Brauer-Bund e.V.

Figure 168: A keg storage room with dispensing equipment

A keg storage room and dispensing equipment should be well maintained and kept clean (Refer to figure 168).

Cleaning and designing a dispensing system

Cleaning thoroughly and regularly

Dispensing systems cannot be sterilised, but they can be cleaned well enough that microbial biofilms cannot become established in the lines or elsewhere in the system. If cleaning is carried out frequently and properly, then it will not take long at all (45 to 60 minutes). The frequency one cleans a dispensing system depends upon the kind of beer being served. Lines through which cloudy, poorly attenuated or yeasty beer is dispensed will require more frequent cleaning than a filtered, well-attenuated beer. If cleaning is put off and carried out less often, then cleaning can take hours.

A dispensing system must be cleaned and sanitised regularly according to a strict cleaning regimen. Beer lines should be cleaned at least every seven days. Any personnel on hand should be made aware that the beer lines will be cleaned prior to commencing the cleaning process. Wear eye protection and any other recommended protective apparel as undiluted beer line cleaner is especially corrosive and is very damaging to eyes and skin. The same applies to the environment; therefore, it should be disposed of properly. Use the detergents and other cleaning chemicals as recommended. Unless otherwise indicated, do not allow the cleaning chemicals to soak in the lines longer than 30 minutes.

An ample amount of time should be allotted for cleaning and sanitising a dispensing system because the keg couplers, taps, FOB detectors, impeller flowmeters, etc. must always be disconnected and disassembled, otherwise the cleaning and sanitising process will not be entirely successful. The only way to successfully remove soil in the recesses and crevices is with a brush and a suitable cleaning agent.

Beer lines should only ever be used to dispense beer. If soft drinks come into contact with hoses and gaskets and beer is dispensed from the same line later, the beer may be tainted. The two should never share lines for this reason. There should be dedicated lines for beers brewed with mixed microbes, i.e. 'sour beers' and 'Brett beers'. These beer lines should be cleaned more frequently than the regular beer lines, usually at least once per week.

Under no circumstances should regular dishwashing liquid be used to clean beer lines or other draught beer equipment out of convenience or to save money. Dishwashing detergent should be avoided entirely as it is hard to rinse off, may be scented, which can also taint the beer, and can cause the foam on the beer to collapse to nothing very rapidly. Only cleaning agents designed for use in dispensing systems should be employed.

If cleaning is not sufficiently frequent and/or executed carelessly (of a lesser quality), bacteria and other microorganisms proliferate and will eventually negatively influence

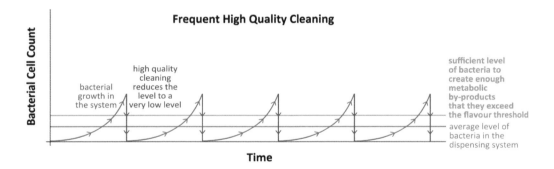

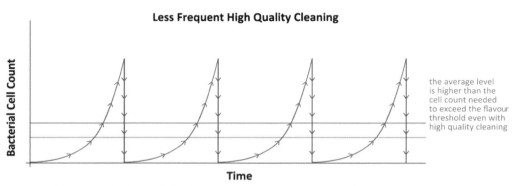

Figure 169: Bacterial cell counts and frequency of cleaning operations

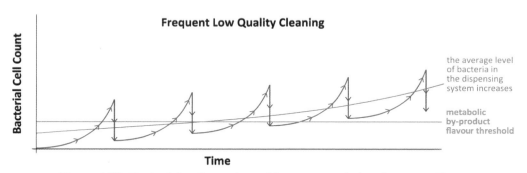

Figure 170: Bacterial cell counts and frequency of cleaning operations

the beer. Although the number of microorganisms in the system may decline to a level below the flavour threshold, they will reproduce rapidly enough that the contamination will endure and spread further. If there is no improvement in the cleaning practices, off-flavours will persist and become impossible to remove, since robust communities of microorganisms forming biofilms will have, by then, become well-established throughout the dispensing system.

Biofilms are especially dangerous in dispensing lines and can negatively influence the flavour and aroma of the beer. Once biofilms have gained a foothold in a dispensing system, they are difficult if not impossible to eradicate and can also spread quickly. Thus, regular, effective line cleaning is paramount in maintaining a high level of quality for cask and keg-dispensed beer. Customer satisfaction depends upon it.

In figure 171, the hose was affixed in the wrong place with the wrong type of clamp. Screw clamps can result in damage to hoses. A better alternative would be a one-eared crimp clamp (on the hose in fig. 171, bottom). On the hose above, the clamp is also positioned too close to the end of the hose. Under the operating pressure of the dispensing system, the hose swells slightly, allowing microbes to enter the space between the connector and the hose where they become established, creating a biofilm. The cleaning cycle misses them, and they thrive, becoming established at other points in the dispensing system. In order to prevent this, the hose should be affixed to the connector using either a wide clamp or two smaller clamps, as shown on the hose in the lower image. Note that one of the clamps is situated close to the end of the connector to keep the microbes out of the interstitial space.

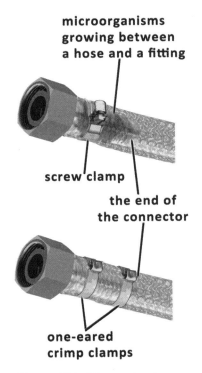

Figure 171: Dispensing hoses and microbial growth

Designing a dispensing system

When designing a dispensing system, one must keep in mind that the simpler a system, the easier it will be to clean. The materials used to manufacture the various components are important, e.g. taps should be made of stainless steel and not be chrome-plated. If pumps, components, automation and other accoutrement are deemed necessary, then it must also become part of the regular cleaning regimen to take these apart and clean them separately from the CIP cycle.

If the beer has to be pushed too far or too high from a deep cellar, it can become overcarbonated because more pressure is needed to transport it to its destination. Pumps and compensator valves are practical in these situations if cleaning is carried out dutifully and consistently. The pressure at the compensator valve always has to be equal to the saturation pressure of the beer. Keeping the saturation pressure low is one of the main reasons that beer line has to be well insulated and should be cooled on the way to the tap tower and at the valve. Consequently, the lines should be thick-walled enough to withstand this pressure. Using a higher diameter beer line will also reduce pressure losses on the way to the taps.

Other remedies for having to push beer further or higher through beer lines is to serve from smaller kegs, to use mixed gas or to simply redesign the system to decrease the length and/or height of the lines may also remedy this issue. Nitrogen and carbon dioxide are able to be mixed in a gas blender, which can be installed as part of the dispensing system. This affords more flexibility to blend the gases as one sees fit. Nitrogen gas, in this case, only serves to push the beer through the line so it does not become overcarbonated. Because it is much less soluble than carbon dioxide in aqueous solutions, it will make beers taste flat if it is overused. (Refer to the section on dispensing with nitrogen below for 'nitro beers'). If the kegs are above the bar, of course, less pressure will be required to push the beer down to the bar due to gravity.

An elegant solution, which has become quite popular in recent years, is to push the beer with compressed air. Of course, the air does not come into contact with the beer, as the beer is filled into a tank equipped with a liner. The compressed air applies pressure to the liner, so the beer is, in fact, well protected against oxidation. These should only be used for a brewery's flagship beers or ones with a higher expected turnover rate, as the lined tanks are quite a bit larger than kegs.

Compensator valves offer a degree of flexibility unavailable with other faucets. When pouring beers with different levels of carbonation or if there are fluctuations in the serving temperature, compensator faucets can compensate for this, hence the name. Furthermore, the valve can be set to a flow rate appropriate for the staff behind the bar.

Temperature control is very important, since carbon dioxide solubility decreases as the beer warms. Glycol or ice water-chilled trunk lines are crucial when pushing beer to the tap over longer distances. This requires the installation of a chiller as part of the dispensing system. Beer can become overcarbonated when stored very cold, especially if it is pushed through long lines to the tap. If kegs are stored at ambient temperature and are chilled in a 'jockey box,' i.e. through a coil in which the beer is chilled between the keg and the tap, the pressure on the beer must be set to maintain the level of carbonation in the beer. This means that more pressure must be applied to the keg to match the saturation pressure of the carbonation in the beer to ensure the beer does not foam upon exiting the tap. (Refer to the graph in the section on carbonation above). Storing beer at ambient temperatures can also lead to hygienic issues. For those pouring beers in the Alps, Himalayas, Rockies or anywhere at higher elevations, this requires more pressure on the beer than at sea level.

Literature and further reading

Tippmann, J., *Richtig reinigen – wie läuft es ab und was kostet es?* Brauwelt, no. 24–25, pp. 694-697, Fachverlag Hans Carl, 2019

Tippmann, J., *Der Aufbau einer Schankanlage: Zapfkopf, Schlauch, Hahn – fertig?* Brauwelt no. 26, pp. 732–735, Fachverlag Hans Carl, 2019

Instructions for cleaning a dispensing system for kegged beer

1. Dispensing systems should be cleaned prior to the busiest period at an establishment. This ensures that the bulk of the beer is being served to customers in optimal condition.
2. Before commencing the cleaning process, any cooling lines, e.g. glycol, should be turned off at least two hours prior or even the night before, so that the cleaning process does not heat it up unnecessarily.
3. Turn off the dispensing gas to the product.
4. Flush the beer lines with fresh water until they run clear. (If the lines are long, the beer can be collected in a pitcher for use in the kitchen, if applicable).
5. Additional hoses or other components used to connect the lines in a cleaning loop should be cleaned prior to attaching them.
6. As mentioned above, never add water to cleaning chemicals. Always add the cleaning chemicals to water. Make the cleaning solution in a vessel set aside for line cleaning according to the manufacturer's instructions.
7. Pump the cleaning solution through the lines.
8. Stop the pump and allow the cleaning solution to soak in the lines for a total 30 min; however, at intervals of 10 min, pump fresh cleaning solution through the lines, unless otherwise directed in the manufacturer's instructions.
9. Insert a fresh sponge ball of an appropriate size and pump it through the line several times. These can mechanically clean areas of the dispensing system where biofilms may be apt to develop.
10. Disassemble and otherwise clean all parts of the valves, taps, keg couplers, FOB detectors, impeller flowmeters and any other components in the dispensing system with cleaning solution and a brush to remove any soil.
11. Rinse the lines well with liberal amounts of fresh water. The water will cease to feel 'slick' once the cleaning solution is completely rinsed out of the lines; however, it is of the utmost importance for the safety of one's customers that pH papers or a pH meter be used to test the water entering and exiting the lines to ensure that there is no change in the pH.
12. Reconnect the dispensing system and turn on the gas. Open the tap and let the rinse water flow out completely until only beer flows from the tap. Check the beer for aroma, flavour and clarity before serving it to customers. Bleed the water out of the FOB detector.
13. Enter the date and time of the line cleaning where records are kept.

For increasing the mechanical cleaning power, a sponge ball can be used to scrub the inner surface of the beer lines. These are manufactured to fit specific diameters of beer lines. They are not meant for reuse since they can harbour microorganisms.

Figure 172: A sponge ball

An additional measure for deterring biofilms

One needs to flush out beer faucets with warm water periodically during dispensing operations. There are a number of devices on the market capable of performing this simple backflushing operation. Products that fit relatively securely over the external surface of the spout are designed for faucets furnished with vent holes (fig. 173). One only needs to firmly yet gently propel warm water up into the faucet. By placing a cup under the vent hole, the rinse water that comes out can be caught and disposed of. The water exiting the vent hole, carries with it any accumulated residues, dried beer foam, etc., all of which encourage bacterial growth. Rinsing the faucet in this manner every couple of hours at a busy bar is helpful in quelling biofilm formation.

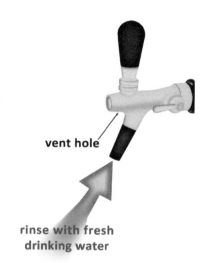

vent hole

rinse with fresh drinking water

Figure 173: A warm freshwater rinse to deter biofilm formation

How to pour beer correctly

Pouring from a tap

Never pour a beer into a dirty glass. This can contaminate the tap and perhaps other parts of the dispensing system. Many bartenders touch the glass to the tap and the beer. It would be better to attempt to avoid doing so as beer adheres to the outer portion of the tap.

Flat or foamy?

This book does not go into detail about dispensing systems, as this topic is worthy of a separate book on its own. There are three primary factors that determine whether a beer will be flat or overly foamy when it exits the tap:

1. **Temperature**: The beer in the keg must be chilled to serving temperature, and the beer in the line on the way to the keg should ordinarily be as well.
2. **Pressure**: Both the level of carbonation already in the beer, and the gauge pressure used to push the beer to the tap are crucial.
3. **The line**: The distance, diameter and roughness of the tubing between the keg and the tap determine how much pressure will or will not be lost to friction before the beer reaches the tap.

These three factors are dependent upon one another. For instance, if the temperature is too high, carbon dioxide bubbles will form in the line, requiring more pressure on the beer or the beer will quickly go flat. Furthermore, if the beer line is too short, then there is not enough pressure loss in the tubing. If the line is too long or climbs too far and the beer drops below the saturation pressure, the beer will begin to lose carbon dioxide, and fobbing problems can occur.

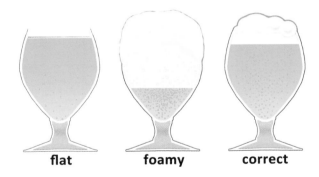

flat   **foamy**   **correct**

Figure 174: Correctly and incorrectly dispensed beer

Engineers are familiar with these kinds of calculations, and in fact, there are programmes available, which allow one to input the factors in order to calculate how to set up the dispensing system. The calculation includes the pressure in the keg, the desired flow rate, whether the beer in the line is chilled or not as well as the length, vertical distance, diameter and roughness of the tubing. Of course, the carbonation level of the beer is an important factor, too.

Cloudy beers versus cask ales

Weissbier, Kellerbier and other hazy beers

Kegs containing suspended solids, for instance *Weissbier* or *Kellerbier*, should be stored upside down until they are ready to be dispensed. When turned over, the yeast and other particles fall slowly to the bottom of the keg. As the beers are dispensed, they are more uniformly turbid; otherwise, the last few beers in the keg will contain of the majority of the sediment.

Pouring from a bottle

The mouth of the bottle should not cross the plane of the glass or touch it when pouring out of a bottle. Some beers with suspended yeast, like Bavarian *Weissbier*, which is meant to be drunk with the beer, should be swirled just before the final few millilitres are poured out so that the yeast sediment is resuspended and it flows into the glass when the bottle is drained. With other styles, especially bottle-conditioned beers, the sediment should not be disturbed. The bottle should rest prior to opening the beer, and the sediment collected at the bottom of the bottle should not be disturbed when pouring. Just before the sediment exits the mouth of the bottle, the pouring should stop.

Pouring from a British-style hand pull

Obviously, the swan neck of the tap does indeed cross the plane of the glass, since it extends down to the bottom. Therefore, extra care should be taken to keep the swan neck clean. Useful information is available from Cask Marque with regard to keeping cask ale, including the proper cleaning and maintenance of beer engines and dispensing lines.

Cask ale

Ales from stillaged casks should not be turbid. Cask ale is served with a beer engine usually pumping the beer up from a cellar below the bar where it is held at 10 °C to 12 °C. By adding the isinglass finings to the cask, the beer will drop bright (become clear) and there will be 'top break' and a 'bottom break', i.e. a small amount of material that floats on the surface and a larger amount of sediment, respectively. Due to the top break, the last pint from the cask is often cloudy. After the ale is mixed with finings, it is placed on a stillage in order to bring about precipitation of the

Figure 175: Stillaged casks

suspended solids (yeast, protein, etc.). Therefore, once cask-conditioned beers have had the finings added and have been properly stillaged (placed on a stillage at the proper angle for serving), they should not be moved (see the picture in figure 175). Stillaging requires at least 24 h but many pubs allow three to four days. Some British breweries chill early to leave residual extract in their ale, while others prime their casks to provide enough CO_2 to the ale, meaning some breweries condition their casks while other trust the publicans to do so. Contrary to popular belief outside the UK, British ale is neither flat nor cloudy. Properly running the cellar in a British pub necessitates a lot of vigilance, sensory evaluation and record-keeping to ensure all the ale is at its best for the customers. British pubs clean their lines quite frequently, as much as four times weekly because cask ale is 'living beer' and thus requires it. A general rule of thumb among publicans is that given line cleaning and other waste, there are 66 drinkable pints in a 72-pint firkin. Refer to Patrick O'Neill's *Cellarmanship* in the list of books below for more information on cask ale.

Dispensing with nitrogen

Nitrogen can also be employed in dispensing in addition to carbon dioxide, but it cannot replace it. Some British publicans use it instead of air to ensure that the volume of the ale pumped out of the cask and up to the bar by hand pull is replaced by pure N_2 rather than air. With nitrogen, the beer does not go 'off' as quickly.

Nitrogen can also be mixed with carbon dioxide gas at a variety of ratios to push beer through dispensing lines; however, one must understand the law of partial pressures and realise that doing so can make a beer taste flat. Nitrogen and mixed gas systems require their own separate gauges.

Some beer styles, such as stout, are regularly dispensed using nitrogen gas under a relatively high pressure. These beers may even be 'nitrogenated' with mixed gas (e.g. 30% N_2/70% CO_2) in a pressure-rated tank a bit over 1 bar of pressure prior to packaging. Serving these beers on tap requires a special dispensing system, a mixed gas or nitrogen bottle and a 'stout tap'. These taps possess a narrower body than taps for dispensing normal, carbonated beer as well as a special restrictor disc, which produces the denser head of foam. By removing the restrictor disc, beers carbonated with no additional nitrogen can usually be served with no problem using the tap. Especially in beers brewed with chit malt or certain adjuncts like unmalted oats, barley, wheat, etc., nitrogen gas imparts a creamy appearance to the foam and alters the mouthfeel to be somewhat smoother, because nitrogen gas bubbles are finer than those created by carbon dioxide and are much less soluble in beer. For this reason, nitrogen gas also causes an attractive cascading effect in the glass when served. The bitterness in the beer fades slightly when served under nitrogen, and the beer may also be perceived as a little less acidic.

Figure 176: A stout dispensed with nitrogen

How to handle glassware

In brewpubs, but also in small breweries with tasting rooms, it has become important for breweries to maintain a close relationship with the brewery personnel, restaurateurs and bar owners who serve their beer. Besides having to ensure that beer lines are kept clean in establishments where their beer is served, brewers also need to instruct those in gastronomy about how to properly serve their beer and treat their glassware. Handling glasses properly should become a habit.

Oils

"Why did the foam collapse so quickly on the beer in this glass?"
Even if one's hands have been washed, oils are still present on them. Fingerprints are unsightly on glasses, anyway, and indicate to a drinker that glasses were handled in an unhygienic manner.

Beverage and food prep

"Why does this pale ale smell like root beer and onions?"
Food preparation or handling soft drink syrup is a bad idea prior to conducting sensory analysis. Strong odours will interfere with the olfactory evaluation of the beer.

Temperature

Hands are warm and alter the temperature of the beer in the glass.

Handwashing

"I just washed my hands." "Yes, and afterwards you dried your hands off on a towel hanging at the sink and then opened the dishwasher!"
Microorganisms are all over everything all of the time, including everything people touch after washing their hands. This has become much clearer to the general public in the wake of the COVID-19 pandemic.

"Why does this pilsner smell like rosemary and lavender?"
Even though one's soap may be unscented, it can still transfer odour or flavour to glass. Touch glasses as far below the rim as possible.

Though washing one's hands is never a bad idea, a neutral smelling soap is best when handling beer glasses. Having washed one's hands does not mean that (1) they are sterile or (2) that they have not touched highly trafficked hot spots since then, such as handles, knobs, etc. Soap also does not remove all the oils or odours from one's hands, especially those from strongly scented foods and beverages.

Washing glasses

If beer glasses are not mechanically cleaned with a dedicated brush or sponge prior to going into the glass washing machine, lipstick can become baked onto the rim.

If beer glasses are washed in the dishwasher with other dishes, this can be detrimental to the foam formation and head retention of the beer.

Liberally added cleaning agent in the glass washing machine cannot be rinsed off sufficiently during the rinse cycle. This can cause the beer to taste soapy and can detrimentally affect the foam formation and head retention.

Touching glassware

Even if a person washes their hands, as mentioned, there are still bacteria, oils, soap residues, etc. which can contaminate or alter the sensory impression of the beer in the glass.

DON'Ts

Figure 177: How not to handle glassware

DOs

Figure 178: How to handle glassware

Servers often stick receipts to the sides of wet glasses for the customers; however, in some cases the receipts are actually placed in the beer foam and stuck to the rim of the glass. This is also unhygienic and contributes nothing to making the beer look inviting for the customer.

TECHNICAL APPENDICES

Appendix 1: Equipping and setting up a laboratory

Considerations for creating a laboratory space:

1. climate-controlled, separate room, if possible, and well-ventilated
   a. a well-ventilated room if handling chemicals
   b. microbiological analysis requires a protected space (little airflow or filtered air)
2. access to water and electricity
3. counters for performing analyses, preferably with chemical and heat-resistant surfaces
4. refrigerator and microwave oven
5. sink and/or dishwasher (laboratory grade or stainless steel)
6. storage closets and/or shelves for laboratory equipment, glassware, supplies, manuals and documentation
7. computer or ledgers for data entry and record-keeping
8. allow additional space for future needs

Having basic equipment on hand to carry out simple microbiological quality control is highly recommended in the following cases:

- unfiltered beer is regularly packaged
- beer is being exported or distributed over longer distances
- multiple strains of yeast or bacteria are being used in the brewery

Sensory analysis with a designated panel that meets regularly is the simplest and least expensive way to monitor quality. The five senses are, however, prone to being compromised by human error, unless carefully prepared protocols are followed. Setting up a basic microbiology laboratory brings with it a number of advantages. Inexpensive and relatively simple microbiological quality control tests include cell count, yeast viability, forced fermentation and the plating of microbiological samples on agar. Counting yeast cells prior to pitching using a haemocytometer provides greater accuracy and consistency, plus further application of the microscope in quality monitoring can aid in the early detection of microbial contaminants. Furthermore, working with agar plates is inexpensive, as they can be used in procedures for checking yeast purity and for the presence of bacteria in samples. A well-organised microbiological quality control programme with regular record-keeping will eliminate or at least greatly limit the impact of problems, such as product recalls, etc.

Laboratory equipment

There are less expensive options to laboratory equipment. Petri dishes, pipettes, agar, chemicals, an autoclave, a laminar flow hood – none of these have to break the bank. Performing basic microbiological and physico-chemical analyses can be done on a budget. Even if laboratory equipment, such as a microscope, is not available, there are alternatives. For example, tests can be purchased that indicate the presence of beer spoilers by means of a colour change or yeast can be evaluated for strain purity by observing the morphology (shape and appearance) of yeast colonies growing on agar, among others.

The laboratory area and glassware should be kept clean to avoid false positive results.

The picture in figure 179 depicts an autoclave full of laboratory glassware. A pressure cooker will serve this purpose as well. For some laboratory equipment, a hot air oven can be used for purposes of sterilisation. Such ovens are safer than autoclaves because they do not require pressurised, heated and sealed containers, that is, if the laboratory equipment is capable of withstanding dry heat at higher temperatures.

Figure 179: An autoclave for sterilising laboratory equipment

Basic laboratory equipment

Every brewery should possess the following at the bare minimum:

hydrometer/refractometer	computer informatics system
laboratory thermometer	dedicated refrigerator/walk-in cooler
pH meter	device for measuring carbonation in the bright tank

For breweries which package their beers in bottles or cans:

archived packaged beer	can double-seam inspection tools
manual crimp gauge for crown caps	template for bottles

For breweries producing approx. 3,000 hl/a and above, the following equipment is indispensable:

density meter	magnetic stir plate with stir bars
microscope	autoclave
haemocytometer	manual bottle cap torque tester
ATP test kit (bioluminescence)	double-seam cross-section inspector
basic digital analytical balance	torque meter for bottles
O_2 meter (ppb)	
can/bottle headspace tester	

In setting up laboratory in a brewery, the following additional equipment is also deemed necessary:

sterilisation indicator tape	isopropyl alcohol (70%)
inoculating loop and handle	plastic spray bottles or wash bottles
Petri dishes	digital pH meter or electrode assembly
screw-top vials	refractometer
parafilm	selective beer spoiler media
Bunsen or portable butane burner	sterile containers or bags for forced wort test
laboratory glassware	sterile swabs and sample vials
beakers	cleaning agents, sanitising agents
Erlenmeyer flasks	test tube rack
pipettes	handheld counter
test tubes	sterile cotton stoppers for flasks
graduated cylinders	water bath (commercial or homemade)
funnels and paper filters	permanent markers
pipette pump	laboratory coat
aluminium foil	gloves (with thermal protection)
microscope slides and cover slips	disposable gloves
immersion oil	eyewash bottle/station
methylene blue solution	eye protection (safety glasses or goggles)
first aid kit	fire extinguisher
titration burette	

Advanced laboratory equipment

As a brewery grows and the laboratory with it, the following equipment can be added for those wishing to delve more deeply into laboratory analysis.

Table 27: Advanced laboratory equipment

burettes and stands for titration	grist sieves
laboratory vacuum pump	hot air oven for sterilisation
laminar flow hood (commercial or DIY)	anaerobic incubator
shaking/rocking/rotating device	spectrophotometer
turbidity measuring device	analytical disc mill
laboratory centrifuge	friabilimeter
dissolved O_2/CO_2 measuring device	HPLC/GC
membrane filtration of samples for microbiological analysis	
multi-function device to measure extract, alcohol, density, colour, etc.	

Microscopy

The parts of the microscope are presented below:

Compound binocular microscopes have become affordable enough that they are within the reach of even small breweries. Their magnification settings usually range from around 40x to 2000x. Most modern microscopes are also able to be connected to a computer display, allowing images to be saved and catalogued for future reference. Other lab paraphernalia for routine analysis includes dyes for staining (e.g. methylene blue), a haemocytometer, a cell counter, microscope slides, cover slips and immersion oil.

For more information, refer to the EBC methods 2.3.5.1 Bright Field Microscopy and 2.3.5.4 Stereo Microscopy. For phase contrast microscopy in the examination of yeast spores and the detection of bacteria in yeast suspensions, refer to EBC method 2.3.5.2 Phase Contrast Microscopy. In a brewery laboratory capable of UV microscopy for examining stained yeast and bacteria cells as well as non-biological sediments in beer, refer to EBC method 2.3.5.3 Fluorescence Microscopy.

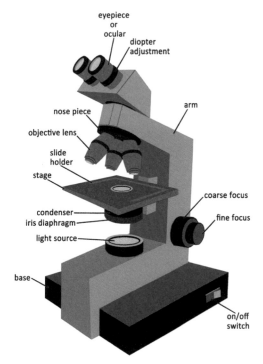

Figure 180: A binocular microscope

Working aseptically on a budget

The main point is simply to be as clean as possible and to prevent any vents or air currents from blowing over the workspace. Similar to the advice one hears during flu season, the first act in practicing aseptic technique is to thoroughly wash one's hands. Then, find a dedicated workspace in a non-draughty corner somewhere. Microbiological contaminants enter clean workspaces from the outside on people (fibres, skin, hair, etc.) and through the air, especially over HVAC systems, both of which bring particles in the millions into a previously cleaned area.

It is no wonder that small breweries whose founders have considerable knowledge of aseptic technique and have dedicated a completely separate room to microbiological analysis. It does not need to be large, simply able to be kept relatively free of microbial contaminants and draughts to prevent airborne contamination from wafting in. A clean room only receives air that has passed through the appropriate, regularly monitored filters, e.g. HEPA (high efficiency particulate air) or ULPA (ultra-low particulate air) filters. Of the two, the HEPA filters allow a higher airflow but do not eliminate as many contaminants as ULPA filters. HEPA filters remove around 99.97% of particulates as small as 0.3 µm, while ULPA filters purify the air to the point that 99.999% of contaminants above a diameter of 0.12 µm are eliminated. When entering a clean area, it is advisable not to traipse into a room with dirty shoes one has worn outdoors or around the brewery. Shoes dedicated for use in the clean space would be desirable, but at the very least, shoe covers are recommended as well as gloves, lab coats, hair cover and eye protection. No food or beverages should enter the space either. Sneezing and coughing should be done away from the clean area, but if necessary, one should do so into the sleeve of one's lab coat.

Materials for use in the clean room should be able to be wiped down with disinfectant (primarily metal and plastic) while porous materials capable of harbouring microorganisms, like wooden pencils, paper, paper towels and tissue, should be avoided. Where micro-biological analysis is crucial to their production process and a clean room is not available, a brewery can nevertheless install a laminar flow hood, which filters air and moves it down toward the workspace. By creating a protected space in which non-turbulent flowing air does not mix with the unclean air from the outside, brewery laboratory personnel can handle and prepare microbiological samples under a clean stream of air. And yet, in a small brewery with few resources, with a little imagination and ingenuity, a relatively clean workspace can be created where microbiological analyses can be carried out in relative safety. Brewery laboratories do not have to meet the strictest ISO standards, but by following these guidelines the particulate matter in the air can be greatly reduced.

Finding a corner with no foot traffic and very little airflow (away from vents, fans, open windows, etc.) and wiping down all of the surfaces with a clean room disinfectant or simply with bleach, isopropyl alcohol (≥ 70%) or peracetic acid, will create a relatively clean space. However, the particulate matter in the air is still slowly falling over the workspace. Some sort of flame which creates an updraught is thus required to maintain a clean workspace. Since an understanding of microorganisms and their role as beer spoilers entered brewers' awareness, they have used fire to flame glass and metal equipment, since heat is a reliable method for killing microorganisms.

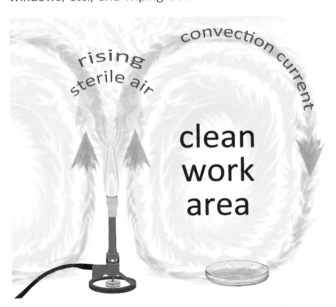

Figure 181: The clean work area around a Bunsen burner

Even more effective would be a laminar flow hood. Laminar flow hoods can be purchased; however, they are rather expensive. Amateur mushroom growers also require a clean space to inoculate their media with fungal spores, and they have posted many DIY plans on the web for building laminar flow hoods with the appropriate filters. There are even plans for portable ones. The airflow is achieved by vacuum cleaner motors or blowers. In order for the laminar flow hood to work, the air forced through the filters should only issue from the vent (refer to the picture). This means the rest of it has to be airtight.

front view

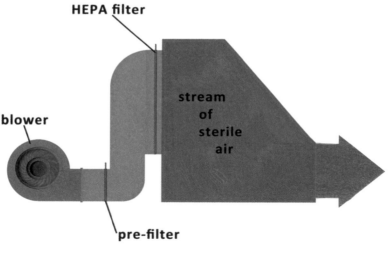

side view

Figure 182: A 'do-it-yourself' laminar flow hood

Appendix 2: Basic laboratory techniques

Using a Bunsen burner safely

1. Place a heat-proof mat under the Bunsen burner.
2. Move any flammable materials, like paper, tissues, etc. away from the Bunsen burner.
3. Check the tube to ensure that there are no tears or cracks.
4. Connect the tube firmly to the gas tap (which should be off, i.e. the valve handle is perpendicular to the gas line).
5. Turn the collar near the base of the burner so that the openings for allowing air to enter the gas stream are closed.
6. Ensure that the needle valve is completely closed by turning it clockwise.
7. Turn the gas on.
8. While holding it above the barrel, ignite the striker.
9. Open the needle valve.
10. The flame should burn bright yellow, which is also called a safety flame (soot may form).
11. To increase the heat of the flame, turn the collar so the openings allow air to enter the gas stream.
12. The flame should turn blue. The hottest part of the flame is just above the white part of the flame, as indicated in figure 183.
13. If the Bunsen burner needs to be moved, touch it only at the base in order to do so.
14. If something goes wrong, immediately turn the valve at the gas tap off.
15. When finished, the Bunsen burner should be turned off as follows:
    *   Turn the collar so the air is turned off in the gas line; the safety flame will appear.
    *   Close the needle valve.
    *   Close the gas tap.
16. Allow the Bunsen burner to stand until it is cool.

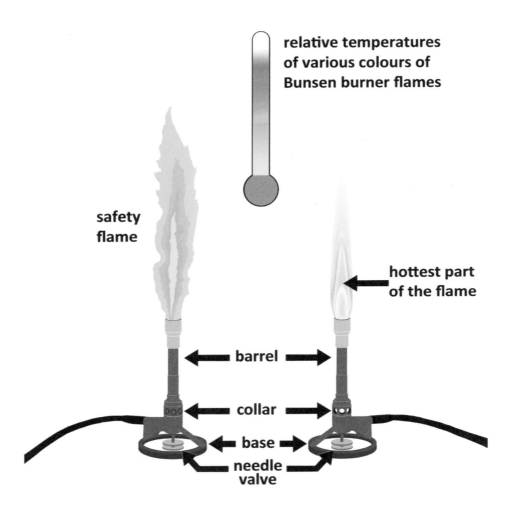

relative temperatures
of various colours of
Bunsen burner flames

safety
flame

hottest part
of the flame

barrel

collar

base

needle
valve

Figure 183: Bunsen burners and flame temperatures

Sterilising laboratory equipment

Laboratory equipment can be sterilised using moist or dry heat. The factors to keep in mind are similar to those for cleaning: time, moisture, temperature and pressure. Sterilisation means that all living cells are killed, even the bacterial spores. Fungal spores are part of these organisms' reproductive process, while bacterial spores represent a means of survival for certain species when environmental conditions become too harsh for their existence in non-spore form. By forming spores, bacteria protect their DNA from incurring damage until conditions improve. Sterilisation methods have to kill these bacterial spores as well, and some are quite resilient.

For both types of sterilisation, there are four similar phases in the process:

1. heating/pressurising
2. uniform temperature distribution
3. sterilisation
4. cooling/drying

Once the air temperature in the autoclave or oven has reached the desired temperature, this does not mean the equipment has. The second phase allows the equipment itself to heat up to the same temperature as the air surrounding it. After this is achieved, the sterilisation phase begins and is held as long as is required, generally with approx. 20 min added to the end, in order to ensure that the process is successful.

Sterilisation in dry heat

Sterilising in an oven takes longer, and the equipment that can be sterilised in dry heat is limited, since the temperatures are considerably higher than in moist heat. Laboratory glassware and stainless steel can be sterilised in an oven but if there is any grease, oil, fat or powder on them, the heat will not penetrate it. Therefore, the equipment must be cleaned and dried first. If a piece of equipment consists, for instance, of glass and metal parts, it must be disassembled, because the two materials expand and contract at different rates. Dry air is a poor conductor of heat, so the air in the oven should be circulated around the oven. The laboratory equipment must be placed in the oven so that there is adequate airflow around each piece. Once the equipment itself has reached the desired temperature, the clock can be set on the sterilisation phase. Refer to the table at right for the temperatures and their corresponding times.

Sterilisation with moist heat

The advantage of moist heat is that sterilisation can be carried out relatively quickly, is very effective, if performed correctly, and can be used with most laboratory equipment, though it can damage some plastics and rubber items. Moist heat requires an autoclave or at least a pressure cooker because the sterilisation occurs under pressure with steam at temperatures above 100 °C. The air is removed from an autoclave and replaced with hot steam using either a vacuum pump or a type of displacement method (in a brewery lab, gravity displacement is common). Equipment in the autoclave is generally heated to between 121 and 132 °C and then sterilised for approximately 20 to 30 minutes before cooling begins.

Table 28: Examples of temperatures and times for dry heat sterilisation

Dry heat sterilisation	
Temperature	Time
160 °C	180 min
170 °C	120 min
180 °C	30 min

Table 29: Examples of temperatures, pressures and times for moist heat sterilisation

Moist heat sterilisation					
Temperature	Pressure				Time
121 °C	203 kPa	2.03 bar	2 atm	1520 mmHg	30 min
134 °C	304 kPa	3.04 bar	3 atm	2280 mmHg	20 min

Indicator tapes are available for autoclaves that change colour if sterilisation has been achieved. In a larger working microbiology lab, autoclaves are subject to testing with these strips or strips containing non-pathogenic heat-resistant spores (*Geobacillus stearothermophilus*) once per week.

Aseptic techniques for microbiological analysis

Collecting samples correctly and in the proper places is an important part of quality control because one must look for the microorganisms where they are most likely to hide.

How to collect samples for laboratory analysis

Aseptic technique involves collecting and transferring cultures without contaminating them. Aseptic technique is a prerequisite for accurate microbiological analysis. In order to work aseptically, all work areas must be cleaned with a disinfectant and hands must be washed with warm, soapy water and dried. All vessels should be sterilised by exposing them to steam or by placing them in a pressure cooker or a hot air oven for an adequate period of time. Inoculating loops must be sterilised by immersing them in 70% ethanol and flaming them. Draughts and contamination from the air should be avoided.

Instructions

1. Wash hands well and dry.
2. Assemble the sample collection equipment close to where the sample is to be taken.

3. Spray the external surfaces of the sampling port or at the point the sample will be taken with ethanol and flame it to sterilise if the surface can withstand heat.
4. Keep the sample container closed. Only open it immediately prior to collecting the sample. Do not touch the inside of the container or the closure with one's fingers.
5. Quickly collect the sample and seal the container.
6. Thoroughly clean the sample port or area where the sample was taken.

Collecting swab samples

Equipment: sterile swab tubes, 70% ethanol, sterile sample containers, gas burner/flame

1. Unscrew the cap containing the swab and remove it from the tube. Do not touch the swab, the inside of the cap or the inside of the tube with one's fingers or with any surface.
2. Place the tip of the swab on the surface to be tested and apply pressure, rotating the swab as it moves across the surface.
3. Insert the swab into the tube and twist the cap to seal.
4. Label the sample with the name, location and date.
5. The swabs can be tested for microbial contaminants by adding a sufficient volume of sterile wort to the tube aseptically. Alternatively, after swabbing a surface, the swab can be used to streak the surface of a plate containing solid nutrient media. Place the tubes or plates in a warm location (30 °C) for three days and monitor for microbial growth (colonies or lawns on plates, turbidity and gas formation in swab tubes).

Collecting samples from ambient air

Air can carry many different kinds of microorganisms, most of which are ubiquitous. These inoculate the wort of 'wild' beers. The number of microorganisms suspended in the air is dependent upon a number of factors. In spring and winter there are fewer microorganisms, but in summer and autumn, when it is warmer, especially during periods with little rain, more microorganisms are airborne. Dust can arise from, for instance, agricultural activities or through milling. If this is the case, microorganisms attached to the particles of dust can become suspended in the air. In wine or fruit-growing regions, there are also usually more airborne microorganisms.

Equipment: closed sterile Petri dishes containing wort agar and/or NBB agar

1. The Petri dishes should be set down and opened at the point one wishes to collect an air sample.
2. Leave the Petri dish open for 10 min.
3. Close the Petri dish again.
4. Return to the lab.

At all locations where wort and beer could come into contact with air, samples should be taken:

- brewhouse
- yeast propagation area
- fermentation area
- maturation area
- filtration area
- bright tank area
- filling area(s)
- laboratory

Only a qualitative analysis is possible; however, one can find out what is floating around in the air at the brewery. Many breweries use air samplers containing membrane filters, which allow much more of the air to be sampled.

In the filling area, there should be fewer than 100 microorganisms per cubic metre of air. This is the reason that in the buildings specially constructed to house filling lines in larger breweries, the air is filtered and the airflow is carefully designed to flow away from the fill heads, that is, away from the unsealed cans and uncapped bottles, in order to prevent airborne microorganisms from landing on them. Even if this is beyond one's capabilities, filters on vents blowing into more sensitive areas would be feasible and the prevention of airflow from less clean areas, such as where returned deposit bottles are received.

Testing for contaminants in wort

Equipment: 70% ethanol, sterile sample containers, gas burner/flame, warm storage location (incubator, water bath, hot room)

This simple test allows brewers to check if microbial contaminants are present in wort.

1. Collect a wort sample in a sterile container using aseptic technique. Close the container and place it in a warm location (around 30 °C) for three days. If bubbles are visible, gas escapes when opening the container or the wort becomes cloudy, then the wort contains microbial contaminants.
2. If proper aseptic technique was used, then contamination is present. The next step is to identify the microorganisms using specific tests to help identify the source of the contamination.

Appendix 3: Laboratory analyses for QC

All of the following are considered essential.

Care and adjustment of laboratory devices

  1.5 Care and Adjustment of Apparatus: pH Meters

The pH of aqueous solutions is determined using a pH meter and electrode system at 20 °C.

  1.6 Care and Adjustment of Apparatus: Density Meters

The density of a liquid is determined at 20 °C using a digital, oscillation U-tube density meter.

Representative sample collection

Water

  EBC method 2.1   Sampling of water

This method describes how to sample water for chemical tests, but not for microbiological tests. Refer to further information on collecting water samples under Appendix 4: Physico-chemical analyses.

Malt, adjuncts, sugars, syrups and caramel

  EBC method 4.1

  EBC method 5.1

  EBC method 6.1.1

  EBC method 6.1.2

These methods describe how to collect a representative sample of malt for analysis.

Hops

  EBC method 7.1   Sampling of Hops and Hop Products

This method describes how to collect a representative sample of hops and hop products for analysis.

Wort

  EBC method 8.1   Sampling of Wort

This method describes the procedures employed to obtain homogeneous and representative samples of wort for analysis.

Beer

EBC method 9.1 Sampling of Beer before Filling

This describes the procedure to obtain a homogenous and representative sample of beer before filling for analysis.

Appendix 4: Physico–chemical analyses

A note on testing water

There are several options available to those interested in independently testing their water. Water samples can be collected on-site and sent to an external laboratory for testing. Some laboratories will provide a container and packaging for sample submission while others will specify the type of container to be used and supply instructions on how to collect the water sample. Always mark the sample clearly with the name of the person or brewery submitting the sample, the type of sample and the date collected. Indicate on the submission form which analyses are to be performed. These should include the primary ions of interest in brewing water: bicarbonate, calcium, chloride, magnesium, sodium and sulphate.

Alternatively, there is a range of water test kits on the market suitable for testing multiple water samples. Kits are convenient because the water can be tested on-site, and results are obtained more rapidly. The kits include instruction manuals on how to properly carry out the tests and contain the supplies needed to conduct the analyses. Some kits are designed to use chemicals such as those typically found in a conventional brewing laboratory, while others utilise no-mess test strips and an all-in-one analysis device with app-based results. Test kits vary in price depending on their complexity, materials and scope, but some entry-level kits are quite affordable.

Water testing kits are available from the following sources: Ward Laboratories, LaMotte, Industrial Test Systems, Craft Brewing Water Test Kit by Hach, Smart Brew Starter Kit by ITS.

Water alkalinity test – p and m value

Alkalinity refers to the acid-neutralising capacity of solutes in water. Highly alkaline or 'hard' water causes several problems in the brewery such as corrosion and mineral scale deposit. Breweries adjust the alkalinity of their water to optimise the brewing process and improve beer flavour. A simple test to determine the hardness levels of water is the p and m alkalinity test.

As carbonic acid comes in contact with various minerals, it dissolves them, causing salts to form. A common example is limestone, which forms calcium and magnesium bicarbonate when it comes into contact with carbonic acid. When heated, these salts dissociate, resulting in mineral deposits on the surfaces of equipment. Removing this type of alkalinity, or temporary hardness as it is termed, prevents the negative effects described above. Several ions in water determine water hardness, but hydroxide, bicarbonate and carbonate ions are those generally measured.

The p and m test involves titrating a water sample with acid until a pH of 8.3 (p-alkalinity) and a pH of 4.3 (m-alkalinity) is achieved. The colour change indicators phenolphthalein (p) and methyl orange (m) signal when the endpoint of each respective titration is reached. The p and m values represent the amount of acid required to neutralise the different types of alkalinity in a particular water sample, bringing it to a predetermined pH. The m value is known as the total alkalinity and is the measure of hydroxide ions and total carbonate alkalinity (carbonate and bicarbonate ions) in the water. The p value is the apparent alkalinity and is a measure of all hydroxide ions and half of the carbonate alkalinity.

Refer to the section on water under Raw Materials for information on how ions in water affect beer and the brewing process.

Literature and further reading

Basarova, G., Savel, J., Basar, P., Lejsek, T., *The Comprehensive Guide to Brewing from Raw Material to Packaging.* Fachverlag Hans Carl GmbH, 2017

Goldammer, T., *The Brewer's Handbook: The Complete Book to Brewing Beer.* Apex Publishers, 2008

Mitteleuropäische Brautechnische Analysenkommission (MEBAK) volume Water, analysis 1.1.11, *Acid consumption*, MEBAK (publisher), 2008

Acidity

Measuring the logarithmic molar concentration of free protons or H^+ ions, i.e. the pH, is not sufficient for characterising the acidity of beer. If one is working with a single strain of yeast like a typical top-fermenting or bottom-fermenting strain, then measuring the pH, that is, the concentration of H^+ ions, may be sufficient. If the spectrum of organic acids in the beer varies widely due to a range of mixed microbes fermenting the beer, measuring the pH cannot satisfactorily characterise how the drinker will perceive the acidity of the beer. Common in other areas of the food industry is the analysis combination of the sugar concentration and titratable acidity for characterising, for instance, when fruit should be harvested to maximise customer acceptance of fruit and fruit juice products. There is no direct correlation between pH and titratable acidity as the former provides an objective measure of the concentration of H+ ions, regardless of how the beer is perceived by the drinker, while the latter provides an idea of how pungent the acid is on the tongue. This is similar to how the sweetness of various sugars is discerned by the human sensory apparatus.

Measuring pH

The pH of the wort should be determined before and after boiling, after leaving the wort chiller prior to pitching, during fermentation, after maturation and in the packaged beer. This should be diligently recorded for every batch. It is imperative that the pH meter be calibrated and maintained according to the manufacturer's instructions.

Titratable acidity

The pH measures the strength of the acidity – the concentration of free (dissociated) H+ ions – while the titratable acidity measures the dissociated and undissociated hydrogen, thus gauging the relative amounts of the various organic acids present in the beer, e.g. acetic, lactic, citric, malic, succinic and tartaric acids. Beers created using mixed cultures contain a number of acids. Measuring the pH is not sufficient for characterising the acidity in beer as perceived by the human sensory apparatus. A beer with a moderately low pH can seem very acidic to a beer drinker, while one with an even lower pH may be considered less acidic. Besides the mixture of acids, the residual extract, carbonation level and alcohol content also affect the perception of sourness. The organic acids created by microorganisms during fermentation are weak acids, which dissociate to a lesser extent than strong acids, meaning that the proton (H+) ion does not separate from the molecule as readily.

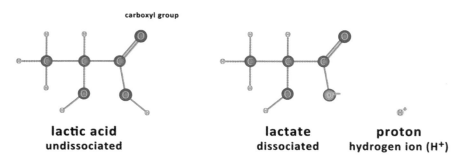

Figure 184: Lactic acid with a dissociated and undissociated hydrogen ion

Lactic and acetic acids are usually the ones brewers are most concerned with, but the synergy among all of them plays a role in how the sourness of a beer is perceived, whether it is, for example, pleasant on the palate or astringent.

Of the relevant organic acids in beer, lactic acid is, of course, produced by lactic acid bacteria and is perceived as imparting a 'softness' to the sourness of beer. It also has the lowest flavour threshold of the organic acids commonly encountered in beer. Citric acid from yeast or fruit additions gives a 'sweet and sour' impression. This acid possesses the highest flavour threshold of the ones mentioned above. Malic acid has a higher flavour threshold than lactic acid, and it is a natural constituent of grape must and of green apples. It contributes a strong perceived acidity and an intense tartness to wine and sour beer. Through malolactic fermentation, lactic acid bacteria can convert malic acid to lactic acid, thus softening the overall acidity as well as increasing the complexity of the aroma and flavour of sour beer, producing a rounder, fuller mouthfeel as well.

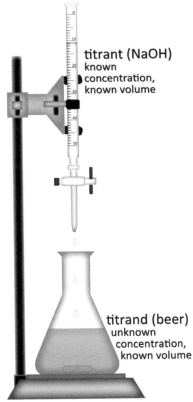

titrant (NaOH) known concentration, known volume

titrand (beer) unknown concentration, known volume

Malolactic fermentation also has the added benefit of reducing the concentration of micronutrients available in the maturing beer, which increases the microbiological stability. The lactic acid bacteria naturally occurring with yeasts in wild cultures or added as starter cultures can accomplish this. If a starter culture is employed, then the lactic acid bacterium *Oenococcus oeni* serves this purpose well, since it exhibits a strong tolerance for ethanol and thrives at a pH of 4.3 to 4.7, though it can tolerate a more acidic environment. In the process, however, diacetyl and compounds, which might impart a 'mousy' or 'breakfast cereal' aroma, may be produced by the lactic acid bacteria. The diacetyl, of course, can be eliminated by yeasts. *Saccharomyces* yeast strains produce succinic acid through respiration (the citric acid cycle), which can exhibit a bitter or even salty taste in beer. 90% of the non-volatile acids resulting from alcoholic fermentation in wine production is succinic acid and thus it plays an important role.

An analysis of the acids present in the beer is valuable, therefore, in understanding how the acidity on the whole will be perceived on the palate. For this reason, the titratable acidity has been compared to measuring the sweetening power of various sugars; for example, sucrose is much sweeter at the same concentration than lactose.

Test kits for measuring the acidity in wine are widely available and are applicable here. The titratable acidity is normally expressed in grams per litre and is a measure of all the acidic compounds in a beer, although the results are usually represented as

Figure 185: Titration – the burette is filled with titrant, in this case a solution of NaOH, and the Erlenmeyer flask with the titrand, beer. The flask is depicted on a magnetic stir plate. This is not necessary; nevertheless, with each addition of the titrant, the contents of the flask must be mixed well.

equivalent to a specific acid. This does not mean that there is only that specific kind of organic acid in the beer. Kits designed for wine yield results for tartaric acid. To convert the result to a value for lactic acid, the results can be multiplied by a certain factor. The requisite multiplication factor will depend upon the lab procedure and thus what dilution one is using. These acidic compounds react with a strong base, which correlates well with the perception of the sourness level of a beer. A strong base (e.g. NaOH) is employed to measure the titratable acidity. The amount of OH⁻ ions needed to titrate the H⁺ is measured with an indicator (phenolphthalein) or a pH meter. The values for titratable acidity (lactic acid) are generally assessed and described as follows:

low, mild, mellow, refreshingly sour:	4.5–8.0 g/l
moderate, tart, tangy:	8.0–10.0 g/l
high, sharp, dry, harsh, astringent:	10.0–18.0 g/l

The titration ends when the equivalence point is reached in this weak acid/strong base reaction. This does not mean that the titrant is added until the pH is 7 (neutral) but rather that in adding the titrant, a certain point in the curve is reached. This is the point at which the quantity of titrant is sufficient to completely neutralise the titrand (beer), the equivalence point in an acid-base titration. The solution contains only salt and water because the moles of the base are equal to the moles of the acids. In this analysis, the pH at this point is normally 8.2.

Although these descriptors become more pronounced as the values for titratable acidity increase, the authors have sampled a beer with a relatively high titratable acidity, a particular Belgian gueuze, which was dry and acidic, but nonetheless reasonably well balanced in its overall impression. The other constituents of the beer also make a difference in how sourness is perceived. Furthermore, the combination and relative concentrations of the organic acids also play a role.

One must also remember that the titratable acidity is often measured in very dry beers, because many but by no means all sour beers are fermented with, among other microorganisms, *Brettanomyces* species. These yeasts leave no stone unturned during fermentation and create extremely highly attenuated beer. Thus, orange juice (unfermented) and beer with a similar value for titratable acidity will each leave a drinker with a very different impression concerning its sourness. In order to preserve some residual sugars to balance the tartness, brewers sometimes choose to pasteurise their sour beers.

In performing the analysis, if a beer possesses a relatively high acidity, the burette may need to be refilled or a larger one may need to be used for the test. Do not empty the burette past the last gradation prior to refilling it. Likewise, a larger Erlenmeyer flask may need to be employed to reach the equivalence point with highly acidic beers. When titrating, ensure that with each addition of titrant, it is well mixed so that the NaOH can react with the acid in the beer. Towards the end of the titration (> 7.6), very little titrant is required to increase the pH, so caution is recommended. Always be careful when mixing or handling a solution of NaOH.

More precise analysis of which specific organic acids are present in a beer is provided by HPLC or enzymatic testing.

Literature and further reading

ASBC Methods of Analysis, Beer 8, *Total Acidity*, American Society of Brewing Chemists, 2020

Suzuki, K., *125th Anniversary Review: Microbiological Instability of Beer Caused by Spoilage Bacteria*. J. Inst. Brew. 117(2), 131–155, 2011

Taylor, K., *Sour Beers: It's more than just pH*. White Labs presentation for the MBAA.

Vaughan, A., O'Sullivan, T. van Sinderen, D., *Enhancing the Microbiological Stability of Malt and Beer – A Review*. J. Inst. Brew. 111(4), 355–371, 2005

Witrick, K. *Characterization of aroma and flavor compounds present in lambic (gueuze) beer*. Dissertation, Virginia Polytechnic Institute and State University, 2012

Colour

The colour of wort/beer should be measured prior to boiling, after boiling, after wort chilling, during fermentation and after filtration and packaging.

Extract measurements

Hydrometer

A hollow, glass or plastic hydrometer possesses a known volume and is precisely weighted at the bottom. Therefore, its buoyancy is also known. This enables measurements to be made to determine the density of the fluid into which it has been submerged. One should note that hydrometers are designed for fluids of different densities. For this reason, a hydrometer specifically made for measuring wort and beer should be obtained; the measurement range is usually indicated directly on the hydrometer. As the density of the fluid to be measured increases, the less the weighted end of the hydrometer can displace the fluid. As a consequence, its hollow body does not sink as far into it. The buoyancy is directly proportional to the density of the displaced wort or beer, revealing how much dissolved extract it contains. This measurement does not establish whether the extract is fermentable or not. Refer to the limit of attenuation under the sections Malt Analysis and Chemical-Technical Analysis for the amount of fermentable extract.

As ethanol is produced by the yeast during fermentation, the reading must be denoted as having been corrected or not, as ethanol is less dense than water. This is the reason readings are labelled 'apparent' (not accounting for the ethanol) or 'real' (having done so).

A hydrometer has to be read at a certain temperature without needing to add or subtract from the reading, since the temperature of the fluid affects its density. Otherwise, if the temperature is higher or lower than that indicated by the manufacturer, the measurement will have to be corrected. Water serves as the solvent for the extract in wort, and as a result wort is most dense at approximately 4 °C. Therefore, the closer the temperature is to 4 °C, the higher the gravity.

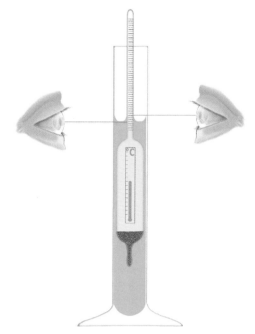

Figure 186: Reading the hydrometer above or below the meniscus

The manufacturer's instructions will indicate whether the hydrometer should be read above or below the meniscus (refer to figure 186). Though the illustration is a bit exaggerated, it is meant to convey the difference between a hydrometer designed to be read at the bottom of the meniscus and one that is meant to be read at the top of the meniscus.

Making a hydrometer reading

1. Take a representative sample of the wort (refer to EBC analysis 8.1).
2. Attemper the sample as required for the hydrometer (most often to 20 °C)
3. Fill the cylinder with the liquid to be analysed (wort, green beer, finished beer). The hydrometer will float when carefully placed in the liquid.
4. Gently submerge the clean, dry hydrometer into the liquid, so that it floats freely, and the meniscus develops immediately; avoid as much vertical movement of the hydrometer as possible.
5. Read the value on the hydrometer (according to hydrometer specifications); a temperature correction may be necessary.
6. Rinse off the hydrometer, dry it and return it to its storage area.

Other methods

Density meter

There are other methods for determining the extract content of wort and beer. Nowadays density meters have become affordable and portable. These devices generally require a sample free of particulate matter with the sample normally attempered to 20 °C. Filtering wort, for instance, from the mash tun, may be required.

 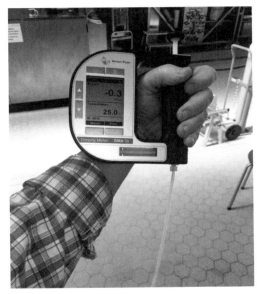

Figure 187: Density meters

Refractometer

Refractometers are robust and durable and therefore popular in breweries. As the name suggests, they measure the index of refraction for mixtures by dropping a small amount of cooled wort on top of a prism over which a cover plate closes. The person performing the measurement then views the reading through an eyepiece and a magnifying glass. As with other methods of measuring extract, a correction must be made when alcohol is present in the sample. This is one reason refractometers are more common in the brewhouse, prior to fermentation.

Figure 188: A refractometer

Visual iodine test

An iodine solution should be used to check for saccharification during mashing and before and after boiling. The time required for saccharification should be recorded on the brewhouse log sheet.

After the starch has been gelatinised in the mash (≥ 60 °C), the amylose and amylopectin drift from the starch granule into the mash where they are attacked by amylolytic enzymes. These molecules are helical even after gelatinisation, though they are single helices, and they react with iodine to produce a dark blue colour. The starch helix happens to be just the right diameter for iodine to enter the hollow spiral portion of the molecule. When iodine forms a line inside of the long spiral glucose chains, it produces a dark blackish blue hue. Therefore, if long polysaccharides derived from starch are present, an iodine test can be performed to determine whether the long chains are still intact, or whether they have been degraded to molecules too small to capture iodine in this way.

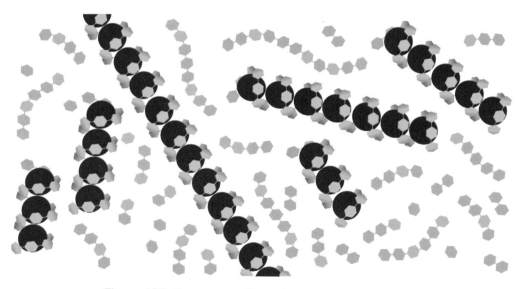

Figure 189: Fragments of starch with iodine molecules

Once starch degradation is underway, and the enzymes are breaking the starch down to smaller molecules, the iodine is no longer dark blue but turns shades of violet. As the process continues, the violet lightens to red and then to rose brown and finally yellowish brown, after which there is no change (the 'achromic point'). Pictured in figure 190 is gelatinised starch in the mash and an approximation of the colours one sees when performing the iodine test. The chains are not depicted in their spiral form for purposes of illustration. A qualitative measure, meaning a visual test, is the method most likely to be used in smaller breweries. In larger breweries with access to a spectrophotometer, the colour can be more precisely determined.

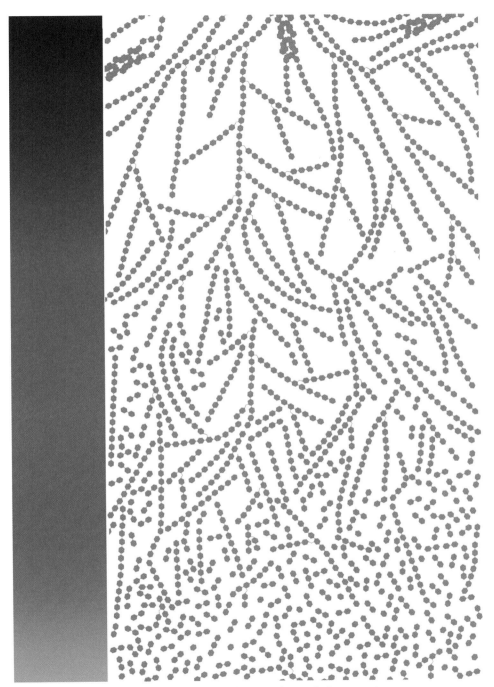

Figure 190: Iodine colour and starch fragments

The simplest test for conversion involves collecting a sample of the mash, taking care to minimise the quantity of solids in the sample:

- Transfer several drops to a white impervious surface, like a ceramic plate with depressions in it or a saucer.
- Add brewer's iodine (1% potassium iodide solution) to the sample and watch for a colour change.
- If the sample turns deep violet or blackish blue, this means that conversion has not taken place and mashing should continue.
- If the sample is yellowish brown and stays this colour after swirling the sample, then the starch in the mash has been converted into fermentable sugars.
- Discard the sample, do not return it to the mash.

The figure at right shows how iodine reacts in samples of the mash using 100% pale malt as conversion is taking place. At the top, the mash has not undergone conversion, while at the bottom, the mash is fully converted.

Figure 191: Changes in the colour of iodine mixed with a liquid sample of converting mash

Appendix 5: Brewing microbiology

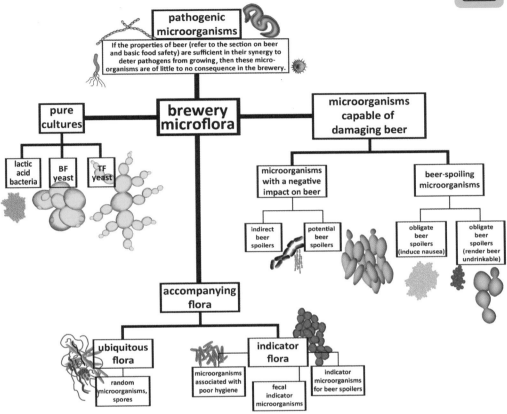

Figure 192: The microorganisms found in a brewery

Source: Back, W., Gastl, M., Krottenthaler, M., Narziss, L., and Zarnkow, M., *Brewing Techniques in Practice*. Fachverlag Hans Carl, 2019

Beer spoilage microorganisms

Beer spoilers are considered not only those microorganisms that are capable of damaging beer to the point that it is unsightly and undrinkable but also those which are not intentionally added to the wort or the beer. In figure 192, the microorganisms brewers are mainly concerned with are the beer spoilers, that is, those on the right side of the diagramme, though the indicator flora are of great interest as well, since they generally signal the presence of said beer spoilers, which are ranked as follows

Obligate beer spoilers: The microorganisms belonging to this category negatively impact beer quality and thus pose the greatest threat to it. They are less intimidated by the barriers to infection inherent in beer and the brewing process, having generally evolved a tolerance to them. Lactic acid bacteria are often culpable, e.g. *Lactobacillus* spp., which make beer sour and turbid, and *Pediococcus* spp., which can do the same in addition to imparting beer with a buttery flavour (diacetyl), even giving it an oily or a ropy texture. For most bacteria, cold maturation represents a barrier to growth but *Pediococcus* ssp. are known to thrive at lower temperatures. *Saccharomyces cerevisiae* var. *diastaticus* and other wild yeasts can contaminate beer, fermenting the dextrins as well as any residual extract (see below).

Potential beer spoilers: Under favourable conditions, these microorganisms can infect beer. If a beer's natural defences are inadequate, which might include a higher pH, a lower hop rate, some oxygen ingress, a lower alcohol content, etc., these microorganisms may be afforded the opportunity to survive or even thrive. Lactic acid bacteria as well as wild and foreign yeasts fall into this category, especially those able to ferment dextrins and longer saccharides, which can cause beer packaging to rupture or burst – a dangerous prospect.

Indirect beer spoilers: When microorganisms that cannot live in beer gain a toehold in raw materials, intermediate products, processing aids or other substances used in the production process, they can cause off-flavours or otherwise damage beer.

As Louis Pasteur and others showed in the 19th century, living organisms do not appear out of thin air through what was then known as 'spontaneous generation'. The means by which beer-spoiling microorganisms succeed in infecting beer are divided into two general categories:

1. Microorganisms, which may or may not be long since dead in the packaged beer, contaminated the raw materials, wort or beer during the production process. They may not be viable, but their metabolic by-products, such as lactic acid, diacetyl or other substances, are present in the finished beer and are apparent as faults.

2. The finished beer reached the packaging process without contamination; nevertheless, at some point during filling or afterwards, microorganisms have tainted the finished beer with their metabolic by-products to the point that they are perceptible as faults.

Contamination

Primary contamination occurs when beer spoilers enter the production process through microbially tainted equipment, raw materials (e.g. malt, hops, yeast), intermediate products (e.g. wort), processing aids (e.g. diatomaceous earth/kieselguhr), etc. and survive to infect the beer. The risk with this kind of infection is that it goes undetected long enough that the microorganisms contaminate a large portion of the brewing process and cultivate biofilms, thus making them difficult to eradicate.

Secondary contamination enters the processes in the filling area at points where less than perfect hygienic conditions and thus biofilms hold sway. The original source of the contamination may be workers on the filling line, gusts of outside air, dripping condensate, etc.

Modern breweries therefore maintain a high level of cleanliness. Every production area, all vessels and piping, especially downstream from the hot side, must be cleaned and disinfected and also tested for contamination according to a strict schedule.

Though they are not beer spoilers, there is another category of microorganisms deserving of attention as well. *Indicator flora*, as they are known, may be the harbinger of as yet undetected beer spoilers in the production process. Indicator microorganisms do not spoil beer but grow in its presence as long as oxygen is present. These microorganisms can encapsulate themselves in biofilms, which may not have been removed through cleaning and sanitizing. The danger: where there are biofilms, there are beer spoilers. Therefore, these indicator microorganisms serve as a warning that the processes of cleaning and sanitizing should be carried out more deeply, regularly and with greater alacrity.

Prominent beer spoilage microorganisms

Though beer possesses attributes which make it relatively microbiologically stable, there are a few genera of bacteria that have evolved the ability to live in this boiled, hoppy, alcoholic, low-oxygen, slightly acidic beverage. They are generally differentiated using the microbiological technique of Gram staining (see below).

Gram-positive bacteria

Among the Gram-positive bacteria (refer to the information about Gram staining below) there are two main genera of lactic acid bacteria that can make brewers, who do not diligently clean and prevent the formation of biofilms, pull their hair out. These genera are *Lactobacillus* and *Pediococcus*. Approximately 60 to 90% of all microbiological beer spoilage is perpetrated by *Lactobacillus* and *Pediococcus*; among them, strains of *L. brevis*, *L. lindneri*, *P. damnosus* and *L. backii* (in that order) are the microorganisms by far wreaking the most havoc. Only those strains of *L. brevis*, as well as the strains of other primary offenders, adapted to the brewery environment are beer-spoilers as they possess a variety of hop resistance mechanisms. The pH value of the beer and the dissolved hop bitter acids are the best defences against most lactic acid bacteria, while the SO_2 concentration in the beer also plays a role. CO_2 at the concentrations normally found in beer also inhibits their proliferation, though below 0.3 g/l, the CO_2 can actually encourage their growth. This is the reason beers with less dissolved CO_2 are more susceptible to contamination by these microorganisms. The use of *Sauergut* (naturally acidified unhopped wort) to acidify the mash and wort is also helpful, not only because it lowers the pH of the wort but also because it contains antibacterial compounds. *Lactobacillus delbrueckii* is among the thermophilic wort-spoilers that can survive in wort under 60 °C, so for those wanting to save energy and employ alternative brewhouse methods, such as boiling below atmospheric pressure, it is nevertheless advisable to raise the wort to a temperature close to 100 °C before doing so. This will also serve to isomerise some of the alpha acids from the hops, which will reduce the number of hop-sensitive bacteria in the wort/beer. Some *Lactobacillus* species and almost all *Pediococcus* species also produce diacetyl, which imparts a buttery and sometimes a butterscotch flavour to beer.

Lactobacillus and *Pediococcus* bacteria are so adept at living in beer that some brewing traditions have simply embraced them. These brewers have learned to create quite excellent beers with their help under the right conditions (e.g. *Gose, Berliner Weisse, Oud Bruin*, Flanders red ale, lambic, among others). In the past, older beers that had become infected with lactic acid bacteria and yeast like *Brettanomyces* would be blended with fresh beer rather than being thrown out. Some breweries began doing this on purpose, and their beers are very drinkable and refreshing, that is, as long as the 'contaminating' organisms do not produce off-flavours or those off-flavours are eliminated in the maturation process.

Strains of *L. brevis, L. buchneri, L. parabuchneri, L. rossiae, Leuconostoc mesenteroides, Leuconostoc paramesenteroides, Pediococcus claussenii* and *Pediococcus damnosus* are all capable of living in wort/beer and excreting exopolysaccharides, creating a gelatine-like ropiness, which does not affect the flavour but imparts a very disagreeable texture to the beer, rending it undrinkable. These exopolysaccharides are also used in biofilm formation. Some brewers of traditional *Berliner Weisse* and lambic, among others, are famous for purposefully employing species of *Brettanomyces* yeast in their fermentations to consume and eliminate these exopolysaccharides. They are also of the opinion that after this has taken place, the beers possess a finer, more pleasantly nuanced flavour than they did before. The diacetyl produced by lactic acid bacteria can also be eliminated by the yeast still active in the maturing beer, which usually ends up being *Brettanomyces* species, as they are better adapted for such environments.

Gram-negative bacteria

There are not many Gram-negative beer spoilers. Those that can live in beer fall into two categories. The first group comprises aerobic and facultative anaerobic bacteria, like acetic acid bacteria, those belonging to the genus *Zymomonas* and the large taxonomic family known as Enterobacteriaceae. Gram-negative bacteria were a significant problem in the mid-20th century when cleaning and sanitation practices were less effective, but now incidents of contamination with them are relatively rare. The second group are obligate anaerobes, such as *Megasphaera* spp. and *Pectinatus* spp., and are primarily a problem when cleaning and sanitation practices are lacking in the filling area. Unpasteurised beer is highly susceptible to these beer spoilers if biofilms become established towards the end of the cold side of production.

Acetic acid bacteria, like *Acetobacter* and *Gluconobacter* species, which impart the pungent acidity of vinegar to wort/beer, were, as mentioned above, a greater problem in the past than today. This is not only due to better cleaning practices but also because dissolved oxygen values in packaging have dropped substantially as well. These aerobic, flagellated, ellipsoidal and short rod-shaped bacteria are sometimes motile and can metabolise ethanol to acetic acid in the presence of oxygen. *Brettanomyces* do this as well. They can be found in wort if the wort passed over a biofilm in a pipe or other equipment. They are a particular nuisance in cask-conditioned ales due to the oxygen and slightly warmer temperatures, which is a good argument for allowing pure nitrogen rather than air to seep into the cask as pints are pulled. If the wood is too porous, barrel-aged beers can also exhibit unpleasant levels after a period of ageing. *Gluconobacter* produce a pellicle and can generate haze and ropiness in beer, too.

Zymomonas was at one time a prevalent beer spoiler. There is only one species in this genus, the facultative anaerobe *Z. mobilis*, which is comparable in many ways to *Gluconobacter* in that it possesses polar flagella, does not form spores and is a short rod-shaped bacterium, which swims rapidly through the liquid medium. *Z. mobilis* metabolises sugars to ethanol and CO_2 more efficiently than brewing yeast but cannot ferment maltose; in fact, when the concentration of maltose is high, these yeast are not active, so at the beginning of fermentation they are less prevalent. This is the reason that cask conditioned ales, which have been primed with sugar, are plagued by these bacteria. Cask beer has declined, for this reason, in favour of kegged beer. *Z. mobilis* can ferment glucose, fructose and the disaccharide they form, sucrose. Fermentation by-products include, not only CO_2 and ethanol, but acetaldehyde and hydrogen sulphide as well, so rotting, sulphurous fruitiness is a sign of this microorganism's presence. Since *Z. mobilis* can very effectively produce both H_2S and ethanol from simple sugars, it has garnered the attention of those in the field of biotechnology. However, for brewers, this bacterium is only considered a nuisance. Ultimately, after further degradation of the fermentation by-products, unpleasant vegetal aromas result if the beer is allowed to mature. Moreover, *Z. mobilis* often appears together with other Gram-negative bacteria, so the off-flavours are commonly accompanied by the pungent sourness of acetic acid.

Enterobacteriaceae is a family of Gram-negative, rod-shaped (bacilli), non-endospore-forming facultative anaerobes. The protective properties of beer outlined in the section devoted to this topic prevent the pathogenic genera of bacteria belonging to this family, such as *Salmonella*, *Shigella*, *Escherichia* and *Klebsiella* from contaminating beer, namely, boiled wort, the ethanol content iso α-acids, low dissolved O_2 content (< 0.3 ppm), high CO_2 concentrations and depleted nutrients as well as pasteurisation. When these inherent properties are less pronounced, for instance, in low-alcohol or non-alcoholic beers, these microorganisms can present a problem. Those able to survive at all are normally indirect beer spoilers, such as *Citrobacter*, *Hafnia*, *Klebsiella* and *Obesumbacterium*. They are not usually able to subsist in the finished beer but contaminate it at certain areas of the production process, e.g. the fermenting wort, the brewing liquor or the pitching yeast, and they can aid in the formation of biofilms, leaving behind a milky haziness in beer smelling unpleasantly of green apples, cabbage and parsnip with a sulphurous, buttery, clove-tinged sourness. The compounds responsible for these aromas comprise DMS, diacetyl, acetaldehyde, higher alcohols, methyl acetate, ethyl acetate, 4-vinyl guaiacol, among others. Some species of Enterobacteriaceae can even produce carcinogenic N-nitrosamines by reducing nitrates to nitrites which subsequently react with amines. One of these is *Obesumbacterium proteus*, the only species belonging to this genus. They appear as short or pleomorphic rods and are aerobes or facultative anaerobes. Fortuitously for sour beer brewers, these microorganisms do not survive below a pH of 3.9; thus, they are a greater threat in the fermenting wort. Fermentation will not occur as expected when they are present. It will be slower and DMS, among other off-aromas, will be more prevalent in the green beer.

Coliform bacteria are an essential part of lambic fermentation but otherwise are a sign that something is terribly wrong with the hygienic situation at a brewery. These genera include *Enterobacter*, *Klebsiella*, *Escherichia*, *Hafnia* and individual strains of *Citrobacter*. Most are sensitive to ethanol, so are only active at the beginning of fermentation, but their presence can have a lasting effect, producing diacetyl, lactic acid, acetaldehyde, 4-vinyl guaiacol and DMS. If water treatment is inadequate, they can enter the brewery through the brewing liquor. If the wort has been boiled and no brewing liquor has been added downstream, then some contaminated water may somehow be leaking into the piping, equipment or vessels. *Pantoea agglomerans*, formerly identified as *Enterobacter agglomerans* and sometimes classified as *Erwinia herbicola*, has been known to contaminate yeast cultures and fermenting wort, leaving green beer with a fruity, buttery and sulphurous aroma accompanied at times by a milky haziness. They have been found in harvested pitching yeast, so they can survive the brewing process. The diacetyl will be noticeable in the aroma and flavour, and the pH of the finished beer will be slightly higher when contaminated with this bacterium, since neutral metabolites are released into the beer as part of the 2,3-butanediol pathway. Again, this species is sensitive to ethanol so does not remain active long after fermentation has begun.

Gram-negative bacteria of the above named genera, among others, are sometimes classified as simply as 'wort bacteria' or 'termo bacteria' (short rods). They are not capable of growth in beer but can establish themselves in biofilms, for instance, on the cooler end of the heat exchanger near the wort outlet. Even though they remain in similar places and do not contaminate any equipment downstream since they cannot tolerate beer, the compounds they create in the wort can persist into the finished beer, giving the beer a sulphurous cabbage, celery or sewage-like note. They can even create substances that give drinkers headaches. Therefore, it is imperative that brewers remain vigilant concerning their presence.

The low oxygen conditions present in the process encourage the growth of strictly anaerobic *Megasphaera* spp. and *Pectinatus* spp. which can produce faecal aromas in beer. The chemicals common in brewery CIP cycles kill them, but they, like many of their fellow microorganisms, survive in biofilms. Keeping oxygen at extremely low concentrations on the cold side is, of course, the goal of every brewer. One consequence of this kind of vigilance is that obligate anaerobes, for which oxygen is nothing but toxic, can survive in beer. Members of the bacterial genera *Pectinatus* and *Megasphaera* cannot grow in the presence of oxygen and are sensitive to ethanol, so they mostly pose a threat to beers with lower concentrations of alcohol. Their presence is evident by turbidity as well as the rotten egg (H_2S) and faecal aromas they produce. This exemplifies why careful attention to the hygienic conditions in a brewery can never be neglected even if beer does possess these inherent protective properties. When they are found to be present, the cleaning and sanitation regimen must be addressed. Very often they reveal the presence of well-established biofilms.

Undesirable and wild yeasts

Any strain that was not pitched by the brewer in a standard brewing process is undesirable. Wild yeasts live outdoors on fruit skins, on people and in many other environments, and through carelessness, poor hygiene, etc. somehow find themselves in the brewing process, where they can become established in biofilms with other microorganisms.

A note on *Saccharomyces cerevisiae* var. *diastaticus*

This yeast can be particularly troublesome for the brewing industry and has recently become an issue among craft brewers because it possesses the enzyme amyloglucosidase (AMG, also known as glucoamylase). This enzyme is encoded by STA genes and can thus be tested for using PCR. AMG is an exoenzyme, so it is excreted by *S. c.* var. *diastaticus* in the presence of normally unfermentable starch or oligosaccharides, which are then degraded to simple sugars. These simple sugars are subsequently fermented by *S. c.* var. *diastaticus* or any residual brewing yeast in the packaged beer. This can cause bottles to gush or even to explode. Strains of *S. c.* var. *diastaticus* yeast can also create phenolic off-flavours in beer. Often, this yeast enters the process through secondary contamination, meaning that it is not present in the yeast or wort itself but develops due to poor hygiene in the filling area or is present in biofilms in the piping or components of the filler. Breweries that add fruit or other plant material, like blooms, to their beers or do not control fruit flies may also be at risk of contamination by super-attenuating yeast, because they, like other wild yeast, including *Saccharomyces cerevisiae*, naturally occur on fruit skins and blooms containing nectar.

Contamination with super-attenuating yeast, like *S. c.* var. *diastaticus*, is difficult to detect, because they can be indistinguishable from brewing yeast under the microscope. In order to test a yeast sample suspected of containing super-attenuating yeast, a volume of wort can first be fermented to the limit of attenuation with a known strain of pure brewing yeast. Afterwards, the resulting beer can be filtered and then inoculated with the yeast sample in question. If signs of alcoholic fermentation occur (ethanol, CO_2), then the yeast sample contains a super-attenuating strain.

Normally, the enrichment media used for the detecting wild yeast in a brewery are lysine agar and crystal violet agar. A starch medium is used for determining glucoamylase activity while media containing copper sulphate are employed for selectively cultivating wild yeasts. Due to recent issues in breweries with super-attenuating yeast, more specific media have been developed, namely Farber Pham Diastaticus Medium, which specifically targets *S.c.* var. *diastaticus*, and PIKA FastOrange Wild Yeast, a medium for detecting wild yeasts and *S.c.* var. *diastaticus*. As mentioned, PCR can detect the presence of the STA genes in a yeast sample.

Super-attenuating yeast, like *Saccharomyces cerevisiae* var. *diastaticus*, are also employed by some traditional Belgian brewers and now by craft brewers to create drier, more fully attenuated beers. *S. c.* var. *diastaticus* grows well above 30 °C and otherwise behaves similarly to brewing yeast. Yeast strains available under the names 'Belgian saison' or 'French saison' or even 'Belgian ale' may contain strains of *S. c.* var. *diastaticus*.

Biofilms

Biofilms are defined as 'matrix-enclosed microbial populations adherent to each other and/or to surfaces or interfaces.' (Costerton, J., Z. Lewandowski, E. Douglas, and R. Korber, in *Microbial biofilms*. Ann. Rev. Microbiol 49:711–745, 1995)

Thus, biofilms are the result of microorganisms assembling in cohesive groups and are usually found on solid surfaces submerged in or exposed to an aqueous solution. Some of the microorganisms exude slime (extracellular polysaccharides), which allow them to attach to a surface or to one other, forming a shelter which protects them to some degree from cleaning and sanitising chemicals. They may perform complementary functions (protection, making nutrients available, attaching to the surface, etc.) enabling the colony of microorganisms to persist where alone they could not. Hygienically designed equipment eliminates some of the spaces where biofilms can develop, but regular cleaning is required to prevent them from forming.

Biofilms are problematic throughout the entire cold side of the brewing process – from the very beginning. For example, wort bacteria can accumulate and flourish in a plate heat exchanger, releasing compounds that can negatively impact the flavour of the beer as well as other aspects of beer quality.

Biofilms attach, grow, mature and reseed themselves very effectively in the absence of countermeasures. This can occur very quickly and once they have become established, they are very difficult to eradicate. This is one reason that sticking to a regular cleaning regimen and microbiological quality control are essential.

Biofilm life cycle

The biofilm life cycle is divided into the following stages (fig. 193):

1. **Attachment:** Free-floating or motile microorganisms (planktonic cells) gain access to the production process and later become attached to the surface of piping or equipment, anchoring themselves to it through cell adhesion.
2. **Formation of a matrix:** Microorganisms release exopolysaccharides, proteins and nucleic acids to create a protective matrix. Some microorganisms are not able to attach themselves directly to the surface but can attach to the matrix.
3. **Proliferation and maturation:** Microorganisms reproduce and can also communicate (quorum sensing), causing the biofilm to grow rapidly through cell division and recruitment. The biofilm may at this stage become visible to the naked eye. Microcolonies of cooperating microorganisms form protective layers enabling them to withstand cleaning chemicals and, in some cases, mechanical cleaning. The biofilm will now be very difficult to remove. Sometimes equipment with more porous surfaces may even have to be replaced.
4. **Dispersion:** The microorganisms in the biofilm can propagate by moving further downstream in the production process through the detachment of pieces of the biofilm or by releasing individual cells.
5. **New life cycle:** The planktonic cells find a new surface where they can begin creating another biofilm.

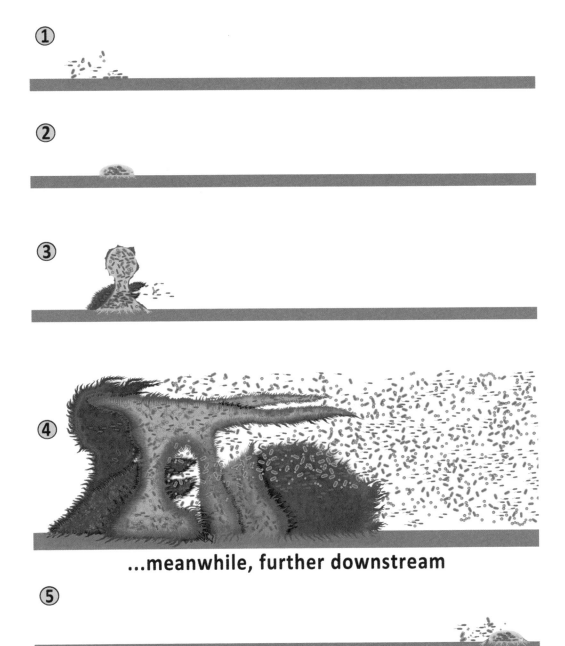

Figure 193: Biofilm formation, growth, maturation and dispersal

Appendix 5-1: Microbiological sample collection in a small brewery

Keeping the yeast healthy and pitching them in the appropriate numbers is essential but not enough. Once the brewing process ceases to involve heat, i.e. starting inside the heat exchanger, hygiene and cleanliness along with the physiological status of the yeast become paramount. Routinely monitoring the microbiological status of the raw materials, the products, the lines and the equipment allows for brewers to react quickly to any problems that may arise at any stage in the process.

Brewing liquor: Testing should be performed on brewing liquor for contaminants, especially for the liquor used for the dilution of beer. The customary method involves the directly plating of samples or the cultivation of a sample from laboratory membrane filtration on an agar plate. The microbiological status of the brewing liquor should be checked weekly or more frequently if deemed necessary. Refer to the recommendations above for how to treat brewing liquor to ensure microbiological purity (e.g. UV light). The activated carbon filters, the lines carrying the brewing liquor, etc. should also be monitored regularly.

Yeast: Since yeast is added on the cold side of the brewing process after the wort is boiled, it must be scrupulously tested to ensure that microbial contaminants, such as lactic acid bacteria, are not present. As mentioned, *Saccharomyces cerevisiae* var. *diastaticus* look like brewing yeast under the microscope and thus cannot be detected visually.

Hops: In order to gain an overview of what sorts of microorganisms are found on hops, particularly those used for dry hopping, a representative sample of hops can be rinsed with sterile water. The rinse water is then prepared as part of a spread or pour plate. The microbes on hops are generally considered not to be beer spoilers; nevertheless, hops added on the cold side will not be boiled and thus represent a potential source of microbial contamination.

Sugars and syrups: Normally, the low water activity prevents any microorganisms from growing in these raw materials; however, spores may survive and flourish under more favourable conditions, namely when diluted or when added to wort. Samples of sugar or syrup can be spread over the surface of an agar plate or be prepared as a pour plate and observed for colony formation.

Air and process gases: Microorganisms are not only found on surfaces; they are also present on dust or in droplets of liquid in the air. For this reason, vessels should be closed or covered in a brewery. Air and process gases are usually checked for contaminants by membrane filtration. As with water or beer samples, the filter is then incubated on wort agar, and the colonies are counted. A general count of the microorganisms in the ambient air can also be performed by removing the lid of an agar plate for a determined amount of time followed by incubation and a colony count.

Wort: Samples from the heat exchanger outlet, pitching tank (if applicable) or from freshly pitched wort in the fermentation vessel can be incubated on an agar plate for the purpose of testing for the presence of, among other microorganisms, enterobacteria and wild yeast. Wort lines may contain biofilms and should be carefully monitored.

Fermentation/Maturation: Brewing yeast should exhibit a high level of vitality and should be the dominant microorganism during fermentation. By outnumbering other microorganisms and rapidly metabolising the substrate, brewing yeast should be capable of suppressing the proliferation of possible contaminants during this stage of the brewing process. The presence of undesirable microorganisms in higher numbers is a sign that something is amiss and is usually indicated by an abnormal fermentation, an unexpectedly precipitous drop in the pH or atypical aromas and flavours.

Filtration: Samples should be collected at least at the inlet and outlet and tested for beer spoilers and indicator flora. Tests for brewing yeast can be performed at the outlet of the filter to monitor the efficacy of the filter.

Bright beer: Bright beer should be tested for contaminants, particularly for lactic acid bacteria, which can negatively affect a beer's aroma and flavour. This is another stage in which the greater sample size provided by membrane filtration is beneficial. Prior to filling the bright tank with beer, a rinse water sample should be taken, membrane filtered and tested for beer spoilers and indicator flora.

Packaged beer: During packaging, beer can become infected through secondary contamination at numerous points of contact with the beer lines and filling equipment. Bacteria belonging to the genera *Pectinatus* and *Megasphaera* are considered to be the most damaging microorganisms in packaged beer, while acetic acid and lactic acid beer spoilers can also appear as uninvited guests. Refer to the section on *Pectinatus* and *Megasphaera* above. Biofilms established between the bright beer tank and the filling line can harbour beer spoilers. For this reason, the beer is very vulnerable at this stage, and a comprehensive regimen of microbiological sampling and testing should be developed and implemented.

Surface testing: Surfaces in a brewery should be hygienically designed and cleaned regularly enough that no microorganisms are given the opportunity to become established on them. ATP testing of the surfaces in the filling areas should be widespread, while contaminants in packaged beer are typically detected using plating or culturing methods.

Swab samples should be taken where weak points exist, i.e. where biofilms are likely to develop. Among these weak points in the filling area are the following:

- any surface with direct contact to beer, including bottles/cans/kegs
- any surface frequently sprayed or covered in beer
- any surface with indirect contact to beer, especially those that rotate and can spread contamination around the filler (e.g. the bottle outlet area of the rinser/washer, empty bottle/can inspector, transport chains, guides, the inner walls of filler cups, lifting pistons, areas around the bottle filler/capper, can filler/seamer, keg filler, etc.)

These surfaces should be tested for beer spoilers and indicator flora.

Membrane filtration: As mentioned above a larger, more representative sample can be collected by membrane filtration to monitor tanks, piping, containers and other equipment (refer to the technique below). A sample can be collected by membrane filtration from equipment, for instance, of brewing liquor, rinse water, wort, beer, compressed air, CO_2, etc. Microbiological samples should also be taken of the ambient air in the packaging area (best with an air sampler with a membrane filter but an open Petri dish containing a cultivation medium also works). The filter is afterwards incubated with the appropriate cultivation medium.

Visual inspection: Aside from being tasted for off-flavours, packaged beer can be visually monitored for signs of contamination. In bottles, these can manifest themselves as rings around the inside of the neck or as the evolution of excessive amounts of carbon dioxide, which can result in gushing, breakage or explosions. If cans rupture or bulge in any way, this is, of course, a sign of a major microbiological problem.

Appendix 5-2: Simple microbiological tests

To find out whether microorganisms are present which may compromise the quality of wort and/or beer, the first logical step is to simply take a sample, add it to sterile wort or beer and see if anything grows in it. But if some unusual growth occurs in the wort or beer, then what? Which microorganisms are there? What measures can be taken to eliminate them? At the risk of stating the obvious, the problem with microorganisms is that they are so small. They can spoil wort or beer and still not exist in sufficient enough numbers to be found and identified under a microscope in an unenriched or unfiltered sample.

In order to monitor the process and take action when they arise, sometimes it is enough to merely know whether they are present or not. Thus, there are media designed for this purpose. They serve as 'yes/no' indicators of beers spoilers . In other cases, brewers want to identify which microorganisms are causing them trouble, so they can take the proper action. For this reason, beverage microbiologists have developed ways to enrich, select and identify wort and beer spoilers.

Given its enormous nutrient content (simple sugars, amino acids, etc.) – even though it is hopped – wort is much more susceptible to microbial spoilage than beer. However, if a few spoilage organisms are present, sufficiently high cell counts of vital yeast can usually outcompete them, overwhelming them to the point that their presence is of little consequence. Only when conditions change, some inadvertent weakness in production is exploited by them or the cleaning regimen consistently fails in some way do they become evident, requiring that action be taken. As discussed in the section on the protective properties of beer, unless a beer has a high pH, is particularly low in alcohol, is unhopped, unboiled or otherwise does not possess the normal defences against spoilage microbes, the vast majority of bacteria and other microorganisms do not come into consideration. This leaves brewers with a fairly narrow field of microorganisms to choose from, unless they are brewing a more vulnerable beverage, like non-alcoholic beer. Consequently, samples containing these microbes can be enriched and identified using selective media with a variety of methods.

A selection of cultivation media for a brewery laboratory

A cultivation medium for finding out whether any of the microorganisms lurking in a brewery are capable of growing in beer is best formulated using the brewery's own beer because the tests are more specific to the characteristics of the in-house products.

The media can be liquid or solid, synthetic (precise constituents) or complex (natural, e.g. wort) and universal, selective or differential media. Universal media allow almost all microorganisms to grow. Selective media permit the cultivation of only a specific type of microorganism while inhibiting the growth of others. Differential media are used to distinguish microorganisms or groups of microorganisms from one another (e.g. colour change) but usually do not inhibit their growth.

Ultimately, microorganisms will grow on a cultivation medium if the following conditions are at or near an optimum for their development:

- nutrients
- temperature
- oxygen conditions (aerobic/anaerobic)
- pH range

For lactic acid bacteria and other microorganisms that may be hop-sensitive, it is practical to create a medium in which they can more readily grow to determine if they are present. This means that aside from using the brewery's finished beer, intermediate products can be taken from the in-house process to create cultivation media for the various microorganisms one is attempting to find. These include first wort, hopped wort, beer brewed from first wort (unhopped), weakly hopped (3 to 5 IBU) beer, aerated beer (for aerobic bacteria) and even wort with ethanol added to it (for acetic acid bacteria). These can ordinarily be mixed with agar powder as well.

The following list represents a selection of the media employed in brewery laboratories to cultivate brewery microorganisms either selectively or non-selectively. It is by no means exhaustive. The normal incubation times, temperatures and other conditions may vary according to the microorganisms or objectives, but they are generally implemented as follows:

Table 30: Cultivation media and incubation conditions

Cultivation media	Solid or liquid	Normal incubation conditions		
		Time	Temp.	Aerobic or anaerobic
hopped wort	liquid	7 d	26–28 °C	aerobic
hopped wort agar	solid	3–4 d		
crystal violet agar or LWYM				
lysine agar		2–5 d		
cupric sulphate agar or LCSM				
Farber Pham Diastaticus Medium	solid	2–5 d	30 °C	aerobic
PIKA FastOrange® Wild Yeast	either		25–37 °C	
weakly-hopped beer	liquid	7 d	26–28 °C	anaerobic
beer fermented from first wort				
fully-attenuated beer				
wort + ethanol				aerobic
aerated beer				
yeast infusion broth	liquid	7 d	26–28 °C	aerobic
yeast infusion agar	solid	3–4 d		aerobic
Lactobacilli MRS agar	solid	24–72 h	34–36 °C	anaerobic
Lactobacilli MRS broth	liquid	18–24 h		
MRS broth		3–7 d	26–28 °C	
MRS broth + beer (50–75% v/v)				
MRS broth + catalase				
Micro Inoculum Broth (MIB)	liquid	18 h – 5 d	26–35 °C	anaerobic
Micro Assay Culture Agar (MACA)	solid	18–72 h	26–37 °C	
NBB-bouillon	liquid	7 d	25–28 °C	mostly anaerobic
NBB-agar	solid	3–4 d		
NBB-concentrate	liquid	3–4 d		anaerobic
VLB-S7 bouillon	liquid	4–5 d	30–35 °C	anaerobic
VLB-S7 agar	solid			
DEV lactose-peptone bouillon	liquid	3–4 d	35–37 °C	aerobic
MacConkey agar	solid	24–48 h	30 °C	aerobic
Wallerstein nutrient agar	solid	2–5 d	30–35 °C	either
Standard I	either	18–48 h	35–37 °C	aerobic
Sodium acetate agar	solid	3d	26–28 °C	aerobic

LWYM = Lin's Wild Yeast Medium   LCSM = Lin's Cupric Sulphate Medium

Table 31: Media and the microorganisms cultivated with them

Cultivation media	Microorganisms
hopped wort	yeast, moulds and beer spoilers, termobacteria
unhopped wort	yeast, moulds and bacteria
wort + ethanol	acetic acid bacteria, among others
weakly-hopped beer	beer-spoiling bacteria incl. somewhat hop-sensitive ones (LAB)
beer fermented from first wort	beer-spoiling bacteria incl. very hop-sensitive ones (LAB)
fully-attenuated beer	super-attenuating yeasts, e.g. *S. c.* var. *diastaticus*
aerated beer	aerobic beer spoilers, e.g. acetic acid bacteria
crystal violet or LWYM	*Saccharomyces* foreign yeasts
lysine	non-*Saccharomyces* yeasts
cupric sulphate or LCSM	
Farber Pham Diastaticus Medium	numerous strains of *S. c.* var. *diastaticus* grow on this medium (brewing yeast are inhibited)
PIKA FastOrange® Wild Yeast	wild yeasts, including *S. c.* var. *diastaticus*
yeast infusion	air analysis, general medium for brewery flora
yeast infusion + raffinose	differentiation between top and bottom-fermenting yeasts
MRS + beer (50–75% v/v)	beer spoilers
MRS + catalase	catalase-positive beer spoilers
Lactobacilli MRS	lactic acid bacteria
MIB	*Megasphaera, Pectinatus*
MACA	*Megasphaera, Pectinatus*
NBB	all known beer spoilers (anaerobes and aerobes)
VLB-S7-S	lactic acid bacteria + other beer spoilers
DEV lactose-peptone	gas in Durham tubes = *E. coli* and coliforms
MacConkey	*E. coli* = large red colonies coliforms = large pink colonies lactose-negative enterobacteria = colourless colonies Gram-positive bacteria are inhibited
Wallerstein	yeasts, moulds and bacteria
Standard I	microorganisms in air, water, etc.
sodium acetate	sporulation medium for yeast

Non-specific tests

Early warning systems for beer spoilers

Spoiled beer can damage a brand over an extended period of time and can even impact sales to the point that the very existence of the brewery is threatened. For this reason, brewers are highly invested in containing any contamination that may occur before it can affect beer leaving the brewery. Consequently, brewers must implement a wide range of routine measures to prevent contamination from arising or to address it in the early stages before the microorganisms can spread through the brewery. In the past, traditional microbiological techniques such as plating samples on selective nutrient media were popular due to their accuracy and the capacity to reveal evidence of beer spoilers. These techniques are still practiced in breweries and have their place in microbiological quality control. However, they require at least several days to yield results, during which time the contamination could spread to other parts of the brewery. For breweries, which do not have ready access to in-house or external laboratories, manufacturers have developed early warning systems in the form of kits. These are designed to detect specific microorganisms which are known to spoil beer. Some are based on a simple colour change, while others require more elaborate procedures and technology.

Colour indicator tests for beer spoilers

For breweries which lack the requisite equipment or training in microbiological techniques, several tests have been developed to detect the presence of beer spoilers by means of a simple colour indicator. If undesirable microorganisms are present, the test medium will change colour. Samples of water, yeast and beer can be collected from various points in the brewing process and tested using these methods.

Simple tests for the development of acid through potential microbial contamination can be carried out by placing samples in nutrient media with a colour indicator. If microorganisms are present, especially lactic acid bacteria, the medium will change colour, for example, from red to yellow.

Figure 194: The clear bottles at the top of the photo contain samples that are being monitored for beer spoilers, while the bottles beneath are reference samples archived for colloidal stability

Enrichment media with a colour indicator for beer spoilers

Beer spoilers can enter the brewery at multiple points in the process, contaminating water, yeast, process gases, wort or beer. As they are generally present in low numbers initially, these trace contaminations are difficult to detect without specific media and larger sample volumes. This is the reason that membrane filtration is recommended, since it allows a much higher volume to be tested for beer spoilage microorganisms. When viewing a sample under a microscope, positive identification of beer spoilage bacteria in the beer means that an infection is quite advanced and drastic measures must be taken to counter it. And yet, the objective of microbiological quality control is to put a halt to contamination before it can advance far enough to be detected under a microscope in an unenriched sample. Special types of enrichment media have been developed to target and promote the growth of beer spoilers to facilitate their detection and identification. During the analysis, the proliferation of harmless microorganisms such as brewing yeast or harmless flora in the sample is inhibited.

The NBB series supplied by Döhler is an example of a product with an integrated indicator which changes colour in the presence of beer spoilers. NBB broth is normally used for detecting beer spoilers in yeast samples, while NBB concentrate is more suitable for unfiltered beer or beer with yeast in suspension. For swab samples, NBB-AM broth is employed.

Membrane filtration

When liquid samples contain too few microorganisms for their detection by plating methods, i.e. less than 1 colony-forming unit (cfu) per ml, then laboratory membrane filtration is recommended. Refer to EBC method 2.3.2.1 Laboratory Membrane Filtration Technique for more information. For the quantitative detection of viable microorganisms collected on a membrane filter, EBC method 2.3.2.2 Filter Membrane Growth Technique is recommended.

Figure 195: Membrane filters incubating on agar

For example, much larger volumes of clarified beer and rinse water samples can be filtered through a membrane and incubated on a special agar medium for the detection of trace microbial contamination (fig. 195). A bypass in a liquor or beer line can be installed to facilitate routine collection of a representative sample on a membrane filter. If NBB agar is used, for instance, which is formulated to selectively cultivate the microorganisms relevant in brewery quality control, the sample would be incubated under anaerobic conditions for five days at 26–28 °C. The liquid broth medium employed in the detection of beer spoilers in yeast samples changes colour from red to yellow after two to three days of incubation, if beer spoilers are present.

A more complex test with NBB concentrate is necessary for samples of unfiltered beer or beer with yeast in suspension. Here, a concentrated (broth) form of the medium (5% of the total volume) is added to the sample in 180 ml swing top bottles followed by an incubation period of seven days at 26–28 °C. The test with NBB and beer (see below) is very selective for obligate beer spoilers; however, a microscope is necessary to detect beer spoilers with this product since this medium does not contain an indicator. Tests for potential and indirect beer spoilers can be performed by following the scheme shown in figure 197.

Figure 196: Incubating bottles

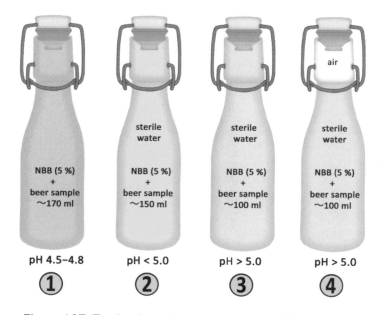

Figure 197: Testing for microorganisms with NBB and beer

The above mixtures test for the following:

(1) obligate beer spoilers

(2) obligate and potential beer spoilers

(3) obligate, potential and indirect beer spoilers

(4) obligate, potential and indirect beer spoilers plus indicator microorganisms

As mentioned above, a microscope is required for the detection of beer spoilers in these samples since there is no indicator in NBB concentrate.

Source: Back, W., Gastl, M., Krottenthaler, M., Narziss, L., and Zarnkow, M., *Brewing Techniques in Practice*. Fachverlag Hans Carl, 2019

Swab tests

Testing with swab samples provides vital insight into the level of cleanliness of various surfaces in the brewery, whether they be the exterior surfaces of production equipment or on the interior surfaces, for instance, of recently cleaned tanks or filling apparatus.

Collecting swab samples

Sterile swab sticks are employed to take samples for detection with liquid or agar media. Alternatively, rapid results can be obtained with ATP measurements.

Refer to EBC analysis 2.3.8.1 for more details on how to take swab samples.

Weak points or areas prone to microbial contamination in production and filling areas are monitored through the collection of samples with sterile swabs. Along with beer spoilers, it is important to test for indicator flora in these areas (especially acetic acid bacteria and wild yeasts). The swab samples are incubated for a maximum of three days. Only tubes exhibiting a colour change from red to yellow, indicating a positive test result,

Figure 198: Incubating swab samples anaerobically

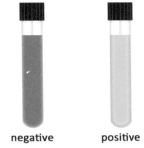

negative   positive

Figure 199: Swab samples yielding positive and negative results for microbial contamination

require further investigation. A positive test usually indicates the presence of a biofilm and thus an area susceptible to contamination which may be colonised by beer spoilers. Swab samples can reveal how effective the cleaning and sanitising processes in the brewery are. After CIPing the equipment and cleaning the entire filling area, swab samples should be taken. The number of swab samples returning positive results (colour change) should be less than 10%. The test results from the swab samples can be depicted graphically to facilitate the early recognition of problematic trends, thus allowing corrective measures to be carried out in a timely manner – no microscope required.

Instructions

1. Collect swab samples once or twice per week in summer and once per week in winter.
2. Incubate for three days in NBB-AM broth at 25–28 °C.
3. Evaluation:
   - Samples collected after cleaning: max. 10% positive
   - Samples collected during production: max. 20–30% positive

ATP testing with swab samples

Adenosine triphosphate (ATP) is an organic molecule that delivers the energy necessary to power living cells. ATP surface testing looks for this molecule, and if it is present in abundance, then biological matter is as well. The test is very simple to perform. Swab a surface with a test swab and insert it into a handheld ATP meter. The result is available in 15 seconds. This test allows brewers to monitor whether their cleaning regimen is effective or not with instant results, and thus is a very valuable tool. In a brewing environment, the higher the amount of ATP, the more microorganisms are present and the higher the reading is on the meter. The monitoring equipment consists of a detection meter which represents a

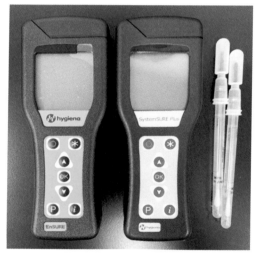

Figure 200: ATP surface testing kit
Photo: *Yuseff Cherney*

moderate cost at the beginning and ongoing material costs for the prepared swabs. The test is temperature-sensitive, so the reagents should be allowed to warm to ambient temperature before they are used. Some meters are rechargeable, while others are battery-operated. Test locations can be programmed into the device. Analysis results are stored and can be reviewed on a computer. This facilitates the location of problem areas to be identified and monitored over time.

One example of an ATP surface testing kit is pictured in figure 200.

For breweries with an on-site laboratory, EBC method 2.3.8.1 describes how to conduct ATP analysis of swab samples in the laboratory using reagents, cuvettes and a luminometer.

General information on ATP bioluminescence methods can be found in EBC 2.3.8. For ATP analysis of rinse water and of the final product, also refer to the EBC methods 2.3.8.2 and 2.3.8.3.

Other rapid methods

PCR and other types of rapid testing based on genetics and molecular biology are not included here but are, of course, available. PCR testing can be used to distinguish yeast strains or to detect and differentiate bacteria and super-attenuating yeast in wort, beer and yeast samples. Methods based on molecular biology are also available in the form of more complex kits, some of which require specialised laboratory equipment. These include the rapid testing kit brewPAL from Invisible Sentinel, the HybriScan system from Sigma-Aldrich, the GeneDisc method from the Pall Corporation and the Microcycler test kit from Weber Scientific.

Literature and further reading

Back, W., Gastl, M., Krottenthaler, M., Narziss, L., and Zarnkow, M., *Brewing Techniques in Practice*. Fachverlag Hans Carl GmbH, 2019

Vogeser, G., S. diastaticus: *geliebt und gefürchtet*. Brauwelt no. 10, 2020, Fachverlag Hans Carl

Specific tests

At smaller breweries, more extensive microbiological testing is becoming more commonplace. This facilitates the identification of microorganisms that may be present at critical stages in the process and likewise allows for greater specificity in the actions taken to cope with them. More precise testing also allows brewers working with a mix of microorganisms to determine which ones are present in the fermentation and/or maturation processes.

General steps in the identification of microorganisms

In order to carry out the tests outlined below, a sample must first be collected and then the following steps carried out:

1. A liquid enrichment, cultivation from a membrane filter or a simple streak culture may need to be performed so that a dilute suspension of the microorganisms in question can be created.

2. This dilute suspension is streak plated over four areas (see below) on a collective medium to obtain a pure culture from a single colony.
3. The microorganisms are taken from the colony on the streak plate and are streaked onto a selective medium for pre-enrichment.
4. From this point, e.g. the Gram/KOH, catalase and/or oxidase tests can be carried out on microscope slides (see below).
5. This starter culture can be inoculated in a liquid enrichment culture and subjected to a set of tests, which are available on the market. These tests can also be carried out without the test sets. Refer to the list of EBC analyses below.

Normally, a minimum of 20 physiological characteristics are tested or genetic analyses are performed on microorganisms to ensure that they are identified correctly. A microscope is necessary, since the shapes of the microorganisms are an important attribute. The EBC methods provided below are used in differentiating the microorganisms in question.

For differentiation of catalase-positive and catalase-negative bacteria:

| EBC Method 2.3.7 | Catalase Test |
| EBC Method 2.3.9.3 | Catalase Test |

For the rapid differentiation of Gram-positive and Gram-negative bacteria:

| EBC Method 2.3.6.2 | KOH Method for Gram Differentiation |
| EBC Method 2.3.9.2 | KOH Method for Gram Differentiation |

The cell wall of Gram-negative bacteria will swell in KOH and make a viscous liquid. The high viscosity is demonstrated by drawing a thread from the suspension.

For the differentiation of Gram-positive and Gram-negative bacteria.

| EBC Method 2.2.6.1. | Gram Staining |
| EBC Method 2.3.9.1 | Gram Staining for Differentiation of Bacteria |

Gram-positive bacteria possess a thick peptidoglycan layer in the cell membrane which is stained permanently with the crystal violet. Gram-negative bacteria do not have this cell layer and the stain washes out with ethanol, which allows them to be counterstained with safranin in the final step of the procedure.

Gram-positive: purple

Gram-negative: pink

For the differentiation of oxidase positive and oxidase negative bacteria:

EBC Method 2.3.9.4   Oxidase Test

A biochemical reaction that tests for the presence of the enzyme cytochrome oxidase.

For the identification of microbial colonies (bacteria or yeasts) from agar plates or membrane filters by their capability to catabolise various nutrients:

EBC Method 2.3.10   Identification of Microorganisms from Single Colonies by Biochemical Testing

Microorganisms are cultivated as single colonies and are subsequently distinguished by their ability to grow in different media. A sugar spectrum analysis can also be performed.

For the detection of *Saccharomyces* wild yeasts in brewing yeast and fermenting beer with $CuSO_4$:

EBC Method 4.2.5.1   Cu-Differentiation

Saccharomyces brewing yeast is more sensitive to Cu^{2+} ions than *Saccharomyces* wild yeasts. Growth of many brewers' yeasts is suppressed at 0.3 g/l $CuSO_4$, whereas *Saccharomyces* wild yeasts grow well at levels above 0.6 g/l $CuSO_4$. Refer to figure 201 below.

A test for detecting the presence of bacteria endospores represents a further method for differentiating bacteria in the brewery. This consists of preparing separate slides and then flooding them with 5% Malachite green solution. They are subsequently steamed for a short time and the stain is washed off with water. Counterstaining occurs for 20 seconds with a couple of drops of safranin solution. After allowing the slides to dry, the specimens are viewed under an oil immersion microscope (100x).

Bacterial endospores: green

Asporogenous, vegetative cells: pink

Examples of schemes for identifying microorganisms

Scheme for differentiating yeasts

Though there are selective media which can more specifically identify yeast, the following selective media provide a simple means for general identification of the yeast in a brewery:

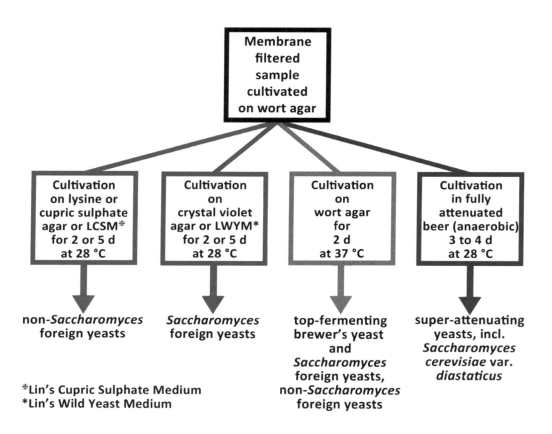

Figure 201: Tests for broadly distinguishing yeasts

Test for S. c. var. diastaticus *using a Durham tube*

Approximately 1 ml of harvested yeast is added to a test tube containing a Durham tube and completely attenuated wort. If a super-attenuating yeasts are present, gas will form in the inverted tube. This test is inexpensive, simple and can detect tens of cells of *S. c.* var. *diastaticus* among billions of brewing yeast cells. However, it can take up to two weeks. This test is not suitable for testing dry yeast right out of the packet.

negative positive

Figure 202: Durham tubes for detecting super-attenuating yeasts

Products designed to detect wild yeast

A solution for smaller breweries wanting to test for wild yeast, such as *S.c.* var. *diastaticus*, *Brettanomyces* species, etc. without a full laboratory is available in sterile, single-use tubes filled with PIKA FastOrange® Wild Yeast Medium. For a *Brettanomyces*-specific medium, FastOrange® BRETT Agar is also available. The sample is carefully added to the sterile bottle, mixed and incubated at ambient temperature. Alternatively, the incubation can occur at 37 °C, if yeasts comfortable at that temperature are targeted. The growth of brewing yeast is suppressed by the medium. The sample is positive if yeast colonies become visible during incubation. Bottles can also be purchased in bulk for mixing in the laboratory.

Farber Pham Diastaticus Medium provides a means for specifically detecting *S. c.* var. *diastaticus* in fermenting beer, finished beer, yeast slurry or swab samples. The medium can detect numerous strains of *S. c.* var. *diastaticus*. Within 48 h, growth should begin to be visible. This medium also suppresses the growth of brewing yeast.

Schemes for differentiating beer-spoiling bacteria

Figures 203 to 206 present methods for generally distinguishing beer-spoiling bacteria. There is a more specific series of tests, for example, for distinguishing lactic acid bacteria; however, this set of tests is useful for generally determining which bacteria are present in a beer sample.

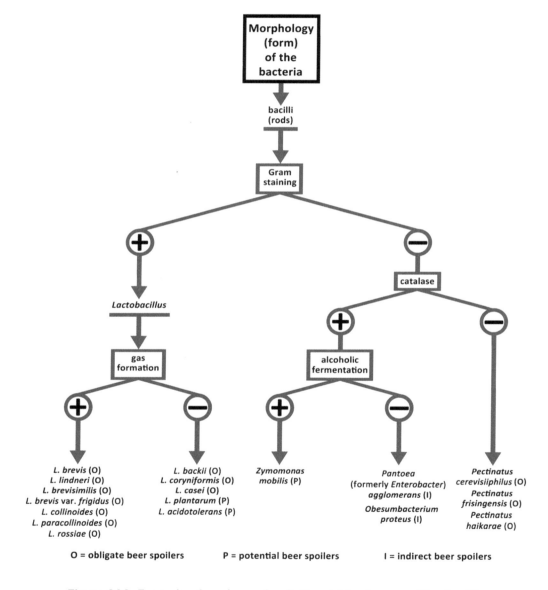

Figure 203: Example of a scheme for distinguishing beer-spoiling bacilli

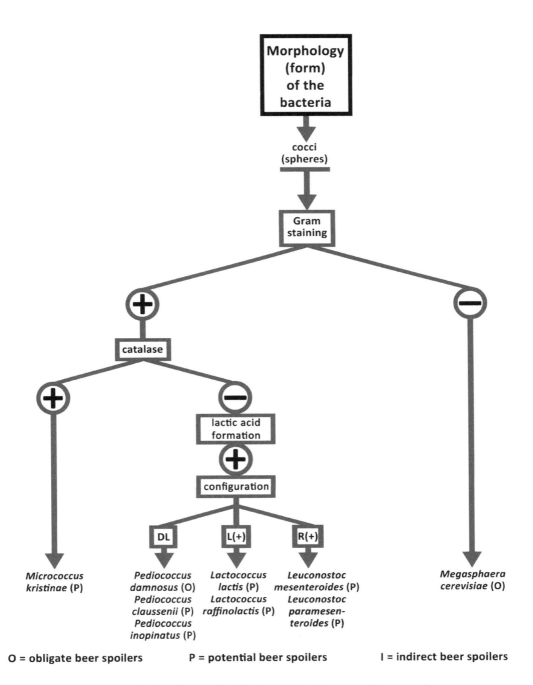

Figure 204: A scheme for distinguishing beer-spoiling cocci

Schemes for differentiating brewery bacteria

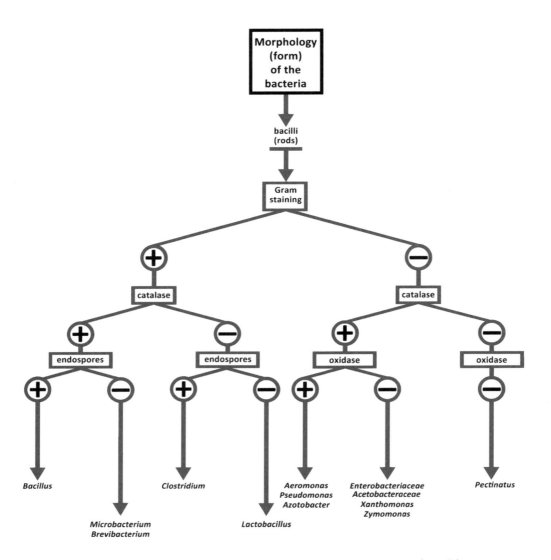

Figure 205: A scheme for distinguishing brewery bacteria (bacilli)

For schemes that allow for greater specificity in identifying yeasts and beer spoilers as well as those for other microorganisms, refer to the EBC analyses and the texts in the reading list.

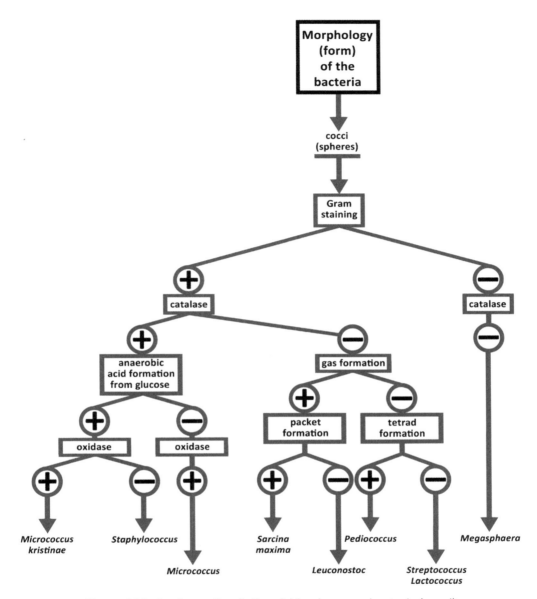

Figure 206: A scheme for distinguishing brewery bacteria (cocci)

The source for figures 203 to 206: Back, W., *Farbatlas und Handbuch der Getränkebiologie, Band 1: Kultivierung, Methoden, Brauerei, Winzerei*. Fachverlag Hans Carl, 1994

Plate counts

Reference methods on the dilution of samples and the following plating and microbiological techniques are provided in the collected EBC analysis methods.

When samples are known to contain too many microorganisms for immediate plating, i.e. more than 1,000 colony-forming units (CFU) per ml, the sample can be diluted using this method:

2.3.1   Dilution of samples

This method can be employed for the detection of microorganisms in liquid samples containing more than one colony-forming units per ml:

2.3.3.1   Pour Plate Technique

For the detection of microorganisms in liquid samples containing more than ten colony-forming units per ml, this method is recommended:

2.3.3.2   Surface Spread Plating Technique

For the isolation of single colonies from a mixture of microorganisms in liquid or solid medium, this method is used:

2.3.3.3   Isolation of Single Colonies

This provides instruction on the incubation of microorganisms, optimal growth condition, selective growth conditions:

2.3.4.1   General Rules for Incubation

Incubation techniques for the cultivation of aerobic and facultative organisms in Petri dishes are found in this method:

2.3.4.2   Aerobic Incubation

An incubation technique for the selective cultivation of anaerobic and microaerophilic microorganisms is presented in this method:

2.3.4.3 Anaerobic, Catalysed Carbon Dioxide Incubation

This method provides an incubation technique for the selective cultivation of the bacterial genera *Lactobacillus* and *Pediococcus*:

2.3.4.4   Anaerobic, Carbon Dioxide Purge Incubation

Remember aseptic technique

When pouring, spreading or streaking plates, care should be taken to ensure that no contamination occurs (e.g. flaming the mouths of test tubes, bottles and other equipment when opening and closing; refer to aseptic technique above). A laminar flow hood is recommended for this kind of work.

Pour plates

With these kinds of plates, the suspension of microorganisms is first pipetted onto the Petri dish and then the cooled yet still molten agar is poured over it. A few colonies grow on the surface, but most grow within the medium. The technique is applicable to most any sample taken in a brewery. Samples may need to be diluted prior to pouring the plate.

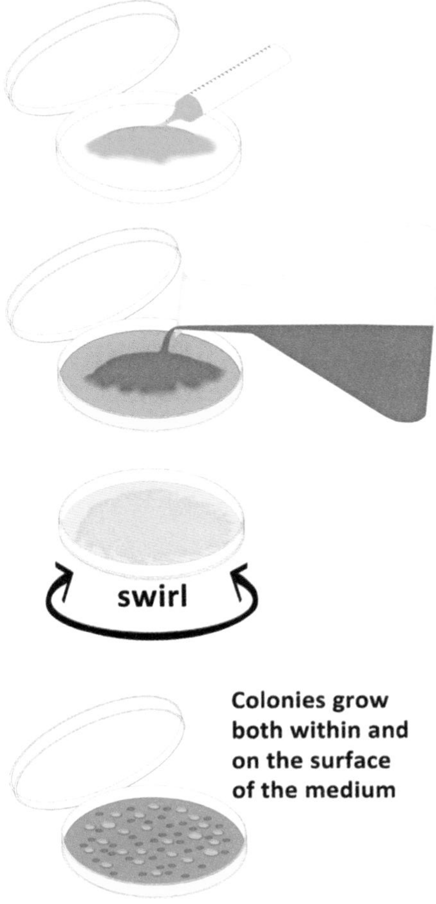

Instructions

1. Melt the agar in boiling water or in a microwave.
2. Set the water bath to 45 °C to attemperate the bottles of molten agar. Avoid contaminating the agar with the water from the bath. Ensure the water is not too deep, that the bottles stand upright, and to wipe the bottles off thoroughly when removing them.
3. Carefully open the Petri dish and pipette 1 to 5 ml of the sample into it. Close it immediately.
4. Open the agar bottle, flame the mouth and carefully open the Petri dish. Pour approximately 20 ml into the Petri dish and close it again. Flame the mouth of the agar bottle and close it.
5. Move the dish gently back and forth to swirl the inoculum and the agar together until they evenly cover the surface.
6. Allow the agar to set.
7. Apply tape to keep the Petri dish closed and incubate in an inverted position to prevent condensate from dripping onto the agar.

swirl

Colonies grow both within and on the surface of the medium

Figure 207: A pour plate

Spread plates

The spread plate technique

This technique is also practiced with viable plate counts, to facilitate counting the total number of colony-forming units on a single plate. It is employed to calculate the concentration of cells in the tube from which the sample was plated. Spread plating is routinely used in enrichment, selection, and screening experiments.

Limitations of the spread plate technique

- Strict aerobes are favoured while microaerophilic microorganisms tend to grow more slowly.
- If the colonies grow together too closely on the medium, this makes counting them difficult.
- The accuracy is not as high as with poured plates.

Instructions

1. The agar in the Petri dishes must be prepared aseptically ahead of time.
2. Make a dilution series from a sample.
3. Carefully pipette out 0.1 ml from the appropriate desired dilution series onto the centre of the surface of an agar plate.
4. Dip the glass spreader into alcohol.
5. Flame the glass spreader over a Bunsen burner.
6. Spread the sample evenly over the surface of agar using the sterile glass spreader, carefully rotating the Petri dish underneath at the same time.
7. Incubate the plate, for instance, at 37 °C for 24 hours.
8. Calculate the CFU value of the sample. Once the colonies have been counted, multiply by the appropriate dilution factor to determine the number of CFU/ml in the original sample.

Source: techniques adapted from microbiologyinfo.com.

Colonies grow only on the surface of the medium

Figure 208: A spread plate

Streak plates

The number of cells per millilitre must be diluted appropriately on a streak plate so that the individual cells become isolated and then will grow into single colonies. If a mixed culture exists, differences should become apparent in the colony morphology (margin, appearance, colour, etc.).

For streak plating yeast, mix 2 g of agar, 30 ml of wort and 70 ml of distilled water together and sterilise.

Preparation and sterilisation of the inoculation loop

1. Place the inoculation loop, samples and labelled plates within reach.
2. Determine which sample is to be streak plated ahead of time.
3. Sterilise the inoculation loop vertically in the hottest part of the flame. The wire will turn glowing red hot.

Inoculation of the nutrient medium: these steps should be carried out as quickly and as aseptically as possible.

1. Carefully open the container holding the sample. The lid or stopper should remain between one's fingers; the portion touching the inside of the container should remain untouched and can be flamed when finished if the material permits.
2. Move the inoculation loop briefly around in the sample as the heat will have killed the first microbes the loop touched.
3. Replace the lid or stopper on the sample; ensure that the inoculation loop does not touch

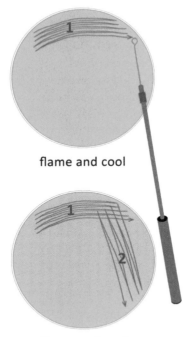

flame and cool

flame and cool

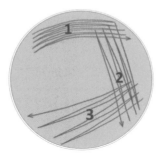

flame and cool

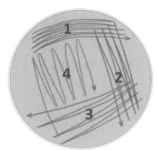

incubate

Figure 209: A streak plate

any surface, keeping it within the sterilised work area.

4. Open the labelled agar plate only enough to slide the loop inside.

5. Streak the sample back and forth on the place as indicated in the area marked 1 on the plate.

6. Sterilise the inoculation loop in the flame again and allow it to cool briefly. (This reduces the number of microbes on the loop and facilitates the growth of colonies from single micro-organisms). Streak the bacteria from area 1 through the inoculum in a single direction across the plate four to six times (fig. 209).

7. Repeat the procedure – flaming and briefly cooling the inoculation loop between streaking each area – until the streaks look like those on the plate in figure 209. Note: the streaks in area 4 of the plate should not be so long that they reach area 1.

8. Sterilise the loop after finishing the streaking of the plate.

9. Close the Petri dish and incubate it accordingly.

10. Inspect the colonies after incubation period is finished.

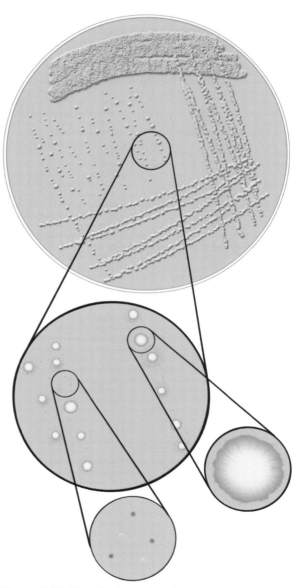

Figure 210: Streak plate showing heavy confluent growth (area 1), heavy growth (area 2), light growth (area 3) and discrete colonies (area 4); magnification showing a colony from a single yeast cell and two types of bacterial colonies

An alternative method for yeast slurry

1. Place three or four tiny droplets of sterile water close to each other on the edge of the agar.
2. Flame the inoculating loop, cool it and then dip it in the yeast slurry.
3. Touch the first droplet with the loop and allow the yeast to become suspended in the water droplet.
4. Flame and cool the loop and then dip the loop in the first droplet until there is a film across the loop.
5. Transfer this film to the second droplet.
6. Repeat this procedure until some yeast cells have been transferred to the third or fourth droplet.
7. With the last droplet, streak the plate without touching the other droplets.

Examining the colonies

A colony's morphological characteristics serve as a set of distinguishing features for the single cell or cells which gave rise to it. The surface of a colony can be smooth, rough, wrinkled, glistening or powdery. Their colour can vary as well. For example, *Saccharomyces cerevisiae* colonies are off-white to cream-coloured and can become very light brown as they age. They are soft, smooth, round, and convex to pulvinate. Their diameter can reach 1 cm.

A few examples of the shapes colonies can exhibit is presented in figure 211:

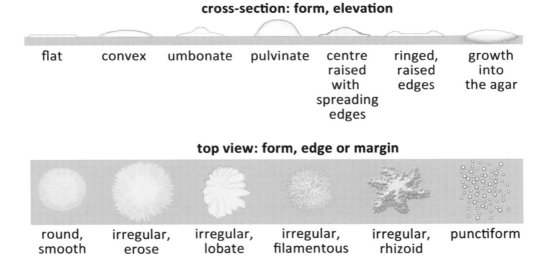

Figure 211: The shapes of colonies on the agar on a streak plate

If tiny colonies exist on the agar next to the yeast, this could be an indication of bacterial contamination. Examination under a microscope at the appropriate magnification would aid in the identification of the bacteria.

Agar slant

An agar slant is created by adding agar to
broth in a test tube, which is then heated
to the point that the agar dissolves and is
sterilised. By allowing the agar to congeal
at a slant, the surface area is increased.
For this reason, a relatively large microbial
culture can be cultivated and stored on
it inside a small tube. Yeast slants are
made this way for temporary or long-term
storage. If the storage is to be long-term,
the slants are stored at around -80 °C.
As with all microbiological procedures,
aseptic technique is paramount.

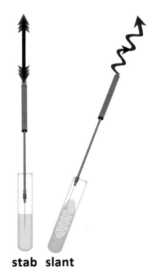

stab slant

Figure 212: A stab and a slant culture

Stab culture

An inoculation needle or loop is flamed to sterilise it and then inoculated by dipping
it into broth. The needle or loop is then stabbed into the agar culture in the test tube,
while avoiding touching the inside walls. A so-called 'deep stab' into the agar does a
fair job of excluding oxygen and allowing obligate anaerobes to grow in the agar. If the
microorganism in question is an obligate anaerobe it will only grow at the bottom of the
stab line. If microbial growth is evident all the way up and down the stab line, then the
microorganisms are facultative anaerobes. If they only grow at the top of the stab line,
they are obligate aerobes.

Appendix 6: Archived samples of packaged beer for reference

As beer ages, it loses colloidal stability or resistance to haze formation. Some breweries
collect filled bottles from each packaging run and store them at ambient temperatures
in an archive for reference. This is not only inexpensive and requires little effort, but the
information gleaned from retaining these samples is invaluable. A representative bottle
should be collected from each filling run. The bottles are placed on a shelf in a room
in chronological order by filling date. Filtered samples are monitored visually for any
development of sediment and turbidity. Also check for a ring of deposits in the bottle
neck at the interface between the beer and the headspace. Installing lighting along the
shelving would be beneficial, since backlit samples are much easier to evaluate.

Literature and further reading

Back, W., Gastl, M., Krottenthaler, M., Narziss, L., and Zarnkow, M., *Brewing Techniques in Practice*. Fachverlag Hans Carl, 2019

Back, W., *Farbatlas und Handbuch der Getränkebiologie, Band 1: Kultivierung, Methoden, Brauerei, Winzerei*. Fachverlag Hans Carl, 1994

Bast, E., *Mikrobiologische Methoden*. 3. Auflage, Spektrum Akademischer Verlag, 1999

Blackburn, C., *Food Spoilage Microorganisms*. Woodhead Publishing Ltd., 2006

Bokulich, N., Bamforth, C., *The Microbiology of Malting and Brewing*. Microbiology and Molecular Biology Reviews, Vol. 77 no. 2, 157–172, June 2013

Costerton, J., Z. Lewandowski, E. Douglas, and R. Korber, in *Microbial biofilms*. Annual Rev. Microbiol. 49:711–745, 1995

Hill, A. (ed.), *Brewing Microbiology*. Woodhead Publishing Ltd., 2015.

Meier-Dörnberg, T., Kory, O., Jacob, F., Michel, M., Hutzler, M., Saccharomyces cerevisiae *var.* diastaticus *friend or foe? —spoilage potential and brewing ability of different* Saccharomyces cerevisiae *var.* diastaticus *yeast isolates by genetic, phenotypic and physiological characterization*. FEMS Yeast Research, Volume 18, Issue 4, June 2018

Paradh, A., Hill, A., *Review: Gram-negative Bacteria in Brewing*. Advances in Microbiology, 2016, 6, 195–209

Paradh, A., Mitchell, W. J., and Hill, A. E., *Occurrence of Pectinatus and Megasphaera in the Major UK Breweries*. J. Inst. Brew. 2011,117(4), 498–506

van Vuuren, J., Cosser, K., Prior, B., *The Influence of* Enterobacter agglomerans *on Beer Flavour*. J. Inst. Brew., January-February, 1980, Vol. 86, 31–33

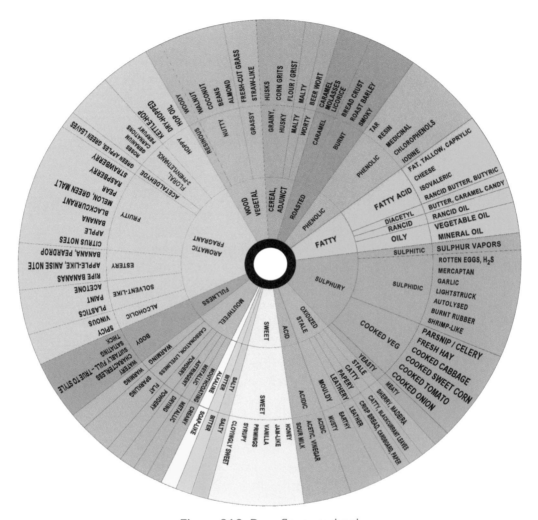

Figure 213: Beer flavour wheel

On the following pages, a sampling of the chemical substances imparting aromas and flavours to beer are presented along with their descriptors and probable causes/sources.

Esters, aldehydes and alcohols derived from the raw materials and the brewing process are responsible for many of the aromas and flavours in beer. Their names can be daunting; however, there is a simple system behind giving them their names:

Table 32: System for naming alcohols and aldehydes

Naming alcohols and aldehydes		
Carbons	**Alcohol**	**Aldehyde**
1 carbon	methanol	formaldehyde
2 carbons	ethanol	ethanal
3 carbons	propanol	propanal
4 carbons	butanol	butanal
5 carbons	pentanol	pentanal
6 carbons	hexanol	hexanal
7 carbons	heptanol	heptanal
8 carbons	octanol	octanal
9 carbons	nonanol	nonanal
10 carbons	decanol	decanal

Table 33: System for naming esters (refer to the example below)

Naming esters		
Carbons	**Alcohol** first word	**Carboxylic acid** second word
1 carbon	methyl	methanoate
2 carbons	ethyl	ethanoate
3 carbons	propyl	propanoate
4 carbons, 3 + 1 branched	2-methyl propyl	2-methyl propanoate
4 carbons	butyl	butanoate
5 carbons	pentyl	pentanoate
6 carbons	hexyl	hexanoate
benzene ring (6 carbons)	benzyl	benzoate
7 carbons	heptyl	heptanoate
benzene ring + 1 carbon (from salicylic acid)		salicylate
8 carbons	octyl	octanoate
benzene ring + 2 carbons		phenylacetate
9 carbons	nonyl	nonanoate
benzene ring + propenol		cinnamate
10 carbons		decanoate

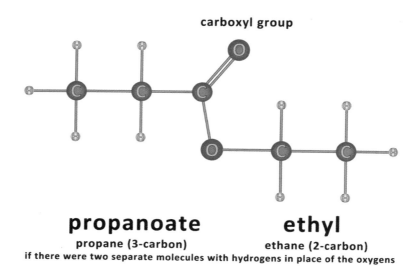

carboxyl group

propanoate
propane (3-carbon)

ethyl
ethane (2-carbon)

if there were two separate molecules with hydrogens in place of the oxygens

Figure 214: Ethyl propanoate, an example of naming an ester

Depending upon their concentrations and their milieu, the following substances can impart different aromas and flavours to a beer. For example, at one concentration or in one type of beer a substance may be pleasantly grassy, while at another concentration or in another type of beer, it may be vegetal, leafy or woody.

Chemical substance	Descriptor	Probable cause/source
acetaldehyde (aka ethanal)	sour, tart green apples	green beer flavour; excessive is a sign of yeast with poor vitality, also a sign of possible microbial contamination
acetic acid (aka ethanoic acid)	sour, vinegar, sharp, acidic	bacterial contamination, esp. if oxygen is present (e.g. barrel); yeast in fatty acid metabolism, ethyl acetate generation
2-acetylfuran (aka 2-furyl methyl ketone)	tobacco, chestnuts, cocoa, coffee, raisins, roasted almonds, tamarind, tea	ageing, thermal stress indicator
2-acetylpyrrole	musty, nutty, bready	Maillard reactions
2-acetyl-3,4,5,6-tetrahydropyridine (ATHP)	mousy, breakfast cereal, cracker, biscuit, urine	found in sour beers or beers contaminated with various microbes, including Brettanomyces or lactic acid bacteria
2-acetyl-1,4,5,6-tetrahydropyridine (ATHP)		ageing
2-aminoacetophenone	fruity, grapes, lime blossom, putty	higher (fusel) alcohol, fermentation, (Brett. as well)
amyl alcohol, active (aka 2-methylbutan-1-ol)	alcohol, acetone	hop aroma compound, an ester
sec-amyl acetate	sweet fruit, slight banana aroma	ageing, thermal stress indicator; exposure to oxygen
benzaldehyde	almonds	Maillard reactions
benzothiazole	malty, pastry	taint
2-bromophenol	India ink, museum interior, old television, electric fire	fusel alcohol (high fermentation temperature)
butanol	alcoholic	fermentation by-product
γ-butyrolactone	fruity, sour	anaerobic bacteria (Megasphaera, Clostridium and Bacillus) contamination in packaged beer or originating in sugar syrups; yeast autolysis
butyric acid	rancid butter, rancid cheese, vomit, putrid, mango	hop aroma compound, a bicyclic monoterpene
camphene	menthol, fresh, minty, woody, fir, camphoraceous	hop aroma compound, a bicyclic monoterpene
3-carene	green fruit	hop aroma compound, a sesquiterpene
β-caryophyllene	cedar, spicy, cloves	hop aroma compound, a terpenoid
carvone	menthol	hop aroma compound, a monoterpenoid phenol
carvacrol	pungent oregano	
chlorophenols -dichlorophenols -trichlorophenols	medicinal, antiseptic mouthwash	chlorination of phenols during disinfection of water; they increase with increasing chlorination; very low organoleptic thresholds
cinnamaldehyde	cinnamon	yeast
citral (aka lemonal)	strong lemon aroma	hop aroma compound
β-citronellol	lime, lychee	hop aroma compound, a natural acyclic monoterpenoid
p-cymene	herbal	a component of hop essential oils; in thyme and cumin, an alkylbenzene
β-damascenone	cooked fruit, stewed apple, rhubarb, strawberry, red fruit, kettle hop aroma, peach, fruity, tobacco, coconut	degradation of neoxanthin, ageing; (E)-β-damascenone is a primary odorant in Kentucky bourbon

Chemical substance	Descriptor	Probable cause/source
decanal	orange peel, floral-fatty, soapy	hop aroma compound; saturated fatty aldehyde
decanoic acid (aka capric acid, decylic acid)	rancid fat, fatty	fermentation by-product (from *Brett.* species as well); a saturated fatty acid; long, warm maturation
diacetyl (aka 2,3-butanedione)	butter, butterscotch, creamy, toffee	fermentation by-product, green beer not adequately matured; product of caramelisation
diallyl disulphide	garlic, vegetal	hop aroma compound
diethyl succinate	fruity, apricot, melon	fermentation by-product; the name is derived from Latin *succinum* for 'amber'
dimethyl sulphide (DMS)	cooked vegetables, sweet corn, blackcurrant, cooked cabbage	from malt; wort not boiled to a suitable intensity or long enough; wort bacteria contamination
dimethyl disulphide (DMDS)	unpleasant garlic aroma, vegetal	hop aroma compound
dimethyl trisulphide	sulphurous, onion	yeast autolysis
2-dodecanone	green fruit	hop aroma compound, a ketone
ethanol	alcoholic	yeast fermentation
ethyl acetate	fruity, pineapple, estery, rum, acetone, solvent, nail polish remover	the most abundant ester in beer; can be an off-flavour, at higher concentrations depending upon the style; fermentation by-product, possible wild yeast or bacterial contamination; has a high sensory threshold; *Brettanomyces* in the presence of oxygen and acetic acid creates high concentrations of this ester to the point that it is unpleasant (acetone, solvent, etc.)
ethyl butanoate (aka ethyl ethyl butyrate, ethyl isobutyrate)	fruity, apple, red berries, orange juice, sweet, rubber	fermentation by-product
4-ethyl catechol (aka 4-ethylbenzene-1,2-diol)	barnyard, medicinal, Band-Aid	produced by some yeasts, esp. *Brett.*
ethyl cinnamate	honey, cinnamon	fermentation by-product
ethyl decanoate (aka ethyl caprate)	fruity, sweet, waxy, apple, grape, oily, brandy	fermentation by-product (*Brett.* species as well)
3-ethyl-2, 5-dimethylpyrazine	chocolate, caramel sweets	Maillard reactions
2-ethyl fenchol	earthy	contaminated water
4-ethyl guaiacol (aka 2-methoxy-4-ethylphenol)	spicy, clove	fermentation by-product (*Brett.* species as well)
ethyl heptanoate	grapes	fermentation by-product
ethyl hexanoate (aka ethyl caproate)	apple peel, sour apple, sweet, pineapple, green banana	fermentation by-product especially in frequently repitched yeast
2-ethyltetrahydropyridine (ETHP)	mousy, breakfast cereal, cracker, biscuit, urine	found in sour beers or beers contaminated with various microbes, including *Brettanomyces* or lactic acid bacteria
cis-3-hexenol	freshly cut grass	lipid derived volatile from degradation of linolenic acid during ageing

Chemical substance	Descriptor	Probable cause/source
ethyl isovalerate	fruity, sweet, metallic, pineapple	fermentation by-product
ethyl lactate	fruity, buttery	fermentation by-product (*Brett.* species as well)
ethyl mercaptan	rotten cabbage	fermentation by-product
ethyl 2-methyl butanoate (aka butyrate)	citrus, apple	fermentation by-product
ethyl-3-methyl butanoate (aka butyrate)	citrus, apple, berry, currant	hop aroma compound
ethyl 4-methyl pentanoate	citrus, pineapple	fermentation by-product
ethyl 2-methyl propanoate	exotic fruit	fermentation by-product
ethyl nicotinate	sweet	thermal stress
ethyl octanoate (aka ethyl caprylate)	fruity, sweet, wine, pineapple, creamy, fatty, mushroom	fermentation by-product (*Brett.* species as well)
4-ethyl phenol (aka 1-ethyl-4-hydroxybenzene)	Band-Aid, medicinal, sweaty, horses	produced by some yeasts, esp. *Brett.*
ethyl 3-phenylpropionate	fruity, red berries	fermentation by-product
ethyl propionate	fruity, sweet, rum, grape, pineapple	fermentation by-product
ethyl valerate	fruity, sweet, apple, pineapple, green, tropical	fermentation by-product
β-eudesmol (β-selinenol)	woody, green	hop aroma compound, a sesquiterpene
eugenol (aka allylguaiacol)	floral, spicy, pleasantly clove-like	hop aroma compound, an allyl chain-substituted guaiacol
farnesene	floral, green apple, woody	hop aroma compound
fatty acids, collectively (middle/short-chain)	old yeast, meaty, rancid fat	dead yeast, autolysis, poor yeast handling
ferrous ion	metallic	corrosion
furaneol	caramel, malty	Maillard reactions, fouling in brewhouse (wort kettle), ageing, tunnel pasteurisation
2-furfural	sweet, woody, freshly baked bread, caramel, phenolic, almonds	hot-side aeration, Maillard reactions
furfuryl ethyl ether	sweet, spicy, nutty, coffee	poor storage and ageing conditions, esp. in dark beers (Maillard)
geosmin	sugar beets, damp soil, smell of rain (petrichor)	sesquiterpene, from surface water sources
geraniol	floral, rose water, geranium	hop essential oil; derived mainly from American hops
geranyl acetate	sweet fruity, citrus	formed by condensation of geraniol with acetic acid
guaiacol	smoky	exposure of raw materials to smoke
heptanal	green, herbal, sage, cognac, fatty	hot-side aeration
2-heptanone	sweet, fruity, spicy, herbal, coconut, woody, green banana, creamy, cheesy	hot-side aeration

Chemical substance	Descriptor	Probable cause/source
1-hexanal	green, leafy	present in pale and pilsner malts; hop aroma compound
(Z)-3-hexenal	green, leafy	hop aroma compound
hexanol	herbaceous, woody, grassy	fermentation by-product, higher alcohol (*Brett.* as well)
hexanoic acid	sweat	fermentation by-product (frequently from *Brett.* species)
2-hexenal	green, grassy, leafy, apple, plum, vegetable	hop aroma compound
hexyl acetate	apple, plum	fermentation by-product
hexyl 2-methyl propanoate	green fruit	hop aroma compound
humulene	floral, grassy	hop aroma compound
humulene epoxide I	hay	hop aroma compound
humulene epoxide II	cedar, lime	hop aroma compound
humulenol II	pineapple, mugwort	hop aroma compound
hydrogen sulphide	rotten eggs	fermentation by-product, sign of yeast with poor vitality; microbial contamination
4-hydroxy-2,5-dimethyl-3-furanone	caramel, strawberry	fermentation by-product
4-(4-hydroxyphenyl)-2-butanone	citrus, raspberry	hop aroma compound
α-ionone	artificial raspberry, cedarwood	hop aroma compound, a "rose ketone"
β-ionone	raspberry, citrus, woodlands, kettle hop aroma, strawberry, floral, berry	hop aroma compound, a "rose ketone"
isoamyl acetate	fruity, banana, apple, pear, solvent	fermentation by-product
isoamyl alcohol (aka 3-methylbutanol)	malty, bitter, alcoholic, solvent	fusel alcohol (high fermentation temperature), *Brett.* as well
isobutanol	medicinal, alcoholic, solvent	fusel alcohol (high fermentation temperature), *Brett.* as well
isobutyl acetate	fruity, sweet, tropical, pear, banana	fermentation by-product
isobutyl alcohol (aka 2-methylpropan-1-ol)	alcoholic	higher (fusel) alcohol
3-isobutyl-2-methoxypyrazine	spicy, 'bell pepper' pyrazine	hop aroma compound, very low sensory threshold (ppt)
2-isopropyl-3-methoxypyrazine	spicy, musty/earthy aromas, green flavour of Sauvignon blanc wine	hop aroma compound, very low sensory threshold (ppt)
2-isopropyl-5-methyl-2-hexenal	woody, green, herbal, sage, lavender, tomato	sesquiterpene, from surface water sources
isovaleric acid	cheesy, old hops, rancid fat	yeast autolysis; oxidised, old hops
limonene	citrus, green	hop aroma compound, a cyclic monoterpene
linalool	lavender, floral	hop aroma compound, a terpene alcohol
p-menthane-8-thiol-3-one	*Ribes*, blackcurrant, tomato plants, tom cat urine	ageing, thermal stress indicator; exposure to oxygen
3-mercaptohexyl acetate (3MHA)	passionfruit, guava	hop aroma compound
3-mercaptohexan-1-ol (3MH)	rhubarb, blackcurrant, citrus, exotic fruit, muscat	hop aroma compound
3-mercapto-4-methylpentane-2-ol	rhubarb, grapefruit	hop aroma compound

Chemical substance	Descriptor	Probable cause/source
4-mercapto-4-methylpentane-2-one (4MMP)	Ribes, blackcurrant, tropical	hop essential oil, derived from hops such as Citra, Cascade, Chinook, Simcoe, Summit, Apollo, Topaz, Cluster, Mosaic
methional	vegetal, mashed potatoes	Strecker degradation, staling and autolysed yeast, non-alcoholic or low-alcohol beers
methyl acetate	estery, fruity, wine, rum, cognac, glue, solvent	bacterial contamination, e.g. Enterobacteriaceae
2-methylbutanal	fruity, sweet, roasted, cocoa	Strecker degradation, hot-side aeration
3-methylbutanal	malty, fruity, toasted bread, baked cereal, cocoa	Strecker degradation, hot-side aeration
3-methyl-2-butene-1-thiol	skunky, lightstruck	UV light striking the beer
3-methylbutyl acetate	banana	fermentation by-product (ester)
methyldecanoate	cream, caramel	hop aroma compound
5-methylfurfural	aged flavour, stale bread, oxidised	staling compound; thermal stress indicator
s-methyl hexanethioate (aka s-methyl thiohexanoate)	green, vegetal, cabbage, cheesy, rancid	hop aroma compound
2-methylpropanal	green, overripe fruit, wet cereal, straw, cocoa	Strecker degradation
2-methylpropyl hexanoate	sweet, fruity, pineapple, peach, tropical	hop aroma compound
methyl thioacetate	cooked cauliflower, cabbage, sulphurous	bottom-fermenting yeast fermentation by-product
myrcene	herbal, green, resinous	hop aroma compound, a monoterpene
1-napthol	mothballs	pesticide residue
neral (an isomer of citral)	strong lemon aroma	hop aroma compound
nerol	floral, lime, citrus	hop aroma compound, a monoterpenoid alcohol
γ-nonalactone	coconut, creamy, waxy, fatty milk, vanilla, glue, rancid, peach, fruity	staling compound, thermal stress indicator, ageing; hop aroma compound
(E,Z)-2,6-nonadienal	cucumber, green, grassy	hop aroma compound
E-2-nonenal	wet cardboard	auto-oxidation/enzymatic oxidation of linoleic acid/linolenic acid with lipoxygenases (LOX) during mashing and malting; yeast can create it; ageing (oxidation)
ocimene (α-, cis-β-, trans-β-)	sweet herbal aroma	hop aroma compound, monoterpenes
octanal	component of fresh green aroma of barley, citrus	pale barley malt
octanoic acid (aka caprylic acid)	goat, waxy, tallowy, wet dog	decarboxylation of tyrosine by bacteria; ageing
octyl acetate	floral, green, earthy, mushroom, herbal, waxy, coconut, vegetable oil, pear, apple	fermentation by-product
2,3-pentanedione	butter, cloying, honey, creamy	fermentation by-product

Chemical substance	Descriptor	Probable cause/source
2-pentanone	sweet, fruity, wine, banana, woody	hot-side aeration
2-phenylethyl acetate	apple, fruity, sweet, tropical, floral, rose, honey	fermentation by-product
phenylacetaldehyde (phenylethanal)	green, floral, honey, sweet, rose, green, grassy, hyacinths, bread, baked cereal	Strecker degradation; ageing, thermal stress indicator; exposure of beer to oxygen
2-phenylethanol	roses, floral, alcohol, honey, sweet	yeast reduction of phenylethanal (*Brett.* as well)
2-phenylethyl acetate	roses, honey, apple, sweet, floral	fermentation by-product, ageing
pinene	spicy, piney	hop essential oil
n-propanol (propan-1-ol)	alcoholic	higher (fusel) alcohol
2-propionylfuran	fruity	ageing
rose oxide	roses, floral, element in aroma of *Gewürztraminer* wine	hop aroma compound, a monoterpene
saponin	astringent, dry, puckering, unripe fruit	raw materials
sodium bicarbonate	caustic, chemical cleaner	baking soda, water
sodium hydroxide	caustic	accidental contamination
sulphite	sulphurous, burning match	fermentation by-product (desirable as antioxidant at lower concentrations)
sulphurous amino acids	onions	raw materials
α-terpineol	lilac, resinous, rose, citrus	hop aroma compound, a monoterpene alcohol
terpinen-4-ol (aka 4-terpineol)	menthol, tea tree oil, juniper	hop aroma compound
thiols ('mercaptans') not listed separately	sulphurous, sewage, garlic, onions, rotten eggs, natural gas	fermentation by-products; yeast autolysis
thymol	herbal, thyme	hop aroma compound, a monoterpenoid phenol, in oil of thyme
2,4,6-trichloroanisole	musty, mouldy	mould, cork taint in wine; poorly cleaned filter
2,4,5-trimethyl-1,3-dioxolane	green, vegetal	yeast
tyramine	savoury	decarboxylation of tyrosine by bacteria; ageing
vanillin	vanilla, cream, caramel	hop aroma compound, a phenolic aldehyde
4-vinyl catechol (3,4-dihydroxystyrene)	plastic, bitter, smoky	produced by some yeasts, esp. *Brett.*
4-vinyl guaiacol (2-methoxy-4-vinylphenol)	cloves	fermentation by-product of certain yeast (high FAN, ferulic acid released during malting/mashing is decarboxylated to 4-vinyl guaiacol)
4-vinyl phenol (4-hydroxystyrene)	phenolic, plastic, smoky	fermentation by-product of certain yeast

SOURCES AND FURTHER READING

AAB staff writer, *Little Spinners: Centrifuge Technology Enters Small Brewing Niche*. All About Beer Magazine, vol. 37, issue 3, 2016

Analytica-EBC on-line: https://brewup.eu/ebcanalytica

ASBC Methods of Analysis, Beer-8, *Total Acidity*, American Society of Brewing Chemists, 2020

ASBC Methods of Analysis, Sensory Analysis-14, *Hot Steep Malt Sensory Evaluation Method*, American Society of Brewing Chemists, 2020

Back, W. *Colour Atlas and Handbook of Beverage Biology*. Fachverlag Hans Carl, 2006 (This is the English edition of the two German volumes listed below combined into one book.)

Back, W., *Farbatlas und Handbuch der Getränkebiologie, Band 1: Kultivierung, Methoden, Brauerei, Winzerei*. Fachverlag Hans Carl, 1994

Back, W., *Farbatlas und Handbuch der Getränkebiologie, Band 2: Fruchtsaft- und Limonadenbetriebe, Wasser, Betriebshygiene, Milch und Molkereiprodukte, Begleitorganismen der Getränke*. Fachverlag Hans Carl, 2000

Back, W., Gastl, M., Krottenthaler, M., Narziss, L., and Zarnkow, M., *Brewing Techniques in Practice*. Fachverlag Hans Carl, 2019

Bast, E., *Mikrobiologische Methoden*. 3. Auflage, Spektrum Akademischer Verlag, 1999

Bamforth, C. (ed.), Russell, I. (ed.), Stewart, G. (ed.), *Beer: A Quality Perspective (Handbook of Alcoholic Beverages)*. Academic Press; 1st edition, 2008

Bamforth, C. W., and A. Lentini. *The flavor instability of beer (Beer: A Quality Perspective)*, Burlington, MA : Academic, 85–109, 2009

Barceló, D. (ed.), Kostianoy, A. (ed.), *The Handbook of Environmental Chemistry*. Springer Nature, 1980–2020

Basarova, G., Savel, J., Basar, P., Lejsek, T., *The Comprehensive Guide to Brewing from Raw Material to Packaging*. Fachverlag Hans Carl GmbH, 2017

Belitz, H.-D., Grosch, W., und Schieberle, P., *Lehrbuch der Lebensmittelchemie*. 6. Auflage, Springer Verlag, 2008 (There is an English translation of this book entitled *Food Chemistry*, published in 2009.)

Berninger, M., *Stickstoff als Alternative zu Kohlendioxid*. Brauwelt no. 46-47, Fachverlag Hans Carl, 2018

Biendl, M., Engelhard, B., Forster, A., Gahr, A., Lutz, A., Mitter, W., Schmidt, R., Schönberger, C., *Hops: Their Cultivation, Composition and Usage*. Fachverlag Hans Carl GmbH, 2014

Blackburn, C., *Food Spoilage Microorganisms*. Woodhead Publishing Ltd., 2006

Bokulich, N., Bamforth, C., *The Microbiology of Malting and Brewing*. Microbiology and Molecular Biology Reviews, Vol. 77 no. 2, 157–172, June 2013

Brauer, J., Lenzini, J., *Fermentability ratios, attenuation scores and drinkability*. Brauwelt international 2021/I, pp. 38-41, Fachverlag Hans Carl

Briggs, D., *Malts and Malting*. Blackie Academic & Professional, 1998

Briggs, D., Boulton, C., Brookes, P., Stevens, R., *Brewing Science and Practice*. Woodhead Publishing Ltd., 2004

Brücklmeier, J., *Bier brauen, Grundlagen, Rohstoffe, Brauprozess*. Eugen Ulmer KG, 2018

BSI – Brewing Science Institute, *Brewing Without the Blindfold – Brewer's Laboratory Handbook*. 2019

Cantwell, D., Bouckaert, P., *Wood & Beer – A Brewer's Guide*. Brewers' Publications, 2016

Cha, J., Debnath, T., Lee, K., *Analysis of α-dicarbonyl compounds and volatiles formed in Maillard reaction model systems*. Nature Scientific Reports, 9:5325, 2019

Costerton, J., Z. Lewandowski, E. Douglas, and R. Korber, in *Microbial biofilms*. Annu Rev Microbiol 49:711–745, 1995.

Cypionka, H. *Grundlagen der Mikrobiologie*. 4. Auflage, Springer Verlag, 2010

Craft Maltsters Guild Quality & Safety Manual, Craft Maltsters Guild, 2017

Dalgliesh, C. E., *Flavour stability*. Proceedings of the European Brewery Convention Congress, 623–659, 1977

De Rouck, G., *System Changes in Wort Production for the Improvement of the Flavour Stability of Lager Beer*. Dissertation KU Leuven Arenberg, Doctoral School, Faculty Of Bioscience Engineering, June 2013

De Keersmaecker, J.; *The Mystery of Lambic*. Scientific American, August 1996

Drexler, G., et. al., *The Language of Hops: How to Assess Hop Flavor in Hops and Beer*. MBAA Technical Quarterly, vol. 54, 2017

Dziedzic, S., Kearsley, M. (ed.), *Handbook of Starch Hydrolysis Products and Their Derivatives*. Springer, 1995

Fischer, M., Glomb, M. *Moderne Lebensmittelchemie*. Behr's GmbH, 2015

Gastl, M., Geißinger, C. Kupetz, M., Becker, T., *Isothermes 65 °C-Maischverfahren löst Kongressmaischverfahren bei der Analytik von hellem Gerstenmalz ab*. Brauindustrie, Vol. 11, 2019

Glas, K. (ed.), Verhülsdonk, M. (ed.), *Wasser in der Getränkeindustrie*. Fachverlag Hans Carl, 2015.

Goldammer, T., *The Brewer's Handbook: The Complete Book to Brewing Beer*. Apex Publishers, 2008

Guichard, E., Salles, C., Morzel, M., Le Bon, A., *Flavour – From Food to Perception*. John Wiley & Sons, Ltd., 2017

Guinard, J.; *Lambic*. Brewers Publications, 1990

Hancock, R., Tarbet, B. *The Other Double Helix—The Fascinating Chemistry of Starch*. Journal of Chemical Education, 77th edition (8), p. 988, 2000

Heyse, K. (ed.), *Praxishandbuch der Brauerei*. Behr' s GmbH, 2000

Hill, A. (ed.), *Brewing Microbiology*. Woodhead Publishing Ltd., 2015

Hutzler, H., Zarnkow, M., Hans, S., Stretz, D., Meier-Dörnberg, T., Methner, Y., Schneiderbanger, H., Jacob, F., *New Yeasts – New Beers*. Brewing and Beverage Industry International, 03-2020, 16–23

Jackson, G., *Achieving Balance in Sour Beer: Understanding and Adjusting Titratable Acidity*. The Beverage People (thebeveragepeople.com), 2019

Kunze, W. (ed.), Hendel, O. (ed.) *Technologie Brauer und Mälzer*. 11. Auflage. Verlag VLB Berlin, 2011

MacKay, R., *The Practical Pumping Handbook*. Elsevier Advanced Technology, 2004

Mattos, R., Moretti, R. *Beer Drinkability—A Review*. MBAA TQ vol. 42, no. 1, pp. 13–15, 2005

McGreger, C., McGreger, N., *Bacteria, Brueghel, Barrels, Blending and Brett* (Parts 1–5). Brauwelt International II–VI, 2018, Fachverlag Hans Carl

McGreger, C., McGreger, N., *Barrels of Beer – A New Perspective on an Old Craft* (Parts 1–5). Brauwelt International III, 2016 – I, 2017, Fachverlag Hans Carl

McGreger,C., McGreger, N. *Beers of the World – Lambic*. Brauwelt International V 2019, Fachverlag Hans Carl

McGreger, C., McGreger, N., *Of Cones and Cauldrons, Hops and Gruit*. Brauwelt International I, 2019, Fachverlag Hans Carl

McGreger, C., McGreger, N., *So the Story Goes, the Story of Gose* (Parts 1–5). Brauwelt International I–V, 2017, Fachverlag Hans Carl,

McGreger, C., McGreger, N., *The Art of Aging Gracefully*. Brauwelt International II, 2019, Fachverlag Hans Carl

MEBAK (Mitteleuropäische Brautechnische Analysenkommission) publishes many useful volumes and guidelines in German, the majority of which have been translated into English. The two referenced in this book are available in English:

    Sensory Analysis. MEBAK (publisher), 2014

    Water. MEBAK (publisher), 2008

Meier-Dörnberg, T., Kory, O., Jacob, F., Michel, M., Hutzler, M., Saccharomyces cerevisiae *var*. diastaticus *friend or foe? —spoilage potential and brewing ability of different* Saccharomyces cerevisiae *var*. diastaticus *yeast isolates by genetic, phenotypic and physiological characterization*. FEMS Yeast Research, Volume 18, Issue 4, June 2018

Morales, F., van Boekel M., *A study on advanced Maillard Reaction in heated casein/sugar solutions: color formation.* Int'l Dairy Journal 8, 907–915, 1998

Narziss, L. *Abriss der Bierbrauerei.* Wiley-VCH Verlag GmbH & Co., 2017

Narziss, L., Back, W., *Die Bierbrauerei, Band 1: Die Technologie der Malzbereitung.* 8. Auflage, Wiley-VCH Verlag GmbH & Co., 2012

Narziss, L., Back, W., *Die Bierbrauerei, Band 2: Die Technologie der Würzebereitung.* 8. Auflage, Wiley-VCH Verlag GmbH & Co., 2009

Narziß, L., *Im Hopfen ist mehr als nur α-Säure.* Brauwelt no. 6, 122–126, 2009

O'Neill, P. *Cellarmanship.* Campaign for Real Ale Ltd, 5th edition, 2010

Palmer, J., Kaminski, C., *Water: A Comprehensive Guide for Brewers.* Brewers Association, 2013

Paradh, A., Hill, A., *Review: Gram-negative Bacteria in Brewing. Advances in Microbiology,* 2016, 6, 195–209

Paradh, A., Mitchell, W. J., and Hill, A. E., *Occurrence of Pectinatus and Megasphaera in the Major UK Breweries.* J. Inst. Brew. 2011,117(4), 498–506

Pellettieri, M., *Quality Management, Essential Planning for Breweries.* Brewers Association, 2015

Rodrigues, J., Almeida, P., *E-2-Nonenal and β-Damascenone in Beer.* Beer in Health and Disease Prevention. Elsevier Inc., 2009

Rogers, L. (ed.), *Discrimination Testing in Sensory Science: A Practical Handbook.* Woodhead Publishing Ltd., 2017

Schwill-Miedaner, A. *Verfahrenstechnik im Brauprozess.* Fachverlag Hans Carl, 2011

Simpson, W., Hammond, J. *The Response of Brewing Yeasts to Acid Washing.* J. Inst. Brew., Vol. 95, pp. 347–354, September-October, 1989

Sovrano, S., Buiatti, S., Anese, M. *Influence of malt browning degree on lipoxygenase activity.* Food Chemistry 99 (2006) 711–717

Speers, R. A., MacIntosh, A. J., *Carbon Dioxide Solubility in Beer.* J. Am. Soc. Brew. Chem. 71(4):242–247, 2013

Steensels, J., Daenen L., Malcorps, P., Derdelinckx, G., Verachtert, H., Verstrepen, K., *Brettanomyces yeasts— From spoilage organisms to valuable contributors to industrial fermentations.* International Journal of Food Microbiology 206 (2015) 24–38

Tippmann, J., *Der Aufbau einer Schankanlage: Zapfkopf, Schlauch, Hahn – fertig?* Brauwelt no. 26, pp. 732–735, 2019, Fachverlag Hans Carl

Tippmann, J., *Richtig reinigen – wie läuft es ab und was kostet es?* Brauwelt, no. 24–25, pp. 694–697, 2019, Fachverlag Hans Carl van Vuuren, J., Cosser, K., Prior, B., *The Influence of Enterobacter agglomerans on Beer Flavour.* J. Inst. Brew., January-February, 1980, Vol. 86, 31–33

Vanderhaegen, B., Neven, H., Daenen, L., Verstrepen, K., Verachtert, H. Derdelinckx, G. *Furfuryl Ethyl Ether: Important Aging Flavor and a New Marker for the Storage Conditions of Beer.* J. Agric. Food Chem. 2004, 52, 1661–1668

Vogeser, G., S. diastaticus: *geliebt und gefürchtet.* Fachverlag Hans Carl Brauwelt no. 10, 2020, pp. 270–273

Wagner, W., *Kreiselpumpen und Kreiselpumpenanlagen.* 3. Auflage, Vogel Buchverlag, 2009

Wagner, W., *Strömung und Druckverlust.* Vogel Buchverlag, 7. Auflage, 2012

White, C., Zainasheff, J., *Yeast: The Practical Guide to Beer Fermentation.* Brewers Publications, 2010

Winter, I.; *Investigations of Possible Location Dependence of Unique Microflora in Lambic Beer.* School of Life Sciences, Heriot Watt, 2013–2014

Zhuang, S., Shetty, R., Hansen, M., Fromberg, A., Hansen, P., Hobley, T., *Brewing with 100% unmalted grains: barley, wheat, oat and rye.* Eur Food Res Technology, Springer-Verlag Berlin Heidelberg, 2016

Lannoo

www.lannoo.com

Register on our website and we will regularly send
you a newsletter with information about new
books and interesting, exclusive offers.

Text: Christopher and Nancy McGreger
Photography: See in the text
Graphic Design: Woomera Communication

If you have observations or questions, please
contact our editorial office:
redactielifestyle@lannoo.com

© The Brewers of Europe/European Brewery
Convention, Lannoo Publishers, Tielt, 2021
D/2021/45/370 – NUR 440, 448
ISBN 978 94 014 79790

Images and photographs